OXFORD THEOLOGICAL MONOGRAPHS

Oxford Theological Monographs

———

CANONS OF THE COUNCIL OF SARDICA
A.D. 343
A Landmark in the Early Development of Canon Law
By HAMILTON HESS. 1958

THE NEW TEMPLE
The Church in the New Testament
By R. J. MCKELVEY. 1968

NEW LITURGICAL FEASTS IN LATER
MEDIEVAL ENGLAND
By R. W. PFAFF. 1970

THE LEONINE SACRAMENTARY
A Reassessment of its Nature and Purpose
By D. M. HOPE. 1971

CLEMENT OF ALEXANDRIA'S TREATMENT
OF THE PROBLEM OF EVIL
By W. E. G. FLOYD. 1971

CLEMENT OF ALEXANDRIA

A STUDY IN
CHRISTIAN PLATONISM
AND GNOSTICISM

BY

SALVATORE R. C. LILLA

OXFORD UNIVERSITY PRESS

1971

Oxford University Press, Ely House, London W.1

GLASGOW NEW YORK TORONTO MELBOURNE WELLINGTON
CAPE TOWN SALISBURY IBADAN NAIROBI DAR ES SALAAM LUSAKA ADDIS ABABA
BOMBAY CALCUTTA MADRAS KARACHI LAHORE DACCA
KUALA LUMPUR SINGAPORE HONG KONG TOKYO

PRINTED IN GREAT BRITAIN
AT THE UNIVERSITY PRESS, OXFORD
BY VIVIAN RIDLER
PRINTER TO THE UNIVERSITY

PREFACE

THE present book is not meant to provide the reader with a general picture of Clement of Alexandria, nor is it concerned with such topics as 'Clement and marriage', 'Clement and family', 'Clement and the use of wealth', 'Clement and original sin', and so on. It aims at being, first of all, an inquiry as comprehensive as possible into his cultural background.

According to a widespread opinion, a Christian author and a non-Christian philosopher can use the same language but mean quite different things. This is what J. Sevenster's book (*Paul and Seneca*, Leiden, 1961) has clearly demonstrated in the case of St. Paul. It would, however, be hazardous to generalize this view and to try to apply it without distinction to *all* Greek apologists and Fathers who, from the second century A.D. on, contributed to the formation of a Christian theology not by disregarding the cultural milieu to which they belonged but by incorporating many elements of it into their systems. This is particularly true in the case of an author like Clement. Only after full light has been thrown on the close connections which exist between him, the so-called Middle Platonism, Neoplatonism, the Jewish-Alexandrine philosophy, and Gnosticism will it be possible, in my opinion, to proceed to a new valuation of him as a Christian thinker.

My book may therefore be of some interest both for the classical scholar who is interested in late antiquity and for the theologian who is not prepared to detach the Christianity of the Greek Fathers from its historical setting. It will, on the contrary, interest far less—and perhaps meet the strong opposition of—those people whose main concern is to deny the existence of any relevant influence of 'profane' or 'heretical' culture on the thought of a Greek Father, whoever he may be.

This book is a revised version of the D.Phil. thesis which I submitted to the Faculty of Theology of the University of Oxford in the spring of 1962. For three years I enjoyed the most kind and fruitful assistance of the Revd. Dr. H. Chadwick, then Regius Professor of Divinity and now Dean of Christ Church, and of Dr. R. Walzer, lecturer in Arabic and Greek philosophy at the University of Oxford. Both of them were extremely generous in giving me suggestions and advice which greatly assisted me during my research work and also in taking pains to correct my still clumsy English style. To both of them I am extremely indebted and can safely maintain that without their help my work would not be such as it is at present. Professor Chadwick was also so kind as to read through the typescript twice before it was handed over to the Press.

My best thanks are due to the Delegates of the Oxford University Press for accepting this book for publication as well as to its readers, for their most careful correction of the proofs and for their suggestions which contributed to improve my English in several points. My colleague and friend Mons. P. Canart, Scriptor at the Vatican Library, also helped me in the correction of the proofs.

S. L.

Rome, March 1971

CONTENTS

ABBREVIATIONS

AAWG	*Abhandlungen der Akademie der Wissenschaften in Göttingen*
ABAWM	*Abhandlungen der königlich Bayerischen Akademie der Wissenschaften, München*
AEHE	*Annuaire de l'École des Hautes Études*
AG	*Analecta Gregoriana*
AHAW	*Abhandlungen der Heidelberger Akademie der Wissenschaften*
AIO	*Annuaire de l'Institut de Philologie et d'Histoire orientales*
ARW	*Archiv für Religionswissenschaft*
ASNSP	*Annali della Scuola Normale Superiore di Pisa*, Classe di lettere, storia e filosofia
BAB	*Bulletin de la Classe des Lettres et des Sciences morales et politiques de l'Académie royale de Belgique*
BAGB	*Bulletin de l'association Guillaume Budé*
BEHE	*Bibliothèque de l'École des Hautes Études*
BGPhM	*Beiträge zur Geschichte der Philosophie des Mittelalters*
BPhM	*Berliner Philologische Wochenschrift*
CAIBL	*Comptes rendus de l'Académie des Inscriptions et Belles Lettres*
CPh	*Classical Philology*
CQ	*Classical Quarterly*
DThC	*Dictionnaire de théologie catholique*
EJ	*Eranos Jahrbuch*
ETL	*Ephemerides theologicae Lovanienses*
FZPhTh	*Freiburger Zeitschrift für Philosophie und Theologie*
HStCPh	*Harvard Studies in Classical Philology*
HThR	*Harvard Theological Review*
JACh	*Jahrbuch für Antike und Christentum*
JCPh	*Jahrbuch für classische Philologie*
JHS	*Journal of Hellenic Studies*
JR	*Journal of Religion*
JRS	*Journal of Roman Studies*
JTS	*Journal of Theological Studies*
LPP	*La parola del passato*
MAB	*Mémoires de l'Académie royale de Belgique*
NGA	*Nachrichten von der Akademie der Wissenschaften in Göttingen*
PG	*Patrologia graeca*
PhM	*Philosophische Monatshefte*
RACh	*Reallexikon für Antike und Christentum*
RAM	*Revue d'ascétique et de mystique*
RE	*Paulys Real-Encyclopädie der classischen Altertumswissenschaft* (begonnen von G. Wissowa)
REG	*Revue des études grecques*
RHE	*Revue d'histoire ecclésiastique*
RHR	*Revue de l'histoire des religions*

RMPh	*Rheinisches Museum für Philologie*
RPh	*Revue de philologie*
RQ	*Römische Quartalschrift*
RSR	*Recherches de science religieuse*
SA	*Studia Anselmiana*
SO	*Symbolae Osloenses*
STh	*Studia theologica*
SVF	*Stoicorum veterum fragmenta* (collegit I. ab Arnim, vols. i–iii, Lipsiae, 1903–5)
ThLZ	*Theologische Literaturzeitung*
TQ	*Theologische Quartalschrift*
TStK	*Theologische Studien und Kritiken*
TU	*Texte und Untersuchungen zur Geschichte der altchristlichen Literatur*
TZ	*Theologische Zeitschrift*
VC	*Vigiliae Christianae*
VSAM	*La Vie spirituelle, ascétique et mystique*
ZAM	*Zeitschrift für Aszese und Mystik*
ZKTh	*Zeitschrift für katholische Theologie*
ZNW	*Zeitschrift für die neutestamentliche Wissenschaft*
ZPhuphK	*Zeitschrift für Philosophie und philosophische Kritik*
ZWTh	*Zeitschrift für wissenschaftliche Theologie*

EDITIONS AND TRANSLATIONS

Acts of John, ed. by M. Bonnet, *Acta Apostolorum Apocrypha*, ed. R. A. Lipsius and M. Bonnet (Lipsiae, 1898).

Albinus, ed. by C. F. Hermann, *Platonis dialogi secundum Thrasylli tetralogias dispositi*, vol. vi (Lipsiae, 1884).

Alexander of Aphrodisias, *In Analytica priora*, ed. M. Wallies, Comment. in Arist. gr. ii. 1 (Berolini, 1883).

—— *In Topica*, ed. M. Wallies, Comment. in Arist. gr. ii. 2 (Berolini, 1891).

Apocalypse of Paul, ed. by A. Böhlig and P. Labib, 'Koptisch-gnostische Apokalypsen aus Codex V von Nag-Hammadi', *Wissenschaftliche Zeitschrift der Martin-Luther Univ.-Halle-Wittenberg* (1963).

Apocryphon of John, ed. and transl. by W. Till, 'Die gnostischen Schriften des koptischen Papyrus Berolinensis 8502', *TU* 60 (Berlin, 1955).

—— ed. and transl. by M. Krause and P. Labib, 'Die drei Versionen des Apocryphon des Johannes im koptischen Museum zu Alt-Kairo', *Abhandlungen des deutschen archäologischen Instituts Kairo*, Band i. (1962).

—— ed. and transl. by S. Giversen, 'The Coptic Text of the Apocryphon Iohannis in the Nag Hammadi Codex II with Translation, Introduction and Commentary', *Acta Theologica Danica*, v (Copenhagen, 1963).

Apuleius, *Apologia*, ed. by R. Helm (Lipsiae, 1963).

—— *De Platone et eius Dogmate*, ed. by P. Thomas (Lipsiae, 1908).

—— *Florida*, ed. by R. Helm (Lipsiae, 1963).

Aristotle, *Prior and Posterior Analytics*, ed. by W. D. Ross (Oxford, 1949).

—— *Eudemian Ethics*, ed. by F. Susemihl (Lipsiae, 1884).

—— *Nicomachean Ethics*, ed. by F. Susemihl (Lipsiae, 1882).

—— *De Caelo*, ed. by D. J. Allan (Oxonii, 1955).

—— *Physics*, ed. by W. D. Ross (Oxford, 1936).

—— *Metaphysics*, ed. by W. D. Ross (Oxford, 1948, reprint of the edition of 1924).

—— *Topics*, ed. by W. D. Ross (Oxonii, 1958).

—— *Fragmenta*, selegit R. Walzer (Testi della Scuola Normale Superiore di Pisa, vol. ii) (Firenze, 1934).

—— *Fragmenta*, collegit V. Rose, in Bekker, vol. v (Berolini, 1870).

[Aristotle], *De Mundo*, ed. by W. L. Lorimer (Paris, Les Belles Lettres, 1933).

Atticus, *Atticos*. Fragments de son œuvre avec introduction et notes par J. Baudry (Paris, Les Belles Lettres, 1931).

Book of Enoch, ed. by H. B. Swete (*The Old Testament in Greek*, vol. iii) (Cambridge, 1899).

Books of Jeu, transl. by C. Schmidt, 2. Auflage bearbeitet von W. Till (Die griech. christl. Schriftsteller der ersten drei Jahrh.) (Berlin, 1954).

Celsus, ed. by R. Bader, 'Der Ἀληθὴς λόγος des Kelsos', *Tübinger Beiträge zur Altertumswissenschaft*, XXXIII. Heft (Stuttgart–Berlin, 1940).

Chalcidius, *Commentary on the Timaeus*, ed. by J. H. Waszink, Plato Latinus, Corpus platonicum medii Aevi (Londinii, 1962).

Cicero, *Academica*, ed. with commentary by J. S. Reid (London, 1885).

—— *De Finibus bonorum et malorum*, ed. by J. Martha (Paris, Les Belles Lettres, 1928–30).

Clement of Alexandria, ed. by O. Stählin (Die griech. christl. Schriftsteller der ersten drei Jahrh.): vol. i, Zweite Auflage (Leipzig, 1936); vol. ii, Dritte Auflage, neu herausgegeben von L. Früchtel (Berlin, 1960); vol. iii (Leipzig, 1909).

—— *The Excerpta ex Theodoto of Clement of Alexandria*, ed. and transl. by R. P. Casey (London, 1934).

—— *Extraits de Théodote*, Texte grec, introduction, traduction et notes de F. Sagnard (Paris, 1948).

Corpus Hermeticum, ed. by A. D. Nock and A. J. Festugière, vols. i–iv (Paris, Les Belles Lettres, 1945–54).

Diogenes Laertius, *Vitae philosophorum*, ed. by H. S. Long (Oxonii, 1964).

Dionysius Areopagita, *De divinis Nominibus*, Migne, *PG* 3.

Epicurus, ed. by C. Bailey (Oxford, 1926).

Epistula Apostolorum, ed. and transl. by C. Schmidt and J. Wainberg, *TU* 43 (Leipzig, 1919).

Eusebius, *Historia ecclesiastica*, ed. by E. Schwartz (Die griech. christl. Schriftsteller der ersten drei Jahrh.) (Leipzig, 1903–8).

—— *Praeparatio Evangelica*, ed. by K. Mras (Die griech. christl. Schriftsteller der ersten drei Jahrh.) (Leipzig, 1954–6).

Galen, *De Methodo medendi*, ed. by C. G. Kühn, vol. x (Lipsiae, 1825).

—— *De Placitis Hippocratis et Platonis*, ed. by C. G. Kühn, vol. v (Lipsiae, 1823).

—— *De Pulsuum Differentiis*, ed. by C. G. Kühn, vol. viii (Lipsiae, 1824).

—— *Institutio logica*, ed. by C. Kalbfleisch (Lipsiae, 1896).

Gellius, *Noctes Atticae*, ed. by C. Hosius (Lipsiae, 1903).

Gnostic authors, fragments collected by W. Völker, *Quellen zur Geschichte der christlichen Gnosis* (Tübingen, 1932).

Gospel of Mary, ed. and transl. by W. C. Till, *TU* 60 (Berlin, 1955), pp. 62–79.

Gospel of Philip, transl. by R. McL. Wilson (London, 1962).

—— transl. by W. C. Till (Berlin, 1963).

Gospel of Thomas, ed. and transl. by A. Guillaumont, H. C. Puech, G. Quispel, W. Till, and Yassah Abd al Masib (Leiden–London, 1959).

Aristotelian,[1] or as a Platonist in his metaphysics and theology and as a Stoic in his ethics.[2] It was this tendency that also gave shape to the image of Clement as an 'eclectic' philosopher. It was very easy, starting from the simultaneous presence of Platonic, Stoic, and Aristotelian elements as well as of so many quotations from classical authors throughout Clement's writings, to speak of Clement's 'eclecticism'; some statements contained in the first book of the *Stromateis* and especially the so often quoted passage of *Strom.* i. 37. 6 seemed to provide the best evidence in support of such a view.[3]

The definition of Clement as an 'eclectic' combines very often with the tendency, characteristic of some modern theologians, to contrast Christianity with Greek culture. In their opinion, the Christian religion and Greek philosophy represent two forces which are substantially extraneous to one another and between which no real synthesis is possible. Christianity, being perfect in itself, needs no help from profane culture: in order to appear more attractive to the 'heathens', it can only deign to borrow a few elements or terms from the philosophical systems which are not so removed from the truth it represents, provided that this

and M. Spanneut, who does not add much to the conclusions reached by Merk, Stelzenberger, and Pohlenz (see particularly pp. 170–1, 234, 235, 244–5, 247–51, 322, 343–4).

[1] See particularly H. J. Reinkens, who bases his arguments mainly on the presence in Clement of elements of Aristotelian logic (see, for instance, pp. 300 and 309).

[2] This view is shared especially by E. Freppel (see particularly p. 316), by E. de Faye, *Clément d'Alexandrie*, 318, and by J. B. Mayor in his introduction to the English translation of the seventh book of the *Stromateis* made by F. J. A. Hort (London, 1892), pp. xxxv–xxxvi.

[3] The scholars who have been led to this conclusion by the passage of *Strom.* i. 37. 6 (ii. 24. 30–25. 2) represent an overwhelming majority. I shall mention at random the following: J. A. Bielcke, who, though being inclined to consider Clement as a Stoic (see footnote 2, p. 1 above), attaches nevertheless some importance to the passage quoted above (see particularly p. 14); F. Tribbechovius, 6; E. Redepenning, who traces Clement's eclecticism back to the eclecticism of his teacher, Pantaenus (Erste Abt., 93–4); H. Ritter, Erster Teil, 442–3; E. Vacherot, i. 250; H. Laemmer, 56; H. Preische, 32; D. Demetreskos, 83; G. Basilakes, 4; F. R. Hitchcock, 53 and 57; J. B. Mayor, pp. xxxiv–xxxv; W. Scherer, 4–5; M. Daskalakis, throughout his dissertation; O. Bardenhewer, Zweiter Band (Freiburg, 1914), 47; H. Eibl, *ZPhuphK* 164 (1917), 42; R. P. Casey, who, though treating Clement generally as a Platonist, is nevertheless inclined to consider him as an eclectic as well, *HThR* 18 (1925), 95; J. Meifort, 9; C. A. Bernouilli in his introduction to the German translation of the *Stromateis* made by F. Overbeck (Basel, 1936), 103; E. Molland, *The Conception of the Gospel . . .*, 166 ff. (about the eclecticism of the Christian school of Alexandria); and E. F. Osborn, 8.

Gospel of Truth, ed. and transl. by M. Malinine, H. C. Puech, and G. Quispel (Zürich, 1956).

Gregory Thaumaturgus, *Thanksgiving to Origen*, ed. by P. Koetschau (Freiburg, 1894).

Hippolytus, *Refutatio omnium Haeresium*, ed. by P. Wendland (Die griech. christl. Schriftsteller der ersten drei Jahr.) (Leipzig, 1916).

Iamblichus, *De Vita Pythagorica Liber*, ed. by L. Deubner (Lipsiae, 1937).

Iohannes Philoponus, *De Aeternitate Mundi*, ed. by H. Rabe (Lipsiae, 1899).

Irenaeus, *Adversus Haereses*, ed. by W. Harvey (Cantabrigiae, 1857) (see also F. Sagnard, *La Gnose valentinienne et le témoignage de Saint Irénée*, pp. 31–50).

Justin, ed. by J. C. Otto (Jenae, 1842).

Maximus of Tyre, *Philosophumena*, ed. by H. Hobein (Lipsiae, 1910).

New Testament, ed. by Eberhard Nestle, Erwin Nestle, and K. Aland (Stuttgart, 1957).

Numenius, fragments collected by E. A. Leemans, *MAB*, Classe des Lettres 27 (1937).

Old Testament, ed. by A. Rahlfs (Stuttgart, 1935).

Origen the Christian, *Contra Celsum*, ed. by P. Koetschau (Die griech. christl. Schriftsteller der ersten drei Jahr.) (Leipzig, 1899).

—— *Contra Celsum*, transl. with an Introduction and Notes by H. Chadwick, (Cambridge, 1953).

Origen the Neoplatonist, fragments collected by K. O. Weber, *Zetemata* 27 (München, 1962).

Philo, ed. by L. Cohn and P. Wendland, vols. i–vi (Berolini, 1896–1915).

—— *De Providentia*, Latin translation from the Armenian version by I. B. Aucher (Venetiis, 1882).

—— *Quaestiones in Genesim*, transl. from the ancient Armenian Version of the original Greek by R. Marcus, the Loeb Classical Library, *Philo*, Supplement i (London, 1953).

Photius, *Bibliotheca*, Migne, *PG* 103–4.

Pistis-Sophia, transl. by C. Schmidt, 2. Auflage bearbeitet von W. Till (Die griech. christl. Schriftsteller der ersten drei Jahrh.) (Berlin, 1954).

—— transl. by H. R. S. Mead, *Pistis-Sophia*, English Translation with Introduction, Notes, Bibliography (London, 1947).

Plato, ed. by I. Burnet, vols. i–v (Oxonii, 1953–5).

—— *Laws*, Book X, Texte établi et traduit par A. Diès (Paris, Les Belles Lettres, 1958).

Plotinus, ed. by E. Bréhier, vols. i–vi (Paris, Les Belles Lettres, 1924–8).

Plutarch, *Moralia*, ed. by G. N. Bernardakis, vols. i–vii (Lipsiae, 1888–96).

Porphyry, *De Abstinentia*, ed. by A. Nauck (Lipsiae, 1886).

—— *Sententiae ad intelligibilia ducentes*, ed. by B. Mommert (Lipsiae, 1907).

Porphyry, *Vita Plotini*, ed. by E. Bréhier (*Plotin, Ennéades* i) (Paris, Les Belles Lettres, 1954).

Proclus, *In Platonis Timaeum*, ed. by E. Diehl, vols. i–iii (Lipsiae, 1903–6).

Sextus Empiricus, *Adversus Mathematicos*, libri i–vi, ed. by J. Mau (Lipsiae, 1954); libri vii–xi, ed. by H. Mutschmann (Lipsiae, 1914).

Simplicius, *in Physica*, ed. by H. Diels, Comment. in Arist. gr. ix–x (Berolini, 1882–5).

Stobaeus, *Anthologium*, ed. by C. Wachsmuth and C. Hense, vols. i–iv (Berolini, 1884–1912).

Stoics, fragments collected by I. von Arnim, vols. i–iii (Lipsiae, 1903–5).

Theon of Smyrna, ed. by E. Miller (Lipsiae, 1878).

Wisdom of Jesus Christ, ed. and transl. by W. Till, 'Die gnostischen Schriften des koptischen Papyrus Berolinensis 8502', *TU* 60 (Berlin, 1955).

Xenocrates, fragments collected by R. Heinze, *Xenocrates* (Leipzig, 1892).

INTRODUCTION

O N Clement of Alexandria a great amount of literature has been piling up during the last 150 years. Either as a mere compilator or as an original philosopher and theologian he has attracted the attention of many a scholar. The question of the sources of some erudite sections of his writings, his views on Greek philosophy, his ethical and theological doctrines, his polemical attitude towards the heretics of his time—these and other aspects of his work have formed the object of so many inquiries that a further study would hardly be expected to add anything new to what we already know. Yet, as far as Clement's 'philosophy' is concerned, things are not so finally settled as might appear at a first glance. First of all, the results of the researches on Clement's cultural background are far from being satisfactory; secondly—and this is perhaps the most important question—modern scholars have generally fallen short of establishing what relations exist between such a background and Clement's Christianity. It is on the solution of both these questions that a right appreciation of the Christian thought of the Alexandrine theologian ultimately depends.

As soon as modern scholars found Platonic, Stoic, or Aristotelian elements in Clement's writings, they traced them immediately back to their original sources: Plato, the Stoics, and Aristotle. In this way, Clement has alternatively been considered either as a Platonist[1] or as a Stoic[2] or even as an

---

[1] This is the view held especially by T. Holzclau, 37–8 and 43–5, P. Hofstede de Groot, C. Bigg, 63–150, R. B. Tollinton, i. 165–6, R. P. Casey, *HThR* 18 (1925), 39–101, and J. Wytzes in his articles in *VC* 9 (1955), 148–58, *VC* 11 (1957), 226–45, and *VC* 14 (1960), 129–53.

[2] Some scholars, by taking Clement's ethical doctrines into special account, came to the conclusion that the influence of Stoicism on Clement is far more relevant than that of any other philosophical system. It will suffice to mention J. A. Bielcke, 15; H. Preische, 42; C. Merk, particularly in the sections 'Wissen und Handeln', 53–9, and 'Ethische Anschauungen', 60–90 (see also his conclusions, p. 90); J. Stelzenberger, 166–70, 226–7, 254–5, 261, 269–70, 283, 323–5; P. Barth and A. Goedeckmeyer, 252–3; M. Pohlenz, *NGA*, phil.-hist. Kl. (1943), 103–80, and *Die Stoa* i. 415–22, who has particularly stressed the importance which the Stoic doctrine of the obedience to the Logos and to the law of *physis* has in Clement's ethics (Pohlenz has not seen, however, that most of his conclusions had been anticipated by the studies of Merk and Stelzenberger, which he does not quote);

does not contaminate its purity and causes no prejudice to its originality. Clement appears, in this way, as a wise Christian philosopher who, being already enlightened by the truth of his own religion, is able to judge what is right and what wrong in the heathen philosophy, and deems it worthy to borrow from it elements which are not in disagreement with his religious principles. This trend of thought, which underlies several studies both of the last and of the present century,[1] appears particularly clear in the recent book by W. Völker, the most important and extensive work on Clement which has ever been published: according to the German theologian, Clement is nothing if not a Christian, who likes to present himself under the guise of a Platonic or Stoic philosopher in order to speak the same philosophical language as the heathens and to convert them to Christianity by showing them that a Christian is not forbidden to express himself in terms of Greek philosophy. Accordingly, the borrowing of elements of Greek philosophy has only an instrumental importance: they are purely exterior terms, covering an orthodox and genuine Christian thought, which, however, is not substantially influenced by them.[2]

The reason why the former studies on Clement's philosophical sources have come to contradictory conclusions is not very far to seek. Nobody has so far examined, in a comprehensive inquiry, the question of the relations between Clement and the dominant philosophy of the second century A.D., namely Middle Platonism[3]

---

[1] See, for instance, H. Laemmer, 56; H. J. Reinkens, 275 and 300 n. 1; V. Hébert-Duperron, 119; J. Huber, 136; J. Cognat, 417–18; J. Patrick, 141–2; and A. C. Outler, *JR* 20 (1940), 237–8.

[2] W. Völker, *Der wahre Gnostiker* . . . See, for instance, p. 8, p. 9, and p. 14 n. 1. But the two following passages indicate better than any other the underlying idea of Völker's book: Clemens bei seiner Methode der Anknüpfung nie die Grenzlinie [sc. between orthodox Christianity and Greek culture] überschritten hat' (p. 9); 'Seit den Tagen der Aufklärung ist es immer behauptet worden, dass die Kirchenväter des Christentum durch die Verwendung der Philosophie hellenisiert hätten. Ich habe das nie geglaubt . . .' (p. 352 n. 3). Völker's views were already clear in his article, *TZ* 3 (1947), 15–40. With him practically agrees E. von Ivanka, who has devoted to Clement two pages of his recent book *Plato Christianus*: 'die platonischen Gedanken bei ihm [sc. Clement] eigentlich nur Bildwert haben' (p. 98).

[3] Some scholars have occasionally hinted at this most important problem, but have fallen short of producing a satisfactory inquiry into it. See especially A. F. Daehne, *De γνώσει Clementis Alexandrini*, 6; E. Redepenning, 92, 93, and 95; Kling, 868; M. Dods, 58; E. de Faye, *Clément d'Alexandrie*, 239; C. Bigg, in the chapter 'The reformed Paganism', 281–316; R. B. Tollinton in the chapter

4 INTRODUCTION

—what C. Andresen has done for Justin[1] has still to be done for Clement; very few scholars have realized the presence, in Clement's thought, of some ideas which are characteristic of Neoplatonism;[2] and the Jewish-Alexandrine philosophy, which

'Six contemporaries', (i. 36–148); J. Meifort, 14 and 34; J. Lebreton, *RSR* 34 (1947), 58–9; R. Arnou's statements in *DThC*, Tome xii (1932–5), are worth noticing, in so far as he is the first who has fully understood the importance which Middle Platonism had for the cultural formation of the Christian Fathers in general (see pp. 2274 and 2275) and particularly of Clement and of Origen (see pp. 2305, 2306, and 2308). Arnou mentions a few points in which the influence of Platonism both on Clement and on Origen is particularly relevant, (see particularly p. 2306), but he seems rather to point to some of the directions in which new research should move than to produce a comprehensive and detailed inquiry on this subject. R. E. Witt also rightly considers Clement as one of the exponents of the Platonism of the second century A.D. in his book *Albinus . . .*, 114; G. Lazzati, though acknowledging the fact that Clement's philosophical studies took place, just as it had happened for Justin, in the Platonic schools of the second century A.D. (see p. 41), makes no attempt to show in detail Clement's dependence on this kind of Platonism, but goes on to speak about his conversion to Christianity, by drawing a parallel between him and Justin (see particularly pp. 48 and 51–3). The article by A. C. Outler is nothing but a repetition of what Meifort had already said; only occasionally does he hint, in general terms, at the influence of Middle Platonism on Clement (p. 237). The three papers by J. Wytzes do not touch the problem of Clement's dependence on Middle Platonism (only two correspondences between Clement and Albinus are mentioned, see pp. 50 and 221 below): Wytzes is mainly concerned with the influence which Plato's ideal of *paideia* had on Clement's thought. As to E. Osborn, he lays strong emphasis on the importance which the first two hypotheses of Plato's *Parmenides* had for the formation of the theology of Middle Platonism and of Neoplatonism, of which he gives a general sketch (see particularly chapter I, pp. 7–24) but does not examine in detail the manifold relations between Clement, Middle Platonism, and Neoplatonism.—The most concrete contributions to the problem of Clement's dependence on Middle Platonism have been made by L. Früchtel, who in his short note in *BPhW* 57 (1937), coll. 591–2 has drawn attention to some correspondences between Clement and Albinus, by J. H. Waszink, whose statements in the paper 'Der Platonismus und die altchristliche Gedankenwelt', *Entretiens Hardt* iii (Genève, 1955), 139–78, should represent the starting-point for anybody wishing to examine closely the problem of the Platonism of the Church Fathers (on Clement see particularly pp. 153–5 and 168), and by J. Daniélou, *Message évangelique . . .* (on his contributions see chapter III, footnote 1, p. 213 below).

[1] C. Andresen, *ZNW* 44 (1952/3), 157–95, has proved beyond any doubt Justin's dependence upon Middle Platonism in the most important points of his ethics, cosmology, and theology, as well as in his attitude towards the different schools of Greek philosophy.

[2] The only exceptions are represented by A. F. Daehne, E. F. Osborn, and R. E. Witt. Both Daehne and Osborn try to establish parallels between Clement's conception of God and of the Logos on the one hand and the Plotinian ἔν and νοῦς on the other (see Daehne, especially pp. 79–112, and Osborn, pp. 25–37 and 41). But also these two problems deserve a closer examination (see pp. 205–7 and 221–3 below). The short paper by R. E. Witt, *CQ* 25 (1931), 195–204, is very important, since it points out further interesting correspondences between some doctrines of

first produced a fruitful synthesis between Hellenism and Judaism, and which was to influence the Alexandrine Fathers so deeply,[1] has not been taken enough into account, the only Clement and of Plotinus: both of them describe the relationship between the human soul and the second hypostasis as φῶς ἐκ φωτός (p. 196), say that the human soul μελετᾷ εἶναι θεός (p. 197), stress the importance of the process κατ' ἀφαίρεσιν in the knowledge of God (pp. 197–8), attribute a cosmological role to the Logos (pp. 199–200), emphasize its property of being inexhaustible, use the terms ἀπόρροια, ἐπιστροφή, and ἐπιστρέφειν (pp. 201–3), and give similar descriptions of the perfect man (p. 204). Witt has also the merit of having drawn attention to the fact that Clement and Ammonius, the founder of Neoplatonism, lived in the same town, Alexandria, for some years and were most probably not unknown to each other (p. 195). I regard the existence of a close relationship between Clement and Ammonius as extremely likely. Clement did not leave Alexandria before Septimius Severus' persecution (A.D. 203). On the other hand Origen the Christian attended the lectures of Ammonius when he was still young (about A.D. 205) and, on this occasion, made acquaintance with another Christian, Heraklas, who had already been attending Ammonius' lectures for five years (see Porphyry in Eusebius, HE vi. 19. 6, vol. ii. 558. 26–560. 1, and a fragment of a letter of Origen preserved by Eusebius, HE vi. 19. 13, vol. ii. 562. 15–17): consequently, the presence of Ammonius in Alexandria must be traced back at least to A.D. 200 (cf., on this point, H. Dörrie, 'Ammonios der Lehrer Plotins', Hermes 83 (1955), 468). I am not persuaded by Dörrie's attempt to deny that Origen the Christian attended the lectures of Ammonius, the founder of Neoplatonism (see art. cit., particularly pp. 471 and 472), who in his opinion could not be teaching in Alexandria at the very beginning of the third century A.D. (art. cit. 468 and 472), and entirely agree with K. O. Weber, who in his book Origenes der Neuplatoniker, 34–9 has shown, in a convincing way, that the Ammonius whose lectures were attended by Origen the Christian must also have been the teacher of Plotinus (this view is shared also by E. R. Dodds, 'Numenius and Ammonius', Entretiens Hardt v. 31 n. 1, H. Chadwick, Early Christian Thought . . ., 68, and W. Theiler, Ammonios der Lehrer Origenes, Forschungen zum Neuplatonismus, 1 and 39). There must have been very close connections between Ammonius and the Christian catechetical school of Alexandria: Ammonius, as Porphyry in Eusebius, HE vi. 19. 7, tells us, had originally been a Christian and received a Christian education (Ἀμμώνιος μὲν γὰρ Χριστιανὸς ἐν Χριστιανοῖς ἀνατραφείς). Such connections have been rightly pointed out by Witt, art. cit. 195, and by H. Langerbeck in his two papers in JHS 77 (1957), 71–2, and AAWG, phil.-hist. Kl. 69 (1967), 162 (as to the criticism, however, of Langerbeck's view, according to which Ammonius remained a Christian throughout his life, see chapter III, footnote 3, p. 225 below) We shall have occasion, in the course of our work, to come back to this very important point (see especially pp. 223–6 below).

---

[1] See especially the exact references produced by C. Siegfried in the second part of his book Philo von Alexandria . . . from p. 300 onwards (on Clement in particular see pp. 343–51) and P. Heinisch, 42. After the works of Siegfried, Heinisch, and Stählin (in the critical apparatus of his edition of Clement) the fact is beyond any doubt that Clement knew Philo virtually by heart and did not refrain from including many excerpts of his writings in his Stromateis (especially in the first and second books). The sections of Philo's writings which have been incorporated in the Stromateis are so evident, that P. Wendland deemed it worth while to use the second book of the Stromateis as another manuscript for the study of the text of Philo (Hermes 31 (1896), 435–56). This will suffice to show what a scanty knowledge

two exceptions being represented by the doctrines of the transcendent God and of the Logos.[1] In other words: nobody has so far tried to explain the presence in Clement of elements coming from different schools of Greek philosophy by taking as a starting-point in his research the nature of the cultural synthesis as it appears in Philo,[2] in Middle Platonism,[3] and in Neoplatonism. Had this been done, the researches on Clement's philosophical sources would have taken a quite different direction.

Another aspect of Clement's cultural background to which very little attention seems to have been paid so far is the substantial agreement between him and the contemporary gnostic systems on some fundamental points of the idea of *gnosis*. Some

A. C. Outler seems to have of the whole problem of the relations between Philo and Clement when he says (pp. 239–40): 'We must resist the temptation... to conclude that Philo is a direct source for Clement. Clement is conscious of no such indebtedness... in a writer like Clement... this seems strongly to suggest that he is indirectly rather than directly related to Philo and that the similarities between them are due rather to a common tradition than to a conscious borrowing on Clement's part.'

[1] See chapter III, footnote 6, p. 199 below.

[2] Whereas Philo's influence on Clement in the most important points of theology has generally been acknowledged (see chapter III, footnote 6, p. 199 below) the same cannot be said about Clement's dependence upon Philo in his ethical doctrines, in which Stoic elements are particularly relevant. Only Ritter and Merk seem to have realized Philo's influence on Clement even in the adoption of Stoic doctrines and terminology: see Ritter, 423, and Merk, 67 and 90. But neither Ritter nor Merk has worked out these true remarks. Even the parallels produced by Heinisch in the definitions of some virtues (pp. 343–51) are incomplete and do not touch the more general problem of Clement's dependence upon Philo in his ethical doctrines.

[3] C. Andresen, art. cit., has clearly shown that Justin received the Stoic doctrines which play such an important role in his philosophy not directly from Stoicism but through the intermediate source represented by the school-tradition of Middle Platonism (see particularly pp. 168–81). It may also be worth while to remember Waszink's remarks on Clement, art. cit., 153–4: 'Eine Analyse seiner [sc. Clement's] Angaben zeigt, dass (genau wie Andresen das für Justin festgesetzt hat) die von ihm angeführten stoischen δόξαι durchgehend nicht aus stoischer Quelle stammen, sondern längst in das System des mittleren Platonismus inkorporiert waren.' The same could be said about the Platonic elements (this has been observed also by Arnou, 2274–5) as well as about some ethical and logical doctrines of Aristotelian origin (see pp. 64–5, 100, and 121–2 below). The results of our inquiry on Clement's cultural background will show, I hope, how wrong is J. Munck's statement 'Das Verhältnis des Klemens zur zeitgenössischen platonischen Philosophie, zum sogenannten "mittleren Platonismus" ist noch nicht untersucht worden. Es muss aber vorderhand als unwahrscheinlich angesehen werden ,dass der Eklektizismus des Klemens selbst innerhalb des eklektischen mittleren Platonismus eingeordnet werden kann' (p. 210).

modern scholars have limited themselves to pointing out the
sharp polemic of Clement against the heretics of his time.[1] It
cannot be denied that such a polemic greatly contributed to
drawing a line between orthodoxy and heresy in the Christianity
of the second century A.D.;[2] this circumstance, however, should
not prevent us from noticing the existence of close links between
Clement's *gnosis* and that of some contemporary gnostic systems.
A comprehensive inquiry into Clement's cultural background
cannot afford to underestimate the importance of this question.

The exact determination of the relations between Clement,
Middle Platonism, Neoplatonism, the Jewish-Alexandrine philosophy, and Gnosticism inevitably leads to the second problem.
Its solution depends on the answer we can give to the following
questions:

1. Does Clement's firm adherence to the Christian faith really
   exclude any influence of Greek philosophy, as Völker seems
   to believe?

2. If it can be demonstrated that Clement's thought starts from
   premisses which are characteristic of Middle Platonism,
   of Neoplatonism, and of the Jewish-Alexandrine philosophy, is there a point beyond which Clement ceases to be
   a Middle-Platonist, a Neoplatonist, and a follower of Philo
   and becomes a Christian?

3. Admitting that the terms of the problems which mostly
   interest Clement are 'Platonic' but their final solution is
   'Christian', as G. Lazzati thinks,[3] must the adjective
   'Christian' necessarily remain abstract? Can it not receive
   a more concrete connotation? Could Gnosticism not be
   helpful in this respect?

Our research on Clement's cultural background must necessarily start from his views on Greek philosophy in general and
on the individual philosophical systems in particular (chapter I):

---

[1] See, for instance, J. Kaye, 263–321, R. B. Tollinton, ii. 47 ff., E. Aleith,
Beiheft 18 zur ZNW (1937), 88–9, and W. Völker, *Der wahre Gnostiker . . .*, 10.

[2] See, on this point, H. Chadwick in his article on Clement in the *Encyclopaedia
Britannica* (1964), 899 and *Early Christian Thought . . .*, 33.

[3] p. 48: 'e però la sua posizione di partenza o impostazione di problemi è
platonica, la soluzione ad essi data è cristiana: solo nel cristianesimo avendo egli
trovato la risposta soddisfacente a quei problemi che il platonismo gli aveva
destati nell'animo.'

not only do they give us a first idea of the sphere in which Clement's thought moves, but also enable us to understand both the reason why in *Strom.* i. 37. 6 he seems to speak as an 'eclectic'[1] and the way in which he interprets Scripture.[2] Next, we shall have to examine Clement's ethical doctrines (chapter II); our inquiry will then be concluded by an analysis of his conceptions of *pistis* and of *gnosis* as well as of his views on cosmology and theology (chapter III).

At the same time, a solution will also be found for the second problem. During our inquiry it will become clear, I hope, that in the study of Clement's thought it is not possible to neglect his cultural background, as Völker and several scholars before him have done; and our examination of Clement's conceptions of the Logos and of *gnosis* will enable us to discover the line which separates the Platonist and the disciple of Philo from the Christian and to determine the nature of the Christianity which provides his 'Platonic' problems with a satisfactory solution.[3]

---

[1] See pp. 51–6 below.   [2] See pp. 56–9 below.

[3] See pp. 162–3, 233–4 below. I think that E. Vacherot, i. 248 is quite right when he says 'si on veut bien comprendre Saint Clément et Origène il faut penser toujours à la Gnose, à Philon et au Platonisme; car ce sont là les trois sources auxquelles ils puisent généralement.'

I

CLEMENT'S VIEWS ON THE ORIGIN
AND VALUE OF
GREEK PHILOSOPHY

THE interest which Clement's work has aroused in most of the
scholars who have dedicated themselves to the study of his
writings lies principally in his attitude towards Greek philosophy. In a period in which most of the Christians showed an open
hostility towards Greek culture, in so far as they regarded it as the
direct product of the devil and as the mainspring of the heresies,
particularly of Gnosticism, Clement was the first who boldly
undertook the task of defending the achievements of Greek
thought against the attacks of some members of the Christian
community to which he belonged. The problem of the recon-
ciliation and synthesis between Christianity and Hellenism was
felt by no other Christian author of the second century A.D. so
deeply as by Clement. He was perfectly aware of the fact that
the religion in which he firmly believed could never have become
a science, or assumed the shape of a philosophical system, without
taking into account the best products of Greek thought. These
important considerations—which alone would suffice to place
Clement's work in the first rank in the history of early Christian
thought and theology—have been pointed out by several modern
scholars[1] and therefore no longer represent a problem waiting
for a solution.

[1] On Clement's defence of Greek philosophy see, for instance, A. F. Daehne,
De γνώσει . . ., 45, Kling, 895 ff., W. Wagner, 9–12, O. Bardenhewer, 18, C.
Bigg, 78–9, J. Lebreton, *RHE* 19 (1923), 491–2, O. Stählin, 1307, P. T. Camelot,
RSR 21 (1931), 555, J. Champomier, *BAGB* N.S. 3 (1947), 85–92, W. Völker,
Der wahre Gnostiker . . ., 333, 342–3, and 347–8, and H. Chadwick, *Early Christian
Thought . . .*, 33–4 and 43, and *The Cambridge History . . .*, 168. The most vivid
picture of Clement's attitude towards those Christians who were afraid of com-
mitting themselves to philosophy and thought that the ψιλὴ πίστις was quite
sufficient for salvation has been made by E. de Faye, *Clément d'Alexandrie*, 137–49
and 150–60. It would also be useful to look at such passages as *Strom.* i. 18. 2–4
(ii. 13. 5–14), i. 20. 1–2 (ii. 13. 27–14. 2), i. 29. 6 (ii. 18. 25–9), i. 35. 2 (ii. 23. 6–8),
i. 35. 3 (ii. 23. 10–11), i. 43. 1 (ii. 28. 18–29. 1), i. 43. 4 (ii. 29. 8–12), i. 50. 4–6
(ii. 33. 3–14), vi. 80. 5 (ii. 472. 1–3), and vi. 159. 1 (ii. 513. 19–21) (this last passage

Almost everyone who has written about Clement has thought it proper to devote some pages of his book, article, or dissertation to the description of Clement's attitude towards Greek philosophy, as it appears especially in the first and sixth books of the *Stromateis*. A considerable amount of literature already exists on this subject.[1] Those people who do not themselves wish to take the trouble of going through the *Stromateis* can read in almost every study on Clement that he believed in the divine origin of Greek philosophy,[2] in the providential role which God had bestowed upon it in any case—i.e. even if one admitted that it had not been sent directly by him[3]—and in the correspondence between

is a refutation of the opinion of those Christians who believed that the devil was the author of philosophy, cf. *Strom.* i. 80. 5, vol. ii. 52. 17, *Strom.* vi. 66. 1, vol. ii. 465. 3 ff., and also de Faye, 189).

[1] Without attempting an exhaustive survey, I shall mention the following scholars: F. Tribbechovius, 31–4; H. F. Guerike, 106–9 and 110–12; P. Hofstede de Groot, 14–21; F. C. Baur, 520 ff.; J. Kaye, 426 and 428; I. A. Möhler i. 450–1; Kling, 899–901; E. Redepenning, Erste Abt., 139–47; H. Ritter, 429–30; E. Vacherot, i. 248–50; V. Hébert-Duperron, 61–76, 105–16, and 116–23; N. Le Nourry in Migne, *PG* 9, coll. 1259–67; J. Cognat, 107–24 and 125–37; J. Huber, 134–6; H. Schürmann, 15–16 and 27–32; E. Freppel, 128–48; H. Preische, 21–9; Knittel, *TQ* 55 (1873), 198–204 and 366–7; C. Merk, 1–15; M. Dods, 54; F. R. Hitchcock, 134–49; W. Christ, *ABAWM*, philos.-philol. Kl. xxi, Abth. iii (1901), 458–69; W. Wagner throughout his dissertation; O. Bardenhewer, 19–21; J. Geffcken, 235–55; E. de Faye, *Clément d'Alexandrie*, 174–90 and 191–200; M. Daskalakis, 22–9 and 29–32; F. H. Chase, 282–5; C. Bigg, 76–9; J. Patrick, 34–64; O. Bardenhewer, 45; W. Bousset, *Jüdisch-christlicher Schulbetrieb...*, 205–18 and 219–36 (the most accurate analysis of the sections of the *Stromateis* dealing with the question of the origin of Greek philosophy); H. Eibl, 33–59; G. Bardy, *Clément d'Alexandrie*, 52–63; J. Meifort, 6–9; P. T. Camelot, *RSR* 21 (1931), 541–69; E. Molland, *SO* xv–xvi. 57–85 and *The Conception of the Gospel...*, 40–69 and 69–75; A. C. Outler, *JR* 20 (1940), 238–9; E. Aleith, 920; P. Barth and A. Goedeckmeyer, 250; M. Pohlenz, *NGA*, phil.-hist. Kl. (1943), 109–10 and *Die Stoa* i. 415; J. T. Muckle, *Phoenix* v (1951), 79–86; W. Völker, 332–52; H. A. Wolfson, *The Philosophy of the Church Fathers*, 21–2; and E. Fascher, *TU* 77. 194–8.

[2] See, for instance, *Strom.* i. 20. 1–2 (ii. 13. 28–30) (with this passage it is worth comparing *Strom.* vi. 110. 3, vol. ii. 487. 9–11, and *Strom.* vi. 42. 1, vol. ii. 452. 21–3); the section of the 7th chapter of the 6th book, from 52. 7 up to 58. 3 (ii. 460. 21–461. 9), where the Logos is represented as the first teacher of all Greek philosophers and consequently as the main source of philosophy; *Strom.* vi. 58. 2 (ii. 461. 15–16), *Strom.* i. 37. 1 (ii. 24. 8–9), i. 94. 2 (ii. 60. 15–18), vi. 62. 4 (ii. 463. 14–16), vi. 156. 3 (ii. 512. 11–18), and vi. 159. 6–8 (ii. 513. 31–2; 514. 1–5).

[3] In *Strom.* i. 81. 4–5 (ii. 53. 5–13) Clement seems to make a concession to his opponents by accepting their view according to which philosophy had not been sent by God, but stolen by some inferior powers or angels who transmitted it to men (*Strom.* i. 80. 5, vol. ii. 52. 17–19; for the origin of this view see p. 29 below); such a theft, however, in Clement's opinion, was allowed by God who, in his providence, knew what a benefit men were to receive from it, *Strom.* i. 81. 5 (ii. 53. 10–13). The same idea underlies the passage of *Strom.* i. 86. 2–3 (ii. 55. 22–9);

it and the Jewish law, in so far as both of them, as two parallel covenants, were to prepare, in the plan of God, the Greeks and the Jews respectively for the reception of the more perfect Christian message, the 'true philosophy';[1] that Greek philosophy, in Clement's opinion, contained some elements of truth;[2] that it had also been 'stolen' by the Greeks from the Old Testament;[3] and finally that, although Greek philosophy was inferior to the perfection of the Christian faith,[4] nevertheless it was still very useful for the Christians, who could find in it the best defence against the attacks of their enemies[5] and an excellent training providing their souls with the best preparation for the study of the Christian doctrines.[6] On these questions the previous studies have said what had to be said, and there is therefore no need to dwell on them at a disproportionate length.

The problems for which no satisfactory solutions have been reached so far are of a different kind and rest upon five fundamental issues:

1. Why does Clement hold so different views on the origin of Greek philosophy, which, at a first glance, seem to conflict with one another?[7] On which sources does he depend? Can the

immediately afterwards, Clement compares the theft of philosophy to the theft of Zeus' fire made by Prometheus, *Strom.* i. 87. 1 (ii. 55. 31). In *Strom.* i. 94. 1 (ii. 60. 12–15) Clement mentions two other possible explanations of the origin of Greek philosophy: the Greek philosophers had succeeded in grasping some elements of truth either by accident (κατὰ περίπτωσιν) or owing to a good fortune (κατὰ συντυχίαν). Here also he does not hesitate to trace both alternatives back to God's providence: θείας οἰκονομίας ἢ περίπτωσις . . . οὐκ ἀπρονόητος ἡ συντυχία; see also *Strom.* i. 18. 4 (ii. 13. 13–14) and vi. 153. 1 (ii. 510. 21–3). On this question Merk's remarks, pp. 9–10, are worth noticing even today.

[1] This view is strongly emphasized by Clement: see *Strom.* i. 28. 3 (ii. 18. 2–5), vi. 42. 1–3 (ii. 452. 21–453. 3), vi. 44. 1 (ii. 453. 16–18), vi. 64. 4 (ii. 464. 6–7), vi. 67. 1 (ii. 465. 19–21), and vi. 159. 9 (ii. 514. 5–6).
[2] See, for instance, *Strom.* i. 80. 5 (ii. 52. 15–16), i. 91. 1 (ii. 58. 17–18), and i. 94. 3 (ii. 60. 20–21).
[3] For the evidence see pp. 31–3 below.
[4] *Strom.* i. 80. 6 (ii. 52. 19–20), i. 98. 4 (ii. 63. 2–4), vi. 62. 1 (ii. 463. 4–5), and vi. 117. 1 (ii. 490. 28–9). This is the point on which Völker, op. cit., 345–50, particularly insists. The question of the subordination of Greek philosophy to Christianity will, however, be discussed more in detail later on (see pp. 56–9 below).
[5] *Strom.* i. 28. 4 (ii. 18. 7–8), i. 35. 6 (ii. 23. 19–21), i. 43. 4 (ii. 29. 9–12), i. 100. 1 (ii. 63. 31–64. 2), vi. 81. 4 (ii. 472. 18–19), and vi. 156. 2 (ii. 512. 11) (the two last passages refer to a particular branch of philosophy, namely dialectic).
[6] See the references given by Völker, 350 n. 2.
[7] Some scholars have pointed out the contradictions in which Clement is apparently involved: see the references given by Völker, 340 nn. 2 and 3. To them I should like to add Daehne, 48, Merk, 4–5, 8 n. 3, and 9, and O. Bardenhewer, 45,

determination of these sources enable us to reconstruct a substantial unity and coherence in his thought?

2. Why does he dwell at such length on the topic of the 'theft of the Greeks'? Is his insistence due *only* to his love for erudition? Can it not find an explanation in the vehement attack which a non-Christian Platonist of the second century A.D. launched against Christianity, and which forced Clement to take up the defence of his own religion? And—what is perhaps more important: in developing his polemic, does Clement resort to ideas which are also characteristic of his opponent?

3. How can Clement's attitude towards the individual philosophical schools be explained? Does it really depend on his Christian faith, which enables him to judge what is right and what is wrong in the different philosophical systems?[1] Is it not rather due to the philosophical education which he received before becoming a Christian, and which plays such an important role even after his conversion?

4. Why does he sometimes seem to speak as an 'eclectic'? Can his 'eclecticism' be regarded simply as 'Christian'? Can it not rather be traced back to a doctrine on which one of his explanations of the origin of Greek philosophy is ultimately based? Is it not also a product of his cultural formation?

5. Is it possible to establish a sort of parallelism between the function which, according to Clement, Greek philosophy has accomplished in the history of mankind and the role which it still plays in the formation of the perfect Christian who must attain *gnosis*? In other words: is the relation between Greek philosophy and Christianity in history analogous to the relation between the study of philosophy on the one hand, and the interpretation of Scripture and *gnosis* on the other?

1. The solutions which Clement adopts in order to explain the problem of the origin of Greek philosophy are substantially the following:

(*a*) the Greek philosophers have discovered some doctrines, and reached a certain degree of knowledge of some elements of truth, either by themselves or by means of a divine inspiration;

---

[1] On this point see the Introduction, p. 3 above.

(b) they have 'stolen' the doctrines which they claim as their own from the Old Testament and, in this way, all of them depend on Moses;

(c) philosophy, which was originally a possession of God, was stolen by some inferior powers or angels, who transmitted it to men.

As to the first solution, it is clear that the Greeks were able to grasp some idea of God owing to a kind of 'natural conception', φυσικὴ ἔννοια, or 'common intellect', κοινὸς νοῦς, which all men possess; in Strom. i. 94. 2 (ii. 60. 15–18) Clement presents this explanation as suggested by somebody else, εἴτ' αὖ φυσικὴν ἔννοιαν ἐσχηκέναι τοὺς Ἕλληνας λέγοι . . . εἴτε μὴν κοινὸν ἐσχηκέναι νοῦν . . .; but in Strom. v. 87. 2 (ii. 383. 21 ff.) he adopts it as his own view: θεοῦ μὲν γὰρ ἔμφασις ἑνὸς ἦν τοῦ παντοκράτορος παρὰ πᾶσι τοῖς εὖ φρονοῦσι πάντοτε φυσική . . . There is no doubt about the Stoic origin of this doctrine and its adoption on the part of Antiochus of Ascalon and of some exponents of Middle Platonism.[1] What, however, is more important to observe here is that Clement shows a strong inclination to bring the φυσικὴ ἔννοια into close connection with human reason, which, in his opinion, is a gift of God. In the section of Strom. v. 87. 2 ff. after maintaining that all wise men, owing to their ἔννοια φυσική, must have some idea of God, and mentioning Xenocrates' view according to which irrational animals also may possess some conception of the divine essence, he lays strong emphasis on the fact that, if so, it would be impossible to state that man is deprived of a 'divine conception' since he alone, among all living beings, possesses reason, which was breathed into him when he was created:

[1] See SVF ii. 83, 106, 473 (p. 154. 29–30), and 841. According to the Stoics, these κοιναί or φυεικαὶ ἔννοιαι are formed in the human mind—which is originally a tabula rasa—by experience, when man is still a child; this is the reason why they call them sometimes προλήψεις: see J. S. Reid's note in his commentary of the Academica of Cicero, 213 (the note is concerned with the notitiae rerum mentioned in Ac. Pr. ii. x. 30). This doctrine occurs also in the eighth book of the Stromateis, dealing mainly with logic and epistemology: ἐχομένους γὰρ καθήκει . . . τῶν ἐννοιῶν τῶν κοινῶν τὰς ζητήσεις ποιεῖσθαι (Strom. viii. 2. 4, vol. iii. 81. 1–2), ἰδίαν λόγου δύναμιν πεφυκυῖαν ἅπαντες ἔχομεν φύσει (Strom. viii. 7. 5, vol. iii. 83. 30). This last passage of Clement reminds us of the words mens enim . . . naturalem vim habet, quam intendit ad ea, quibus movetur which reproduce the view of Antiochus of Ascalon (Cic. Ac. Pr. ii. x. 30). For Antiochus' adoption of the Stoic doctrine of the φυσικαὶ ἔννοιαι see H. Strache, Der Eklektizismus . . ., 17, and R. E. Witt, Albinus . . ., 58. As to its presence in Middle Platonism see, for instance, Albinus, Did. 155. 23 and 27–8 (cf. K. Praechter in Überweg–Heinze, Grundriss . . . i. 542, and Witt, op. cit. 47–54).

πολλοῦ γε δεῖ ἄμοιρον εἶναι θείας ἐννοίας τὸν ἄνθρωπον, ὅς γε καὶ τοῦ ἐμφυσήματος ἐν τῇ γενέσει μεταλαβεῖν ἀναγέγραπται, καθαρωτέρας οὐσίας παρὰ τὰ ἄλλα ζῷα μετασχών (Strom. v. 87. 4, vol. ii. 383. 20–384. 3). If we want to grasp the real meaning of this passage, we must remember that Clement is thinking here of the words of Gen. 2: 7, καὶ ἔπλασεν ὁ θεὸς τὸν ἄνθρωπον χοῦν ἀπὸ τῆς γῆς καὶ ἐνεφύσησεν εἰς τὸ πρόσωπον αὐτοῦ πνοὴν ζωῆς, and that he interprets the πνοὴ ζωῆς as meaning 'reason', as it is easy to infer from the words καθαρωτέρας οὐσίας παρὰ τὰ ἄλλα ζῷα μετασχών, which represent his own explanation of the biblical passage. That Clement identifies the πνοὴ ζωῆς with reason is proved by the passage which immediately follows. Eager as he is to show the agreement between the Greek philosophical doctrines and the teaching of Scripture, he adds that the followers of Pythagoras and of Plato held also the view that reason was something which had been given by God to man: ἐντεῦθεν οἱ ⟨μὲν⟩ ἀμφὶ τὸν Πυθαγόραν θείᾳ μοίρᾳ τὸν νοῦν εἰς ἀνθρώπους ἥκειν φασί, οἱ δὲ ἀμφὶ τὸν Πλάτωνα νοῦν μὲν ἐν ψυχῇ θείας μοίρας ἀπόρροιαν ὑπάρχοντα (Strom. v. 88. 1–2, vol. ii. 384. 3–7).[1] The same inter-

---

[1] I am personally inclined to believe that the sentence of Strom. v. 88. 2 (ii. 384. 5–6), ἀλλ' ἡμεῖς μὲν τῷ πεπιστευκότι προσεπιπνεῖσθαι τὸ ἅγιον πνεῦμά φαμεν, has been put in a wrong place by the copyist either of L or of one of its predecessors, since it breaks, without any reason, the two references to the Greek schools. Its proper place would be before the clause which introduces the biblical quotation in Strom. v. 88. 3 ἀναφανδὸν γὰρ διὰ 'Ιωὴλ . . . In the text as it stands in Stählin's edition the γάρ of this introductory clause has no meaning, since there is no relation between it and the immediately preceding reference to the Platonic school. The sentence ἀλλ' ἡμεῖς . . . represents on the contrary the natural introduction to the biblical quotation of Strom. v. 88. 3 dealing with prophecy, since it is meant to draw attention to the fact that prophecy is originated by the Holy Ghost. As to the words καθάπερ Πλάτων καὶ Ἀριστοτέλης ὁμολογοῦσιν, they seem to me to be a gloss of some erudite commentator; Clement had no reason to say καθάπερ Πλάτων if he was to add, immediately afterwards, a longer statement about the Platonic school. I suggest therefore the following reading of the whole section of Strom. v. 88. 1–3: ἐντεῦθεν οἱ ⟨μὲν⟩ ἀμφὶ τὸν Πυθαγόραν θείᾳ μοίρᾳ τὸν νοῦν εἰς ἀνθρώπους ἥκειν φασί, [καθάπερ Πλάτων καὶ Ἀριστοτέλης ὁμολογοῦσιν] οἱ δὲ ἀμφὶ τὸν Πλάτωνα νοῦν μὲν ἐν ψυχῇ θείας μοίρας ἀπόρροιαν ὑπάρχοντα, ψυχὴν δὲ ἐν σώματι κατοικίζουσιν. ἀλλ' ἡμεῖς τῷ πεπιστευκότι προσεπιπνεῖσθαι τὸ ἅγιον πνεῦμά φαμεν. ἀναφανδὸν γὰρ διὰ 'Ιωὴλ . . . Clement's words νοῦν μὲν ἐν ψυχῇ . . . ψυχὴν δὲ ἐν σώματι κατοικίζουσιν seem to have been directly originated by Timaeus 30 b 4–5, νοῦν μὲν ἐν ψυχῇ, ψυχὴν δὲ ἐν σώματι συνιστάς. This passage, however, is not concerned with the origin of human reason, but with the order established by the Demiurge in the universe by means of the world-soul. The doctrine of the divine origin of human reason can be observed in another passage of the Timaeus, namely 41 c 7–d 1, θεῖον λεγόμενον ἡγεμονοῦν τε . . . σπείρας καὶ ὑπαρξάμενος ἐγὼ παραδώσω (these words are part of the speech which the Demiurge addresses to the astral

pretation of the passage of Genesis is given by Clement later on, *Strom.* v. 94. 3 (ii. 388. 10–11), ψυχὴν δὲ τὴν λογικὴν ἄνωθεν ἐμπνεῦσθαι ὑπὸ θεοῦ εἰς πρόσωπον. That reason is something divine in man is also the idea which underlies Clement's interpretation of two other passages of Genesis: ποιήσωμεν ἄνθρωπον κατ' εἰκόνα ἡμετέραν καὶ ὁμοίωσιν (Gen. 1: 26) and ἐποίησεν ὁ θεὸς τὸν ἄνθρωπον, κατ' εἰκόνα θεοῦ ἐποίησεν αὐτόν (Gen. 1: 27). He thinks that the word εἰκών, which appears in both passages, hints at the divine Logos, the Son or image of God. Consequently for him the two biblical passages mean that God bestowed upon man a rational principle which was an imitation of his own image, the Logos; this is the reason why he says: διὸ "κατ' εἰκόνα καὶ ὁμοίωσιν τὸν ἄνθρωπον" γεγονέναι. εἰκὼν μὲν γὰρ θεοῦ λόγος θεῖος καὶ βασιλικὸς ... εἰκὼν δ' εἰκόνος ὁ ἀνθρώπινος νοῦς (*Strom.* v. 94. 4–5, vol. ii. 388. 13–16). What Clement says here is in perfect agreement with what he had said before, when he had remarked on the suggestion that the Greek philosophers had grasped some elements of truth by means of the φυσικὴ ἔννοια or of the κοινὸς νοῦς: τὸν τῆς φύσεως δημιουργὸν ἕνα γινώσκομεν, and τίς ὁ τούτων πατὴρ σκοπήσωμεν (*Strom.* i. 94. 2); and with what he will say later on, *Strom.* vi. 62. 4: τὰς γραφὰς εὑρίσκω τὴν σύνεσιν θεόπεμπτον εἶναι λεγούσας. All this proves also that there is for Clement a close kinship between the human mind and the universal Logos, the Son of God. It could not therefore be surprising if some Greek philosophers succeeded in reaching some exact idea of the first principle by means of the divine element dwelling in them, κἀκ τοῦ ἐν ἡμῖν θείου τὸ ποιητικὸν αἴτιον ὡς οἷόν τε συνθεωροῦντες (*Strom.* i. 94. 4, vol. ii. 60. 24–5), or discovered some doctrines which may be regarded as the reflection of the eternal truth, ναὶ μὴν κατ' ἔμφασιν ἀληθείας ἄλλοι θέλουσιν εἰρῆσθαί τινα τοῖς φιλοσόφοις (*Strom.* i. 94. 3, vol. ii. 60, 20–2: cf. *Strom.* i. 20. 1 φιλοσοφίαν ... ἀληθείας οὖσαν εἰκόνα ἐναργῆ, θείαν δωρεὰν Ἕλλησι δεδομένην).[1] The idea of the *revelatio*

gods). As to the presence of this doctrine in the Platonic and Pythagorean schools see, for instance, Albinus, *Did.* 176. 7–8, Plutarch, *Quaest. Plat.* 1004 d 2–4, and Aetius, *Plac.* iv. 5. 1, 392 b 2 (= Xenocrates, fr. 69 Heinze, p. 187). For the use of the terms ἀπόρροια and ἀπορροή in Neoplatonism see the references given by R. E. Witt in *CQ* 25 (1931), 201 nn. 4 and 9.

[1] E. Molland, *SO* 15–16 (1938), 57–85, rightly translates Clement's expression κατ' ἔμφασιν ἀληθείας with 'reflection of truth' (see pp. 69 ff.). He points out the Platonic origin of the idea of reflected knowledge, and produces some interesting

naturalis, which appears in *Strom.* i. 94. 2 and *Strom.* v. 87. 2, is thus developed by Clement himself into the idea of the intuition or discovery of some true principles: directly in *Strom.* i. 94. 3–4 and by way of implication in the section of *Strom.* v. 87. 3–88. 1. That between the two ideas there is a climax has been rightly shown by E. Molland.[1]

The Greek philosophers could discover some true doctrines not only by means of their reason, but also by means of a divine inspiration, which also comes from the Logos. In other words: not only did God in creation provide man with a divine principle which represents his reason but, in the history of mankind, he also inspired a few selected people. We can thus understand why in *Strom.* i. 26. 2 (ii. 17. 4–5) Clement says: ἔχουσι μέν τι οἰκεῖον φύσεως ἰδίωμα οἱ "σοφοὶ τῇ διανοίᾳ", λαμβάνουσι δὲ "πνεῦμα αἰσθήσεως" παρὰ τῆς κυριωτάτης σοφίας.[2] The σοφοὶ τῇ διανοίᾳ mentioned here include also the Greek philosophers (cf. *Strom.* i. 26. 4, vol. ii. 17. 12–13); the πνεῦμα αἰσθήσεως ('spirit of sensitivity') represents the divine inspiration, and the κυριωτάτη σοφία the Logos.[3] That among the σοφοὶ τῇ διανοίᾳ the Greek philosophers must be included is also shown by two other passages, *Strom.* i. 87. 2 (ii. 56. 6), ἴσως γὰρ καὶ πνεῦμα αἰσθήσεως ἐσχήκασι [sc. οἱ φιλόσοφοι], and *Strom.* vi. 154. 1 (ii. 511. 3–5), οἱ τοίνυν φιλόσοφοι... πνεύματι αἰσθητικῷ συνασκηθέντες. This πνεῦμα inspiring the philosophers is practically identical with the Holy Ghost, which inspired the prophets of the Old Testament and which is represented as something distinct from human reason (cf. *Strom.* v. 88. 2–3, vol. ii. 384. 5–8, ἀλλ' ἡμεῖς [μὲν] τῷ πεπιστευκότι προσεπιπνεῖσθαι τὸ ἅγιον πνεῦμά φαμεν. ἀναφανδὸν γὰρ διὰ 'Ιωὴλ... εἴρηται).[4] A passage of the fifth book of the *Stromateis*

parallels to it collected from some later authors such as Philo and Plutarch (see pp. 76–85).

[1] See Molland's acute and penetrating analysis of the section of *Strom.* i. 94. 1–4, art. cit. 65–75, especially p. 71 (a short summary of it can be found in his book *The Conception of the Gospel* . . ., 49–53).

[2] The expressions "σοφοὶ τῇ διανοίᾳ" and "πνεύματι αἰσθήσεως" go back to the passage of Exod. 28: 3 which Clement quotes a few lines before, *Strom.* i. 26. 1 (ii. 17. 2–3): see Stählin's apparatus, ii. 17.

[3] On the identity between the Logos and the divine wisdom see chapter III, pp. 208–9 below.

[4] For the text see footnote 1, p. 14 above. This passage, as it stands in Stählin's edition, has provided Völker with a beautiful occasion to point out the radical opposition between the Christian doctrines of Clement and those of the Greek philosophers (see p. 284 n. 7). Were this true, this would be the only passage

is particularly instructive in this respect. In *Strom*. v. 29. 4 (ii. 344. 26–345. 2) Clement does not hesitate to represent Pythagoras, his disciples, and Plato as inspired prophets who had attained a partial knowledge of the truth: 'Having with the help of God come into harmony ⟨with the teachings of the lawgiver⟩, owing to some acute utterance inspired by a prophetic power, and grasped partially the truth in some prophetic sayings, they honoured it with appellatives which proved to be clear and in keeping with the explanations of reality; they got some reflection of the proper sense of the truth.' Clement lays a particularly strong emphasis on the close parallelism which, according to him, exists between the Old Testament and Greek philosophy.[1] Accordingly, for Clement the Greek philosophers, like the prophets, are divinely inspired men, in so far as they also are filled with the πνεῦμα coming from the divine Logos.

In order to describe the way in which this divine inspiration took place, Clement likes to resort to the picture of the shower: God inspired the philosophers by dropping particles of the Logos into their minds. This idea is implied in *Protr*. 68. 2 (i. 52. 2–4), πᾶσιν γὰρ ἁπαξαπλῶς ἀνθρώποις, μάλιστα δὲ τοῖς περὶ λόγους διατρίβουσι, ἐνέστακταί τις ἀπόρροια θεϊκή,[2] and makes clearer what Clement says later on, *Protr*. 74. 7 (i. 57. 8–9), καὶ τὰ μάλιστα

in the whole work of Clement in which a Platonic and Pythagorean doctrine is rejected. The sentence ἀλλ' ἡμεῖς . . . , if put before the sentence ἀναφανδὸν γὰρ διὰ 'Ιωὴλ . . ., is not meant to oppose the Christian doctrine of the Holy Ghost as the source of inspiration to the Pythagorean and Platonic doctrine of the origin of the human mind; Clement aims here simply at distinguishing the reason which all men possess from the divine inspiration which God bestows *in addition* to those who believe in him (either the prophets or the philosophers). This is the reason why he uses the verb προσεπιπνεῖσθαι (to be breathed into in addition to something else) instead of the simple ἐπιπνεῖσθαι; cf. *Strom*. vi. 134. 2 (ii. 500. 3–5), where the διὰ τῆς πίστεως προσγινόμενον ἁγίου πνεύματος χαρακτηριστικὸν ἰδίωμα, which is mentioned immediately after the ἡγεμονικόν, recalls the expression τῷ πεπιστευκότι προσεπιπνεῖσθαι τὸ ἅγιον πνεῦμα of *Strom*. v. 88. 2.

[1] See footnote 1, p. 11 above.

[2] This sentence has a double meaning. The ἀπόρροια θεϊκή which all men possess is obviously human reason: in this way, Clement virtually adopts the view of the Platonists and of the Pythagoreans, who also regard the human mind as an ἀπόρροια coming from God (see *Strom*. v. 88. 1–2 and footnote 1, p. 14 above); the same idea appears also in the 'Υποτυπώσεις, fr. 23 (iii. 202. 20–22), ἀλλὰ δύναμις τοῦ θεοῦ οἷον ἀπόρροια τοῦ λόγου αὐτοῦ νοῦς γενόμενος τὰς τῶν ἀνθρώπων καρδίας διαπεφοίτηκε. On the other hand, the ἀπόρροια θεϊκή which is dropped *especially* (μάλιστα) on the philosophers cannot be identified with human reason, but must hint at the divine inspiration which a few selected people receive from God.

ἐναύσματά τινα τοῦ λόγου τοῦ θείου λαβόντες "Ελληνες ὀλίγα ἄττα τῆς ἀληθείας ἐφθέγξαντο. Clement therefore finds it easy, at the beginning of chapter VII of the first book of the *Stromateis*, to compare Greek philosophy with the showers falling upon the earth: καταφαίνεται τοίνυν ἡ προπαιδεία ἡ Ἑλληνικὴ σὺν καὶ αὐτῇ φιλοσοφίᾳ θεόθεν ἥκειν εἰς ἀνθρώπους . . . ὃν τρόπον οἱ ὑετοὶ καταρρήγνυνται, *Strom.* i. 37. 1 (ii. 24. 8 ff.). A few lines below Clement, in order to give another picture of the origin of philosophy, resorts to the Gospel parable of the sower; the different philosophical systems are compared to the different seeds which the same husbandman drops on different places at different times (*Strom.* i. 37. 2–3, vol. ii. 24. 16–23). Even here, however, Clement cannot refrain from using the image of the rainfall, in close connection with that of the dropping of the seeds: εἷς γὰρ ὁ τῆς ἐν ἀνθρώποις γῆς γεωργὸς ὁ ἄνωθεν σπείρων . . . τὰ θρεπτικὰ σπέρματα, ὁ τὸν κύριον καθ' ἕκαστον καιρὸν ἐπομβρίσας λόγον (*Strom.* i. 37. 2, vol. ii. 24. 17–19; cf. *Paed.* i. 41. 3, vol. i. 115. 7–8, τοῦ φιλοστόργου καὶ φιλανθρώπου πατρὸς ἐπομβρήσαντος τὸν λόγον). The Logos is thus represented as the multitude of the seeds which like a rainfall are dropped on the soil; it is, needless to say, one and the same thing with the πνεῦμα which inspires the philosophers.

If we want now to understand why Clement had so many ideas and images floating in his mind when he attempted to set forth one of the possible explanations of the origin of Greek philosophy, we must remember that he found them already formed in the Jewish-Alexandrine philosophy and in Justin. In the Wisdom of Solomon,[1] which Clement knew nearly by heart and which he quotes so many times, the σοφία of God is described as ἀτμὶς τοῦ θεοῦ δυνάμεως καὶ ἀπόρροια τῆς τοῦ παντοκράτορος δόξης εἰλικρινής (7: 25).[2] Moreover, it contains the 'Holy Ghost' in itself (ἔστι γὰρ ἐν αὐτῇ πνεῦμα νοερόν, ἅγιον, μονογενές, 7. 22) and, descending upon the souls of some blessed men, enables them to become prophets (εἰς ψυχὰς ὁσίας μεταβαίνουσα φίλους θεοῦ καὶ προφήτας κατασκευάζει, 7: 27). In Ecclesiasticus (or the Wisdom of Jesus, Son of Sira), science and knowledge are represented as a rainfall produced by the divine wisdom, ἐπιστήμην καὶ γνῶσιν

---

[1] On this product of Hellenistic Judaism and its philosophical sources see E. Schürer, Band iii. 505, 512 (especially 507), and E. Zeller, *Die Philos. der Griechen* iii. 2. 292–6.

[2] R. E. Witt, *CQ* 25 (1931), 201, has also noticed the use of the term ἀπόρροια in the Wisdom of Solomon.

συνέσεως ἐξώμβρησεν [sc. σοφία], 1: 19. These passages remind us at once of the expressions used by Clement: the words ἀτμὶς τοῦ θεοῦ δυνάμεως καὶ ἀπόρροια recall the ἀπόρροια θεϊκή of *Protr.* 68. 2;[1] the mention of the Holy Ghost and the descent of the wisdom of God upon some blessed men who, in this way, become prophets find their exact counterpart in what Clement says in *Strom.* i. 26. 2, v. 88. 2–3, and v. 29. 4 (see also pp. 16–17 above), and the image of the rainfall used in connection with the dropping of scientific knowledge is the same both in Ecclesiasticus and in Clement, *Strom.* i. 37. 1.

In Philo these ideas assume an even clearer shape and are closely connected with the question of the origin of philosophy. Philo openly maintains that philosophy is the source of all good things, *De spec. Leg.* iii. 186 (v. 202. 7),[2] and resorts very often to the image of the shower in order to represent the way in which God bestows His blessings on men, as the following evidence shows:

Leg. Alleg. iii. 164 (i. 149. 2): τὸν θεὸν ὀμβρήσειν . . . ἀγαθά.
De Sobr. 64 (ii. 227. 76): τὸ θεοφιλὲς ὤμβρησεν ἀγαθόν [sc. ὁ θεός].
De Migr. Abr. 121 (ii. 291. 25–6): ὁ δὲ τὸν οὐράνιον ἀνοίξας θησαυρὸν ὀμβρεῖ καὶ ἐπινίφει τὰ ἀγαθὰ ἀθρόα.
De Migr. Abr. 156 (ii. 299. 6–7): ἀγαθὰ ἀθρόα . . . ὀμβρήσαντος.
Quis Rer. div. Her. 280 (iii. 64. 1): ἀθρόα καὶ νέα ὤμβρησεν ἀγαθά.
De Mut. Nom. 141 (iii. 180. 25): τοῦ χάριτας ἐπομβροῦντος θεοῦ.
De Somn. i. 162 (iii. 239. 20): διὰ τὰς ὀμβρηθείσας ἄνωθεν δωρεάς.

Since philosophy contains all divine blessings in itself and these blessings are dropped like a shower from heaven onto the earth, Philo, like the author of Ecclesiasticus, does not hesitate to represent philosophy itself as a shower, which falls straightway into the human mind, *De spec. Leg.* iii. 185 (v. 202. 5), φιλοσοφίαν ὤμβρησε ὁ οὐρανός, ἐχώρησε δὲ ὁ ἀνθρώπινος νοῦς, cf. *De Fuga et Inv.* 166 (iii. 146. 12–13), εὐτρεπισμένην εὗρε σοφίαν [sc. ὁ αὐτομαθὴς καὶ αὐτοδίδακτος σοφός] ἄνωθεν ὀμβρηθεῖσαν ἀπ᾽ οὐρανοῦ,

[1] The author of the Wisdom of Solomon describes the emanation of σοφία from God, whereas in *Protr.* 68. 2 Clement hints at the dropping of the particles of the Logos into the minds of the philosophers; the image of the effluence of a stream (ἀπόρροια) out of its source (i.e. God) is, however, the same in both passages.
[2] These words of Philo find their exact counterpart in Plato, *Timaeus* 47 b 1–2, φιλοσοφίας γένος, οὗ μεῖζον ἀγαθὸν οὔτ᾽ ἦλθεν οὔτε ἥξει ποτὲ τῷ θνητῷ γένει δωρηθὲν ἐκ θεῶν; Clement also may have thought of this passage of Plato when he wrote in *Strom.* i. 20. 1–2 (ii. 13. 28–30), φιλοσοφίαν . . . ἀληθείας οὖσαν εἰκόνα ἐναργῆ, θείαν δωρεὰν Ἕλλησι δεδομένην.

and *Leg. Alleg.* iii. 162 (i. 148. 17–19), οὐ γηΐνοις καὶ φθαρτοῖς τρέφεται ἡ ψυχή, ἀλλ' οἷς ὁ θεὸς ὀμβρήσῃ λόγοις ἐκ μεταρσίου καὶ καθαρᾶς φύσεως. Clement found therefore in the Jewish-Alexandrine philosophy the image of philosophy as a shower, which he reproduced in chap.VII of the first book of the *Stromateis*.[1]

But there are still some more similarities between Philo and Clement. Like Clement (*Strom.* i. 37. 2), Philo maintains that the Logos is the source of wisdom . . . λόγον θεῖον, ὃς σοφίας ἐστὶ πηγή, *De Fuga et Inv.* 97 (iii. 131. 1), and in order to represent the way in which the Logos is originated by God he uses the image of the effluence of a stream out of its source: ἀκροτάτης καὶ πρεσβυτάτης . . . ἀρχῆς, ἀφ' ἧς ἡ τῶν ὄντων γένεσις ὤμβρησε καὶ τὸ σοφίας ἐπλήμμυρε νᾶμα, *De Somn.* ii. 221 (iii. 294. 8–9); in this passage the πρεσβυτάτη ἀρχή hints at God, whereas the expressions ἡ τῶν ὄντων γένεσις ὤμβρησε and σοφίας . . . νᾶμα indicate the divine Logos. Here we have a very close kinship with the ἀπόρροια which appears both in Clement and in the Wisdom of Solomon, with the ὤμβρησε of Ecclesiasticus, and with the expressions τὸν κύριον . . . ἐπομβρίσας λόγον or ἐπομβρήσαντος λόγον which we have met in Clement.[2]

Moreover, Clement depends closely on Philo both in the doctrine of the divine origin of human reason—the discoverer of philosophy—and in the interpretation of the passages of Genesis concerning the creation of the first man. That for Philo the human νοῦς is something divine is proved by the following evidence, which shows a striking similarity with the passages of Clement quoted above (pp. 14–15):

> *Quis Rer. divin. Her.* 64 (iii. 15. 19–20): ὁ καταπνευσθεὶς ἄνωθεν, οὐρανίας τε καὶ θείας μοίρας ἐπιλαχών, ὁ καθαρώτατος νοῦς.
> *Quis Rer. divin. Her.* 184 (iii. 42. 11–12): . . . ὁ ἀκραιφνέστατος νοῦς ἐστιν, ὃς ἀπ' οὐρανοῦ καταπνευσθείς . . .

---

[1] H. A. Wolfson has drawn attention to the image of the shower used by Philo in *De spec. Leg.* iii. 185 as well as to the use made of it by Clement (*Philo* i. 142 and 160–1, and *The Philosophy of the Church Fathers*, 22). He goes too far, however, when he says that Clement quotes Philo 'almost verbatim' (*Philo* i. 160–1 and *The Philosophy of the Church Fathers*, 22).

[2] This passage of Philo contains therefore the same doctrine as that which we have met in the Wisdom of Solomon (see footnote 1, p. 19 above). Further remarks on the doctrine of the origin of the divine Logos both in Clement and in Philo will be added in chapter III, pp. 203–5 below.

De Somn. i. 34 (iii. 212. 7): νοῦς, ἀπόσπασμα θεῖον ὤν.

Like Clement, Philo explains the expression κατ' εἰκόνα of Gen.
1: 26 and 27 in the sense that human reason is an image or
imitation of the divine Logos, who is himself the image of
God; the following passages are particularly important in this
respect:

> *Opif. M.* 139 (i. 48. 11–15): For he [i.e. the creator] thought it
> proper to employ for its making [i.e. of the human soul] no
> pattern taken from creation but only, as I have said, his own
> Logos. This is the reason why he says that man became a likeness
> and imitation of the Logos when he received the breath into his
> face.
> *Quis Rer. divin. Her.* 230–1 (iii. 52. 6–13): . . . two reasons, the one,
> which is above us, being the archetype, the other, which dwells
> in us, being its imitation. Moses calls the reason which is above
> us the image of God, and the reason which dwells in us the
> cast of the image. For 'God' he says 'made man' not the image of
> God but 'after the image'. Consequently the mind which each of
> us possesses . . . is the third impression coming from the creator,
> whereas the reason which stays in the middle is the pattern of
> human reason and the image of God.
> *De spec. Leg.* iii. 207 (v. 207. 17–18): For the human mind is god-
> like, in so far as it has been formed after the archetypal idea, the
> Logos who is above all.
> *De Proem. et Poen.* 163 (v. 374. 15–18): For God presented the
> human race with an extraordinary and most important gift, viz.
> the kinship with his Logos; it was from him, who served as
> an archetype, that the human mind was born.
> *De Decal.* 134 (iv. 299. 4–5): Man . . . possessing in his mind the
> most faithful image and imitation of the eternal and blessed idea.
> *Quaest. in Gen.* i. 4: . . . But the man made in accordance with
> God's form is intelligible and incorporeal and a likeness of the
> archetype . . . And he is a copy of the original seal. And this is
> the Logos of God, the first principle, the archetypal idea, the
> pre-measurer of all things.[1]

In Justin it is possible to observe ideas which show a close parallelism with the views held by Clement and Philo. Like Clement,

---

[1] In quoting the passages of *Quaest. in Gen.* I follow the English translation of the
Armenian version made by R. Marcus (Loeb Library, vol. i *Supplementum*). On
the influence of Philo on Clement in the interpretation of Gen. 1: 26 and 27 see
also P. Heinisch, 161–2.

Justin traces Greek philosophy back either to human reason, which is an imitation of the divine Logos and closely related to him, or to the direct inspiration of the Logos himself. That Justin regarded Greek philosophy first of all as a product of human reason is shown by the two following passages:

Apol. ii. 13. 6: οἱ γὰρ συγγραφεῖς πάντες διὰ τῆς ἐμφύτου τοῦ λόγου σπορᾶς ἀμυδρῶς ἐδύναντο ὁρᾶν τὰ ὄντα. ἕτερον γάρ ἐστι σπέρμα τινὸς καὶ μίμημα κατὰ δύναμιν δοθὲν καὶ ἕτερον αὐτό, οὗ κατὰ χάριν [τὴν ἀπ᾽ ἐκείνου] ἡ μετουσία καὶ μίμησις γίνεται. *Apol.* ii. 8. 1 : διὰ τὸ ἔμφυτον παντὶ γένει τῶν ἀνθρώπων σπέρμα τοῦ λόγου.[1]

The last sentence of the first passage points to the distinction between human reason (the copy or imitation) and the divine Logos (the original model) and, at the same time, stresses the close kinship between the former and the latter. A close connection can be observed between σπέρμα, μίμημα, μετουσία, and μίμησις:[2] human reason is represented as a 'seed', i.e. as a particle of the divine Logos, and, in this sense, it also partakes of him (μετουσία) and is his imitation (μίμημα, μίμησις). The underlying idea of Justin's sentence recalls both Philo's interpretation of the expression κατ᾽ εἰκόνα of Gen. 1 : 26 and 27, according to which human reason is a copy or image of the divine Logos,[3] and the Platonic teaching which regarded the human νοῦς as a divine fragment.[4] Owing to this part of the divine Logos which is im-

---

[1] In my opinion, the σπέρμα τοῦ λόγου and the λόγου σπορά of these two passages refer also to human reason and not simply to the Stoic and Middle Platonic πρόληψις-doctrine as R. Holte believes, *STh* 12 (1958), 139 and 141.

[2] The connection between σπέρμα, μετουσία, μετέχειν, μέθεξις, and μίμημα has been observed by Holte (art. cit. 147 and 153) and by J. Waszink, *Bemerkungen zu Justins Lehre vom Logos Spermatikos*, *JACh*, Ergänzungsband 1 (Münster, 1964), 387. The term σπέρμα does not, however, imply *only* the idea of μετέχειν, μετουσία, and μίμημα: see my remarks in footnote 4, p. 23 below.

[3] See p. 21 above. The similarity between *Apol.* ii. 13. 6 and Philo's theory of the origin of human reason has unfortunately not been observed by Holte and Waszink, who have recently reexamined (artt. citt.) the problem concerning the meaning of the expressions σπέρμα τοῦ λόγου and λόγος σπερματικός in Justin (Holte, pp. 147–8, mentions *en passant* Philo's interpretation of Gen 1 : 27 but falls short of bringing it into connection with Justin's passage).

[4] I cannot agree with Holte when he says: 'the σπέρμα τοῦ λόγου does not mean that Logos or some part of him is sown in Man. The meaning is on the contrary that a seed is sown in Man by the personal Logos, a seed that is clearly distinguished from him but is nevertheless an imitation of the Logos' (p. 146); nor do I think that he is completely right in saying: 'Justin has already directly denied the idea

planted in all men (ἔμφυτος)[1] the Greek philosophers could reach a 'dim' knowledge of the truth. The same idea, expressed by the same words, occurs in the second passage, *Apol.* ii. 8. 1. Philosophy, however, according to Justin, does not owe its origin only to human reason: the divine Logos also 'sows' it

of the soul's kinship with God in the form in which it appears in Plato; that the soul as part of Divine reason (τοῦ βασιλικοῦ νοῦ μέρος) can be described as divine . . . He at least indirectly rejects the idea of the soul as τοῦ βασιλικοῦ νοῦ μέρος' (pp. 154-5). It is true that in chapters 4 and 5 of the *Dialogue with Trypho* the old man rejects the Platonic doctrines according to which the soul is ungenerated and immortal and, in order to be punished, transmigrates into other bodies after seeing God; but, on the other hand, it should not be forgotten that he does not criticize at all the doctrine of the divine origin of the νοῦς, the highest part of the soul: on the contrary, he maintains quite openly that what imparts life and any other faculty to the soul is the ζωτικὸν πνεῦμα (*Dial.* 6. 5) which is present in it; this πνεῦμα, according to Justin, is practically identical with the divine Logos (*Apol.* i. 33. 7, τὸ πνεῦμα οὖν καὶ τὴν δύναμιν τὴν παρὰ τοῦ θεοῦ οὐδὲν ἄλλο νοῆσαι θέμις ἢ τὸν λόγον). I. M. Pfättisch is therefore quite right in saying 'der Logos . . . die Vernunft des Menschen wird' (p. 110) or 'dem ihm eingepflanzten Teil des Logos' (p. 117). Waszink virtually agrees with Pfättisch (art. cit. 388-9 'man . . . anerkennen kann, dass Justin die Anwesenheit eines Teils des Logos im Menschen annahm, was Holte bestritten hat') with the only difference, that he seems to interpret the λόγου σπορά and the σπέρμα τοῦ λόγου of *Apol.* ii. 13. 6 and ii. 8. 1 from a purely gnoseological point of view, i.e. as referring not to human reason, but only to those philosophical doctrines which are originally part of the Logos. Justin's view, according to which it is a small fragment or particle of the Logos (i.e. the σπέρμα τοῦ λόγου, the λόγου σπορά, and the πνεῦμα ζωτικόν) that represents human reason, is perfectly in keeping with the whole Platonic tradition: see, for instance, Plato, *Timaeus* 41 c 7–d 1, θεῖον λεγόμενον ἡγεμονοῦν τε . . . σπείρας καὶ ὑπαρξάμενος ἐγὼ παραδώσω, Clem. *Strom.* v. 88. 2, οἱ δὲ ἀμφὶ τὸν Πλάτωνα νοῦν μὲν ἐν ψυχῇ θείας μοίρας ἀπόρροιαν ὑπάρχοντα, and Philo, *De Somn.* i. 34, νοῦς ἀπόσπασμα θεῖον ὤν. Most probably, Justin chose the terms σπορά and σπέρμα τοῦ λόγου because he had still floating in his mind the passage of *Tim.* 41 c 7–d 1 in which the Demiurge is represented in the act of 'sowing' (σπείρας) reason in man: he thought that what is dropped by the 'sower' can be easily regarded as a 'seed'. The terms σπέρμα and σπορά must necessarily hint at something which is dropped by the divine principle and which, before being dropped, is part of it: in this way, the σπέρμα τοῦ λόγου of Justin is practically identical with the θείας μοίρας ἀπόρροιαν of the Platonists (Clem. *Strom.* v. 88. 2) and with the ἀπόσπασμα θεῖον of Philo. The fact that this σπέρμα, when in man, is something distinct from the universal Logos (ἔτερος . . . ἔτερον, *Apol.* ii. 13. 6) and appears as his copy does by no means exclude its close kinship with him, i.e. its divine origin: it is interesting to notice, in this respect, that for Philo also human reason is, at the same time, a divine fragment and an image of the Logos.

[1] Besides *Apol.* ii. 13. 6 and ii. 8. 1 see *Apol.* i. 46. 4–5, τὸν Χριστὸν πρωτότοκον τοῦ θεοῦ εἶναι ἐδιδάχθημεν καὶ προεμηνύσαμεν λόγον ὄντα, οὗ πᾶν γένος ἀνθρώπων μετέσχε, and *Apol.* ii. 10. 9, Χριστῷ δέ . . . λόγος γὰρ ἦν καί ἐστιν ὁ ἐν παντὶ ὤν. Waszink, 389, has drawn attention to the last passage and has also noticed the close connection which exists between *Apol.* ii. 13. 6, ii. 8. 1, and i. 46. 4–5 (p. 387). He, however, interprets these passages only from a gnoseological point of view (see also the preceding footnote).

directly into the mind of the Greek philosophers. This idea is clearly implied in the following passages:

Apol. ii. 10. 1: ὅσα γὰρ καλῶς ἀεὶ ἐφθέγξαντο καὶ εὖρον οἱ φιλοσοφήσαντες ἢ νομοθετήσαντες κατὰ λόγου μέρος ⟨δι'⟩ εὑρέσεως καὶ θεωρίας ἐστὶ πονηθέντα αὐτοῖς. *Apol.* ii. 13. 4: ἕκαστος γάρ τις [i.e. each philosopher or each poet] ἀπὸ μέρους τοῦ σπερματικοῦ καὶ θείου λόγου τὸ συγγενὲς ὁρῶν καλῶς ἐφθέγξατο. *Apol.* ii. 8. 4: οὐ κατὰ σπερματικοῦ λόγου μέρος.[1]

It is R. Holte's merit to have distinguished the λόγος σπερματικός mentioned in *Apol.* ii. 13. 4 and 8. 4 from the λόγου σπορά or σπέρμα τοῦ λόγου which occurs in *Apol.* ii. 13. 6 and 8. 1.[2] Whereas the λόγου σπορά or σπέρμα τοῦ λόγου represents what is dropped by the Logos, the λόγος σπερματικός is nothing but the divine Logos himself engaged in a special activity. Both Holte and Waszink have rightly pointed out that the expression λόγος σπερματικός must be interpreted in an active sense:[3] the Logos, in the three passages quoted above, is represented in the act of 'sowing' philosophical doctrines; the Greek philosophers are the object of this activity, i.e. they receive what the Logos sows. Since

[1] The close connection between these three passages has been rightly pointed out by Waszink, 385 and 387.

[2] Art. cit., 136, 'all scholars have taken it for granted that the conceptions λόγος σπερματικός and σπέρμα τοῦ λόγου in Justin are identical . . . could not one of these terms be thought to imply something divine and the other something human?' and 146, '. . . the question of whether the terms λόγος σπερματικός and σπέρμα τοῦ λόγου are really identical has never been raised in research. The identity has been unreflectingly postulated.' On the exact meaning of σπέρμα τοῦ λόγου and λόγου σπορά, however, see my remarks in footnote 4, pp. 22–3 above.

[3] See Holte, 147, 'the epithet σπερματικός . . . refers to Logos in a special activity, i.e. sowing his σπέρμα', and Waszink, 384 and 387, 'ich bin mit ihm [i.e. Holte] einverstanden wenn er . . . betont dass die Bedeutung von spermatikos aktiv sein muss und dass es somit beim Logos spermatikos nicht um etwas menschliches, einen in die Menschen eingesäten Logos, sondern um eine aktive und göttliche Potenz, den säenden Logos, handelt.' As to the view held by Andresen, according to which Justin has inherited the doctrine of the λόγος σπερματικός from Middle Platonism (ZNW 44 (1952/3), 170–3, and also *Logos u. Nomos*, 336), see the criticism of Holte, 137–8 and 145–6, and of Waszink, 382–4. I have nothing to object to the remarks with which Waszink concludes his paper, art. cit. 390 'Die Wahl des Terminus λόγος σπερματικός lässt sich erklären aus einem Zusammentreffen von drei Faktoren: erstens der Tatsache, dass es sich hier um einen allbekannten stoischen Terminus handelte . . . zweitens des Einflusses der Parabel vom Säer (Matt. 13: 3) und drittens der Frequenz des Bildes des Säens und Pflanzens in Philonschriften.' I should only like to add that Justin most probably thought also of the passage of Plato, *Timaeus* 41 c 7–d 1, in which the term σπείρας occurs (see also footnote 4, p. 23 above).

the Logos is the absolute truth, and what he sows is represented by philosophical doctrines which are part of him,[1] Justin can easily maintain that the Greek philosophers, when they receive what the Logos sows, partake of him (κατὰ λόγου μέρος, *Apol.* ii. 10. 1; ἀπὸ μέρους τοῦ σπερματικοῦ καὶ θείου λόγου, *Apol.* ii. 13. 4; κατὰ σπερματικοῦ λόγου μέρος, *Apol.* ii. 8. 4); in this way, they can see what is closely related to their mind, i.e. truth (τὸ συγγενὲς ὁρῶν)[2] and utter something good (καλῶς ἐφθέγξατο).

By tracing Greek philosophy back to human reason and to the direct inspiration of the Logos Justin sketches a twofold stage of knowledge: by means of the rational principle which is implanted in all men and which is a particle of the Logos the philosophers can already reach a 'dim' knowledge of the truth (ἀμυδρῶς); when, on the other hand, they receive some doctrines directly from the divine Logos who sows them into their minds they can utter something good (καλῶς). The two expressions chosen by Justin, ἀμυδρῶς and καλῶς, seem to hint at such distinction between two stages of knowledge. In both these stages the image of the sower is applied to the Logos: by way of implication in *Apol.* ii. 13. 6 and 8. 1 since the λόγου σπορά or σπέρμα τοῦ λόγου, which is to form human reason, represents the seed dropped by him;[3] and directly in *Apol.* ii. 10. 1, 13. 4, and 8. 4. It must, however, be remembered that, whereas in the first case reason is not dropped by the Logos only on the philosophers but on the whole of mankind (παντὶ γένει τῶν ἀνθρώπων, *Apol.* ii. 8. 1), in the second case only the philosophers and the poets seem to partake of the benefits deriving from the activity of the λόγος

---

[1] Waszink, 386, is quite right in translating the expression ἀπὸ μέρους τοῦ σπερματικοῦ καὶ θείου λόγου of *Apol.* ii. 13. 4 'auf Grund (d. h. durch die Hilfe) des in ihm vorhandenen Teils des göttlichen, (Kenntnis der Wahrheit) säenden Logos' and in remarking: 'Die Verwandtschaft beruht eben darauf, dass die Wahrheit mit dem Logos identisch ist und dass jeder einen Teil des Logos in sich (d. h. in seiner Seele) trägt.' I do not think that the activity of Justin's λόγος σπερματικός is limited to the sowing of a few general conceptions, such as the idea of God (this view is held by Holte, art. cit. 163). In *Apol.* ii. 10. 1 Justin refers quite clearly to the various doctrines discovered by the philosophers and to the laws established by the lawgivers.

[2] Holte, 147, considered the words τοῦ σπερματικοῦ καὶ θείου λόγου in *Apol.* ii. 13. 4 as dependent on τὸ συγγενές and translated 'each man spoke well according to his partial insight into things related to the divine Logos, the sower'; against this interpretation Waszink, 385-6, rightly observed that the expression τοῦ σπερματικοῦ καὶ θείου λόγου does not depend on τὸ συγγενές but on ἀπὸ μέρους. His translation of the whole passage of *Apol.* ii. 13. 4 is worth noticing, p. 386.

[3] See my remarks in footnote 4, pp. 22-3 above.

σπερματικός.[1] Since the Logos is, for Justin, practically identical with the πνεῦμα,[2] he does not seem to be very far removed from the conception which we have noticed in Clement: the Greek philosophers are, like the prophets,[3] divinely inspired men. We can now proceed to notice some very close correspondences between Justin and Clement. Like Justin, Clement maintains that the Greek philosophers could attain only a partial and 'dim' knowledge of the truth represented by the Logos: the passages of Justin, *Apol.* ii. 10, ἐπειδὴ δὲ οὐ πάντα τὰ τοῦ λόγου ἐγνώρισαν, ὅς ἐστι Χριστός, and ii. 13. 6, οἱ γὰρ συγγραφεῖς πάντες διὰ τῆς ἐνούσης τοῦ λόγου σπορᾶς ἀμυδρῶς ἐδύνατο ὁρᾶν τὰ ὄντα,[4] must be compared with *Strom.* i. 80. 5 (ii. 52. 15–16), ἡ μὲν οὖν Ἑλληνικὴ φιλοσοφία . . . ἐπήβολος ἀληθείας ἀμῇ γέ πῃ, ἀμυδρῶς δὲ καὶ οὐ πάσης, γίνεται.[5] Moreover, the ἀπόρροια θεϊκή which falls especially into the minds of the philosophers (*Protr.* 68. 2) and the ἐναύσματά τινα τοῦ λόγου τοῦ θείου which the Greeks receive (*Protr.* 74. 7) represent the equivalent of what Justin's λόγος σπερματικός drops on the Greek philosophers. In this connection it is important to remember

[1] I do not think that Waszink is right in bringing the passages of *Apol.* ii. 13. 6 and ii. 8. 1 concerning the σπέρμα τοῦ λόγου and the λόγου σπορά into connection with the passages of *Apol.* ii. 10. 1, ii. 13. 4, and ii. 8. 4 in which the λόγος σπερματικός occurs, and in referring consequently *Apol.* ii. 13. 6 and ii. 8. 1 also to the activity of the λόγος σπερματικός as sower of philosophical doctrines (see for instance p. 387, 'Justin das Vorhandensein eines Teils des mit Christus identischen "säenden Logos" und damit der ebenfalls mit Christus identischen Wahrheit *in jedem* der vor Christi Menschenwerdung lebenden Menschen angenommen hat . . . vor der Menschwerdung Christi *jeder Mensch* teilhatte an dem säenden Logos der in ihm einen Teil seiner selbst, d. h. der Wahrheit, säte', and p. 390, 'der Teile der Wahrheit *in alle Menschen* eingesät hat'). He comes to this conclusion because he interprets the σπέρμα τοῦ λόγου and the λόγου σπορά of *Apol.* ii. 13. 6 and ii. 8. 1 from a purely gnoseological point of view; in my opinion, instead, neither expression hints at the philosophical doctrines, but at human reason (see above, footnote 4, p. 22, and footnote 1, p. 23).

[2] See the passage of *Apol.* i. 33. 7 quoted in footnote 4, p. 22 above.

[3] See *Apol.* i. 36. 1, τοῦ κινοῦντος αὐτοῦ θείου λόγου, *Apol.* ii. 10. 9, λόγος γὰρ ἦν . . . καὶ διὰ τῶν προφητῶν προειπὼν τὰ μέλλοντα γίνεσθαι, and *Dial.* 7, . . . μακάριοι καὶ δίκαιοι καὶ θεοφιλεῖς, θείῳ πνεύματι λαλήσαντες . . . προφήτας δὲ αὐτοὺς καλοῦσιν. See also Andresen, *Logos und Nomos,* 342–3.

[4] The adverb ἀμυδρῶς is a technical term in Plato's theory of knowledge: for its presence both in Plato and in the Platonic school-tradition see the evidence collected by Andresen, op. cit. 338 n. 71.

[5] Clearly connected with this passage is *Strom.* i. 94. 7 (ii. 61. 1–3), κατ' ἔμφασιν δὲ καὶ διάφασιν οἱ ἀκριβῶς παρ' Ἕλλησι φιλοσοφήσαντες διορῶσι τὸν θεόν, where the expression κατ' ἔμφασιν καὶ διάφασιν, 'by way of reflection', suggests an imperfect stage of knowledge, i.e. a kind of knowledge which is distinct from the direct knowledge πρόσωπον πρὸς πρόσωπον: see Molland, *SO* 15–16 (1936), 69 and 76–85, and cf. footnote 1, p. 15 above.

that Clement does not hesitate to adopt directly the doctrine of the λόγος σπερματικός in *Strom*. i. 37. 2–4 where, in order to explain the origin of Greek philosophy, he resorts to an allegorical interpretation of the Gospel parable of the sower: the Lord ὁ ἄνωθεν σπείρων . . . τὰ θρεπτικὰ σπέρματα (*Strom*. i. 37. 2, vol. ii. 24. 18) is practically one and the same thing with Justin's λόγος σπερματικός; and the θρεπτικὰ σπέρματα and the κύριον λόγον mentioned by Clement are, like the ἀπόρροια θεϊκή and the ἐναύσματα τοῦ λόγου, nothing but the philosophical doctrines which, as we have seen, the λόγος σπερματικός of Justin also sows.[1] It is most likely that Clement had read the writings of his predecessor, although he never mentions him directly.

To sum up. If we consider the idea of the derivation of philosophy from a divine inspiration, we can notice at once that, from the Wisdom of Solomon to Clement, it represents a piece of coherent doctrine which, in the different authors, is expressed in nearly the same images and terms: ἀπόρροια and πνεῦμα ἅγιον in the Wisdom of Solomon, ὤμβρησε in Ecclesiasticus, φιλοσοφίαν ὤμβρησε, σοφίαν ἄνωθεν ὀμβρηθεῖσαν, σοφίας νᾶμα in Philo, πνεῦμα and λόγος σπερματικός in Justin, πνεῦμα αἰσθήσεως, ἀπόρροια θεϊκή, ἐναύσματα τοῦ λόγου, ὑετοί, ὁ ἄνωθεν σπείρων . . . τὰ θρεπτικὰ σπέρματα, ὁ τὸν κύριον . . . ἐπομβρίσας λόγον in Clement. The terms πνεῦμα, ἀπόρροια, ὑετοί, σπέρματα, λόγος are for Clement equivalent, since all of them indicate for him Greek philosophy; he was able to use them indifferently since they had already been employed, for the same purpose, by the exponents of the Jewish-Alexandrine philosophy and by Justin.

One last remark must be added before we conclude our inquiry into the first explanation on the origin of Greek philosophy given by Clement. The Platonist of the second century A.D. who strongly attacked Christianity in his work Ἀληθὴς λόγος, namely Celsus, stresses the identity between the πνεῦμα which inspired the prophets and the πνεῦμα which filled the 'old men', i.e. those

[1] I do not agree, therefore, with M. Pohlenz, who denies that Clement ever employed Justin's doctrine of the λόγος σπερματικός, *NGA*, phil.-hist. Kl. (1943), 161 and *Die Stoa* (Göttingen, 1959), i. 147. It is interesting to notice that the doctrine of the λόγος σπερματικός is applied by the Valentinians to Jesus and Σοφία: λόγοι ἄνωθεν κατεσπαρμένοι ἀπὸ τοῦ κοινοῦ τοῦ πληρώματος καρποῦ καὶ τῆς Σοφίας εἰς τοῦτον τὸν κόσμον, Hippol. *Ref*. vi. 34. 6 (iii. 163. 16–18). The common fruit of the *pleroma* is obviously Jesus (cf. Irenaeus, *Adv. Haer*. i. 2. 6, ἄστρον τοῦ πληρώματος, τέλειον καρπὸν τὸν Ἰησοῦν).

exponents of the παλαιὸς λόγος among whom, according to him, the Greek philosophers must be included: καὶ πνεῦμα εἴ τι οἴεσθε κατιὸν ἐκ θεοῦ προαπαγγέλλειν τὰ θεῖα, τοῦτ᾽ ἂν εἴη τὸ πνεῦμα τὸ ταῦτα κηρύττον, οὗ δὴ πλησθέντες ἄνδρες παλαιοὶ πολλὰ κἀγαθὰ ἤγγειλαν (fr. vii. 45, p. 189. 2–4).[1] We have already noticed that for Justin and Clement the Greek philosophers are, like the prophets, inspired by the divine πνεῦμα or Logos. There can be no doubt about the fact that Justin, Clement, and Celsus show a substantial agreement on this point. As we shall have opportunity to see later on (p. 37 below), Clement, besides Justin's writings, also most probably knew Celsus' Ἀληθὴς λόγος.

Something must now be said about the two other solutions. The second solution, namely that of the 'theft of the Greeks' and of their dependence on the Old Testament, represents one of the main topics of the *Stromateis*: Clement resorts to it very frequently throughout his work. This theory, however, occurs also in Philo and in Justin, who both adopt it together with the first solution. In *De Somn.* ii. 244 (iii. 297. 23–6) Philo maintains that the words βασιλεὺς παρὰ θεοῦ εἶ σὺ ἐν ἡμῖν, which in Gen. 23: 6 refer to Abraham, represent the model of the maxim ὅτι μόνος σοφὸς ἄρχων καὶ βασιλεύς; in *De Aet. M.* 19 (vi. 78. 9–11) the Platonic doctrine according to which the universe has been generated and will not perish is presented as an original discovery not of Plato but of Moses, who had already expounded it in his sacred books; in *Quaest. in Gen.* iv. 152 Heraclitus is represented as a thief, since he stole from Moses the saying 'we live their death and we die their life'; in *De spec. Leg.* iv. 10. 61 (v. 223. 1–2) the Jewish law is considered as the model for the Greek legislations; in *De mut. Nom.* 167–8 (iii. 185. 5–6) Moses is regarded as the author of the doctrine according to which virtue is a εὐπάθεια; in *Quis Rer. div. Her.* 214 (iii. 48. 21–3) Heraclitus' theory of the unity of opposites is considered as being already present in Moses.[2]

Very similar ideas are adopted by Justin. In *Apol.* ii. 44 (i. 122. 27–124. 1) Plato's statement αἰτία ἑλομένου, θεὸς δ᾽ ἀναίτιος (*Rep.* x. 617 e) is regarded as dependent on Moses, who had lived much earlier than any Greek writer; a few lines after (i. 124. 1–5)

---

[1] Cf. Andresen, *Logos und Nomos*, 138–40 and 306.

[2] See also Wolfson, *Philo* i. 141–2, who does not seem, however, to have taken into account the passage of *De Somniis* ii. 244 and *De Aet. M.* 19.

Justin openly maintains that all the most important philosophical doctrines owe their origin to the prophets; and in *Apol.* i. 59 (i. 158–60) he does not hesitate to say that the whole Platonic doctrine of the origin of the world has been borrowed from Scripture (see also *Apol.* i. 60, vol. i. 160).[1]

As to the third solution, according to which philosophy has been stolen by some powers or angels who transmitted it to men, Clement adopts and discusses it at some length in *Strom.* i. 81. 1–5. Two other passages in which it appears are those of *Strom.* v. 10. 2 (ii. 332. 16–19), where Clement promises to give later on an account of the story of the descent upon the earth of certain angels who revealed secret doctrines to some women, and *Strom.* vii. 6. 4 (iii. 6. 16–17), οὗτός ἐστιν ὁ διδοὺς καὶ τοῖς Ἕλλησι τὴν φιλοσοφίαν διὰ τῶν ὑποδεεστέρων ἀγγέλων. The original source of this theory can be found in the Book of Enoch, 16: 3: ὑμεῖς ἐν τῷ οὐρανῷ ἦτε, καὶ πᾶν μυστήριον ὃ οὐκ ἀνεκαλύφθη ὑμῖν καὶ μυστήριον τὸ ἐκ θεοῦ γεγενημένον ἔγνωτε, καὶ τοῦτο ἐμηνύσατε ταῖς γυναιξὶν ἐν ταῖς σκληροκαρδίαις ὑμῶν.[2] The story of the fall of some angels and of their intercourse with women represented one of the favourite arguments of the Christian apologists—especially of those who, like Tertullian, aimed at showing the demonic origin of Greek philosophy.[3] Clement, however, by tracing this story back to God's providence, treats it in a completely different way;[4] Philo and Justin also seem to know it, although they do not bring it into direct connection with the question of the origin of Greek philosophy.[5]

If we want now to establish what Clement really thought about the origin of Greek philosophy we must not try to ascertain, as some scholars have done, which of these three solutions he personally preferred, nor must we start from the assumption that they contradict one another and that Clement is unable to make up his mind and to choose one of them. On the contrary, in Clement's thought there is no contradiction between these three

[1] Andresen's remarks on the presence of this topic in Justin (op. cit. 341–3) are also worth noticing.

[2] For detailed information on the Book of Enoch see E. Schürer, Band iii (Leipzig, 1909, 4th ed.), 268–94.

[3] On the presence of this theory in Christian apologetic—especially in Tertullian—see the references given by F. C. Baur, 530 n. 38, by C. Otto in his edition of Justin, i. 210 n. 6, and by W. Wagner, 23 n. 8.

[4] See footnote 3, p. 10 above.

[5] Philo, *De Gig.* 17 (ii. 45. 9 ff.); Justin, *Apol.* ii. 5.

theories, as can be seen from five passages of the *Stromateis*. In *Strom.* i. 87. 2 (ii. 56. 1–6) Clement maintains that, among the philosophical doctrines, some have really been stolen from the prophets, whereas some others have been discovered by the philosophers themselves, who perhaps possessed a kind of πνεῦμα αἰσθήσεως. This statement is taken up again in *Strom.* vi. 55. 4 (ii. 459. 27–460. 3). In the well-known passage of *Strom.* ii. 100. 3 containing a eulogy of the Platonic formula ὁμοίωσις θεῷ Clement points out the close similarity between Plato's teaching and that of the Jewish law and, in order to explain it, says that Plato either was by some chance in harmony with the law through his own excellent nature, or was directly instructed by the oracles of Scripture. The same idea appears in *Strom.* v. 29. 3–4 (ii. 344. 23–345. 3): here Pythagoras, his disciples, and Plato are first represented as closely dependent on Moses (σφόδρα τῷ νομοθέτῃ ὡμίλησαν), and then regarded as inspired prophets who were able to attain a partial knowledge of the truth. In *Strom.* v. 10. 1–2 Clement promises to deal later on in greater detail with the plagiarism of the Greeks from Scripture as well as with the story of the fall of certain angels. This passage proves, beyond any doubt, that the second and third solutions do not contradict each other; in the same way, the passages of *Strom.* i. 87. 2, vi. 55. 4, v. 29. 3–4, and ii. 100. 3 show that there is no conflict between the first and second solutions. What E. Molland has rightly said about the section of *Strom.* i. 94. 1–3[1] is equally true if referred to the three different solutions adopted by Clement.

But something more must be said. We should not be far from the truth if we assume that Clement did not find any contradiction between these three theories just because his predecessors, Philo and Justin, were indifferent whether they should attribute the origin of Greek philosophy to the divine Logos or to the plagiarism of the Greeks from Scripture. The views of Philo and Justin on the origin of Greek philosophy are substantially the same as those adopted by Clement: it does not make much

---

[1] 'The four possibilities . . . which Clement sketches out in *Strom.* i. 94 are not thought of as alternatives between which we have to choose, one excluding the others. Clement is a most non-scholastic thinker who does not work with clear distinctions and sharply elaborated alternatives. He will not make distinctions or separations where reality exhibits connexions and inseparability' (Molland, art. cit. 75).

difference if Clement apparently develops the theory of the plagiarism of the Greeks to a greater extent than Philo[1] and Justin by resorting directly to the material which he was able to find already formed in the Jewish and Christian apologetic, or if he is inclined to consider the story contained in the Book of Enoch as another possible solution. What really mattered for Clement, as well as for Philo and Justin, was to show the substantial identity between the content of the Greek philosophical doctrines and the teaching of Scripture and, in this way, also the divine origin of Greek philosophy. That this was the main purpose of Clement has been rightly shown by some modern scholars; they have, however, limited their inquiry to him and thus fallen short of pointing out his dependence on his two predecessors in this most important question.[2]

2. The idea that Greek philosophy is not an original output of the Greek thinkers but depends mainly on the Old Testament is expounded in many sections of the *Stromateis*. Clement starts dealing systematically with it at the end of chapter XIV of the first book: after mentioning the most important Greek philosophical schools, he goes on to speak about the chronology of the oldest among them, in order to show that Jewish philosophy

[1] My statement is of course true only if referred to the works of Philo which we still possess. P. Wendland, in the appendix to his article in *JCPh*, Suppl. 22 (1896), 770, rightly observes: 'denn dies Ansicht wird wohl gelegentlich von Philo vorausgesetzt, aber in den erhaltenen Schriften nie ausführlicher entwickelt.' Philo may, however, have dealt with the plagiarism of the Greeks in greater detail in some of his lost writings: Clement, *Strom.* i. 72. 4 (ii. 46. 15–17) says that Philo had produced much evidence in support of the thesis of the greater antiquity of the Jews in comparison with the Greeks: διὰ πολλῶν ὁ Πυθαγόρειος ἀποδείκνυσι Φίλων. Clement's passage can refer only to some lost work of Philo, perhaps to the Ὑποθετικά, as Wendland, loc. cit., is inclined to believe (of the Ὑποθετικά only some fragments have come down to us: see Philo, vol. ix of the Loeb edition, 414–43).

[2] See, for instance, Baur, 533, H. Preische, 27, and de Faye, *Clément d'Alexandrie*, 189. The similarity between the first explanation given by Clement about the origin of Greek philosophy and Justin's doctrine of the relations between the Logos and mankind has occasionally been observed: see, for instance, Cognat, 107 and 113, and de Faye, op. cit. 188. Nobody has, however, sufficiently pointed out so far that the main features of *two* of the explanations adopted by Clement (i.e. the relationship between the Logos and mankind and the plagiarism of the Greeks) are already present in Justin. As to Clement's dependence on Philo, H. A. Wolfson, *Philo* i. 160–1, and *The Philosophy of the Church Fathers*, 21–2, has observed some similarities between Clement's views and those of the Jewish author (see also footnote 1, p. 20 above). His remarks are, however, rather general and do not examine the question in detail.

was much earlier.¹ The following chapter (the fifteenth) shows
the barbarian origin of most of the Greek philosophers, who had
also learnt many doctrines from barbarian teachers,² and lays
strong emphasis on the fact that philosophy, before coming to the
Greeks, had flourished among many barbarian races.³ Chapter
XVI proceeds on the same lines, since it is mainly a survey of
the discoveries made not by the Greeks but by the Barbarians.⁴
In Chapter XVII Clement openly maintains that the Greek
philosophers had stolen some parts of the truth from the prophets,
and that not only had they not admitted their theft, but had
even treated the doctrines they had borrowed from Scripture
as their own discoveries.⁵ This statement is taken up again at
the end of chapter XX.⁶ The long chronological survey of
chapter XXI (vol. ii. 64–92) aims at showing that Jewish philosophy was much older than any other philosophy.⁷ In chapter
XXII Clement mentions the Greek translation of the Old
Testament which had been made under Ptolemy Philadelphus
and quotes a fragment of a work by Aristobulus stating that
Plato owed much to Moses, since he knew the Old Testament
from a much earlier translation. Immediately afterwards he
quotes a sentence of Numenius of Apamea, τί γάρ ἐστι Πλάτων
ἢ Μωυσῆς ἀττικίζων;⁸ chapters XXIII and XXIV are a eulogy
of Moses, in many sections of which Clement follows Philo
almost verbatim.⁹ At the end of chapter XXIV the strategy of
some Greek generals such as Miltiades or Thrasybulus is traced
back to the strategy of Moses.¹⁰ In chapter XXV Clement mentions again Plato's indebtedness to Moses in every branch of his
philosophy. In chapters XXVI and XXVII the Jewish law is
warmly praised and considered as the source of the best Greek
legislations.¹¹ At the beginning of chapter XXVIII a strong
emphasis is laid upon the similarity between the fourth branch of
Moses' philosophy, namely theology, and what in Greek philosophy was called metaphysics or dialectic.¹² In the twenty-ninth

---

¹ *Strom.* i. 64. 5 (ii. 41. 6–8).   ² *Strom.* i. 66. 1 (ii. 41. 23–4).
³ *Strom.* i. 71. 3 (ii. 45. 19–21).   ⁴ *Strom.* i. 74. 1 (ii. 47. 20–1).
⁵ *Strom.* i. 87. 2 (ii. 56. 1–4).   ⁶ *Strom.* i. 100. 4 (ii. 64. 10–12).
⁷ *Strom.* i. 101. 1 (ii. 64. 20–2). A summary of the main arguments contained in
this chapter can be found in Molland, *The Conception of the Gospel* . . ., 58–60.
⁸ *Strom.* i. 150. 4 (ii. 93. 11).   ⁹ See Stählin's app. crit., vol. ii. 93 ff.
¹⁰ See especially *Strom.* i. 160. 1–164. 4 (ii. 100. 29–103. 7).
¹¹ *Strom.* i. 170. 4 (ii. 106. 8–11).   ¹² *Strom.* i. 176. 1–2 (ii. 108. 24–30).

chapter (the last of the first book) Clement interprets the passage of *Timaeus* 22 b, ὦ Σόλων, Σόλων . . . Ἕλληνες ὑμεῖς ἀεὶ παῖδές ἐστε . . . γέρων δὲ Ἑλλήνων οὐκ ἔστιν οὐδείς, as referring to the greater antiquity of the Jews in comparison with the Greeks.[1] At the opening of the second book Clement promises to produce later on more evidence for the dependence of the Greeks on the Old Testament.[2] He renews his promise in the introduction of the fourth book, where he sets forth the arguments he has still to deal with in the remaining books of the *Stromateis*.[3] This promise is fulfilled in the fifth chapter of the fifth book,[4] where the Pythagorean σύμβολα are considered as dependent on the Old Testament,[5] and in the last, long chapter of the same book,[6] which aims at showing in detail the close dependence on Scripture both of the Greek philosophers and of the Greek poets.[7] The beginning of the sixth book provides the reader with some additional proofs of the inclination of the Greeks to steal what does not belong to them: not only had they borrowed many doctrines from Scripture, but also had not hesitated to copy one another's works; this is the underlying idea of the second chapter of the sixth book, which shows the mutual plagiarism of many Greek authors.[8] The following chapter (the third of the sixth book) deals with the dependence of the Greek παράδοξα on those of the Jews, and is the last in which the theory of the 'theft of the Greeks' is expounded at some length.[9]

The reader who goes through these sections of the *Stromateis* may at first be led to think that Clement insists so much on this topic because it provides him with the best opportunity of displaying his erudition and greatly contributes to confer upon the

[1] *Strom.* i. 180. 2 (ii. 110. 15–18).   [2] *Strom.* ii. 1. 1 (ii. 113. 5–11).
[3] *Strom.* iv. 1. 2 (ii. 248. 9–10).   [4] ii. 342–6.
[5] *Strom.* v. 27. 1 (ii. 342. 20–1).
[6] ii. 384–421. For a detailed analysis of this chapter see W. Bousset, *Jüdisch-christlicher Schulbetrieb* . . ., 219–29.
[7] See especially *Strom.* v. 89. 1 (ii. 384. 16–17), τὴν ἐκ τῆς βαρβάρου φιλοσοφίας Ἑλληνικὴν κλοπὴν σαφέστερον ἤδη παραστατέον.
[8] ii. 442–3; see particularly *Strom.* vi. 5. 3–4 (ii. 424. 6–14).
[9] Two more detailed analyses of the sections of the *Stromateis* dealing with the topic of the 'theft of the Greeks' can be found in Bousset, op. cit. 205–18 and 219–36, and in E. Molland, op. cit. 52–65. As to Bousset's hypothesis, according to which the sections of the *Stromateis* dealing with the 'theft of the Greeks' represent an extraneous and already composed body, a 'quellenmässiger Zusammenhang' which Clement incorporated in the *Stromateis* at a later stage, when they had already been written (op. cit. 216–18), see J. Munck's criticism, 136–42.

Stromateis that composite character at which he himself hints on some occasions.[1] Without underestimating this fact we must, however, point out that it cannot be regarded as the only reason that induced Clement to produce such a huge mass of material in support of the thesis of the lack of originality in Greek philosophy and of its substantial dependence on the Old Testament.

In the second century A.D. the growth of a Christian theology was threatened by a twofold danger. On the one hand, the completely negative attitude of many uneducated Christians towards Greek philosophy prevented Christianity from assuming a scientific and philosophical character, and thus limited greatly its chances of success; on the other hand, the pagan world did not refrain from attacking the new religion. If in chapters I–XIV and XVIII–XIX of the first book of the *Stromateis* Clement had faced the first danger and taken up the defence of Greek philosophy, in the sections of the *Stromateis* mentioned above he was forced to reaffirm the originality of his religion and of the tradition on which it rested. Let us examine this question more closely.

In the second half of the second century A.D., about twenty-five years before the appearance of the *Stromateis*, a non-Christian philosopher, Celsus, undertook in his work Ἀληθὴς λόγος[2] the ambitious task of destroying the philosophical foundations of the religion which, at that time, was dangerously growing up. The only way to achieve this purpose was, in Celsus' opinion, to assert,

---

[1] See especially *Strom.* iv. 4. 1 (ii. 249. 19–21), *Strom.* vi. 2. 1 (ii. 422. 24–423. 6) and *Strom.* vii. 111. 1 (iii. 78. 23–7).

[2] It was written in A.D. 178 (see Andresen, *Logos und Nomos*, 309); on the other hand, the *Stromateis* were most probably written at the very beginning of the third century A.D., i.e. between 200 (the year of the death of Pantaenus) and A.D. 203 (the year of Septimius Severus' persecution, which compelled Clement to leave Alexandria): see T. Zahn, 173–4 and 176. I entirely agree with the dating proposed by Zahn and do not think that O. Bardenhewer, 66–7, is right in taking the year 202/3 as *terminus a quo*; it is true that Clement, in the *Stromateis*, hints at the persecutions of the Christians, but it does not follow from this that he must necessarily have thought of the persecution of A.D. 202/3: he may have thought of other previous persecutions. It is far more likely that Clement should have composed the *Stromateis* soon after the death of Pantaenus, when he was still teaching at the catechetical school of Alexandria: the way in which he speaks of his teacher (*Strom.* i. 11. 2, ii. 8. 23–9. 3) seems strongly to suggest that the latter was already dead when the former started writing the *Stromateis*; and the *Stromateis* themselves seem to be closely connected with Clement's activity as director of the catechetical school of Alexandria after the death of his teacher, since, as will be seen later on (chapter III, footnote 4, p. 189 below) they are meant to be a kind of introduction to the study of the highest doctrines.

on the one hand, the sacred character of history and tradition, and consequently also of Greek culture in so far as it was the most relevant expression of the cultural tradition of mankind; and, on the other hand, to demonstrate that Judaism and Christianity could not be regarded as true representatives of this tradition, but only as bad imitations of it.[1] Accordingly, Celsus tried to ridicule both of them by showing that what had been said by their founders, Moses and Jesus, was nothing but a misunderstanding and a counterfeit of some doctrines of the παλαιὸς λόγος, i.e. of Greek philosophy. He must have devoted long sections of his work to the demonstration of this thesis.[2] Although the original text of the Ἀληθὴς λόγος was considerably cut by Origen, who left aside especially its erudite sections,[3] the extant fragments nevertheless enable us to realize the strong emphasis laid by Celsus on the dependence both of Judaism and of Christianity on the Greek philosophical tradition. In i. 21 Moses' account of creation is traced back to analogous accounts present in the religious traditions of other races or made by other wise men;[4] in iv. 11 and iv. 41 the flood of which the book of Genesis speaks is presented not as original but as derived from Deucalion's myth;[5] in iii. 16 b Celsus maintains that what the Christians preach is actually a misunderstanding of the παλαιὸς λόγος;[6] in v. 65 b the Christians are represented in the act of misunderstanding and corrupting the ancient doctrines;[7] in vi. 12 St. Paul's sentence ἡ σοφία τοῦ κόσμου μωρία παρὰ θεῷ ἐστι (1 Cor. 3: 19) is traced back to the distinction, present in Greek philosophy, between the divine and the human wisdom;[8] in vi. 15 and 16 the Christian praise of humility and poverty is regarded as a misunderstanding of what Plato had said;[9] in vi. 71 the inclination of the Christians to consider God as πνεῦμα is regarded as directly influenced by Stoicism;[10] in vii. 58 the Christian maxim 'to him who slaps thee offer the other cheek' is ridiculed and represented as a counterfeit

---

[1] That these are the underlying ideas of Celsus' work has been shown by Andresen: see the section 'Die Polemik des Kelsos wider das Christentum' of his book *Logos und Nomos*, 108–238.
[2] Cf. Andresen, op. cit. 32–3.
[3] Cf. Andresen, op. cit. 22–3 and also 373.
[4] Cf. Andresen, op. cit. 1 and 354.
[5] Cf. Andresen, op. cit. 151 and 354 n. 16.
[6] Cf. Andresen, op. cit. 162.
[7] Cf. Andresen, op. cit. 154.
[8] Cf. Andresen, op. cit. 155.
[9] Cf. Andresen, op. cit. 150–1.
[10] Cf. Andresen, op. cit. 73–4.

of the passages of Plato's *Crito*, in which Socrates maintains that injustice should not be repaid by another injustice; in the same fragment Celsus makes it clear that he who wishes to go on with such research could easily find further material in support of his thesis.¹ In these passages Celsus does not limit himself to stressing the idea of the borrowing of doctrines of the παλαιὸς λόγος on the part of the Jews and Christians (ἐπακούειν, λαμβάνειν); what he particularly insists on is the misunderstanding (παρακούειν, παράκουσμα), the corruption (διαφθείρειν), and the counterfeiting (παραχαράττειν) of these doctrines, for which both the Jews and the Christians make themselves responsible when they borrow them.

Small wonder, therefore, if Clement felt the necessity of answering back to Celsus' attack and of producing as much material as he could in support of the exactly opposite thesis: Judaism and Christianity were not, as Celsus maintained, a rough copy of philosophy; on the contrary, it was Greek philosophy that was dependent on Jewish tradition, since the Greek philosophers had stolen many doctrines from the Old Testament. It is important to notice, in this connection, that Clement retorts against the Greek philosophers the charges of 'counterfeit' (παραχαράττειν) and of 'misunderstanding' (οὐ συνιέναι) which Celsus had addressed against the Jews and Christians: in *Strom.* i. 87. 2 (ii. 56. 2–5) Clement, after maintaining that the Greek philosophers had considered as their own the doctrines which they had stolen from the prophets without acknowledging their indebtedness to their sources, makes it clear that they had counterfeited them (παρὰ τῶν Ἑβραϊκῶν προφητῶν μέρη τῆς ἀληθείας οὐ κατ᾽ ἐπίγνωσιν λαβόντες ἀλλ᾽ ὡς ἴδια σφετερισάμενοι δόγματα καὶ τὰ μὲν παραχαράξαντες); at the beginning of the second book he renews this charge (τὰ κυριώτατα τῶν δογμάτων σκευωρουμένους καὶ παραχαράσσοντας), *Strom.* ii. 1. 1 (ii. 113. 7); and in *Strom.* v. 89. 2–4 (ii. 384. 18–385. 5) he asserts that the Stoic doctrine that identified God with the πνεῦμα which permeates everything was actually based on a misunderstanding of the passage of the Wisdom of Solomon, διήκει καὶ χωρεῖ διὰ πάντων διὰ τὴν καθαρό-

---

¹ Cf. Andresen, op. cit. 146–9. I have here drawn attention only to some passages of Celsus in which his polemical attitude towards Judaism and Christianity appears particularly clear. Further evidence is produced by Andresen, op. cit. 146–66, 167–88, 209–24, and 225–38.

τητα (7. 24). It is difficult to resist the hypothesis that Clement had already read Celsus' Ἀληθὴς λόγος and bore in mind his charges against Judaism and Christianity when he wrote the *Stromateis*. As the Ἀληθὴς λόγος was meant to be an answer to Justin's writings,[1] in the same way the sections of the *Stromateis* dealing with the topic of the 'theft of the Greeks' represent, in Clement's intentions, the answer of Christianity to the charges which Celsus, on behalf of the non-Christian world, had addressed against it. Origen's work *Contra Celsum* cannot therefore be regarded as the first attempt at a refutation of Celsus' theses; actually, the *Stromateis* represent its natural predecessor.

And yet, in spite of this vehement polemic, it is possible to notice a close link between the Alexandrine theologian and the pagan philosopher. What they have in common is represented by their conception of the history of culture in general and of philosophy in particular, i.e. by their tendency to regard Greek culture not as an original invention of the Greeks, but as something which they had inherited from other, much more ancient races, as the expression of a tradition going back to prehistoric times: in other words, philosophy had flourished first among the oriental peoples, such as the Indians, the Persians, the Chaldeans, and the Egyptians, and only later had it come to the Greeks. This view, which was widespread not only in the first centuries of our era but also in the Classical and Hellenistic ages,[2] enabled Celsus to build up his theory of the παλαιὸς λόγος: the philosophical and religious doctrines go back to very ancient, 'wise', and 'divine' races, and in so far as they are 'old' they possess

[1] This has been clearly shown by Andresen: see op. cit., especially 306 and 307, 344–5, 347.
[2] See the material collected by A. J. Festugière, *La révélation d'Hermès Trismégiste* i. 19–44. Here I shall limit myself to drawing attention to the proem of Diogenes Laertius, i. 1, and to Numenius, fr. 9a Leemans (both passages are translated by Festugière, 19–20). In fr. 9a Numenius points out the agreement between the doctrines of Plato and Pythagoras and the religious beliefs of the Brahamans, the Jews, the Magians, and the Egyptians. The philosopher of Apamea was very interested in the culture of the oriental races and interpreted Scripture allegorically also (frr. 9a, 9b, and 32). To this important aspect of Numenius' thought H. C. Puech has rightly drawn attention, *AIO*, Tom. ii (1934), 745–78 (see particularly pp. 747–8 on fr. 9a and pp. 751–4 on Numenius' admiration for Judaism); cf. also E. R. Dodds, 'Numenius and Ammonius', *Entretiens Hardt* v. 5. It must not be forgotten that Clement seems to have read Numenius, since in *Strom.* i. 150. 4 (ii. 93. 11) he quotes one of his sentences, stressing the identity between the teaching of Plato and that of Moses.

a sacred character and form all together throughout the history of mankind a holy tradition (the ἀρχαῖος or παλαιὸς λόγος) which was handed down to the Greeks. Both the barbarian and the Greek philosophers and poets are the exponents of this tradition.[1] These topics occur very frequently in Celsus' work, as the following evidence shows:

i. 2 (pp. 39–40): Celsus praises the Barbarians for being capable of discovering doctrines; but he adds to this that the Greeks are better able to judge the value of what the Barbarians have discovered and to establish the doctrines and put them into practice by virtue.

i. 14 a (p. 44): Thinking that between many of the nations there is an affinity in that they hold the same doctrine, Celsus names all the nations which he supposes to have held this doctrine originally.

i. 14 c (pp. 44–5): Hear Celsus' words: there is an ancient doctrine which has existed from the beginning, which has always been maintained by the wisest nations and cities and wise men. And he would not speak of the Jews as being a very wise nation on a par with the Egyptians, Assyrians, Indians, Persians, Odrysians, Samothracians, and Eleusinians.

i. 16 a (p. 45): I am surprised that Celsus numbers the Odrysians, Samothracians, Eleusinians, and Hyperboreans among the most ancient and wise nations, and yet does not reckon the Jews worth including with the wise or the ancient.

vi. 80 (p. 175): After this Celsus thought fit to say that the Chaldeans have been a race endowed with the highest inspiration from the beginning . . . Celsus also reckons the Magi among the most inspired races.

vi. 80 (pp. 175–6): Yet now Celsus thought fit to remark that the nation of the Egyptians is also endowed with the highest inspiration, and that from the beginning . . . the Persians . . . appear to Celsus to be an inspired race; and the Indians also . . . But . . . not only does he not call the Jews endowed with the highest inspiration but even says that they will presently perish.

i. 16 b (p. 45. 8–10): Again, when he makes a list of ancient and wise men who were of service to their contemporaries and to posterity by their writings, he rejects Moses from the list of wise men.

i. 16 b (p. 45. 12–15): For he says that Linus, Musaeus, Orpheus, Pherecydes, Zoroaster the Persian, and Pythagoras understood

[1] See Andresen, op. cit. 108–45 and 189–208.

these doctrines and their opinions were put down in books and are preserved to this day.

i. 21 (p. 48): Accordingly, he says, Moses heard of this doctrine which was current among the wise nations and distinguished men and acquired a name for divine power.

vii. 41 (p. 187): He refers us to inspired poets, as he calls them, and wise men and philosophers without giving their names; and although he promises to show us the guides, he points to the inspired poets and wise men and philosophers without stating precisely whom he means.¹

Since the Greek philosophers are representatives of this holy tradition, it necessarily follows that Plato also, the most outstanding among them, depends on it. Celsus does not hesitate to bring him into connection with the ancient wise men, παλαιοὶ τοίνυν ἄνδρες καὶ σοφοὶ δηλούσθωσαν τοῖς ἐπίστασθαι δυναμένοις καὶ δὴ καὶ Πλάτων ὁ τοῦ Ἀρίστωνος τὰ περὶ τοῦ πρώτου ἀγαθοῦ διασημαινέτω, vi. 3 (141. 1–3).² According to Celsus, Plato had never tried to conceal his indebtedness to the old tradition, ὁ Πλάτων οὐκ ἀλαζονεύεται καὶ ψεύδεται φάσκων αὐτὸς καινόν τι εὑρίσκειν ἢ ἀπ᾽ οὐρανοῦ παρὼν ἀγγέλλειν, ἀλλ᾽ ὁπόθεν ἐστὶ τοῦθ᾽ ὁμολογεῖ, vi. 10 b (144. 7–8),³ and had always admitted that what he said had already been said by his predecessors: in vi. 9 (144. 4–5) Celsus quotes *Epist.* vii. 342 a–b, ἔστι γάρ τις λόγος ἀληθής, ἐναντίος τῷ τολμήσαντι γράφειν τῶν τοιούτων ὁτιοῦν, πολλάκις μὲν ὑπ᾽ ἐμοῦ καὶ πρότερον λεχθείς, and interprets the word πρότερον in the sense that Plato hints here at the old sources on which he himself depends;⁴ in vii. 58 (191. 17–19) also Celsus, after quoting *Crito* 49 d–e, ἐμοὶ μὲν γὰρ πάλαι οὕτως καὶ νῦν δοκεῖ, interprets the adverb πάλαι as referring to the previous philosophers, Πλάτωνι μὲν οὕτως ἤρεσεν, ἦν δὲ καὶ πρόσθεν ἔτι θείοις ἀνδράσι δεδογμένα.⁵

Very similar views are expounded by Clement. Before tackling directly the topic of the 'theft of the Greeks' (*Strom.* i, chap. XVII) he wants to make it clear to his readers that not only philosophy but also all other disciplines and the most important discoveries go back to the barbarian peoples (*Strom.* i. 74. 1, vol. ii. 47. 20–1); he devotes two chapters of the first book of the *Stromateis* (the

---

¹ I have followed H. Chadwick's translation (*Origen: Contra Celsum*, Cambridge, 1953).
² Cf. Andresen, op. cit. 127.
³ Cf. Andresen, op. cit. 129.
⁴ Cf. Andresen, op. cit. 129–30.
⁵ Cf. Andresen, op. cit. 128–31.

15th and the 16th) tot he demonstration of this thesis. In *Strom.* i. 71. 3–4 (ii. 45. 19–26) he sets forth practically the same conception of history as that which underlies the passages of the Ἀληθὴς λόγος quoted above: φιλοσοφία τοίνυν πολυωφελές τι χρῆμα πάλαι μὲν ἤκμασε παρὰ βαρβάροις κατὰ τὰ ἔθνη διαλάμψασα, ὕστερον δὲ καὶ εἰς Ἕλληνας κατῆλθεν. The words πάλαι μὲν ἤκμασε παρὰ βαρβάροις κατὰ τὰ ἔθνη διαλάμψασα recall analogous expressions of Celsus: ἔστιν ἀρχαῖος ἄνωθεν λόγος περὶ ὃν δὴ ἀεὶ καὶ τὰ ἔθνη τὰ σοφώτατα καὶ πόλεις καὶ ἄνδρες σοφοὶ κατεγένοντο, i. 14 c. Moreover, the list of the barbarian races given in *Strom.* i. 71. 4 shows a very close kinship with the catalogues present in the fragments i. 14 c and vi. 80 of the Ἀληθὴς λόγος.[1]

The agreement between Celsus and Clement appears also in their tendency to regard the Greek philosophers as directly dependent on the Barbarians. Clement openly maintains that most of the Greek philosophers had been instructed by some barbarian teachers (*Strom.* i. 66. 1, vol. ii. 41. 24): Plato (he says) always showed a great respect for the Barbarians and acknowledged that both he and Pythagoras had learnt the best doctrines from them (ὁ δὲ Πλάτων δῆλον ὡς σεμνύνων ἀεὶ τοὺς βαρβάρους εὑρίσκεται, μεμνημένος αὐτοῦ τε καὶ Πυθαγόρου τὰ πλεῖστα καὶ γενναιότατα τῶν δογμάτων ἐν βαρβάροις μαθόντος, *Strom.* i. 68. 2, vol. ii. 42. 26–8).[2] It would be difficult to deny the existence of a close relationship between these words of Clement and what Celsus says in vi. 9, vi. 10 b, and vii. 58 (see p. 39 above).

It is, then, the same conception of the history of philosophy that appears in both Celsus and Clement. Only the use they make of it is dictated by opposite intentions. In developing his theory of the παλαιὸς λόγος Celsus aimed at showing that Greek philosophy represented the climax of the cultural tradition of the whole of mankind and consequently that Judaism and Christianity were nothing but bad imitations of this tradition. Clement, who had read Celsus' work and become aware of the danger it represented, borrowed from him the main features of his conception in order to emphasize the dependence of the Greek philosophers on the barbarian races and consequently also on the Jews: the fifteenth and sixteenth chapters of the first book of the *Stroma-*

---

[1] To the importance of Clement's catalogue for ancient ethnography attention has recently been drawn by A. Dihle, *JACh*, Ergänzungsband 1, 60–9.

[2] Cf. *Protr.* 70. 1 (i. 53. 12–15).

teis must, in his intention, prepare the reader for the topic of the 'theft of the Greeks' (which begins in chapter XVII) and represent a kind of introduction to it; it is not by a simple chance that Clement, already in the fifteenth chapter, hints at the greater antiquity of the Jews in comparison with other races.[1] Celsus' Ἀληθὴς λόγος explains therefore both Clement's adoption of the topic of the 'mirage oriental'[2] and the use he makes of it; like the topic of the 'theft of the Greeks', it is present in the *Stromateis* not only because of Clement's love of erudition: it provided Clement with the best opportunity of refuting the views of his opponent.

3. On the question of Clement's attitude towards the individual philosophical systems it is important to establish whether or not it is possible to share the view of those scholars who regard Clement's acceptance or rejection of determinate philosophical doctrines as simply due to his Christian faith. The only way to reach a solution for this problem is by a thorough comparison of Clement's views on the Pythagorean, Platonic, Epicurean, Aristotelian, and Stoic systems with those of Justin and of some exponents of Middle Platonism. The close correspondences which it is possible to discern between Clement, Justin, and Middle Platonism in this respect show that, exactly as in the case of Justin, Clement's utterances about the different philosophical schools go ultimately back to that school-Platonism of the second century A.D. which must have represented the basis of the cultural formation of both Christian authors before their conversion to Christianity.[3]

The agreement between Clement, Justin, and Middle Platonism appears particularly evident in the following points:

(*a*) the warm praise of Plato and of Pythagoras;

(*b*) the condemnation of the 'atheistic' philosophy of Epicurus;

---

[1] *Strom.* i. 72. 4 (ii. 46. 15–19); cf. *Strom.* i. 64. 5 (ii. 41. 7–8).

[2] The author of this expression is Festugière: see op. cit. 20, and cf. also E. R. Dodds, art. cit. 5.

[3] Völker, *Der wahre Gnostiker* . . ., 1 n. 2, is wrong in excluding any possibility of analogy between the history of the conversion of Justin and that of Clement. If Clement was converted to Christianity only at a certain stage of his life, it is most likely that his cultural formation before his conversion should have taken place in the Platonic schools of the second century A.D., just as had happened for Justin.

(c) the condemnation of the Peripatetic doctrine which limits divine providence to the world above the moon;
(d) the condemnation of Stoic materialism and determinism.

(a) No Greek philosopher is so warmly praised by Clement as Plato.[1] In chapter VI of the *Protrepticus* Plato is directly invoked by Clement to be his companion in his search for God: τίνα γὰρ λάβω συνεργὸν τῆς ζητήσεως;[2] εἰ βούλει, τὸν Πλάτωνα. πῇ οὖν ἐξιχνευτέον τὸν θεόν, ὦ Πλάτων; (*Protr.* 68. 1, vol. i. 51. 25–7). Immediately afterwards Clement quotes the well-known passages *Timaeus* 28 c, τὸν γὰρ πατέρα καὶ ποιητὴν τοῦδε τοῦ παντὸς εὑρεῖν τε ἔργον καὶ εὑρόντας εἰς ἅπαντας ἐξειπεῖν ἀδύνατον, and *Epist.* vii. 341 c, ῥητὸν γὰρ οὐδαμῶς ἐστι, which, as we shall see, represent two important elements of the background of Clement's conception of the highest divinity.[3] After these quotations, Clement again addresses his words directly to Plato, and renews his invitation to accompany him in his search for the Good: εὖ γε, ὦ Πλάτων, ἐπαφᾶσαι τῆς ἀληθείας· ἀλλὰ μὴ ἀποκάμῃς· ξύν μοι λαβοῦ τῆς ζητήσεως τἀγαθοῦ πέρι (*Protr.* 68. 2, vol. i. 52. 1–2). In *Strom.* i. 42. 1 (ii. 28. 2–4) Plato is represented as ὁ φιλαλήθης . . . οἷον θεοφορούμενος and in *Strom.* ii. 100. 3 he is again praised because of his definition of the human τέλος as ὁμοίωσις θεῷ κατὰ τὸ δυνατόν.

Although Clement maintains several times that Plato owes much to Scripture,[4] such a dependence does not induce the Christian author to condemn him, but on the contrary to praise the divine character of his philosophy. The best proof is given by chapter XXV of the first book of the *Stromateis*: what Clement wants to stress here is not Plato's dependence on Moses in the different branches of his philosophical system, but on the contrary the excellence of his conceptions, particularly that of the βίος θεωρητικός. Plato's indebtedness to the Jewish law giver becomes therefore a further reason to adopt and follow his teaching.

---

[1] 'Clemens in Platon lebt und webt', W. Bousset, *Jüdisch-christlicher Schulbetrieb* . . ., 227.

[2] These words were most probably suggested to Clement by Plato, *Phaedo*, 65 a 9–b 1, πότερον ἐμπόδιον τὸ σῶμα ἢ οὔ, ἐάν τις αὐτὸ ἐν τῇ ζητήσει κοινωνὸν συμπαραλαμβάνῃ;

[3] See chapter III, pp. 219 and 220 below.

[4] See, for instance, *Protr.* 70. 1 (i. 53. 16–17), *Paed.* ii. 18. 1 (i. 166. 24–5), 18. 2 (i. 167. 1–2), ii. 89. 2 (i. 211. 14–15), ii. 91. 1 (i. 212. 9), iii. 54. 2 (i. 267. 20–1), *Strom.* i. 10. 2 (ii. 8. 5–6), i. 165. 1 (ii. 103. 14–15), i. 166. 1 (ii. 103. 25–6), ii. 133. 2 (ii. 186. 13–15), v. 99. 3 (ii. 392. 2–5).

Pythagoras also is praised by Clement in warm terms. In *Strom.* v. 29. 3–4 (ii. 344. 23–345. 3) he and Plato are regarded as those philosophers who, more than anybody else, followed the teachings of Moses and succeeded in grasping some elements of the truth: 'In short, Pythagoras and his disciples together with Plato above all other philosophers were very familiar with the teachings of the lawgiver, as it is possible to infer from their doctrines. Having with the help of God come into harmony with them, owing to some acute utterance inspired by a prophetic power, and grasped partially the truth in some prophetic sayings, they honoured it with appellatives which proved to be clear and in keeping with the explanation of reality; they got some reflection of the proper sense of the truth.'[1]

Clement is thus inclined to interpret the philosophy of Plato and of Pythagoras in a religious sense in so far as he regards them as two theologians who possessed some true knowledge of the highest divinity. This way of interpreting Plato and Pythagoras underlies also Justin's utterances about them. In the first part of the *Dialogue with Trypho* the Christian apologist, referring to a period of his life preceding his conversion, presents himself as a follower of the Platonic philosophy of the second century A.D.; he does not hesitate to represent Plato and Pythagoras as 'wise men, who were our wall and our pillar' (*Dial.* 5),[2] and maintains that the aim of the Platonic philosophy is the contemplation of the highest divinity, ἤλπιζον αὐτίκα κατόψεσθαι τὸν θεόν· τοῦτο γὰρ τέλος τῆς Πλατωνικῆς φιλοσοφίας, *Dial.* 2 (ii. 10. 3–5), cf. *Dial.* 4 (ii. 16. 14–18. 1), φησὶ γὰρ Πλάτων . . . αὐτὸ τοιοῦτον εἶναι τὸ τοῦ νοῦ ὄμμα καὶ πρὸς τοῦτο ἡμῖν δεδόσθαι, ὡς δύνασθαι καθορᾶν ἐκεῖνο τὸ ὂν εἰλικρινεῖ αὐτῷ ἐκείνῳ ὃ τῶν νοητῶν ἁπάντων ἐστὶν αἴτιον. It is important to observe that Justin, even after his conversion, does not disavow Plato's theology—or, more exactly, the theology which he had learnt in the Platonic schools of his time, before becoming a Christian. This is clearly shown by *Apol.* ii. 10 (i. 226. 16–228. 1–2) where he cannot refrain from quoting the hackneyed passage of *Timaeus* 28 c.[3] Even as

---

[1] On this passage see also pp. 17 and 30 above.
[2] A reference to this passage can also be found in Andresen, *ZNW* 44 (1952/3), 161.
[3] That Justin's quotation of this passage of the *Timaeus* is not based directly on Plato's text but on a school-tradition has been shown by Andresen by means of a comparison between Justin, *Apol.* ii. 10, and Albinus, *Did.* 179. 32 ff. (art. cit. 167–8).

a Christian Justin continues to express his conception of the highest divinity in Platonic terms.

The tendency to regard Plato and Pythagoras as the highest theologians among the Greek philosophers, which can be recognized both in Clement and in Justin, is also characteristic of Middle Platonism and represents an important feature of the culture of the second century A.D.[1] Both philosophers are often mentioned together and praised because of the excellence of their doctrines. Plutarch celebrates both Pythagoras and Plato because of their doctrines of the harmony of the universe and of the immortality of the soul, *De Mus.* 1147 a 9–17 and *De Vita et Poes. Hom.* 122 (vii. 395. 15–17). The school-Platonism identifies also the Platonic definition of the human τέλος as ὁμοίωσις θεῷ (*Theaet.* 176 b) with that characteristic of the Pythagorean school, ἕπου θεῷ.[2] Taurus praises Pythagoras' way of teaching (Gellius, *Noct. Att.* i. 9. 1–8, vol. i. 59. 5–60. 6);[3] Theon of Smyrna points out that Plato very often followed Pythagoras, *De Ut. Math.*, p. 12. 10;[4] and Maximus of Tyre represents Plato as an 'interpreter of God' and as a 'seer', *Or.* xi. 6 e.[5] It is this religious interpretation of Plato that also underlies some typical writings of Middle Platonism, such as the *Didaskalikos* of Albinus, the *De Platone et eius dogmate* of Apuleius, the *Quaestiones Platonicae* and the *De Animae Procr. in Tim.* of Plutarch, and the speech bearing the title Τίς ὁ θεὸς κατὰ Πλάτωνα of Maximus of Tyre. The passages of the *Timaeus* and of the seventh letter, which are so praised both by Clement and by Justin, represent also the fundamental background of the theology which was taught in the Platonic schools of the second century.[6] There is no better picture of this school-Platonism than that given by Justin himself at the opening of his *Dialogue with Trypho*: 'I occupied myself as much as possible with the study of the Platonic doctrines; I made good progress and advanced in the knowledge of them every day. My whole being was captured by the thought of the incor-

---

[1] For the admiration of Pythagoras during the first centuries of our era see especially A. J. Festugière, op. cit. i. 14–18. Andresen's remarks are also worth noticing, art. cit. 162, and op. cit. 124 and 239–40.

[2] See the evidence collected by Andresen, art. cit., n. 20 on pp. 162–3.

[3] Cf. K. Praechter in his article 'Taurus', *RE*, Zweite Reihe, neunter Halbband, col. 61.

[4] Cf. Andresen, art. cit. 161.   [5] Cf. Andresen, op. cit. 275 n. 6.

[6] See pp. 212, 219–20, below.

poreal realities, and the contemplation of the ideas furnished my
intellective faculty with new wings;[1] in a short time, I thought
I had become a wise man, and in my naïvety I hoped to be able
to see God very soon: for this is the aim of the Platonic philosophy' (*Dial.* 2, vol. ii. 8. 27–10. 5). We can therefore easily
understand why Clement and Justin were led to interpret Plato
and Pythagoras from a religious point of view and to praise
their doctrines in such warm terms.

(*b*) The condemnation of the Epicurean system can be found
in the following passages of Clement:

Protr. 66. 5 (i. 51. 6–7) : Ἐπικούρου μὲν γὰρ μόνου καὶ ἑκὼν ἐκλήσομαι,
ὃς οὐδὲν μέλειν οἴεται τῷ θεῷ, διὰ πάντων ἀσεβῶν.
Strom. i. 50. 6 (ii. 33. 8–10): φιλοσοφίαν μὲν οὐ πᾶσαν, ἀλλὰ τὴν
Ἐπικούρειον, ἧς καὶ μέμνηται ἐν ταῖς Πράξεσι τῶν ἀποστόλων ὁ
Παῦλος διαβάλλων, πρόνοιαν ἐξαιροῦσαν καὶ ἡδονὴν ἐκθειάζουσαν . . .
Strom. ii. 16. 3 (ii. 121. 9): ὁ Ἐπίκουρος, ὁ μάλιστα τῆς ἀληθείας
προτιμήσας τὴν ἡδονήν.

The same kind of polemic against those philosophers who denied
God's providence is present in Justin as well, as the following
passage clearly shows:

Apol. i. 28 (i. 88. 10 ff.): εἰ δέ τις ἀπιστεῖ μέλειν τούτων τῷ θεῷ,
ἢ μὴ εἶναι αὐτὸν διὰ τέχνης ὁμολογήσει ἢ ὄντα χαίρειν κακίᾳ φήσει
ἢ λίθῳ ἐοικότα μένειν . . . ἥπερ μεγίστη ἀσέβεια καὶ ἀδικία ἐστί.

Justin does not specify who these philosophers are, but that Epicurus and his followers must be included among them can be
easily inferred from the argument which Justin produces in order
to justify the condemnation of them, namely the denial of God's
providence.

In another passage Justin puts Epicurus and Sardanapalus on
the same level:

Apol. ii. 7. 3: Σαρδανάπαλον δὲ καὶ Ἐπίκουρον ἐν ἀφθονίᾳ καὶ δόξῃ
δοκεῖν εὐδαιμονεῖν.[2]

---

[1] Ἀνεπτέρου μοι τὴν φρόνησιν. The words ἀναπτερόω, πτερόω, πτέρωμα, and so
on in connection with the contemplation of the ideas go back to Plato, who uses
them especially in the *Phaedrus*: see, for instance, *Phaedr.* 246 c 1, 249 c 4, 249 d 6,
251 b 7.
[2] On this passage of Justin see also Andresen, art. cit. 187 n. 121.

The two main arguments which appear in the polemic of
Clement and Justin against the Epicurean system (namely the
denial of divine providence and the deification of pleasure) are
also characteristic of Middle Platonism. Already Antiochus of
Ascalon had made it clear to the Epicureans that virtue and
pleasure contradicted each other, *non igitur potestis voluptate omnia
derigentes aut tueri aut retinere virtutem* (Cicero, *De Fin.* ii. 22.
71);[1] Taurus in Gellius, *Noct. Att.* ix. 5. 8 does not conceal his
polemical attitude towards Epicurus' identification of pleasure
with the highest good and his denial of God's providence;[2]
Plutarch, *Adv. Col.* 1111 b 10–12, addresses exactly the same
charges against Epicurus; moreover, in *De Stoic. Rep.* 1052 b
6–10, he sharply criticizes both Epicurus and Chrysippus and
puts them on the same level: as the former had destroyed the
providence of the gods, in the same way the latter had denied
their incorruptibility.[3] Atticus is particularly violent against
Epicurus. In a fragment preserved by Eusebius (fr. III Baudry)
he condemns him together with Aristotle, since both of them
had excluded the notion that God can care about man. Three
passages of the fragment are especially worth noticing, namely
Eusebius, *Praep. Ev.* xv. 5. 7–8 (ii. 357. 9–15), xv. 5. 9 (ii. 357.
20–4), and xv. 5. 11 (ii. 358. 3–7). In the same fragment Atticus
expresses himself ironically about the Epicurean doctrine of
pleasure:

Praep. Ev. xv. 5. 6 (ii. 357. 3 f.): ἐκεῖνος μὲν γὰρ καὶ πάνυ χρηστός
ἐστιν, ὅστις τὴν ἡδονὴν ἡμῖν προτείνας ὡς ἀγαθόν . . .[4]

---

[1] For the reference to this passage see Andresen, art. cit. 186 n. 119.

[2] See also K. Praechter in his article on Taurus, coll. 61 and 66, and Andresen,
art. cit. 186 and footnote 120 on the same page.

[3] It must be observed that Plutarch has nothing to object against Chrysippus'
criticism of the Epicurean doctrine which denies God's providence: πρὸς τὸν
Ἐπίκουρον μάλιστα μάχεται [sc. Chrysippus] καὶ πρὸς τοὺς ἀναιροῦντας τὴν πρόνοιαν
ἀπὸ τῶν ἐννοιῶν ἃς ἔχομεν περὶ θεῶν εὐεργετικοὺς καὶ φιλανθρώπους ἐπινοοῦντες,
De Stoic. Rep. 1051 e 1–4. He simply mentions it immediately after condemning
Chrysippus' doctrine of ἀνάγκη which practically limits divine providence (*De
Stoic. Rep.* 1051 d 10–12); in this way, he wants to draw the attention of the reader
to the contradiction which, according to him, exists between Chrysippus' doc-
trine of ἀνάγκη and his defence, against Epicurus, of divine providence.

[4] On this fragment see especially Praechter in Überweg–Heinze, Band i, 548,
and in his article on Taurus, col. 61, and Andresen, art. cit. 186. Together with
Eudorus, Taurus, Nicostratus, and Hierax, Atticus represents the tendency of
Middle Platonism which opposed any contamination between the Platonic and
Peripatetic doctrines: see E. Zeller, *Die Phil. der Griechen* iii/1. 837, Praechter,

(c) Closely connected with the rejection of the Epicurean
system is the criticism directed against Aristotle's view according
to which divine providence does not work below the sphere of
the moon. In *Protr.* 66. 4 (i. 51. 2 f.) Clement mentions this
Peripatetic doctrine[1] and condemns it together with Aristotle's

op. cit. 529–30, 530–1 (on Eudorus), 546 (on Taurus), 548 (on Nicostratus and
Atticus), 551–2 (on Hierax), art. cit. on Taurus, col. 61, and his two articles
'Hierax der Platoniker', *Hermes* 41 (1906), 616, and 'Nikostratos der Platoniker',
Hermes 57 (1922), 495 ff., and Merlan, 63 (on Taurus) and 73–4 (on Atticus).
The opposite tendency of Middle Platonism, which, following the example of
Antiochus of Ascalon, had given shape to a kind of syncretism of Platonic, Peripatetic, and Stoic doctrines, is represented especially by the school of Gaius:
see Praechter, art. cit. on Taurus, col. 61, and op. cit. 527–9 and 548, H. Diels,
76–7, R. E. Witt, *Albinus* . . ., 8–20 and 42–103, and Ph. Merlan, 64. Plutarch
occupies an intermediate position between these two tendencies: if, on the one
hand, his writings against the Stoics and the Epicureans prove that he wanted to
preserve the distinction between Platonism and the other philosophical systems,
on the other hand he did not refrain from incorporating Stoic and Peripatetic
doctrines into his system (see Praechter, op. cit. 535). We shall have occasion to
examine this question more in detail later on (chapter II, especially pp. 65, 67,
and 101 below).
  [1] For the presence of this doctrine in Aristotle see E. Zeller, ii/2 468 n. 1 (I
owe this reference to Stählin, app. crit., vol. i, p. 51); cf. also Diogenes Laertius
v. 32 (i. 213. 6–7 Long), διατείνειν δὲ αὐτοῦ τὴν πρόνοιαν μέχρι τῶν οὐρανίων. An
interesting parallel is represented by [Aristotle], *De Mundo* 397ᵇ30–398ᵇ6; in this
section the author maintains that the more things are removed from God, the
less they enjoy divine providence (κατὰ τὸ ἔγγιόν τε καὶ πορρωτέρω θεοῦ εἶναι
μᾶλλόν τε καὶ ἧττον ὠφελείας μεταλαμβάνοντα), denies that God cares directly about
earthly things (μᾶλλον ἢ ὡς . . . αὐτουργεῖ τὰ ἐπὶ γῆς), and compares God to the
Great Persian King: as the provinces of his empire are administered not by him
personally but by his satraps, so the inferior parts of the universe are under the
guardianship not of God but of some of his powers. Similar ideas are expounded
by Philo: in *De Decal.* 178 (iv. 307. 14–17) the Jewish author maintains that,
whereas God, 'the Great King', cares only about the general order of the universe,
the task of punishing the transgressors of his law is allotted to his assistant, justice;
and in the same work, *De Decal.* 61 (iv. 282. 16–22), he compares God to the Great
King and the sensible universe to the satraps. The views held by the Stoic Chrysippus were not very different: as Plutarch, *De Stoic. Rep.* 1051 c 4–11, tells us, in his
work Περὶ οὐσίας, he had maintained that, although the universe as a whole
was well administered, there were nevertheless a few things about which divine
providence did not care (ἀμελουμένων τινῶν) and which were under the guardianship of mean daemons (ἢ διὰ τὸ καθίστασθαι ἐπὶ τῶν τοιούτων δαιμόνια φαῦλα).
In refuting Chrysippus' view Plutarch, *De Stoic. Rep.* 1051 d 4–9, resorts to the image
of the Persian king and of the satraps which is employed both by the author of *De
Mundo* and by Philo. A trace of this doctrine, according to which the highest
divinity allots the guardianship of man to some inferior divinities, can be found in
Plato's *Timaeus*: at the end of his speech addressed to the astral gods the Demiurge
orders that they must look after man, τροφήν τε διδόντες αὐξάνετε, 41 d 2–3.
On the other hand, however, Plato strongly criticizes those who deny that God
can care about man (see *Laws* x. 899 d 5–6, 900 b 2–3, 904 e 5, 905 a 4, 905 b 6)
and maintains quite openly that divine providence is concerned also with the

tendency—which had been inherited by his school—to identify God with the soul of the universe.[1] Aristotle's view about divine providence is mentioned again in *Strom.* v. 90. 3 (ii. 385. 19–20); according to Clement, Aristotle was led to formulate this doctrine by his misunderstanding of Ps. 35: 6, κύριε, ἐν τῷ οὐρανῷ τὸ ἔλεός σου καὶ ἡ ἀλήθειά σου ἕως τῶν νεφελῶν. That such a condemnation of Aristotle comes from Middle Platonism can be seen from the passages of Atticus quoted above, where Aristotle is put on the same level as Epicurus, because he too denied that God cares for man.[2] Justin also must have held the same views as Clement, since the passage of *Apol.* i. 28 quoted in the previous section can equally refer to Epicurus and to the teaching of the Peripatetic school.[3]

(*d*) The condemnation of Stoic pantheism is particularly clear in the following passages of Clement, which seem to repeat one another:

Protr. 66. 3 (i. 50. 24–7): οὐδὲ μὴν τοὺς ἀπὸ τῆς Στοᾶς παρελεύσομαι, διὰ πάσης ὕλης, καὶ διὰ τῆς ἀτιμωτάτης, τὸ θεῖον διήκειν λέγοντας, οἳ καταισχύνουσιν ἀτεχνῶς τὴν φιλοσοφίαν.

Strom. i. 51. 1 (ii. 33. 12–14): ἀλλὰ καὶ οἱ Στωϊκοί, ὧν καὶ αὐτῶν μέμνηται [sc. St. Paul], σῶμα ὄντα τὸν θεὸν διὰ τῆς ἀτιμωτάτης ὕλης πεφοιτηκέναι λέγουσιν, οὐ καλῶς.

Strom. ii. 14. 3 (ii. 120. 7–8): . . . τὸ ἁπλοῦν, ὃ οὔτε σὺν ὕλῃ ἐστὶν οὔτε ὕλη οὔτε ὑπὸ ὕλης.

Strom. v. 89. 2 (ii. 384. 18–19): φασὶ γὰρ σῶμα εἶναι τὸν θεὸν οἱ Στωϊκοὶ καὶ πνεῦμα καὶ οὐσίαν, ὥσπερ ἀμέλει καὶ τὴν ψυχήν.

Strom. v. 89. 3 (ii. 384. 22–385. 1): ἀλλ' οἱ μὲν διήκειν διὰ πάσης οὐσίας τὸν θεόν φασι . . .

The same rejection of Stoic pantheistic materialism appears also in Justin, as the following evidence shows:

smallest things (*Laws* x. 900 c 9–d 1, 901 b 1–4, 902 c 1–2, 902 e 4–903 a 3). Atticus in his polemic against Aristotle and Epicurus (see p. 46 above) and Plutarch in his criticism of Chrysippus (*De Stoic. Rep.* 1051 d 4–9) may have thought of these passages of the tenth book of the *Laws*.

[1] On this doctrine see Aristotle, Περὶ φιλοσοφίας, fr. 26 Walzer (= Cicero, *De Nat. Deor.* i. 13. 33: *modo mundum ipsum deum dicit esse* [sc. Aristotle]); cf. also *De Nat. Deor.* i. 13. 35: *nec audiendus eius* [sc. *Theophrasti*] *auditor Strato . . . qui omnem vim divinam in natura sitam esse censet.*

[2] Praechter, *RE*, Zweite Reihe, Vierter Halbband, col. 61, thinks that Taurus also, like Atticus, may have criticized this Peripatetic doctrine: he composed a work 'About the differences between the doctrines of Plato and those of Aristotle'.

[3] On Justin's attitude towards the Peripatetic school see also Andresen, art. cit. 160–1.

Apol. i. 20. 3: οἱ λεγόμενοι δὲ Στωϊκοὶ φιλόσοφοι καὶ αὐτὸν τὸν θεὸν
εἰς πῦρ ἀναλύεσθαι δογματίζουσι καὶ αὖ πάλιν κατὰ μεταβολὴν τὸν
κόσμον γενέσθαι λέγουσιν. ἡμεῖς δὲ κρεῖττόν τι τῶν μεταβαλλομένων
νοοῦμεν τὸν πάντων ποιητὴν θεόν.
Apol. ii. 7. 3: ὡς δηλοῦσθαι ἐν τῷ περὶ ἀρχῶν καὶ ἀσωμάτων οὐκ
εὐοδοῦν αὐτούς [sc. the Stoics].
Apol. ii. 7. 4: ἢ μηδὲν εἶναι θεὸν παρὰ τρεπόμενα καὶ ἀλλοιούμενα
καὶ ἀναλυόμενα εἰς τὰ αὐτὰ ἀεί, φθαρτῶν μόνων φανήσονται κατάληψιν
ἐσχηκέναι. καὶ αὐτὸν τὸν θεὸν διά τε τῶν μερῶν καὶ διὰ τοῦ ὅλου
ἐν πάσῃ κακίᾳ γινόμενον . . .

This polemic against Stoic materialism, which both Christian
authors have in common, is also characteristic of Middle
Platonism. In *De Stoic. Rep.* 1051 f 9–1052 a 9 Plutarch strongly
criticizes Chrysippus' view according to which the gods are
material and corruptible; and in *De Def. Or.* 426 b 3–c 3 he says:

It is not right to consider the gods as the chiefs of a swarm who
cannot get out of it and to keep them closed or, more exactly,
blocked up in matter, as these people [i.e. the Stoics] do: considering the gods simply as determinate states of air or as composite powers of water and fire, they think that they came into
existence together with the material universe and let them burn
together with it. In this way, the gods are neither independent
nor free like the charioteer or the helmsman but, as statues are
nailed to their basements or fused together with them, so they
are closed in the corporeal substance and united to it; they
must share its destiny till its destruction, dissolution, and trans-
formation.

Albinus also maintains quite openly that God can by no means
be regarded as corporeal:

Did. 166. 2 ff.: If God is corporeal, he must be composed of matter
and form . . . but it is absurd to think that God is composed of
matter and form, since in this case he would be neither simple
nor primal; accordingly, God is incorporeal. And, in the same
way: if he is corporeal, he is composed of matter; in this case,
he would be either fire or water or earth or air or something
composed of these elements; but none of these elements is
primal. Moreover, he would come into existence after matter,
if he is composed of matter. All these conclusions being absurd,
it is necessary to consider him as incorporeal. In fact, if he
is corporeal, he is also corruptible, originated, and subject to
change; each of these attributes is absurd if applied to him.

With the beginning of this passage of Albinus it is worth comparing Clement, *Strom.* ii. 14. 3 (ii. 120. 7–8) ... τὸ ἁπλοῦν, ὃ οὔτε σὺν ὕλῃ ἐστὶν οὔτε ὕλη οὔτε ὑπὸ ὕλης.[1]

Another point on which Stoicism is violently criticized is the doctrine of εἱμαρμένη : destiny, according to the Stoics, regulated human actions in such a way that the possibility of a free choice and consequently also the idea of personal responsibility seemed to be completely destroyed. Clement, on the contrary, lays a very strong emphasis on the power of free choice which man possesses, and, polemizing indirectly against the Stoics, maintains that prizes and punishments could not exist, if the human soul were devoid of it :

Strom. i. 89. 1 (ii. 57. 19) : ἑκούσιος γὰρ ἥ τε αἵρεσις ἥ τε τῆς ἀληθείας ἐκτροπή.

Strom. i. 83. 5 (ii. 54. 12–14) : οὔτε δὲ οἱ ἔπαινοι οὔτε ψόγοι οὔθ᾽ αἱ τιμαὶ οὔθ᾽ αἱ κολάσεις δίκαιαι, μὴ τῆς ψυχῆς ἐχούσης τὴν ἐξουσίαν τῆς ὁρμῆς καὶ ἀφορμῆς ἀλλ᾽ ἀκουσίου τῆς κακίας οὔσης.

Justin maintains that the acceptance of the Stoic doctrine of εἱμαρμένη would imply the destruction of the ideas of good and evil, which are both based on the assumption that man is endowed with a free power of choice : the long section of *Apol.* i. 43 (i. 118–22) as well as some passages of chapter VII of the second apology (i. 218. 9–11 ; 218. 15–22 ; 220. 5 ff.) show clearly Justin's opinion on this problem.[2]

But exactly the same ideas appear in Middle Platonism. A correspondence between Albinus and Clement, which J. Wytzes also has noticed,[3] is particularly striking :

Clem. *Strom.* i. 83. 5 (ii. 54. 12–14) : οὔτε δὲ οἱ ἔπαινοι οὔτε ψόγοι οὔθ᾽ αἱ τιμαὶ οὔθ᾽ αἱ κολάσεις δίκαιαι, μὴ τῆς ψυχῆς ἐχούσης τὴν ἐξουσίαν τῆς ὁρμῆς καὶ ἀφορμῆς ἀλλ᾽ ἀκουσίου τῆς κακίας οὔσης.

Clem. *Strom.* i. 89. 1 (ii. 57. 19) : ἑκούσιος γὰρ ἥ τε αἵρεσις ἥ τε τῆς ἀληθείας ἐκτροπή.

Albinus, *Did.* 179. 6–7 : ἐπεὶ καὶ τὸ ἐφ᾽ ἡμῖν οἰχήσεται καὶ ἔπαινοι καὶ ψόγοι καὶ πᾶν τὸ τούτοις παραπλήσιον.

Albinus, *Did.* 179. 9–10 : ἀδέσποτον οὖν ἡ ψυχὴ καὶ ἐπ᾽ αὐτῇ μὲν τὸ πρᾶξαι ἢ μή, καὶ οὐ κατηνάγκασται τοῦτο.

---

[1] On the criticism of Stoic pantheism in Middle Platonism Andresen's remarks are particularly worth noticing : see art. cit. 170 and op. cit. 304.
[2] On Justin's criticism of Stoic determinism see also Andresen, art. cit. 183–7.
[3] *VC* 9 (1955), 149.

Plutarch stresses the incompatibility between the Stoic doctrine of εἱμαρμένη and the idea of human freedom, and points out the contradictions which would necessarily derive from the attempt to adopt both of them at the same time:

> De Stoic. Rep. 1056 d 1–11 : Should we say that assent, virtue, vice, success, and failure do not depend on us or should we regard destiny as defective, fate as unbounded, and the movements and the stationary conditions of Zeus as defective? Of these two conclusions, the former must be drawn if we say that destiny is an absolute cause, the latter if we say that it is only the initial cause. As absolute cause of everything, it destroys our free and voluntary choice, as initial cause it loses its propriety of being unhindered and effective.[1]

The author of the treatise 'About destiny' also maintains that the existence of εἱμαρμένη does not exclude that of the free power of choice in man (τὸ ἐφ᾿ ἡμῖν); the passages of Plutarch, *De Fato* 570 e 7–11, 570 f 4–5, 571 d 1–7, and of Calcidius, *Comm. on the Timaeus*, 156, p. 190. 12–13 Waszink (*erit ergo . . . optio penes hominem qui utpote rationale animal cuncta revocat ad rationem atque consilium*), and 179, p. 208. 11–12 Waszink (*quae res ostendit optionem quidem esse in hominibus nec eandem in omnibus*), are very clear on this point.[2]

Like Justin, therefore, Clement judges the individual philosophical systems from the point of view of Middle Platonism. His philosophical education has not been effaced by his conversion to Christianity.

4. Some passages of the *Stromateis* have induced many scholars to regard Clement as an 'eclectic' philosopher.[3] It has often been assumed that Clement, owing to his belief that the universal truth had been torn into pieces like Pentheus' body and that fragments of it had been dropped like seeds in all Greek philosophical systems,[4] showed a strong inclination towards a kind of

---

[1] On the critical attitude of Middle Platonism towards Stoic determinism see Andresen, art. cit. 184–7.

[2] See also E. Zeller, *Die Philos. der Griechen* iii/2. 230–1 ; that the author of *De Fato* and Calcidius depend on a common Middle Platonic source has been shown by A. Gercke, *RMPh* 41 (1886), 266–91 (especially 269–79).

[3] Besides the very famous passage of *Strom.* i. 37. 6 see *Strom.* i. 57. 4 (ii. 36. 18–22) and *Strom.* vi. 55. 3 (ii. 459. 25–7).

[4] See particularly *Strom.* i. 57. 1–2 (ii. 36. 8–14) and *Strom.* i. 57. 6 (ii. 36. 29–31).

eclecticism to which either he personally or his teacher Pantaenus[1] had given shape: like a bee flitting from flower to flower, he was thus able to find, in the different systems of Greek philosophy, some true doctrines, and to gather them together so as to reconstruct that universal truth which the individual philosophical systems had only partially grasped.[2] This assumption seemed to be confirmed by the view held by E. Molland of the practice then current in the catechetical school of Alexandria; for he supposes that in the catechetical school the works of the most important Greek philosophers were read, discussed, and commented upon, and that what the pupils learnt from their teachers was, first of all, how to select the best doctrines from all Greek philosophical systems.[3] It will be the purpose of the present section to determine in what sense these views may be accepted and how they can be inserted into the general frame of Clement's thought.

There is no doubt about the fact that in the first book of the *Stromateis* Clement seems to speak as an 'eclectic'. But it would be misleading to detach his 'eclecticism' from one of the most important aspects of his theological thought and from his cultural background. In other words, it is not sufficient simply to point out Clement's 'eclecticism' by quoting the sections of the *Stromateis* in which it appears, without trying to determine the reasons to which it ultimately goes back. These reasons are

---

[1] See E. Redepenning, 93–4.

[2] The metaphor of the bee as the best picture of Clement's eclectic attitude has been pointed out by G. Basilakes (see footnote 3, p. 2 above) and, in more recent times, by W. Telfer, in his interesting paper in *JTS* 28 (1926/7), 167–8. Telfer draws attention to some passages in which Clement, by quoting the sentence of Prov. 6. 8a ἢ πορεύθητι πρὸς τὴν μέλισσαν καὶ μάθε ὡς ἐργάτις ἐστί, advises the gnostic or perfect Christian to imitate the tireless activity of the bee so that he may become πολυμαθής (see *Strom.* i. 33. 6, vol. ii. 22. 13–15, and *Strom.* iv. 9. 2, vol. ii. 252. 9–10: both passages are quoted by Telfer, 171). Telfer is certainly right when he says: 'Honey, for Clement, symbolizes the sweet and profitable knowledge of the Logos, which is to be culled from all over the varied garden of the universe. The bee symbolizes the active principle of truth in man, which enables him to do this; or, by a derived use, it symbolizes a "gnostic" soul as actualizing this principle. Because the sweets of the Logos are to be found anywhere, the gnostic will be πολυμαθής' (art. cit. 177). It must, however, be observed that his following statement, 'And he himself [sc. Clement] is like a bee, gathering divine sweets from all over the garden . . . of his encyclopaedic knowledge', though substantially true, is supported by no direct evidence, since the passage of *Strom.* vii. 111. 1 (iii. 73. 28–9) to which he refers does not contain any identification of Clement with the bee, but simply a picture of the various and composite nature of the *Stromateis*.

[3] E. Molland, *The Conception of the Gospel* . . ., 166.

fundamentally two: the first, which may be called 'theological', is directly connected with the first explanation which Clement gives of the origin of Greek philosophy and with the sources on which this explanation is based; the second, which may be defined as 'historical', rests upon the nature of the cultural milieu on which the Christian author depends.

Clement's theory according to which each Greek philosophical system contains some elements of truth in itself finds its explanation in the fact that, according to him, the Greek philosophers could reach a certain knowledge of the truth either by means of their own reason, the divine element dwelling in all men which is intimately connected with the universal Logos, or by means of that divine inspiration with which they, like the prophets, were filled.[1] In both cases, what gives origin to Greek philosophy is the divine Logos,[2] i.e. that ἀπόρροια θεϊκή of *Protr.* 68. 2 which can be regarded both as the origin of the rational principle which all men possess, and as the inspiration which God bestowed upon the philosophers.[3] But Clement goes even beyond these statements; in chapter VII of the first book of the *Stromateis* he practically identifies philosophy with the Logos himself by representing it first as a shower and then as the seeds dropped by the husbandman.[4]

Considered from this twofold point of view, the different systems of Greek philosophy appear as fragments of the divine Logos. This imposing conception of Clement's cannot, however, be regarded simply as 'Christian'. The two doctrines which represent its basis are already present in his philosophical sources: the doctrine of the divine origin of human reason is characteristic both of Philo and of the Platonic school-tradition;[5] and the doctrine of the effluence of the divine Logos or 'Holy Ghost' out of its source and of its dropping into the mind of the philosophers and the prophets goes back to the Wisdom of Solomon, to Ecclesiasticus, and to Philo, and occurs in effect also in Justin and in Clement's great antagonist, Celsus.[6]

The first reason for Clement's 'eclecticism' then appears clear. In observing that parts of the truth are contained in all Greek philosophical systems Clement does not think in abstract terms

---

[1] See p. 16 above.
[2] See pp. 17–18 above.
[3] See footnote 2, p. 17 above.
[4] See p. 18 above.
[5] See especially footnote 4, p. 23 above.
[6] See pp. 27–8 above.

nor does he behave like a narrow-minded Christian who limits himself to comparing the truth represented by his religion with the different philosophical systems, in order to establish to what extent they agree with each other, and who, after this comparison, comes to the conclusion that, after all, it should not be very dangerous to borrow some 'terms' or 'expressions' of the Greek philosophers;[1] he is under the direct influence of Jewish-Hellenistic and Middle Platonic doctrines which both determine the way in which he approaches and resolves this problem, and actually represent the constitutive elements of a most important aspect of his theological thought. It is not by a simple chance that the famous passage of *Strom.* i. 37. 6, which has been constantly quoted by the scholars who have regarded Clement as an 'eclectic',[2] occurs immediately after the representation of Greek philosophy as a shower and as a multitude of seeds and its identification with the divine Logos.

Since the universal truth represented by the Logos is scattered in the different systems of Greek philosophy, it naturally follows, in Clement's opinion, that he who wants to know the whole truth must gather together the best doctrines of the different systems: in this way he can build up a kind of absolute philosophy which is also identical with the truth.[3] Clement, however, is well aware of the fact that neither he nor any other Christian theologian is the first who must perform this task. During his philosophical studies before his conversion Clement had come into contact with the Platonic schools of the second century A.D. and noticed that the exponents of many of them, following the example of Antiochus of Ascalon, did not refrain from adopting doctrines of the Porch and of the Lycaeum, thus conferring an eclectic character upon Platonism;[4] moreover, after his arrival in Alexandria, he, as a Christian theologian, had had the best opportunity of reading the writings of Philo as well as other products of Hellenistic Judaism and of observing that these writings contained a selection of the best Greek philosophical

---

[1] A list of the scholars who hold this view is given in the Introduction, p. 3 above, footnotes 1–2.

[2] See the Introduction, footnote 3, p. 2 above.

[3] See particularly *Strom.* i. 57. 6 (ii. 36. 31–37. 2), ὁ δὲ τὰ διῃρημένα συνθεὶς αὖθις καὶ ἑνοποιήσας τέλειον τὸν λόγον ἀκινδύνως εὖ ἴσθ' ὅτι κατόψεται, τὴν ἀλήθειαν.

[4] On the eclectic tendency of some schools of Middle Platonism see footnote 4, pp. 46–7 above.

doctrines which, under many aspects, was analogous to the cultural synthesis present in some of the Platonic schools of the second century: in particular, it could hardly have escaped him that Philo's philosophy was mainly based on a syncretism of Pythagorean, Platonic, Stoic, and also Peripatetic doctrines, and that such a syncretism did not substantially differ from that characteristic of Middle Platonism.[1] Clement's insistence on the necessity of realizing a synthesis of the 'best' philosophical doctrines finds therefore its exact counterpart in the teaching both of Middle Platonism and of the Jewish-Alexandrine philosophy.

We are now also able to appreciate the real character of the Christian catechetical school of Alexandria. E. Molland, starting from the description of Origen's way of teaching made by Gregory Thaumaturgus in his 'Thanksgiving to Origen', deemed it right to draw attention to the 'eclectic' attitude of its teachers.[2] Gregory Thaumaturgus tells us that in Origen's school the works of all Greek philosophers were taken into account, except those which were regarded as 'atheistic'.[3] Among such works there were obviously included those of Epicurus and of his followers as well as some Stoic and Peripatetic treatises on theology.[4] In this way, a close parallelism can be established between such practices of the catechetical school and the tendencies characteristic of some contemporary Platonic schools: the acceptance and rejection on the part of Origen and of Clement of determinate philosophical doctrines is in keeping with the attitude of some exponents of Middle Platonism who, on the one hand, missed no opportunity of attacking the Epicurean, Peripatetic, and Stoic conceptions of the divinity[5] but, on the other, did not hesitate to borrow some ethical and epistemological doctrines of the Porch and of the Lyceum. And the same— though even stronger—'eclectic' tendency can be ascertained in the teaching of the most important non-Christian philosopher contemporary with Origen, Plotinus. Porphyry tells us that in Plotinus' school the Stoic and Peripatetic works, as well as those of several exponents of Middle Platonism, of Numenius, and

[1] This will be shown more in detail in the following chapters of the present work.
[2] See footnote 3, p. 2 above.
[3] Chapter XIII, 151–3, p. 29 Koetschau.
[4] See pp. 47 f. above.
[5] See pp. 46 ff. above.

of some commentators of Aristotle were carefully read.[1] The natural conclusion is that the curriculum of the Christian school of Alexandria was planned after the example of the contemporary Platonic schools, which the Christian teachers wanted to emulate. Like Clement's eclecticism, the 'eclectic' tendency of the Alexandrine catechetical school must therefore be understood in the light of the character of the Platonism of the time.

5. It has already been noticed that, according to Clement, Greek philosophy, in the history of mankind, accomplishes a most important task: it prepares the Greeks for the reception of the Christian message, the 'true philosophy'.[2] In our study of Clement's conception of *gnosis* we shall have occasion to observe that the 'true message', the highest aspect of Christianity, does not consist for him simply in some general conceptions about God, or in what can be read and understood by everybody but, first of all, in the ἀλήθεια which is one and the same thing with the divine Logos,[3] i.e. in a system of doctrines which can be known only by a select few and which, therefore, represent the object of an esoteric *gnosis*.[4] The teacher of this esoteric *gnosis* is the historical Christ, the incarnation of the divine Logos.[5] Not only did he communicate 'secret' doctrines to some of his apostles, but also taught them the right way of interpreting Scripture:[6] only by means of a right interpretation of Scripture is it possible to grasp the truth which is hidden behind its literal meaning and reach the treasure of *gnosis*.[7] If we now remember how strongly Clement is inclined to consider Greek philosophy as a product of the Logos,[8] we cannot keep from observing the intimate connection which, according to him, exists between the Logos, philosophy, and the right interpretation of Scripture or *gnosis*: if the Logos is the source both of philosophy and of the right interpretation of Scripture; if philosophy is meant to prepare,

---

[1] *Vita Plot.* chap. XIV. Cf. A. von Harnack, *Lehrbuch der Dogmengeschichte*, Erster Band, 641: 'Der Lehrgang [of the catechetical school] war mutatis mutandis natürlich derselbe, wie bei den Neuplatonikern.'

[2] See p. 11 above and footnote 1 on the same page.

[3] See *Strom.* i. 32. 4 (ii. 21. 18–19), ἀλήθεια δὲ αὕτη, περὶ ἧς ὁ κύριος αὐτὸς εἶπεν "ἐγώ εἰμι ἡ ἀλήθεια" (Clement quotes here John 14: 6).

[4] This point will be examined more in detail later on in the section on *gnosis*, chapter III, pp. 144 ff. below.

[5] See p. 159 below.   [6] See p. 155 below.

[7] See pp. 137–42 and 154–5 below.   [8] See p. 18 above.

in the history of mankind, the higher Christian message, i.e. the Christian *gnosis*; if the higher *gnosis* can only be attained by means of a determinate interpretation of Scripture, it necessarily follows that Greek philosophy and interpretation of Scripture are, for Clement, practically one and the same thing:[1] in other words, whenever a Christian wants to reach *gnosis*, i.e. to grasp the inner meaning of Scripture, he must resort to Greek philosophy. This is the reason why Clement insists so much on the necessity, for those who want to become γνωστικοί, of studying and taking into account philosophy.[2]

Philosophy is, therefore, something more than a simple tinge covering a Christian thought which is not influenced by it,[3] or a cloak which the Christian theologian deigns to put on in order to convert the heathen philosophers:[4] it provides the rules for the right interpretation of Scripture, it is the key which discloses its inner meaning.[5] The interpretation which Clement gives of some passages of Scripture is very instructive. In each case, a determinate philosophical doctrine provides him with the clue

---

[1] See *Strom.* i. 28. 1 (ii. 17. 32–3), φιλοσοφία ... προπαιδεία τις οὖσα τοῖς τὴν πίστιν δι' ἀποδείξεως καρπουμένοις: it will be seen later on (pp. 138 ff.) that the ἀπόδειξις mentioned here is nothing but the interpretation of Scripture. It is worth noticing also the passage of *Strom.* i. 18. 1 (ii. 13. 1–2), περιέξουσι δὲ οἱ Στρωματεῖς ἀναμεμιγμένην τὴν ἀλήθειαν τοῖς φιλοσοφίας δόγμασι, μᾶλλον δὲ ἐγκεκαλυμμένην καὶ ἐπικεκρυμμένην.

[2] Those who want to remain ignorant will never be able to attain wisdom, *Strom.* ii. 45. 6 (ii. 137. 6–9). It is true that in *Strom.* i. 100. 1 (ii. 63. 29–32) Clement maintains that the Christian teaching is self-sufficing and is not made stronger by Greek philosophy; Völker, of course, sees in this passage a very powerful piece of evidence in support of his views: 'durch die Philosophie erfährt sie keinen Zuwachs an Wahrheit' (op. cit. 352). Against this interpretation it must, however, be observed that Clement sees no real distinction or opposition between the 'good' doctrines of Greek philosophy and the higher Christian teaching (ἡ ἀλήθεια or σοφία) since, according to him, both of them are originally part of the divine Logos: they are, therefore, substantially identical with each other. The higher Christian teaching contains the 'good' parts of philosophy in itself: what Justin says in *Apol.* ii. 13. 5, ὅσα οὖν παρὰ πᾶσι καλῶς εἴρηται ἡμῶν τῶν Χριστιανῶν ἐστι, reflects also Clement's thought. Clement can say that Greek philosophy does not make truth stronger because he does not regard philosophy as something extraneous to the higher Christian doctrines, but as the constitutive element of them. What, in his opinion, philosophy *does* make stronger, is not the higher *gnosis*, but the ψιλὴ πίστις (i.e. the acceptance of the literal meaning of Scripture) which, with the aid of it, becomes *gnosis*: see *Strom.* i. 28. 1 (ii. 17. 32–3), φιλοσοφία ... προπαιδεία τις οὖσα τοῖς τὴν πίστιν δι' ἀποδείξεως καρπουμένοις, and pp. 138–40 below.

[3] See the Introduction, p. 3 above and footnote 2 on the same page.

[4] This is Völker's view: see the Introduction, footnote 2, p. 3 above.

[5] On the presence of an inner meaning in Scripture see pp. 137 and 154 below.

which enables him to lift the veil of allegory which keeps the true meaning of the sacred text hidden to the many: the beginning of the book of Genesis is interpreted with the aid of the Platonic distinction between the sensible and the intelligible world;[1] the expressions πνοὴ ζωῆς and κατ' εἰκόνα (Gen. 2: 7; 1: 26 and 1: 27) are considered as referring to the doctrine of the divine origin of human reason;[2] the expression καθ' ὁμοίωσιν of Gen. 1: 26 is brought into direct connection with the Platonic formula ὁμοίωσις θεῷ of *Theaetetus* 176 b;[3] the interpretation of the story concerning Abraham's relations with his handmaid Agar and his wife Sarah (Gen. 16: 1 ff.) goes ultimately back to the Platonic doctrine of the propaedeutic role of the encyclical disciplines;[4] and the interpretation of the Jewish tabernacle and of the high priest is based on the cosmological system of the *Timaeus* as well as on the distinction between sensible and intelligible things.[5]

Since the interpretation of Scripture, on which the acquisition of wisdom ultimately depends, can only be achieved with the aid of philosophy, it is easy to understand why Clement calls philosophy a 'cultivation of wisdom'[6] and 'search for the truth and for the nature of beings'[7] and is inclined to consider it as subordinate to theology[8] and as its 'handmaid'.[9] The relationship which can be observed between Greek philosophy and Christian theology in history finds its exact counterpart in the role which philosophy plays in the interpretation of Scripture: in both cases, philosophy represents a kind of preparation for the

---

[1] See pp. 191–2 below.

[2] See pp. 14–15 above.

[3] See p. 108 below.

[4] On the role of the encyclical disciplines see pp. 169–73 below; on Clement's interpretation of the story of Gen. 16: 1 ff. see footnotes 2 and 3, p. 59 below.

[5] See pp. 174–5 below.

[6] *Strom.* i. 30. 1 (ii. 19. 15), ἔστι γὰρ ἡ μὲν φιλοσοφία ἐπιτήδευσις σοφίας; immediately afterwards he defines wisdom as 'scientific knowledge of divine and human things and of their causes', ἐπιστήμη τῶν θείων καὶ ἀνθρωπίνων πραγμάτων καὶ τῶν τούτων αἰτίων.

[7] *Strom.* i. 32. 4 (ii. 21. 17–18), cf. *Strom.* vi. 91. 1 (ii. 477. 20–1), and *Strom.* ii. 45. 6 (ii. 137. 7–9) (with this last definition it is worth comparing [Plato], *Ὅροι* 414 b: see Stählin's apparatus, vol. ii. 137).

[8] *Strom.* i. 30. 1 (ii. 19. 16–17), κυρία τοίνυν ἡ σοφία τῆς φιλοσοφίας.

[9] *Strom.* i. 32. 1 (ii. 21. 9–10), ἀσπάζομαι μὲν τὴν κοσμικὴν παιδείαν ὡς σὴν θεραπαινίδα (these words are part of Clement's allegorical interpretation of the well-known biblical story of Abraham's relations with Agar and Sarah: see *Strom.* i. 30. 3–32. 3, vol. ii. 19. 21–21. 16).

Christian *gnosis*.¹ This is the real nature of its subordination to Christianity.

Clement's views on the relations between philosophy and theology cannot be fully appreciated without taking Philo and Middle Platonism duly into account. The section of *Strom.* i. 30. 1–2, in which Clement explains the relations between philosophy and wisdom, is directly dependent on Philo, *De Congr. Er. Gr.* 79.² Philo gives exactly the same definitions of philosophy and of wisdom as those present in Clement³ because he also, like Clement, attempts to interpret the Old Testament in terms of Greek philosophy. On this most important question the Jewish author is the direct teacher and model of the Alexandrine theologian.⁴ In Middle Platonism Albinus expounds practically the same views: in perfect agreement with Philo and Clement, he maintains that philosophy consists in longing for wisdom,⁵ defines wisdom as 'scientific knowledge of divine and human things',⁶ and considers theology as the highest part of philosophy.⁷

¹ On the preparatory function of philosophy in the building of *gnosis* see the evidence collected by Völker, 350 n. 2 and, besides, *Strom.* i. 28. 1 (ii. 17. 32–3).
² See Stählin, app., vol. ii. 19, and Heinisch, 188. In the allegorical interpretation of the story of Abraham also Clement follows Philo (*De Congr. Er. Gr.* 1–24 and 154, 158, 177) very closely: the exact correspondences between Philo and Clement can be found in Stählin's apparatus, vol. ii, pp. 19–21, and in Heinisch, 188–9 and 191; see also, on this question, Wolfson, *Philo* i. 155–7, and *The Philosophy of the Church Fathers*, 97–8.
³ *De Congr. Er. Gr.* 79 (iii. 88. 1–3); cf. Stählin's apparatus, vol. ii, p. 19. On the origin of this definition of σοφία see p. 73 n. 1 below.
⁴ See also pp. 140–1, 154–5 below.   ⁵ *Did.* 152. 4.
⁶ *Did.* 152. 6–7. The correspondence between Albinus and Clement in the definition of σοφία has been noticed by L. Früchtel, *BPhW* 57 (1937), 592 (see also his addition to Stählin's apparatus in the reprint of Stählin's edition, Berlin, 1960, p. 19).
⁷ *Did.* 152. 28–9, τοῦ μὲν θεωρητικοῦ [sc. βίου] τὸ κεφάλαιον ἐν τῇ γνώσει τῆς ἀληθείας κεῖται.

II

ETHICS

SOME scholars both of the last and of the present century have studied Clement's ethical views, and have attempted either to give a general sketch of them[1] or to stress their dependence on Stoicism[2] or to point out their Christian character which, according to them, remains uncorrupted even if the language used is sometimes borrowed from Greek philosophy.[3] But, as far as I know, no comprehensive inquiry has been undertaken on the problem of the relations between Clement's ethical doctrines and those of Philo, of Middle Platonism, and of Neoplatonism.[4] If we succeed in our attempt to show how strongly this cultural background has influenced both the general structure of Clement's ethical system and its climax—i.e. the ideal of ἀπάθεια and of ὁμοίωσις θεῷ—we shall also be able to produce a picture of Clement's ethics different from that with which the book by W. Völker presents us. In order to achieve this result, it will be best to examine thoroughly the following points:

1. The doctrine of virtue in general.
2. The four cardinal virtues and their relations with the different parts of the soul.
3. The doctrine of πάθος.
4. The lower ethical stage: the ethics of μετριοπάθεια in connection with the maxim 'to live according to nature'.
5. The higher ethical stage: the ethics of ἀπάθεια and the portrait of the perfect Christian or γνωστικός.
6. Ὁμοίωσις θεῷ.

[1] See, for instance, the works by F. J. Winter, K. Ernesti, W. Capitaine, J. Patrick, 141–87, and R. B. Tollinton, i. 239–69 and 270–92 and ii. 72–101.

[2] See the literature quoted in the Introduction, footnote 2, p. 1 above.

[3] See particularly W. Völker, 109–82, 183–219, 254–300, and 446–609. As to the scholars who have held this view before Völker see the literature quoted in the Introduction, footnote 1, p. 3 above.

[4] Prunet, though admitting in his recent book *La Morale de Clément d'Alexandrie*... that 'Clément marque un tournant décisif dans le processus d'hellénisation du Christianisme' (p. 243), does not study Clement's ethics from this point of view: his main concern is to establish to what extent Clement's ethical system agrees with the ethics of the New Testament.

ETHICS 61

After pointing out the close connections which exist between Clement's ethics and the ethics of Philo, of Middle Platonism, and of Neoplatonism, we shall also have to say something about the element which is characteristic of Clement and which Philo, Middle Platonism, and Neoplatonism do not possess, namely the role of Christ. In this connection, it will be necessary to find an answer for the two following questions:

1. Is there any relationship between the role which Christ plays in Clement's ethics and the ethical ideal of Philo and of Neoplatonism?
2. Can Christ's role in ethics be regarded as the exact counterpart of the function He accomplishes on the theoretical side of *gnosis*? If so, are we not already introduced into the atmosphere of *gnosis*?

1. We meet two general definitions of virtue in two passages of the *Paedagogus*:

Paed. i. 101. 2 (i. 150. 27–8): ἡ ἀρετὴ αὐτὴ διάθεσίς ἐστι τῆς ψυχῆς σύμφωνος τῷ λόγῳ περὶ ὅλον τὸν βίον.

Paed. iii. 35. 2 (i. 257. 3–4): ἡ ἀρετή, ὅς ἐστι λόγος διὰ τοῦ παιδαγωγοῦ παραδιδόμενος.

To these two definitions it will be convenient to add another passage, which, though not a definition itself, is closely related to them:

Paed. i. 102. 4 (i. 151. 24–6): καὶ γὰρ ὁ βίος ὁ Χριστιανῶν ... σύστημά τί ἐστιν λογικῶν πράξεων, τουτέστι τῶν ὑπὸ τοῦ λόγου διδασκομένων ἀδιάπτωτος ἐνέργεια.

The words βίος ... σύστημά τι ... λογικῶν πράξεων of this last passage remind us of the διάθεσις ... σύμφωνος τῷ λόγῳ περὶ ὅλον τὸν βίον in the first definition, whereas the words τῶν ὑπὸ τοῦ λόγου διδασκομένων recall the λόγος διὰ τοῦ παιδαγωγοῦ παραδιδόμενος in the second definition.

It has already been pointed out that the first definition is of Stoic origin.[1] It must, however, also be observed that, in Clement's

---

[1] See, for instance, C. Merk, 47 n. 7 and 71, W. Capitaine, footnote 3, pp. 329–330, M. Daskalakis, 100, J. Stelzenberger, 226–7 and 323–4, and M. Pohlenz, *NGA*, phil.-hist. Kl. (1943), 162, and *Die Stoa* i. 422. With *Paedagogus* i. 101. 2 it is worth comparing Stobaeus, *Ecl.* ii, p. 60 7–8 W. (= *SVF* iii. 262 end) and Diog. Laert.

62 ETHICS

thought, the words σύμφωνος τῷ λόγῳ do not express simply a Stoic doctrine, but hint also at the Platonic view according to which virtue is nothing but the harmony of the soul, i.e. the agreement between its inferior parts and reason, its ruling principle.[1] Clement himself refers directly to Plato when he maintains that it is the harmony of the soul (i.e. virtue) that makes right life possible:

Strom. iv. 18. 1 (ii. 256. 20–3): ἐν τῷ τρίτῳ τῆς Πολιτείας ὁ Πλάτων εἶπεν . . . ἐπιμελεῖσθαι σώματος δεῖν ψυχῆς ἕνεκα ἁρμονίας, δι' οὗ βιοῦν τέ ἐστι καὶ ὀρθῶς βιοῦν.[2]

The definitions of virtue given by Albinus and Apuleius show an analogous mixture of Stoic and Platonic elements and substantially agree with Clement's first definition:

Albinus, Did. 182. 13 f.: αὐτὴ μέν ἐστι διάθεσις ψυχῆς τελεία καὶ βελτίστη,[3] εὐσχήμονα[4] καὶ σύμφωνον καὶ βέβαιον παρέχουσα τὸν ἄνθρωπον.

vii. 89 (= SVF iii. 197). These references can be found in Stählin's app. crit., vol. i, p. 150 of his edition of Clement, and in Merk, 47 n. 7. A passage of Plutarch can be added to them: κοινῶς δ' ἅπαντες οὗτοι τὴν ἀρετὴν τοῦ ἡγεμονικοῦ τῆς ψυχῆς διάθεσίν τινα καὶ δύναμιν γεγενημένην ὑπὸ λόγου, μᾶλλον δὲ λόγον οὖσαν αὐτὴν ὁμολογούμενον καὶ βέβαιον καὶ ἀμετάπτωτον ὑποτίθενται (De Virt. m. 441 c = SVF i. 202). This reference is also given by Völker, 285 n. 1.

1 See, for instance, Phaedo 93 c 3–7 and 93 e 8–9, Rep. iv. 430 e 3–4, 443 d 6–e 2 (about man who practises justice), and viii. 554 e 4–5, Laws ii. 653 b 6, ii. 659 e 2–3, iii. 689 d 5–7, and 696 c 8–10. It is worth noticing that the sentences λαβόντων δὲ λόγον συμφωνήσωσι τῷ λόγῳ (Laws ii. 653 b 4–5) and καὶ τὰς ἡδονὰς καὶ λύπας . . . συμφώνους τοῖς ὀρθοῖς λόγοις (Laws iii. 696 c 8–10) are in keeping with the expression σύμφωνος τῷ λόγῳ of Paed. i. 101. 2.
2 Cf. Plato, Rep. iii. 410 c and also Rep. ix. 591 d, ἀλλ' ἀεὶ τὴν ἐν τῷ σώματι ἁρμονίαν τῆς ἐν ψυχῇ ἕνεκα συμφωνίας ἁρμοττόμενος φανεῖται. Both references are given by Stählin, app. crit., vol. ii, p. 256. My own impression is that Clement, though mentioning the third book of the Republic, has the words of the other passage of Rep. ix. 591 d still floating in his mind.
3 R. E. Witt, Albinus . . ., has pointed out (p. 89) that the beginning of Albinus' definition is not Stoic but occurs in the [Platonic] definitions and shows also a Peripatetic influence: see his footnotes 1 and 2 on p. 89, with the references to [Plato], Ὅροι 411 c διάθεσις ἡ βελτίστη, to Stobaeus Ecl. ii. 51. 1–2 W., and to Aristotle, Polit. 1323ᵇ13 and EE 1218ᵇ38 (the reference to this last passage of Aristotle can also be found in Wachsmuth, app. crit. to Stob., Ecl. ii. 51, and in K. Praechter, Grundr. der Gesch. der Philos. 544). It must be remembered that many of the definitions which occur in the Ὅροι are derived not from Plato, but either from the Lyceum or from the Porch, as J. Souilhé, Platon, Œuvres complètes, Tome xiii, 3ᵉ partie (Paris, Les Belles Lettres, 1930), 156–7, rightly points out.
4 On εὐσχήμονα it is worth comparing Maximus of Tyre, Or. xxvii. 115 a (p. 323. 1–2), ἄλλο τι ἡγεῖ εἶναι τὴν ἀρετὴν ἢ ψυχῆς ὑγίειάν τε καὶ εὐσχημοσύνην;

Apuleius, *De Plat. et eius Dogm.* ii. 227: *sed virtutem Plato habitum esse dicit mentis optime ac nobiliter figuratum, quae concordem sibi . . . constantem etiam eum facit, cui fuerit fideliter intimata, non verbis modo sed factis secum et cum ceteris congruentem.*[1]

The words σύμφωνον and *concordem sibi* of Albinus and Apuleius have practically the same meaning as the expression σύμφωνος τῷ λόγῳ of *Paed.* i. 101. 2: they do not recall only the διάθεσιν σύμφωνον and ὁμολογουμένην of *SVF* iii. 262 and 197 or the λόγον ὁμολογούμενον of *SVF* i. 202,[2] but also the Platonic doctrine of virtue as harmony between the inferior parts of the soul and reason.[3] As to the expressions βέβαιον and *constantem . . . factis secum . . . congruentem*, they show an even clearer Stoic character, in so far as they recall such words as περὶ ὅλον τὸν βίον (*SVF* iii. 262 end), πρὸς ὁμολογίαν παντὸς τοῦ βίου (*SVF* iii. 197) and λόγον . . . βέβαιον καὶ ἀμετάπτωτον (*SVF* i. 202) and completely agree with what Clement says in *Paed.* i. 101. 2 (περὶ ὅλον τὸν βίον) and i. 102. 4 (βίος . . . σύστημά τι . . . λογικῶν πράξεων).[4]

Philo also practically identifies virtue with the harmony of the

This passage of Maximus depends most probably on Plato, *Rep.* iv. 444 d–e, ἀρετὴ μὲν ἄρα . . . ὑγίειά τις ἂν εἴη καὶ κάλλος καὶ εὐεξία ψυχῆς (see Hobein, app. crit. ad loc.).

[1] The correspondence between the definitions of virtue given by Albinus and Apuleius has been observed by Sinko, *Rozprawy Akademji Umiejętności. Wydział Filologiczny*, Serya ii, Tom. 26 (Cracoviae, 1906), 153. Sinko's view, according to which the doctrines of Albinus and Apuleius go back to the teaching of Gaius (cf. also his article 'Apuleiana', *Eos* 18 (1912), 139) has been accepted by K. Gronau, 296–7, and, with some modifications, by K. Praechter in his two articles, 'Zum Platoniker Gaios', *Hermes* 51 (1916), 510 (see especially footnote 1) and 513, and 'Gaios', *RE*, Suppl. iii, coll. 535–7 (see also *Grundr. der Gesch. der Phil.*, 541). On Albinus in general see E. Zeller, *Die Philos. der Griech.* iii/1. 835, footnotes 1 and 2, K. Praechter, 'Zum Platoniker Gaios', *Hermes* 51 (1916), 513–17, and *RE*, Suppl. iii, coll. 535–7, and Witt, *Albinus . . .*, 1–7 and 104–13. To Apuleius as 'Middle Platonist' a young Italian scholar, C. Moreschini, has recently devoted two particular studies, '*La posizione di Apuleio . . .*', *ASNSP*, Serie ii, 33 (1964), 17–56, and *Studi sul 'De dogmate Platonis' di Apuleio* (Pisa, 1966).

[2] See footnote 1, pp. 61–2 above.

[3] For the evidence see footnote 1, p. 62 above.

[4] A further correspondence between Clement and Middle Platonism can be observed in a particular point which is closely related to the doctrine of virtue: πρᾶξις is defined by Clement, *Paed.* i. 102. 3, as ψυχῆς ἐνέργεια λογικῆς . . . διὰ τοῦ συμφυοῦς καὶ συναγωνιστοῦ σώματος ἐκτελουμένη. The same definition occurs in Albinus, *Did.* 153. 3–4, ψυχῆς λογικῆς ἐνέργεια διὰ σώματος γινομένη, and in Hierax, Stobaeus, *Anth.* 9. 54 (iii. 366. 5–6), πᾶσα δὲ πρᾶξις ἐνέργεια ψυχῆς διὰ σώματος. The correspondence between Clement and Albinus has been noticed by L. Früchtel in *BPhW* 57 (1937), 592; to the presence of this doctrine in Hierax attention has been drawn by Praechter, *Hermes* 41 (1906), 608–9.

soul, and maintains that on this harmony a right and coherent
system of life ultimately depends:

Quod D. sit imm. 25 (ii. 61. 15–18): ὅπερ [sc. the soul] εἰ καλῶς
ἁρμοσθείη, τὴν πασῶν ἀρίστην συμφωνίαν ἀπεργάσεται, ἥτις ...
ἐν ὁμολογίᾳ τῶν κατὰ τὸν βίον πράξεων ἔχει τὸ τέλος.

In this passage the Platonic topic of the harmony of the soul is
closely connected with the Stoic conception ἐν ὁμολογίᾳ τῶν κατὰ
τὸν βίον πράξεων.[1] The same Stoic conception appears also in
another passage of Philo, Leg. Alleg. i. 58 (i. 75. 16), ὅλου γὰρ
τοῦ βίου ἐστὶ τέχνη ἡ ἀρετή, which must be compared both with
the Stoic fragments quoted above and with Paed. i. 101. 2 and
102. 4.

As to the second definition of virtue given by Clement, Paed.
iii. 35. 2, it is possible to observe in it a mixture of Christian and
Stoic conceptions. The παιδαγωγός whom Clement mentions is
none other than Christ.[2] But Christ is, in Clement's thought, one
and the same thing with the universal Logos. Clement completely accepts the Stoic doctrine according to which the Logos
is the ruler both of nature and of human morals.[3] This Stoic
idea of the universal Logos as source of virtue appears clearly
also in Philo, as can be seen from Leg. Alleg. i. 65 (i. 78. 1–3),
De Post. C. 127 (ii. 28. 6–7), De Post. C. 129 (ii. 28. 14), De Plant.
121 (ii. 157. 13–14), De Somn. ii. 243 (iii. 297. 18–19). In his
Paedagogus Clement is also inclined to adopt the doctrine of virtue
as μεσότης, as can be inferred from the following passage:

Paed. ii. 16. 4 (i. 166. 2–4): ἀγαθὴ μὲν ἡ μέση κατάστασις ἐν πᾶσι ...
ἐπεὶ αἱ μὲν ἀκρότητες σφαλεραί, αἱ μεσότητες δὲ ἀγαθαί.[4]

This doctrine is Aristotelian.[5] It is, however, extremely unlikely
that Clement should have taken it directly from Aristotle, as

---

[1] See footnote 1, on pp. 61–2 above.

[2] The title of Clement's second work, the Παιδαγωγός, is directly derived from
the function of educator which Clement ascribes to Christ; about the λόγος
παιδαγωγός see Witt's pertinent remarks in CQ 25 (1931), 199.

[3] This has been pointed out especially by Pohlenz, NGA, phil.-hist. Kl. (1943).
However, see also my remarks, pp. 93 ff. below.

[4] Clement does not say here openly that virtue is a μεσότης, but this can easily be
inferred from his praise of the 'middle way' and from his condemnation of the
opposite extremes.

[5] See, for instance, EE 1227ᵇ8, EN 1106ᵇ15, 1106ᵇ36, and 1107ᵃ7.

Daskalakis seems to believe.¹ It is far easier to explain its presence in Clement if we remember that it appears both in Philo and in some authors of Middle Platonism. Philo calls virtue τὴν μέσην ὁδόν, *Quod D. sit imm.* 164 (ii. 90. 22), cf. 165 (ii. 90. 26), αὗται μέσαι τῶν παρ᾽ ἑκάτερα ἐκτροπῶν εἰσι, and does not hesitate to identify the μέση ὁδός with the βασιλικὴ ὁδός leading to God: τῇ δὲ μέσῃ ὁδῷ παρέρχεσθαι, ἣν κυριώτατα καλεῖ βασιλικήν, *De Post. C.* 101 (ii. 22. 1–2).² As to Middle Platonism, it will suffice to mention Plutarch, *Quomodo quis suos in Virt. sent. Prof.* 84 a, . . . εἰ μέλλομεν εἰς τὸ μέσον καθίστασθαι, *De Virt. m.* 444 c, τὰς ἠθικὰς ἀρετάς . . . μεσότητας, and 444 d, τῷ ποσῷ δὲ μεσότης γίνεται,³ Albinus, *Did.* 184. 13 f., κατ᾽ ἄλλον τρόπον μεσότητες ἂν εἶεν [sc. αἱ ἀρεταί],⁴ and Apuleius, *De Plat.* ii. 228, *hinc medietates easdemque virtutes . . . vocat non solum quod careant redundantia et egestate, sed quod in meditullio quodam vitiorum sitae sint.*⁵ The presence of this Aristotelian doctrine in these authors is most probably due to the fact that Antiochus of Ascalon and Arius Didymus, who both greatly influenced the growth of Middle Platonism, expounded it at some length in their works.⁶

---

¹ p. 101. Daskalakis is also wrong in maintaining (p. 100) that Clement, following Aristotle, defines virtue as an ἕξις προαιρετικὴ μεσότητος: he is not able to produce any passage of Clement containing such a definition.

² See also *Quod. D. sit imm.* 159 (ii. 90. 3–5) and 160 (ii. 90. 7–8) and *De Migr. Abr.* 146 and 147.

³ The references to the last two passages of Plutarch are also given by Praechter, *Grundr. der Gesch. der Phil.* 539. It is worth pointing out that both in Plutarch and in Philo the doctrine of virtue as μεσότης is closely connected with the view according to which virtue is the harmony of the soul. The soul is thus compared to a musical instrument: as the harmony produced by a musical instrument avoids the extreme notes, in the same way the soul, in order to produce a perfect harmony (i.e. virtue), must keep itself away from the opposite extremes: see Plutarch, *De Virt. m.* 444 f–445 a and 451 f and Philo, *Quod D. sit imm.* 24 (ii. 61. 9–14). The use of the terms ἐπιτείναι and ἀνείναι which occurs in this passage of Philo goes ultimately back to Plato: see, for instance, *Rep.* iv. 441 e 9–442 a 1, τὴν μὲν ἐπιτείνουσα . . . τὸ δὲ ἀνείσα.   ⁴ See also Praechter, op. cit. 545, and Witt, *Albinus* . . ., 90.

⁵ See Witt, op. cit. 101, and also C. Moreschini, *Studi sul 'De dogmate Platonis' di Apuleio*, 79.

⁶ The presence in Antiochus' system of the Aristotelian doctrine of virtue as μεσότης can be inferred from his adoption of the doctrine of μετριοπάθεια, of which we shall have to speak more in detail later on (see p. 100 below). As to Arius Didymus, see Stobaeus, *Ecl.* ii. 39. 11 f. and the whole section 20 (ii. 137. 14–142. 13) especially in the passages ii. 138. 19–20, ii. 139. 23, and ii. 140. 12–14 (quotation of Aristotle, *EN* 1106ᵇ36–1107ᵃ2). The importance both of Antiochus and of Arius Didymus for Middle Platonism has been pointed out by Witt, op. cit. 42–94 and 95–103 (for more details on this question see C. Andresen, *ZNW* 44 (1952/3), 172 n. 65).

Although Clement, in a passage of the fifth book of the *Stromateis*, seems to consider the virtue of the perfect Christian or γνωστικός as a divine gift which God bestows as a privilege only on certain men,[1] on the other hand he lays strong emphasis on the importance of the human efforts without which it would be impossible to attain virtue. There is no real contradiction between these two views. Clement's real thought must have been that virtue is the product of the combined activity of God and man: he seems therefore to be in favour of what is called 'synergism'. Völker is quite right on this particular point.[2] What, however, matters more for us here is to observe that Clement, when speaking only of human efforts, maintains that men, though endowed with a natural disposition towards virtue, nevertheless do not possess it from their birth, but must acquire it by means of a constant training and instruction: in other words virtue, though having a basis in the human φύσις, must be developed by means of ἄσκησις and μάθησις. This idea is particularly clear in such passages as *Strom*. i. 31. 5 (ii. 20. 17–21. 1), i. 34. 1 (ii. 22. 20–1), i. 38. 4 (ii. 25. 15), ii. 75. 2 (ii. 152. 24–5), iv. 124. 1 (ii. 303. 9–11), vi. 95. 5 (ii. 480. 3–5), vi. 96. 3 (ii. 480. 16–20), vii. 19. 3 (iii. 14. 9–11), vii. 64. 6 (iii. 46. 19–20), vii. 98. 5 (iii. 69. 27–9).[3]

[1] See the whole section of *Strom*. v. 83. 2–4 (ii. 381. 21–8) with the quotations of Plato, *Meno* 100 b and 99 e. Clement expounds here practically the same idea of the divine origin of virtue as that which we have observed in *Paed*. iii. 35. 2 (see p. 61 above). The Platonic expression θείᾳ μοίρᾳ (it occurs very frequently also in the *Ion*) has met with the favour of some later authors: I shall mention Aristotle who, speaking about the origin of happiness, says ὅθεν καὶ ἀπορεῖται πότερόν ἐστι μαθητὸν ἢ ἐθιστὸν ἢ καὶ ἄλλως πως ἀσκητόν, ἢ κατά τινα θείαν μοῖραν ἢ δια τύχην παραγίνεται, *EN* 1099ᵇ9–11; the title of a speech of Maximus of Tyre (*Or*. xxxviii, p. 437 Hobein), Εἰ γένοιτό τις θείᾳ μοίρᾳ ἀγαθός (cf. also, in the same speech, § 133 a, p. 442. 15–16); and Philo *De Somn*. i. 190 (iii. 246. 5–6) and *Quod omn. prob. lib. sit* 44 (vi. 12. 6–7). Clement also uses this Platonic expression when he sets forth the view held by the Pythagoreans and by the Platonists on the divine origin of human reason: see the passage of *Strom*. v. 88. 1–2 quoted in the first chapter, p. 14 above. On the idea of θεία μοῖρα before Plato see R. S. Bluck's note in his commentary on the *Meno* (Cambridge, 1961), pp. 435–6.

[2] See Völker, 121 ff. and 254–6, as well as the references to Clement's passages given in the footnotes on these pages. I shall only observe that a clear instance of this 'synergism' is provided by *Paed*. iii. 35. 2, ἡ ἀρετή, ὅς ἐστι λόγος διὰ τοῦ παιδαγωγοῦ παραδιδόμενος εἰς ἄσκησιν. Clement's synergism is certainly Christian; a passage of Maximus of Tyre, *Or*. xxxviii. 134 a (p. 445. 11 ff. Hobein) provides, however, a striking correspondence with Clement's views: αἱ δὲ ἄρισται . . . φύσεις . . . ἐν μεθορίᾳ τῆς ἄκρας ἀρετῆς πρὸς τὴν ἐσχάτην μοχθηρίαν καθωρμισμέναι, δέονται συναγωνιστοῦ θεοῦ καὶ συλλήπτορος τῆς ἐπὶ θάτερα τὰ κρείττω ῥοπῆς τε καὶ χειραγωγίας.

[3] On the presence in Clement of the ideas of ἄσκησις and μάθησις see also Völker, 280–2 and 288–9.

The doctrine according to which virtue is produced by the combination of φύσις, μάθησις, and ἄσκησις or ἔθος is Aristotelian. It is possible to find in Aristotle exactly the same ideas which are expounded by Clement.[1] This is the reason why Daskalakis was led to suppose here also a direct influence of Aristotle on Clement.[2] But just as in the case of the definition of ἀρετή as μεσότης, this Aristotelian doctrine is adopted by Antiochus of Ascalon[3] and is mentioned by Arius Didymus in his well-known account of the Peripatetic ethics;[4] moreover, under the direct influence both of Antiochus and of Arius Didymus, it also occurs in the writings of some exponents of Middle Platonism:

[Plutarch], *De Lib. ed.* 2 a: ὡς εἰς τὴν παντελῆ δικαιοπραγίαν τρία δεῖ συνδραμεῖν, φύσιν καὶ λόγον καὶ ἔθος· καλῶ δὲ λόγον μὲν τὴν μάθησιν, ἔθος δὲ τὴν ἄσκησιν.

Idem, *De Lib. ed.* 2 b: ἡ μὲν γὰρ φύσις ἄνευ μαθήσεως τυφλόν, ἡ δὲ μάθησις δίχα φύσεως ἐλλιπής, ἡ δ᾽ ἄσκησις χωρὶς ἀμφοῖν ἀτελής.

Idem, *De Lib. ed.* 2 f: καὶ γὰρ τὸ ἦθος ἔθος ἐστὶ πολυχρόνιον . . .

Idem, *De Lib. ed.* 3 a: καὶ τὰς ἠθικὰς ἀρετὰς ἐθικὰς ἄν τις λέγῃ, οὐκ ἄν τι πλημμελεῖν δόξαιεν.[5]

Plutarch, *De Virt. m.* 443 c: ἔστι μὲν γάρ, ὡς τύπῳ εἰπεῖν, ποιότης τοῦ ἀλόγου τὸ ἦθος, ὠνόμασται δ᾽ ὅτι τὴν ποιότητα ταύτην καὶ τὴν διαφορὰν ἔθει λαμβάνει τὸ ἄλογον.[6]

---

[1] Aristotle, *Pol.* 1332ᵃ38–40, *EN* 1103ᵃ17–19, 1103ᵃ23–6 (with this passage it is worth comparing Clement, *Strom.* vi. 95. 5, φύσει μὲν γεγόναμεν πρὸς ἀρετήν . . . πρὸς τὸ κτήσασθαι ἐπιτήδειοι) and 1170ᵃ11–12 (see also E. Zeller, *Die Philos. der Griechen* ii/2. 626 nn. 2 and 7). As to Plato, he seems to limit the role of training to the inferior virtues of the soul: see *Rep.* vii. 518 d 9–e 3 and *Phaedo* 82 a 11–b 3 (see also Zeller, ii/1. 882 and H. Strache, *Der Eklektizismus . . .*, 44).

[2] pp. 100–1.

[3] *Ac. Post.* i. 20: *morum autem putabant studia esse et quasi consuetudinem, quam partim exercitationis adsiduitate, partim ratione formabant* and *Ac. Post.* i. 38: *cumque superiores . . . quasdam virtutes natura aut more perfectas . . .* See also H. Strache, *De Arii Didymi in morali philosophia auctoribus* (Diss. Berlin, 1909), 10, and A. Lueder, 33 and 36–8.

[4] Stob. *Ecl.* ii. 38. 3 f., ii. 51. 5 (cf. Strache, *De Arii Didymi . . .*, 10), ii. 116. 21–117. 2 (cf. Aristotle, *EN* 1103ᵃ17–19), ii. 118. 5–6, and ii. 136. 16 (the reference to this last passage is given also by Strache, *Ekl. des Ant. v. Ask.* 44 n. 7).

[5] On the spurious origin of *De Lib. ed.* see K. Ziegler in his article 'Plutarchos', *RE* xxi/1, coll. 810–12 (Ziegler, loc. cit., provides an excellent survey of the literature dealing with this question). The work can, however, also be regarded as belonging to Middle Platonism since it was most probably written by one of Plutarch's pupils (see Ziegler, art. cit., col. 810). The two passages of *De Lib. ed.* 2 f and 3 a should be compared with Aristotle, *EN* 1103ᵃ17–19 as well as with Arius Didymus, Stob. ii. 116. 21–117. 2.

[6] This passage of Plutarch shows a close correspondence with Arius Didymus,

68 ETHICS

Albinus, *Did.* 182. 3–5: ἐφικοίμεθα δ' ἂν τοῦ γενέσθαι ὅμοιοι θεῷ φύσει
τε χρησάμενοι τῇ προσηκούσῃ ἔθεσί τε καὶ ἀγωγῇ καὶ ἀσκήσει
τῇ κατὰ νόμον, καὶ κυριώτατον λόγῳ καὶ διδασκαλίᾳ . . .[1]
Apuleius, *De Plat.* ii. 222–3: *hominem a stirpe ipsa neque absolute
malum nec bonum nasci, sed ad utrumque proclive ingenium eius esse;
habere semina quidem quaedam utrarumque rerum cum nascendi origine
copulata, quae educationis disciplina in partem alteram debeant emicare.*

Maximus of Tyre also maintains that virtue cannot be regarded
simply as the product of nature (*Or.* i. 5 d, p. 9. 11 f.) and is
inclined to consider φύσις, ἔθος, and λόγος as the three sources of
it (*Or.* i. 4 d, p. 116. 10–11, cf. *Or.* xxvii. 9 b, p. 331. 8–9).

In Philo the same doctrine is to be found. Although he seems
to believe that virtue can be produced *either* by φύσις *or* by ἄσκησις
or by μάθησις (*De Somn.* i. 167, vol. iii. 240. 20–1, τὴν ἀρετὴν
ἢ φύσει ἢ ἀσκήσει ἢ μαθήσει περιγίνεσθαί φησι) and to regard
Abraham, Isaac, and Jacob as the symbols of these three different kinds of virtue (Abraham representing for him the διδα-
σκαλικὴ ἀρετή, Isaac the φυσική, and Jacob the ἀσκητική, *De Abr.*
52, vol. iv. 13. 2–6, cf. *De Congr. Er. Gr.* 35, vol. iii. 79. 6–9, and
36, vol. iii. 79. 12–14), on the other hand he makes it clear that
such a distinction is not absolute, since nature, training, and instruction cannot be completely separated from one another,
De Abr. 53 (iv. 13. 6–10), cf. *De Jos.* 1 (iv. 61. 3–4) and *De Praem.
et Poen.* 65 (v. 350. 15–16).

It now remains to examine the presence in Clement of the
doctrine according to which virtue is the only real source of
happiness. Clement, referring to a passage of Plato's *Republic*
(ii. 361 e), maintains that the perfect Christian does not let his
happiness depend on external events but only on his own conviction (*Strom.* iv. 52. 1–2, vol. ii. 272. 11–15), since his inner
virtue would suffer no harm from dishonour, exile, confiscation
of property, or even death (*Strom.* iv. 52. 3, vol. ii. 272. 15–17).
Moreover, in the chapter of the fifth book of the *Stromateis* which
deals with the dependence of the Greeks on the Old Testament,
he does not hesitate to say that the maxims μόνον τὸ καλὸν ἀγαθόν

Stob. *Ecl.* ii. 38. 3 f. and with the definition of ἦθος given by Galen (see R. Walzer,
CQ 43 (1949), 85–6).
[1] To the presence in Albinus of the doctrine of virtue as a product of ἔθος
attention has been drawn also by Witt, 90.

and ἀρετὴ αὐταρκὴς πρὸς εὐδαιμονίαν were already known to Jewish philosophy (*Strom.* v. 96. 5, vol. ii. 389. 23–5). It can be inferred from this passage that Clement regards this philosophical doctrine as being a part of his own ethical system.[1] The idea of the αὐτάρκεια of virtue had been stressed especially by the Porch, where it had become a hackneyed topic, although it was not unknown to Plato and the Academy.[2] Some scholars were therefore inclined to consider this fact as a proof of Clement's dependence on Stoicism.[3] They have, however, failed to observe that this doctrine occurs also in Antiochus of Ascalon, in Middle Platonism, in Justin, and in Philo. Antiochus is of the opinion that happiness can be based on virtue alone, *itaque omnis illa antiqua philosophia censuit in una virtute esse positam beatam vitam* (Cicero, *Ac. Post.* i. 22–3) ;[4] Plutarch maintains that only virtue,

---

[1] See also the passage of *Strom.* v. 97. 6 (ii. 390. 10–14) containing a reference to the Stoic Antipater, who had attempted to show the agreement between Plato and the Porch in the doctrine of the αὐτάρκεια of virtue. Closely related to this doctrine is the idea that the perfect Christian must attain *gnosis* (which, according to Clement, is the highest form of virtue) for its own sake, without bothering about other things: see for instance *Strom.* iv. 136. 2 (ii. 308. 20–3), iv. 136. 2 (ii. 308. 23–5), iv. 136. 2 (ii. 308. 27–33) (here *gnosis* is preferred even to salvation!), iv. 145. 2–146. 1 (ii. 312. 21–31), vi. 98. 3 (ii. 481. 14–17), vi. 99. 1 (ii. 481. 21), and vi. 99. 3 (ii. 481. 25–6).

[2] On the Stoic origin of this topic see *SVF* i. 187, iii. 29–45 and 49–67. As to Plato see, for instance, the whole section of *Rep.* iii. 387 d–e and especially 385 d 11– e 1, ὁ τοιοῦτος μάλιστα αὐτὸς αὑτῷ αὐτάρκης πρὸς τὸ εὖ ζῆν καὶ διαφερόντως τῶν ἄλλων ἥκιστα ἑτέρου προσδεῖται. Further evidence concerning both Plato and the Academy has been collected by R. Walzer, *Aristotelis Dialogorum Fragmenta*, 63–4 and 63 n. 1. To the passages quoted by Walzer it is possible to add *Strom.* ii. 133. 7 (ii. 186. 28–187. 2). I do not understand how C. Moreschini can deny the presence of this doctrine in Plato (*ASNSP* (1964), 20–1: 'Tale dottrina non può essere attribuita a Platone senza un grave fraintendimento di quanto egli ha realmente insegnato, senza attribuirgli cioè un dogma che egli non formulò mai'). He has, however, considerably modified his view in his subsequent study on Apuleius, p. 79.

[3] See, for instance, M. Spanneut, 244–5, and M. Pohlenz, *Die Stoa* i. 422.

[4] Antiochus distinguishes, however, the *vita beata*, which depends only on virtue, from the *vita beatissima*, which requires also the possibility of using external goods: ... *nec tamen beatissimam, nisi adiungerentur et corporis et cetera, quae supra dicta sunt, ad virtutis usum idonea, Ac. Post.* i. 22, cf. *Ac. Pr.* ii. 134: *Zeno in una virtute positam beatam vitam putat. Quid Antiochus?* '*Etiam*' inquit '*beatam, sed non beatissimam.*' This view of Antiochus can be regarded as the attempt to conciliate the Stoic and Platonic doctrine of the αὐτάρκεια of virtue with the Peripatetic teaching, which considered happiness as dependent also on the use of the external goods (see, for instance, *EN* 1099^{a}31 f., φαίνεται δ' ὅμως καὶ τῶν ἐκτὸς ἀγαθῶν προσδεομένη [sc. εὐδαιμονία]; this passage is quoted by Praechter, *Hermes* 41 (1906), 616 n. 1): on this argument see also Strache, *Ekl. d. Ant. v. Ask.* 73–9, A. Lueder, 56, G. Luck, 56, and Pohlenz, *Die Stoa* i. 252.

70 ETHICS

and not external things, can make man really happy, *De Virt. et Vit.* 100 c, τὸ δ' ἡδέως ζῆν καὶ ἱλαρῶς οὐκ ἔξωθέν ἐστιν, ἀλλὰ τοὐναντίον ὁ ἄνθρωπος τοῖς περὶ αὐτὸν πράγμασιν ἡδονὴν καὶ χάριν ὥσπερ ἐκ πηγῆς τοῦ ἤθους προστίθησιν, and 100 d, οὕτω μετ' ἀρετῆς καὶ δίαιτα πᾶσα καὶ βίος ἄλυπός ἐστι καὶ ἐπιτερπής, cf. *De Tranq. An.* 466 f., οὐ γὰρ ἡ συνήθεια ποιεῖ τοῖς ἑλομένοις τὸν ἄριστον βίον ἡδύν ... ἀλλὰ τὸ φρονεῖν ἅμα τὸν αὐτὸν βίον ποιεῖ καὶ ἄριστον καὶ ἥδιστον.[1] Maximus of Tyre regards virtue as the highest good and, like Clement, maintains that it can by no means be taken away: τὸ δὲ ἀγαθὸν τί ἂν εἴη ἄλλο ἢ ἀρετή; ἡ δὲ ἀρετὴ ἀναφαίρετον, *Or.* xii. 62 b (p. 148. 12–14).[2] Albinus repeats almost verbatim the Stoic formulas μόνον τὸ καλὸν ἀγαθόν and ἀρετὴ αὐταρκὴς πρὸς εὐδαιμονίαν (*Did.* 180. 33–5)[3] and, referring most probably to the passage of *Rep.* ii. 361 e which Clement also had in mind in *Strom.* iv. 52. 1–3, sets forth the idea that virtue and happiness cannot be influenced by any kind of pain: 'that Plato considered virtues as eligible in themselves can be regarded as a consequence of the fact that he thought that only beauty was good; this is demonstrated in most of his works, and especially throughout the *Republic*; for he who possesses the science mentioned above is the luckiest and the happiest man ... even if he remains unknown to all men and is seized by the so-called evils, such as dishonour, exile, and death' (*Did.* 181. 5 ff.).[4] Apuleius holds practically the same view, *De Plat.* ii. 238, *primum bonum atque laudabile est virtus ... solum quippe quod honestum est bonum ducimus,* cf. ii. 253, *utrarumque autem felicitatum origo ex virtute manat. et ad ornamentum quidem genialis loci, id est virtutis, nullis extrinsecus eorum, quae bona ducimus, adminiculis indigemus.*[5] Atticus and

---

[1] See also Zeller, iii/2. 202–3. In order to demonstrate that Plutarch did not believe in the αὐτάρκεια of virtue, C. Moreschini, *ASNSP* (1964), 20, refers to *De audiendis Poetis* 36 d; this passage, however (ἆρ' οὐκ ἀπόδειξίς ἐστιν ὧν οἱ φιλόσοφοι λέγουσι περὶ πλούτου καὶ τῶν ἐκτὸς ἀγαθῶν, ὡς χωρὶς ἀρετῆς ἀνωφελῶν ὄντων καὶ ἀνονήτων τοῖς ἔχουσι), does not support his thesis at all: Plutarch does not say here that the external goods are necessary for the existence of happiness ('il concorso dei beni esterni alla felicità è sostenuto ... da Plutarco', loc. cit.), but simply that they, if separated from virtue, are completely useless.

[2] See also Zeller, iii/2. 220.   [3] See also Witt, 88.

[4] The correspondence between Clement, *Strom.* iv. 52. 1–3 and Albinus, *Did.* 181. 8 ff. has been pointed also by Andresen, *ZNW* 44 (1952/3), 181 n. 44.

[5] I cannot, therefore, agree with Moreschini, who denies that Apuleius believed in the αὐτάρκεια of virtue (*ASNSP* (1964), 19. The passage he refers to (*De Plat.* ii. 253) has most probably been influenced by the teaching of Antiochus, who had distinguished the *vita beata* from the *vita beatissima* (see footnote 4, p. 69

Hierax openly criticize the Peripatetic teaching which regarded happiness as dependent also on the external events and on welfare :[1]

Atticus in Eusebius, *Praep. Ev.* xv. 4. 2 (ii. 350. 9–13 = fr. ii Baudry): He [i.e. the Peripatetic philosopher] introduced a change in respect of Plato; for he did not keep the right measure and did not regard virtue as self-sufficient, but abandoned the belief in its power and thought that it needed the benefits of fortune, so as to destroy happiness.
Eusebius, *Praep. Ev.* xv. 4. 11 (ii. 352. 18–19 = fr. ii Baudry): How can it be excluded that in this way the dignity of virtue is destroyed and overthrown?
Hierax in Stobaeus, *Anth.* iv. 31. 92 (v. 767. 8–9 Hense): How can the possession of wealth lead anybody towards justice and the other virtues? For what is subordinate to the inferior things opposes the acquisition of the best.[2]

Like the other exponents of Middle Platonism, Atticus lays a strong emphasis on the doctrine of the self-sufficiency of virtue:

Eusebius, *Praep. Ev.* xv. 4. 16 (ii. 354. 4–8 = fr. ii Baudry): Virtue is something powerful and beautiful; it needs nothing in respect of the acquisition of happiness and is never deprived of it; even if poverty, illness, ill repute, tortures, pitch, the cross, and the misfortunes described in tragedies should stream on all together, nevertheless the righteous man always remains happy and blessed.[3]

Plotinus also points out the self-sufficiency of the wise man, as far as his happiness is concerned: αὐτάρκης οὖν ὁ βίος τῷ οὕτως ζωὴν ἔχοντι ... αὐτάρκης εἰς εὐδαιμονίαν καὶ εἰς κτῆσιν ἀγαθοῦ· οὐδὲ γάρ ἐστι ἀγαθὸν ὃ μὴ ἔχει, *Enn.* i. 4. 4.

The same views occur in Justin and in Philo. According to Justin, only virtue can lead to the real happiness, even if it, at a first glance, may look unpleasant and unattractive (*Apol.* ii.

---

above). Moreschini himself, loc. cit., takes this possibility into account. In his book on Apuleius (p. 79) he seems, however, to have changed his view.

[1] The agreement between Hierax and Atticus on this question has been pointed out by Praechter, *Hermes* 41 (1906), 615–16.

[2] This passage is quoted by Praechter, *Hermes* 41 (1906), 615.

[3] On the presence in Atticus of the doctrine of the αὐτάρκεια of virtue see also Andresen, art. cit. 180 and footnote 94 on the same page.

ETHICS

11, vol. i. 230. 6–12).[1] As to Philo, it will suffice to draw attention to such passages as *De Post. C.* 95, *De Post. C.* 133 (= *SVF* iii. 131), *Quod det. pot. ins. sol.* 9 (= *SVF* iii. 33), and *De spec. Leg.* ii. 48 and 73.

2. Let us now go on to examine more in detail each of the four cardinal virtues (φρόνησις, ἀνδρεία, σωφροσύνη, and δικαιοσύνη).

(a) *Φρόνησις.* In the second book of the *Stromateis* Clement is led by his eulogy of πίστις to quote a passage of Ecclesiasticus, σοφία ἐν στόματι πιστῶν (15: 10). The word σοφία which occurs in the sentence gives him the opportunity of reporting a doctrine of Xenocrates:

Strom. ii. 24. 1 (= Xenocrates, fr. 6 Heinze): ἐπεὶ καὶ Ξενοκράτης ἐν τῷ Περὶ φρονήσεως τὴν σοφίαν ἐπιστήμην τῶν πρώτων αἰτίων καὶ τῆς νοητῆς οὐσίας εἶναί φησι, τὴν φρόνησιν ἡγούμενος διττήν, τὴν μὲν πρακτικήν, τὴν δὲ θεωρητικήν, ἣν δὴ καὶ σοφίαν ἐνυπάρχειν ἀνθρωπίνην.

The way in which Clement speaks implies that he completely accepts the Xenocratic doctrine of the twofold φρόνησις. Traces of this doctrine can also be found in two other passages of the *Stromateis*:

Strom. i. 177. 3–178. 1 (ii. 109. 14–20): αὕτη γὰρ τῷ ὄντι ἡ διαλεκτικὴ φρόνησίς ἐστι περὶ τὰ νοητὰ διαιρετική . . . ἢ δύναμις περὶ τὰ τῶν πραγμάτων γένη διαιρετική . . . παρεχομένη ἕκαστον τῶν ὄντων οἷόν ἐστι φαίνεσθαι. διὸ καὶ μόνη αὕτη ἐπὶ τὴν ἀληθῆ σοφίαν χειραγωγεῖ, ἥτις ἐστὶ δύναμις θεία, τῶν ὄντων ὡς ὄντων γνωστική.
Strom. vi. 154. 4 (ii. 511. 16–19): φρόνησίς ἐστι, δύναμις ψυχῆς θεωρητικὴ τῶν ὄντων καὶ τοῦ ἀκολούθου ὁμοίου τε καὶ ἀνομοίου διακριτική τε αὖ καὶ συνθετικὴ καὶ προστακτικὴ καὶ ἀπαγορευτική.

The sentence of *Strom.* i. 178. 1, μόνη αὕτη ἐπὶ τὴν ἀληθῆ σοφίαν χειραγωγεῖ, ἥτις ἐστὶ δύναμις θεία, τῶν ὄντων . . . γνωστική, is closely related to *Strom.* ii. 24. 1 (= Xenocrates, fr. 6 Heinze), τὴν δὲ θεωρητικήν, ἣν δὴ καὶ σοφίαν ἐνυπάρχειν ἀνθρωπίνην. Moreover, both *Strom.* vi. 154. 4 and *Strom.* i. 177. 3–178. 1 should be compared with another fragment of Xenocrates, which Aristotle has preserved:

---

[1] For further detail on the presence of this topic in Justin see Andresen, art. cit. 179–81.

ETHICS 73

Xenocrates, fr. 7 Heinze (p. 161)
(= Aristotle, *Top.* vi. 3. 141ᵃ6 ff.):
οἷον εἰ ὡς Ξενοκράτης τὴν φρόνησιν ὁριστικὴν καὶ θεωρητικὴν τῶν
ὄντων φησὶν εἶναι.

Strom. vi. 154. 4: φρόνησίς ἐστι,
δύναμις ψυχῆς θεωρητικὴ τῶν
ὄντων καὶ τοῦ ἀκολούθου ὁμοίου τε
καὶ ἀνομοίου διακριτική...
cf. *Strom.* i. 177. 3–178. 1 : φρόνησίς
ἐστι περὶ τὰ νοητὰ διαιρετική...
διὸ καὶ μόνη αὕτη ἐπὶ τὴν ἀληθῆ
σοφίαν χειραγωγεῖ, ἥτις ἐστὶ δύναμις θεία, τῶν ὄντων ὡς ὄντων γνωστική.

The expression θεωρητικὴ τῶν ὄντων which occurs in Aristotle is
used by Clement in *Strom.* vi. 154. 4 and shows a very close
similarity with the expression τῶν ὄντων... γνωστική of *Strom.*
i. 178. 1 ; the term ὁριστικήν used by Aristotle is parallel to the
terms διακριτική and διαιρετική which appear in Clement's passages.

For Clement φρόνησις is therefore the pure activity of mind,
which leads man to the knowledge of the intelligible realities
and also directs his behaviour in practical life. As far as its
theoretical activity is concerned, φρόνησις is practically, in
Clement's thought, one and the same thing with σοφία, as the passages of *Strom.* i. 178. 1 and ii. 24. 1 clearly show.[1] By adopting the
Xenocratic doctrine of φρόνησις, Clement attaches to this word
the same meaning as that which it assumed in Plato. For Plato
also φρόνησις was both a theoretical and a practical virtue.[2] The
same cannot be said about Aristotle, who, by allotting theoretical

---

[1] See also *Strom.* ii. 24. 2 (ii. 125. 23–4), διόπερ ἡ μὲν σοφία φρόνησις, οὐ μὴν πᾶσα
φρόνησις σοφία. However, Clement also defines σοφία as ἐπιστήμη θείων καὶ ἀνθρωπίνων πραγμάτων (*Paed.* ii. 35. 3, *Strom.* i. 30. 1, iv. 40. 3, iv. 163. 4, vi. 133. 5, vii. 60.
2, vii. 70. 5). This definition, which is more comprehensive than those given by
Xenocrates (*Strom.* ii. 24. 1) and by Aristotle (see footnote 1, p. 74 below), is of
Stoic origin : see *SVF* ii. 35–6 (but cf. also Plato, *Symp.* 186 b, as Witt, 42 n. 1, has
rightly pointed out). It also occurs in Antiochus, in Middle Platonism, and in
Philo : see *De Fin.* ii. 37 : *adhibita primum rerum divinarum humanarumque scientia,
quae potest appellari rite sapientia* (on the dependence of *De Fin.* ii on Antiochus see
Witt, 29, and the literature quoted by G. Luck, 56) ; Albinus, *Did.* 152. 6–7 (cf.
Praechter, *Grundr. der Gesch. der Philos.* 541 and Witt, 42) and Apuleius, *De Plat.*
ii. 228; *quarum sapientiam disciplinam vult videri divinarum humanarumque rerum.* As
to Philo, see footnote 3 on p. 59 above.
[2] See for instance *Phaedo* 79 d 6–7, where Socrates, speaking about the contemplation of the intelligible world which the soul enjoys when it is completely detached from the body, defines such condition of the soul as φρόνησις : καὶ τοῦτο
αὐτῆς τὸ πάθημα φρόνησις κέκληται. On the practical role of φρόνησις see *Symp.*
209 a 5–7.

knowledge to σοφία, eventually confined φρόνησις to the practical sphere.¹

If we consider for the moment only the theoretical part of Clement's φρόνησις we can observe a close correspondence between him and Albinus:

Albinus, *Did*. 153. 4–6: ἡ ψυχὴ δὴ   Clem. *Strom*. vi. 154. 4 (ii. 511.
θεωροῦσα μὲν τὸ θεῖον καὶ τὰς   16–17) : τὸ δὲ οὐδὲν ἀλλ᾽ ἢ φρόνησίς
νοήσεις τοῦ θείου εὐπαθεῖν τε   ἐστι, δύναμις ψυχῆς θεωρητικὴ τῶν
λέγεται καὶ τοῦτο τὸ πάθημα αὐτῆς   ὄντων . . .
φρόνησις ὠνόμασται.

Therefore Albinus also reproduces the Platonic and Xenocratic doctrine of φρόνησις.² Plutarch and Philo on the contrary, following Aristotle, regard φρόνησις only as a practical virtue and distinguish it sharply from σοφία.³

We can now proceed to examine the practical function of Clement's φρόνησις. The first thing to observe is that the expression προστακτικὴ καὶ ἀπαγορευτική which in *Strom*. vi. 154. 4 refers to the practical role of φρόνησις is the same expression as that which Clement uses when speaking about the divine Logos or the Jewish νόμος ; see *Paed*. i. 8. 3 (i. 85. 3–4), *Paed*. i. 65. 2 (i. 128. 12–13), *Strom*. i. 166. 5 (ii. 104. 10–12) = *SVF* iii. 132, *Strom*. ii. 34. 4 (ii. 131.

---

¹ Aristotle defines σοφία as ἐπιστήμη καὶ νοῦς τῶν τιμιωτάτων τῇ φύσει, *EN* 1141ᵇ2, cf. *Met*. A 981ᵃ27–9 (his conception of σοφία is therefore substantially identical with that of Xenocrates, as R. Heinze, 5, has observed) ; as to his idea of φρόνησις see *EN* 1140ᵇ20–1 and 1141ᵇ8 (Aristotle distinguishes it from ἐπιστήμη, see *EN* 1141ᵃ5–7). There is, however, an evolution in the Aristotelian conception of φρόνησις : in his earlier works, which are still under Plato's influence, Aristotle uses φρόνησις in its Platonic meaning : see for instance *Protr*., fr. 6 Walzer, p. 35. 18–36. 4 and p. 36. 16–19 (cf. W. Jaeger, *Aristoteles*, 67 ; p. 67 also in the English translation made by R. Robinson, Oxford, 1948, 2nd ed.). On the distinction between σοφία and φρόνησις in the Peripatetic school see Arius Didymus, Stob. *Ecl*. ii. 145. 19 ff.

² The influence of Xenocrates on Albinus' conception of φρόνησις has been observed by Witt, 14 ; it is important to notice that Albinus' words καὶ τοῦτο τὸ πάθημα αὐτῆς φρόνησις ὠνόμασται go directly back to *Phaedo* 79 d 6–7.

³ Plutarch, *De Virt. m*. 443 d (cf. also Praechter, *Grundr. der Gesch. der Philos*. 539) ; Philo, *De Praem. et Poen*. 81 (v. 354. 13–14) (it must be remembered that for Philo the θεραπεία θεοῦ is one and the same thing with the θεωρία τοῦ πρώτου αἰτίου). As to Apuleius, he seems to adopt the Platonic and Xenocratic doctrine of φρόνησις, *De Plat*. ii. 228: *illam virtutem, quae ratione sit nixa et est spectatrix diiudicatrixque omnium rerum prudentiam dicit atque sapientiam*. Immediately afterwards, however, he distinguishes σοφία from φρόνησις just as Aristotle, Arius Didymus, Plutarch, and Philo do : *quarum sapientiam disciplinam vult videri divinarum humanarumque rerum, prudentiam vero scientiam esse intelligendorum bonorum et malorum* (on this point see also Moreschini, *Studi sul 'De dogm. Plat.' di Apuleio*, 81–2).

ETHICS 75

9–10), *Strom.* iii. 84. 1 (ii. 234. 25–7). Pohlenz has rightly pointed
out that the definition of νόμος as λόγος προστακτικὸς μὲν ὧν
ποιητέον, ἀπαγορευτικὸς δὲ ὧν οὐ ποιητέον is Stoic and that, more
exactly, it goes back to Chrysippus.[1] But he is wrong in tracing
Clement's conception of νόμος as λόγος ὀρθός straight back to
Chrysippus without attaching great importance to the use made
by Philo of this Chrysippean formula in the definition he gives
of the Jewish law, and without pointing out the role of mediator
which Philo necessarily plays between Clement and Stoicism,
especially in this particular case.[2] And even stranger does this
seem to be, since Pohlenz himself as little as one year before the
publication of his article on Clement showed the connection
which exists between the Chrysippean formula and Philo's definition of νόμος.[3] It is worth while quoting the passages of Philo
in which the use of the Chrysippean formula in the definition
of the Jewish law is particularly clear:

Leg. Alleg. i. 94 (i. 86. 6–7): νόμων προστάξεις καὶ ἀπαγορεύσεις
ἐχόντων.

Quod D. sit imm. 53 (ii. 68. 14–15): ἐν ταῖς προστάξεσι καὶ ἀπαγο-
ρεύσεσι νόμων . . .

De Migr. Abr. 130 (ii. 293. 13–14): νόμος δὲ οὐδὲν ἄρα ἢ λόγος θεῖος,
προστάττων ἃ δεῖ καὶ ἀπαγορεύων ἃ μὴ χρή.

De Jos. 29 (iv. 67. 17–18): λόγος δέ ἐστι φύσεως προστακτικὸς μὲν
ὧν ποιητέον, ἀπαγορευτικὸς δὲ ὧν οὐ ποιητέον (= *SVF* iii. 323).

De Vita Mos. ii. 4 (iv. 201. 4–5): πρόσταξις δὲ τῶν πρακτέων καὶ
ἀπαγόρευσις τῶν οὐ πρακτέων ἴδιον νόμου.

De Praem. et Poen. 55 (v. 248. 11–12): νόμος δὲ οὐδέν ἐστιν ἕτερον ἢ
λόγος προστάττων ἃ χρὴ καὶ ἀπαγορεύων ἃ μὴ χρή.

There is no doubt that Clement, in the passage of *Strom.* i. 166. 5
quoted above, is referring to the Stoics, whose dependence on
the Old Testament he particularly stresses. But we must not
forget that his conception of the Jewish νόμος is identical with
that of Philo. Clement, when defining νόμος in Stoic terms, has
the definition of νόμος given by Philo still floating in his mind.[4]

---

[1] *NGA*, phil.-hist. Kl. (1943), 143; see also *Die Stoa* i. 418 with the reference to
SVF iii. 314. For the Stoic origin of the formula see also the references given by
Stählin, app. crit., vol. i. 95.
[2] *NGA*, phil.-hist. Kl. (1943), loc. cit.
[3] *NGA*, phil.-hist. Kl. (1942), 442 and 464; *Die Stoa* i. 377; see also his note
S 377 Z 39 in his vol. ii. 184, with the references to Philo's passages.
[4] The correspondence between the definitions of νόμος given by Philo and by

Both for Clement and for Philo the Mosaic law was nothing but the expression of the divine Logos; for both, moreover, a spark of this universal Logos was present in the human mind.[1] This is the reason why Clement, speaking about the practical φρόνησις, resorts to the Stoic terms which he employs in the definitions of νόμος: since φρόνησις is the activity of reason, and reason comes directly from the divine Logos, which is also νόμος, the practical function of φρόνησις can be defined in the terms which are usually applied to νόμος. The same view is shared by Philo: exactly as Clement does, he defines φρόνησις (which for him has only a practical role, see p. 74 above) in a way which reminds us of the definitions he gives of νόμος: λογισμοῦ γάρ ἐστιν ἐπιστήμη ὧν τε δεῖ ποιεῖν ὧν τε μή (Leg. Alleg. i. 70, vol. i. 79. 18–19), ἡ μὲν φρόνησις περὶ τὰ ποιητέα ὅρους αὐτοῖς τιθεῖσα (Leg. Alleg. i. 65, vol. i. 78. 7–8).

A similar definition of the practical φρόνησις is given by Albinus, ἡ μὲν δὴ φρόνησίς ἐστιν ἐπιστήμη ἀγαθῶν καὶ κακῶν καὶ οὐδετέρων, Did. 182. 23–4, cf. Apuleius, De Plat. ii. 228, prudentiam vero scientiam esse intelligendorum bonorum et malorum, eorum etiam quae media dicuntur. This definition is Stoic, as both Praechter and Witt have shown,[2] and is also adopted by Antiochus;[3] that it is nothing but an equivalent of the definition of the practical φρόνησις given by Clement is proved by SVF iii. 262 (= Stob. Ecl. ii. 59. 4 W.): φρόνησιν εἶναι ἐπιστήμην ὧν ποιητέον καὶ οὐ ποιητέον καὶ οὐδετέρων ἢ ἐπιστήμην ἀγαθῶν καὶ κακῶν καὶ οὐδετέρων. A further correspondence can be observed between Clement, Philo, and Albinus in the conception of the practical φρόνησις: Albinus, just as Clement and Philo do, brings φρόνησις into close connection with the ὀρθὸς λόγος: ὁ δὲ ὀρθὸς λόγος ἀπὸ φρονήσεως γίνεται, Did. 183. 5–6.[4]

Clement has been noticed by Merk, 46 n. 2 and 50 n. 5, by Stählin, app. crit., vol. i. 95, and by Heinisch, 227.

[1] See chapter I, pp. 17–18 and 19–20 above.

[2] Praechter, Grundr. der Gesch. der Philos., 544, and Witt, 89. It is worth observing that the same Stoic definitions of φρόνησις adopted by Clement, Philo, and Albinus occur also in [Plato], Ὅροι 411 d, φρόνησις . . . ἐπιστήμη ἀγαθῶν καὶ κακῶν . . . διάθεσις καθ᾽ ἣν κρίνομεν τί πρακτέον καὶ τί οὐ πρακτέον.

[3] Cicero, De Fin. v. 67: prudentia in delectu bonorum et malorum: cf. Strache, Ekl. des Ant. v. Ask., 48, and Witt, 89 n. 4.

[4] Since Albinus defines the practical φρόνησις in Stoic terms, the ὀρθὸς λόγος which he mentions together with it can be of Stoic origin (cf. Praechter, Grundr. 544, Witt, 90 n. 1); Praechter, however, rightly points out that the ὀρθὸς λόγος

(*b*) *Ἀνδρεία*. A definition of ἀνδρεία is given by Clement in the second book of the *Stromateis*:

Strom. ii. 79. 5 (ii. 154. 17–21): ἐπεὶ δ' οὖν τὴν μὲν ἀνδρείαν ὁρίζονται ἐπιστήμην δεινῶν καὶ οὐ δεινῶν καὶ τῶν μεταξύ . . . παράκειται τῇ μὲν ἀνδρείᾳ ἥ τε ὑπομονή, ἣν καρτερίαν καλοῦσιν, ἐπιστήμην ἐμμενετέων καὶ οὐκ ἐμμενετέων.

That these definitions are Stoic is clear from the comparison with *SVF* iii. 262 and 266. The whole section to which they belong (*Strom.* ii. 79. 5, vol. ii. 154. 17–23) contains definitions of σωφροσύνη, μεγαλοψυχία, and εὐλάβεια and has been incorporated by Arnim in his *SVF* (iii. 275) since it must come from a Stoic source. But Philo also, in defining ἀνδρεία, uses the same Stoic terms as those which we find in the definitions of ἀνδρεία and καρτερία given by Clement:

Leg. Alleg. i. 65 (i. 78. 8): ἡ δὲ ἀνδρεία τοῖς ὑπομενετέοις (= *SVF* iii. 263).

Leg. Alleg. i. 68 (i. 79. 3–4): ἐπιστήμη γάρ ἐστιν ὑπομενετέων καὶ οὐχ ὑπομενετέων καὶ οὐδετέρων (= *SVF* iii. 263).

De spec. Leg. iv. 145 (v. 241. 19–22): τὴν ἀνδρείαν, ἀρετὴν περὶ τὰ δεινὰ πραγματευομένην . . . τῶν ὑπομενετέων οὖσαν ἐπιστήμην.[1]

The same Stoic definition of ἀνδρεία is practically adopted by a Middle Platonic philosopher, namely Hierax, who gives the following definition of δειλία, Stob. *Anth.* 8. 19 (iii. 345. 4–6 Hense): δειλία τοίνυν ἐστί . . . ἢ ἄγνοια δεινῶν τε καὶ οὐ δεινῶν καὶ οὐδετέρων.[2]

occurs also in Aristotle, who connects it with virtue: see *EN* 1138ᵇ19–20 and 1138ᵇ 24–6. It must not be forgotten that Albinus, as we have seen (p. 65 above), adopts the Aristotelian doctrine of virtue as μεσότης. In Albinus' doctrine of the λόγος ὀρθός Stoic and Aristotelian elements seem therefore to be strictly combined.

¹ The correspondence between the definitions of ἀνδρεία adopted by Clement and by Philo has been observed by Heinisch, 278, and by Völker, 291 n. 6.

² Hierax defines δειλία also in Platonic terms, διαφθορὰ δόξης ἐννόμου δεινῶν τε πέρι καὶ μή, loc. cit. (on both definitions of δειλία given by Hierax see Praechter, *Hermes* 41 (1906), 600–1). Albinus, *Did.* 182. 30–31 defines ἀνδρεία as δόγματος ἐννόμου σωτηρία περὶ τοῦ δεινοῦ τε καὶ μὴ δεινοῦ, thus repeating what Plato had said in the *Republic*: see *Rep.* iv. 429 c 7–8 and 433 c 7–8 (cf. Witt, 89, and Praechter, *Grundr.* 544). Between the Platonic and the Stoic definition there is, however, no substantial difference; the Platonic definition was adopted by the Stoic Sphaerus, as can be seen from Cicero, *Tusc.* iv. 53: *fortitudo est conservatio stabilis iudicii in eis rebus quae formidulosae videntur subeundis et repellendis* (= *SVF* i. 628): for this reference see Witt, 89 n. 5.

(c) Σωφροσύνη. Two passages of the *Stromateis* are particularly important for Clement's conception of σωφροσύνη:

Strom. ii. 79. 5 (ii. 154. 18–19): τὴν δὲ σωφροσύνην ἕξιν ἐν αἱρέσει καὶ φυγῇ σώζουσαν τὰ τῆς φρονήσεως κρίματα. *Strom.* iv. 151. 1 (ii. 315. 15–16): ἐπὶ δὲ τῇ ἐπιθυμίᾳ τάττεται ἡ σωφροσύνη.

The first definition, belonging to the same context in which that of ἀνδρεία appears, is of Stoic origin, as the comparison with *SVF* iii. 262 and 266 again shows. But, just as in the case of ἀνδρεία, we meet very similar Stoic terms in Philo, *Leg. Alleg.* i. 65, ἡ δὲ σωφροσύνη τοῖς αἱρετέοις [sc. ὅρους τιθεῖσα = *SVF* iii. 263], cf. *De Virt.* 14, σωφροσύνη, σωτηρίαν τῷ φρονοῦντι τῶν ἐν ἡμῖν ἀπεργαζομένη.[1]

As to the second passage, it can be traced back to the Platonic and Aristotelian doctrine according to which the main task of σωφροσύνη is to control desires and pleasures, as can be seen, for instance, from Plato, *Rep.* iv. 430 e 6–7 and *Laws* i. 647 d 3–6,[2] and Aristotle, *Top.* 136^{b}13–14, 138^{b}4–5, *EN* 1107^{b}4–6 and 1117^{b}25–6.[3]

But this doctrine also has become part of a school-tradition, since it occurs in Antiochus, in Arius Didymus, and in some exponents of Middle Platonism, as can be seen from the following evidence:

Cicero, *De Fin.* v. 67: *temperantia in praetermittendis voluptatibus.*[4]

---

[1] The correspondence between Clement and Philo in the doctrine of σωφροσύνη has been pointed out by Heinisch, 279.

[2] It should, however, not be forgotten that in the *Republic* σωφροσύνη is not related only to the ἐπιθυμητικόν but is also the virtue owing to which the two inferior parts of the soul (namely the θυμοειδές and the ἐπιθυμητικόν) recognize the sovereignty of reason: 'sie ist vielmehr die zwischen Regenten und Beherrschen bestehende Einigkeit darüber, wer zu herrschen ist' (Praechter, *Grundr. der Gesch. der Philos.* 273): see *Rep.* iv. 432 a 6–8 and 442 c 10–d 1; the same idea appears in one of the definitions of σωφροσύνη given in [Plato], Ὅροι 411 e, συμφωνία ψυχῆς πρὸς τὸ ἄρχειν καὶ ἄρχεσθαι. On Plato's σωφροσύνη see also Zeller, *Die Philos. der Griech.* ii/1 (Leipzig, 1889), footnote 2 on pp. 884–5.

[3] Völker, 291, is therefore wrong in maintaining that Clement's conception of σωφροσύνη has no close parallel in Greek philosophy. He says the same about φρόνησις (loc. cit.). On the Aristotelian doctrine of σωφροσύνη see Zeller, ii/2. 658–61, and Praechter, *Grundr. der Gesch. der Phil.* 390. The first definition of σωφροσύνη which occurs in [Plato], Ὅροι 411 e, μετριότης τῆς ψυχῆς περὶ τὰς ἐν αὐτῇ κατὰ φύσιν γινομένας ἐπιθυμίας, may be of Peripatetic origin (but see also Plato, *Rep.* iv. 430 e 6–7).

[4] Cf. Strache, *Ekl. des Ant. v. Ask.* 51, and footnote 6 on the same page.

Arius Didymus (= Stob. ii. 124. 4–5) : τῆς σφοδρότητος ἀπολύουσα τῶν παθῶν ἡμᾶς [sc. σωφροσύνη]. Cf. ii. 141. 5 ff.: σώφρονά τε γὰρ εἶναι οὔτε τὸν καθάπαξ ἀνεπιθύμητον οὔτε τὸν ἐπιθυμητικόν ... τὸν δὲ μέσον τούτων. Albinus, *Did.* 182. 24–6: ἡ δὲ σωφροσύνη τάξις περὶ τὰς ἐπιθυμίας καὶ τὰς ὀρέξεις καὶ τὴν εὐπείθειαν αὐτῶν πρὸς τὸ ἡγεμονικόν, τοῦτο δ' εἴη ἂν τὸ λογιστικόν.[1] Apuleius, *De Plat.* ii. 229: *tertia pars* ... *cupidinum et desideriorum, cui necessario abstinentia comes est, quam vult esse servatricem convenientiae eorum, quae natura recta pravaque sunt in homine.*[2] Hierax in Stob. *Anth.* iii. 5. 44 (iii. 269. 11–12 Hense): ὅθεν τὴν λειπομένην ἀρετὴν ἐπιστῆσαι δεῖ τῇ τῶν ἡδονῶν φυλακῇ.[3]

For Philo also the function of σωφροσύνη is to moderate desires and passions, which have their origin in the ἐπιθυμητικόν: it is worth looking at such passages as *Opif. M.* 31 (i. 28. 7–8), *Leg. Alleg.* i. 69 (i. 79. 7–9 and 9–11), *Leg. Alleg.* i. 70 (i. 79. 19–20), *Leg. Alleg.* i. 71 (i. 80. 3–4), *Leg. Alleg.* ii. 79 (i. 106. 5), *Leg. Alleg.* ii. 99 (i. 110. 20–1), *Leg. Alleg.* ii. 105 (i. 111. 25–6), *De Agr.* 98 (ii. 115. 10–11), *De Agr.* 106 (iii. 116. 19–21).[4]

(*d*) Δικαιοσύνη. In the definitions of δικαιοσύνη given by Clement we notice at once a mixture of Stoic and Platonic elements:

Paed. i. 64. 1 (i. 127. 28): δικαιοσύνη ... τοῦ κατ' ἀξίαν ἑκάστῳ ἐστὶν ἀπονεμητική.

Strom. iv. 163. 4 (ii. 321. 3–4): δικαιοσύνη δὲ συμφωνία τῶν τῆς ψυχῆς μερῶν.

The first definition, the Stoic origin of which can be inferred from the comparison with *SVF* iii. 262, can also be found in Antiochus (*De Fin.* v. 67, *iustitia in suo cuique tribuendo*)[5] and in

---

[1] In this passage of Albinus it is possible to notice both the conception according to which σωφροσύνη is related *particularly* to the ἐπιθυμητικόν (Praechter, *Grundr.* 544, regards this doctrine simply as Aristotelian, but the two passages of *Rep.* iv. 430 e 6–7 and *Laws* i. 647 d 3–6 quoted above, p. 78, should also be taken into account) and the idea of the obedience of the inferior parts of the soul to reason, which is expounded by Plato in the fourth book of the *Republic* (see footnote 2, p. 78 above).

[2] On the doctrine of σωφροσύνη in Apuleius see also Moreschini, *Studi sul 'De dogm. Platonis' di Apuleio*, 83–4.

[3] Cf. Praechter, *Hermes* 41 (1906), 594–5.

[4] What Philo says in this passage—and also in *Leg. Alleg.* ii. 99 (i. 110. 20–1) and in *Opif. M.* 81 (i. 28. 7–8)—should be compared with Arius Didymus, in Stob. *Ecl.* ii. 124. 4–5.

[5] See also Strache, *Ekl. des Ant. von Ask.* 70.

Philo, *Leg. Alleg.* i. 65 (i. 78. 9), ἡ δὲ δικαιοσύνη τοῖς ἀπονεμητέοις, i. 87 (i. 84. 2–3), ὅτι ἀπονεμητικὴ τῶν κατ' ἀξίαν ἐστὶ ἡ δικαιοσύνη (= *SVF* iii. 263), and i. 87 (i. 84. 7–8), ἡ δικαιοσύνη . . . ἀπονέμει τὸ κατ' ἀξίαν ἑκάστῳ πράγματι.[1]

As to the second definition, it shows at once its origin from the fourth book of Plato's *Republic*: justice is considered by Plato as the harmony between the different parts of the soul (443 d 6–7, ξυναρμόσαντα τρία ὄντα, ὥσπερ ὅρους τῆς ἁρμονίας ἀτεχνῶς) since it is the virtue through which each part of the state or of the human soul is given a particular function and accomplishes it without interfering with that of the others: καὶ ταύτῃ ἄρα πῃ ἡ τοῦ οἰκείου τε καὶ ἑαυτοῦ ἕξις τε καὶ πρᾶξις δικαιοσύνη ἂν ὁμολογοῖτο (*Rep.* iv. 433 e 12–434 a 1).[2] But the same idea, expressed in the same terms as in Clement, can be found in Philo, *Leg. Alleg.* i. 72 (i. 80. 7–8), πότε οὖν γίνεται; ὅταν τὰ τρία μέρη τῆς ψυχῆς συμφωνίαν ἔχῃ, and in Albinus, *Did.* 182. 32–4, ἡ δὲ δικαιοσύνη ἐστὶ συμφωνία τις τούτων πρὸς ἄλληλα, δύναμις οὖσα, καθ' ἣν ὁμολογεῖ καὶ συμφωνεῖ πρὸς ἄλληλα τὰ τρία μέρη τῆς ψυχῆς.[3]

It is now interesting to notice another point on which Clement, Philo, Albinus, and Apuleius show perfect agreement: all of them adopt the Platonic partition of the soul into λογιστικόν, θυμοειδές, and ἐπιθυμητικόν (*Rep.* iv. 436 a) and, according to the Platonic teaching as set forth in *Timaeus* 69 d–70 a, 70 d–e, locate each of these parts in a particular part of the body; moreover, they ascribe a particular virtue to each part of the soul, thus forming a piece of coherent doctrine which remained the same throughout Middle Platonism and was also adopted, without any noticeable variation, even by exponents of Neoplatonism such as Plotinus and Porphyry. According to this doctrine, φρόνησις is allotted to the λογιστικόν, which is located in the head, whereas ἀνδρεία and σωφροσύνη are the virtues peculiar to the θυμοειδές and ἐπιθυμητικόν which are located in the breast or heart and in

[1] On the presence in Philo of the same Stoic definition of δικαιοσύνη which is adopted by Clement see also Völker, 291 n. 1. Heinisch, 278–9, has not mentioned this further correspondence between Philo and Clement. The Stoic definition of δικαιοσύνη occurs also in the Ὅροι, 411 e, ἕξις διανεμητικὴ τοῦ κατ' ἀξίαν ἑκάστῳ.

[2] See also [Plato], Ὅροι 411 d–e, δικαιοσύνη . . . εὐταξία τῶν τῆς ψυχῆς μερῶν πρὸς ἄλληλά τε καὶ περὶ ἄλληλα.

[3] The correspondence between the two definitions of δικαιοσύνη given by Clement and Albinus has been noticed by Früchtel, *BPhW* 57 (1937), 592. As to the agreement between Clement and Philo in this respect see also Völker, 291.

the belly or liver respectively.¹ Let us examine it in its details in each of the four authors.

That, for Clement, the natural seat of the λογιστικόν is represented by the head, whereas heart and liver are the appropriate places of the θυμοειδές and ἐπιθυμητικόν is proved by the following evidence:

Paed. i. 5. 2 (i. 92. 17): ἐνθρονίζεται δ᾽ οὗτος [sc. ὁ λογισμός] ἐν ἐγκεφάλῳ.

Paed. ii. 34. 2 (i. 117. 9–11): οὕτω τοίνυν ὁ ἐγκέφαλος ἄνωθεν ἰλιγγιάσας ὑπὸ μέθης ἐπὶ τὸ ἧπαρ καὶ τὴν καρδίαν, τουτέστιν ἐπὶ τὴν φιληδονίαν καὶ τὸν θυμόν . . .

Paed. ii. 72. 2 (i. 201. 17): ἐν ἐγκεφάλῳ τοῦτον ἱδρυμένον [sc. τὸν λόγον].

Strom. v. 94. 4 (ii. 388. 11–12): ἐνταῦθα γὰρ [sc. ἐν τῷ προσώπῳ] τὸ ἡγεμονικὸν ἱδρῦσθαι λέγουσιν.

The Platonic partition of the soul in Clement is clear as well.² The attribution of a single virtue to each part of it can be

¹ The attribution of the single virtues to the different parts of the soul can be observed especially in *Rep.* iv. 441 e–442 d; it must, however, be remembered that Plato prefers to use σοφία rather than φρόνησις (see, for instance, 441 e 4, τῷ μὲν λογιστικῷ . . . σοφῷ, 442 c 5 σοφὸν δέ γε ἐκείνῳ τῷ . . . μέρει, τῷ ὃ ἦρχέν τ᾽ ἐν αὐτῷ) and gives a more general function to σωφροσύνη (see the passages quoted in footnote 2, p. 78 above).

² *Paed.* iii. 1. 2 (i. 236. 4–8), *Strom.* iii. 68. 5 (ii. 227. 9–10), and *Strom.* v. 80. 9 (ii. 379. 25–6). Daskalakis, 68–9, mentions only the passage of *Paed.* iii. 1. 2 without giving any indication about the others. Clement is sometimes inclined to regard the soul as consisting only of two parts, a rational and an irrational (which comprehends, however, both the θυμοειδές and the ἐπιθυμητικόν): see, for instance, *Strom.* iv. 9. 4 (ii. 252. 12 ff.) and cf. *Strom.* v. 53. 1 (ii. 362. 8–9). This bipartition of the soul occurs in Antiochus (*De Fin.* v. 34, cf. Strache, *Ekl.* 28, and Witt, 80) as well as in Middle Platonism: see Albinus, who divides the soul into λογιστικόν and παθητικόν and considers the θυμικόν and the ἐπιθυμητικόν as belonging to the latter, *Did.* 173. 9 ff. (cf. Clement, *Strom.* v. 53. 1, vol. ii. 362. 8–9) and Plutarch, *De Virt. m.* 441 d and 442 a. Philo holds the same view: see *De spec. Leg.* i. 333 (v. 80. 21–2), *Quis rer. div. Her.* 132 (iii. 31. 4), and *Leg. Alleg.* iii. 116 (i. 139. 10–11). The reference to *Strom.* v. 52. 2 given by Daskalakis (p. 69) in order to prove that Clement adopts the distinction between a rational and an irrational part of the soul is wrong, since in this passage such a distinction is by no means clearly stated. Daskalakis' words, 'Diese beide Seelen, oder die beiden πνεύματα wie er sie auch nennt, vergleicht er mit zwei Tafeln, welche die Gebote für das ἡγεμονικόν und πλασθέν enthalten' (loc. cit.), must be related not to this passage, but to *Strom.* vi. 134. 1 (ii. 499. 28–30) and vi. 136. 4 (ii. 501. 1–3), which Daskalakis does not bother to mention. As to the division of the soul into ten parts, *Strom.* vi. 134. 2 (ii. 500. 1–5) and *Strom.* ii. 50. 3, Daskalakis is right in pointing out its Stoic origin (see his quotation of Diog. Laert. vii. 110, p. 70 n. 1) and in maintaining that Clement added, to the original Stoic division into eight parts,

inferred from the definition of σωφροσύνη quoted above (p. 78) and from the close connection between φρόνησις and λογισμός or λόγος ὀρθός which we have already observed (pp. 74–5 above). As to Philo, the following sections of the *Legum Allegoriarum libri* are particularly worth noticing:

Leg. Alleg. i. 70 (i. 79. 13–20): It must be remembered that our soul is composed of three parts, namely the rational, the irascible, and the concupiscible; the seat and the dwelling-place of the rational part is the head, that of the irascible the breast, that of the concupiscible the belly. To each of these parts a suitable virtue has been closely attached: to the rational part has been allotted prudence, to the irascible courage, to the concupiscible temperance.

Leg. Alleg. i. 71 (i. 79. 24–80. 5): Of virtues, the first is prudence, which is concerned with the first part of the soul, namely the rational, and which dwells in the head, the first part of the body; the second is courage, because it is concerned with the second part of the soul, namely the seat of anger, and dwells in the breast, the second part of the body; the third is temperance, because it is active in the belly, which is the third part of the body, and in the concupiscible part of the soul, which is the third.

As to Albinus and Apuleius, attention should be drawn to the following passages:

Albinus, *Did.* 173. 5–6; 9–12: They [i.e. the gods] placed the authoritative part of the soul in the head . . . in this seat there is a rational part, which also judges and contemplates; they placed below the part of the soul which is the seat of passions: the irascible part was allotted to the heart, the concupiscible to the belly.

Did. 176. 12–13: They allotted it [i.e. the rational part] to the head . . . 16–18: They allotted the irascible part to the heart, and the concupiscible to that seat which stays in the middle between the navel and the head . . .[1]

τὸ κατὰ πλάσιν πνευματικόν and τὸ διὰ πίστεως προσγινόμενον ἁγίου πνεύματος χαρακτηριστικὸν ἰδίωμα. It must, however, be remembered that Philo adopts the same Stoic partition in *Opif. M.* 117, *Leg. Alleg.* i. 11, *Quod det. pot. ins. sol.* 168, *De Agr.* 30, *Quis rer. div. Her.* 232, *De mut. Nom.* 110, *Quaest. in Gen.* i. 75 and ii. 11. Of these passages, only the first is mentioned by Daskalakis, 71 (he is wrong in adding the reference, according to Mangey's edition, to *Opif. M.* 27).

[1] Albinus' words ἐν τῷ μεταξὺ τόπῳ τοῦ τε πρὸς τὸν ὀμφαλὸν ὅρου καὶ τῶν φρενῶν go directly back to Plato, *Timaeus* 70 e, εἰς τὸ μεταξὺ τῶν τε φρενῶν καὶ τοῦ πρὸς τὸν ὀμφαλὸν ὅρου.

ETHICS 83

Did. 182. 19–23: Since the irascible, the concupiscible, and the rational part are different from each other, the virtues which are characteristic of each of them are also different: for the virtue of the rational part is prudence, that of the irascible courage, that of the concupiscible temperance.

Apuleius, *De Plat.* i. 207: *at enim cum tres partes animae ducat esse, rationabilem, id est mentis optumam portionem, hanc ait capitis arcem tenere, irascentiam vero procul a ratione ad domicilium cordis deductam esse . . . cupidinem atque adpetitus, postremam mentis portionem, infernas abdominis sedes tenere ut popinas quasdam et latinarum latebras, deversoria nequitiae atque luxuriae.*

Idem, *De Plat.* ii. 228–9: *virtutes omnes cum animae partibus dividit et illam virtutem, quae ratione sit nixa et est spectatrix diiudicatrixque omnium rerum, prudentiam dicit atque sapientiam . . . in ea vero parte, quae iracundior habeatur, fortitudinis sedes esse et vires animae . . . tertia pars mentis est cupidinum et desideriorum, cui necessario abstinentia comes est, quam vult esse servatricem convenientiae eorum, quae natura recta pravaque sunt in homine.*[1]

Another doctrine which Clement has in common with Middle Platonism and with Philo is that of the mutual implication (ἀντακολουθία) between the different virtues, which in the wise man cannot be separated from one another:

Strom. ii. 45. 1 (ii. 136. 23): ὡς μὲν οὖν ἀντακολουθοῦσιν ἀλλήλαις αἱ ἀρεταί, τί χρὴ λέγειν;
Strom. ii. 80. 2 (ii. 154. 25–6): ἀντακολουθοῦσι δὲ ἀλλήλαις αἱ ἀρεταί.
Strom. ii. 80. 3 (ii. 155. 3–4): ὅτι μίαν ἔχων ἀρετὴν γνωστικῶς πάσας ἔχει διὰ τὴν ἀντακολουθίαν.
Strom. iv. 59. 2 (ii. 275. 11–12): εἰ δὲ ἀνδρὸς ἀρετὴ σωφροσύνη δήπουθεν καὶ δικαιοσύνη καὶ ὅσα τούτοις ἀκόλουθα νομίζονται.
Strom. iv. 163. 3 (ii. 320. 28; 321. 1): καὶ δὴ ἡ ἀντακολουθία τῶν τριῶν ἀρετῶν . . .
Strom. viii. 30. 2 (iii. 99. 16–17): οὕτως καὶ αἱ ἀρεταὶ αἴτιαι τοῦ μὴ χωρισθῆναι διὰ τὴν ἀντακολουθίαν.

That this doctrine is Stoic is shown by the comparison with *SVF* i. 199 and iii. 295 ff.;[2] this is the reason why some scholars have seen a direct influence of Stoicism also on this particular

---

[1] On the presence of the same doctrine in Neoplatonism see Plotinus, *Enn.* i. 2. 1 and Porphyry, *Sent.* xxxii. 2 (pp. 17. 21–18. 4 Mommert).

[2] This doctrine can, however, be found also in Plato and in Aristotle: see, for instance, *Protag.* 329 e 4 (on the unity of virtue in Plato see also Zeller, ii/1. 880 and 882–3) and *EN* 1145ᵃ2–3.

point of Clement's ethics.[1] But the same Stoic doctrine is adopted by Antiochus[2] and consequently occurs also in Middle Platonism: it will suffice to mention Albinus, *Did.* 183. 2–3, ὅθεν καὶ ἀντακολουθεῖν ἡγητέον τὰς ἀρετάς, and 183. 14, ἀχώριστοι ... ἀρεταὶ ἀλλήλων,[3] Apuleius, *De Plat.* ii. 228, *eas vero, quae perfectae sint, individuas sibi et inter se conexas esse . . . arbitratur,*[4] and in the anonymous commentator of the *Theaetetus*, cols. 9. 39–10. 1–3 (p. 8 ed. Diels–Schubart) and col. 11. 16 f. (p. 9).[5] Philo also maintains that he who has one of the virtues must necessarily have all of them, *De Vita Mos.* ii. 7 (iv. 202. 3–4), ἐφ᾽ ὧν δεόντως εἴποι τις ἄν, ὃ καὶ ἐπὶ ἀρετῶν εἴωθε λέγεσθαι, ὅτι ὁ μίαν ἔχων καὶ πάσας ἔχει (= *SVF* iii. 303) : according to Philo, virtue is one in origin, and its different names are nothing but species of the same genus, τὸ γὰρ ὅλον ἐν γένει ἡ ἀρετή, ἣ κατὰ εἴδη τὰ προσεχῆ τέμνεται, φρόνησιν καὶ σωφροσύνην καὶ ἀνδρείαν καὶ δικαιοσύνην (*De Sacr. Ab. et C.* 84, vol. i. 237. 3–4 = *SVF* iii. 304). What Philo says in this passage reminds us of the doctrine of the origin of virtue from the Logos, which we have already examined (p. 64 above).

3. We have now to go through a very important aspect of Clement's ethics and psychology, namely the doctrine of πάθος, which has so far been regarded as one of the strongest arguments in support of the assumption that Clement depends directly upon Stoicism in his ethical doctrines.[6] It will be our purpose to see whether such a view can be accepted, or whether here also it is possible to trace Clement's views back to Middle Platonism and to Philo. In this way we shall also be able to show, in the next section, the close relationship which exists between a part of

[1] See especially Merk, 72: 'Mit der Stoa stimmt ferner Clemens überein in der Lehre von der Einheit der Tugend. Wer die eine Tugend hat, hat die andern alle.'

[2] *De Fin.* v. 67: *nam cum ita copulatae connexaeque sint, ut omnes omnium participes sint nec alia ab alia possit separari*; cf. A. Lüder, 50, Strache, *Der Eklektizismus . . .*, 48, and Witt, 90.

[3] On the ἀντακολουθία of virtues in Albinus see Praechter, *Grundr.* 544, and Witt, 89–90. For the presence of this doctrine in Neoplatonism see Plotinus, *Enn.* i. 2. 7 and Porphyry, *Sent.* xxxii. 4.

[4] See also Moreschini, *Studi sul 'De dogm. Plat.' di Apuleio*, 80.

[5] For some general remarks on this anonymous commentator see Praechter, op. cit. 552–3.

[6] See, for instance, Merk, 50, 64, and 65, Daskalakis, 97, and especially Pohlenz, *NGA*, phil.-hist. Kl. (1943), 125–7 and 162, and *Die Stoa* i. 420.

Clement's ethical system and the ethics characteristic both of Middle Platonism and of Philo. That the general definition of πάθος given by Clement in *Strom.* ii. 59. 6 goes back to Zeno and Chrysippus is proved by the following comparison:

Clem. *Strom.* ii. 59. 6 (ii. 145. 3–9): πάθος δὲ πλεονάζουσα ὁρμὴ ἢ ὑπερτείνουσα τὰ κατὰ τὸν λόγον μέτρα, ἢ ὁρμὴ ἐκφερομένη καὶ ἀπειθὴς λόγῳ· παρὰ φύσιν οὖν κίνησις ψυχῆς κατὰ τὴν πρὸς τὸν λόγον ἀπείθειαν τὰ πάθη . . . αὐτίκα καθ᾽ ἓν ἕκαστον τῶν παθῶν εἴ τις ἐπεξίοι, ἀλόγους ὀρέξεις λέγοι ἂν αὐτά (= *SVF* iii. 377).

Diog. Laert. vii. 110 (= *SVF* i. 205): ἔστι δὲ τοῦτο τὸ πάθος κατὰ Ζήνωνα ἡ ἄλογος καὶ παρὰ φύσιν ψυχῆς κίνησις, ἢ ὁρμὴ πλεονάζουσα. Galen, *De Plac. Hipp. et Plat.* iv, c. 5, vol. v Kühn, p. 397. 7 ff. ἡ δ᾽ οὖν ῥῆσις ἡ κατὰ τὸ θεραπευτικὸν τῶν παθῶν βιβλίον ὧδ᾽ ἔχει· "οἰκείως δὲ καὶ ὁρμὴ πλεονάζουσα λέγεται εἶναι τὸ πάθος, ὡς ἄν τις ἐπὶ τῶν ἐπιφερομένων κινήσεων πλεονάζουσαν κίνησιν εἴποι . . . ὑπερβαίνουσα γὰρ τὸν λόγον ἡ ὁρμὴ καὶ παρὰ φύσιν ἀθρόως φερομένη· οἰκείως τ᾽ ἂν πλεονάζειν ῥηθείη καὶ κατὰ τοῦτο παρὰ φύσιν γίνεσθαι καὶ εἶναι ἄλογος" (= *SVF* iii. 479. 130). Cf. *De Plac. Hipp. et Plat.* iv, c. 2, vol. v Kühn, p. 368. 1 ff. (= *SVF* iii. 462, p. 113).

The definitions of the single πάθη are formulated in the same terminology, and it is therefore easy to trace them back to their origin.[1]

In order, however, to reconstruct Clement's exact view on πάθος, it is necessary to establish what he thought about its origin. Two other passages of the *Stromateis* are worth noticing in this respect:

Strom. vi. 135. 3 (ii. 500. 16–21): αὐτίκα μὲν τὴν ζωτικὴν δύναμιν, ᾗ ἐμπεριέχεται τὸ θρεπτικόν τε καὶ αὐξητικὸν καὶ καθ᾽ ὅλου κινητικόν, τὸ πνεῦμα εἴληχε τὸ σαρκικόν, ὀξυκίνητον ὂν καὶ πάντη διά

---

[1] *Paed.* i. 101. 1 (i. 150. 21–5 = *SVF* iii. 445): this passage should be compared with *SVF* iii. 391, which contains the same definitions of the single πάθη. See also *Paed.* iii. 102. 1 (i. 218. 11), iii. 53. 1 (i. 226. 27), *Strom.* ii. 32. 3 (ii. 130. 8), *Strom.* ii. 119. 3 (ii. 177. 21–2).

τε τῶν αἰσθήσεων καὶ τοῦ λοιποῦ σώματος πορευόμενόν τε καὶ πρωτοπαθοῦν διὰ σώματος, τὴν προαιρετικὴν δὲ τὸ ἡγεμονικὸν ἔχει δύναμιν. *Strom.* iv. 136. 1 (ii. 500. 23–5): διὰ τοῦ σωματικοῦ ἄρα πνεύματος αἰσθάνεται ὁ ἄνθρωπος, ἐπιθυμεῖ, ἥδεται, ὀργίζεται, τρέφεται, αὔξεται.

It is clear from the first passage that Clement regards the πνεῦμα σαρκικόν as the expression of the animal life in man, and that he connects it also with body and sensations (διά τε τῶν αἰσθήσεων καὶ τοῦ λοιποῦ σώματος πορευόμενον); in the second passage the πνεῦμα σαρκικόν or σωματικόν is closely related not only to the animal life (τρέφεται, αὔξεται) but also to such functions as ἐπιθυμεῖν, ἥδεσθαι, ὀργίζεσθαι, i.e. to πάθος (see also the term πρωτοπαθοῦν which occurs in the first passage).

The πνεῦμα σαρκικόν, in so far as it comprehends all the irrational functions in itself, represents for Clement the inferior and irrational part of the human soul. The rational faculty is sharply distinguished from it: τὴν προαιρετικὴν δὲ τὸ ἡγεμονικὸν ἔχει δύναμιν, *Strom.* vi. 135. 3. This is the reason why Clement comes to speak about the two different πνεύματα dwelling in man, with which the two tables of stone containing the ten commandments are concerned (see *Strom.* vi. 134. 1, vol. ii. 499. 28–30 and vi. 136. 4 501. 1–2). This distinction of two πνεύματα is practically one and the same thing with the partition of the soul into a rational and irrational part, which we have already observed.[1]

A conclusion can be drawn from Clement's doctrine of the πνεῦμα σαρκικόν. Since, as we have seen, the ἐπιθυμεῖν, ἥδεσθαι, and the ὀργίζεσθαι are functions peculiar to it, it follows that ἐπιθυμία, ἡδονή, and ὀργή, which are three of the main πάθη, must have their natural seat in the irrational part of the soul, and also be connected, in some way, both with sensation and with body. Consequently Clement could hardly have shared the view of those who, like Chrysippus, considered πάθος simply as the product of a wrong judgement of reason and, in this way, traced it back to the rational part of the soul. Actually Clement, as Pohlenz has rightly pointed out, never mentions this Chrysippean doctrine in his writings.[2] Though adopting Chrysippus' definition

---

[1] See footnote 2, p. 81 above.
[2] See Pohlenz, *NGA*, phil.-hist. Kl. (1943), 126, cf. *Die Stoa* i. 420. The only exception is represented by *Strom.* v. 67. 4 (ii. 371. 8–9), ἄνευ τῆς σωματικῆς φλυαρίας καὶ τῶν παθῶν πάντων, ὅσα περιποιοῦσιν αἱ κεναὶ καὶ ψευδεῖς ὑπολήψεις. This

of πάθος, he keeps himself close to the view of Posidonius according to which πάθος cannot be related to reason, but is connected with body and must be regarded as an irrational impulse peculiar to the two inferior functions of the soul, namely the ἐπιθυμητική and the θυμοειδής.[1] We are now able to discover the link which connects Clement with Middle Platonism, Neoplatonism, and Philo. The three points on which Clement's doctrine of πάθος is based (namely the tendency to consider it as produced by the irrational parts of the soul, the tendency to connect it with sensation and body, and the implied refusal to regard it as a wrong judgement of reason) occur also in such authors as Galen, Plutarch, and Albinus, as well as in Plotinus and Philo. Like Clement, all of them adopt Posidonius' view of its origin.[2]

apparent contradiction with Clement's general doctrine of πάθος is, however, of no importance, since the present passage comes directly from Philo, *De Sacr. Ab. et C.* 84, προστέτακται μέντοι καὶ τὸ "ὁλοκαύτωμα δείραντας εἰς μέλη διανεῖμαι" ὑπὲρ τοῦ πρῶτον μὲν γυμνὴν ἄνευ σκεπασμάτων, ὅσα περιποιοῦσιν αἱ κεναὶ καὶ ψευδεῖς ὑπολήψεις τὴν ψυχὴν φανῆναι. It is evident that Clement has replaced Philo's word σκεπασμάτων with the expression ἄνευ τῆς σωματικῆς φλυαρίας καὶ τῶν παθῶν πάντων but kept the following words of Philo, ὅσα περιποιοῦσιν αἱ κεναὶ καὶ ψευδεῖς ὑπολήψεις, without remembering that, by doing so, he contradicted his own view on πάθος. The dependence of this passage of Clement on Philo has been observed by Stählin, app. ad loc., and by Heinisch, 254. Pohlenz, though mentioning Clement's passage (art. cit. 126 n. 2), has however not pointed out its dependence on Philo. Prunet, 72, is wrong in maintaining that, according to Clement, 'elles [i.e. passions] sont, en effet, entièrement dépendantes de l'assentiment'.

[1] The fourth book of Galen's *De Placitis Hippocratis et Platonis* provides us with the best evidence for both Chrysippus' theory about the origin of πάθος and Posidonius' criticism of it. Galen quotes large sections of the Περὶ παθῶν of Chrysippus, and refers to his doctrine, adding his own criticism (*De Plac. Hipp. et Plat.* iv, c. 5, vol. v Kühn, p. 392. 2–8 = *SVF* iii. 476, p. 127, cf. *De Plac. Hipp. et Plat.* iv, c. 6, vol. v Kühn, p. 403. 11–13 = *SVF* iii. 473). He reports also how Posidonius criticized Chrysippus' doctrine of πάθος, and points out that Posidonius kept himself closer to Plato's partition of the soul and in this way gave a better explanation of the origin of πάθος: see *De Plac. Hipp. et Plat.* iv, c. 6, vol. v Kühn, p. 421. 5 ff. (cf. Zeller, iii/1. 599 n. 2), v, c. 1, vol. v Kühn, p. 429. 14 ff. (cf. Zeller, iii/1. 601 n. 3), and v, c. 5, vol. v Kühn, p. 464. 6–7 (cf. Zeller, iii/1. 602 n. 1, and A. Schmekel, 262 n. 1). Posidonius considered the Platonic ἐπιθυμητικόν and θυμοειδές not as real parts (μέρη) but simply as functions (δυνάμεις) of the soul: see Zeller, iii/1. 602 and footnote 2 on the same page, and Schmekel, 258 and 260. On Posidonius' doctrine of πάθος see especially Zeller, iii/1. 600–2, A. Schmekel, 262–3, K. Gronau, 253–4, Pohlenz, *Die Stoa* i. 226, Praechter, *Grundr. . . . .*, 480, W. Theiler, *Die Vorbereitung des Neuplatonismus*, 85–9 (who deals mainly with Plotinus' dependence on Posidonius in this respect), and R. Walzer, *CQ* 43 (1949), 87.

[2] For Antiochus see, for instance, *Ac. Post.* i. 39: *cumque eas perturbationes antiqui naturales esse dicerent et ratione expertes, aliaque in parte animi cupiditatem, in alia rationem*

Galen is very clear on this point. In the fourth book of his
De Plac. Hipp. et Platonis he does not conceal his polemical attitude
towards Chrysippus, but does his best to point out his contradictions and incongruities; reason, he maintains, cannot be the
cause of πάθος, which must have its origin in the irrational functions of the soul: 'We ask you, which cause has given origin to
this irrational movement which, though not being produced by
reason, is clearly produced by some cause? We say that sometimes
it is the irascible faculty, and sometimes the concupiscible faculty
that produces it' (c. 5, vol. v Kühn, p. 393. 2–5); 'consequently,
Chrysippus, reason is not the cause of this runaway and im-
moderate movement; you yourself admit that it takes place
against reason. It is not possible that something is produced by
reason and against reason at the same time; since this movement
must be produced at any rate by some cause, the faculty which
produces passions is not the rational, but an irrational one'
(c. 5, vol. v Kühn, pp. 394. 18–395. 5). Moreover, in order to
prove the real existence of the conflict between the rational and
the irrational functions of the soul, and to show how wrong and
full of contradictions is Chrysippus' view on πάθος, he quotes two
lines of Euripides' *Medea* (1078–9) which, as he himself says, he
found in Chrysippus' Περὶ παθῶν: ἡ δέ γε Μήδεια βιασθεῖσα πρὸς
τοῦ θυμοῦ, περὶ ἧς οὐκ οἶδ᾽ ὅπως ὁ Χρύσιππος οὐκ αἰσθάνεται
καθ᾽ ἑαυτοῦ τοῦ Εὐριπίδου μεμνημένος ἐπῶν·

collocarent, ne his quidem adsentiebatur [sc. *Zeno*]. *Nam et perturbationes voluntarias
esse putabat opinionisque iudicio suscipi* . . . This passage is quoted by Strache, *Ekl.*, 33.
Strache (op. cit. 33–4) thinks that Antiochus opposed the teaching of the old
Porch on πάθος. Pohlenz holds the opposite view on this point, since he thinks that
Antiochus adopted Chrysippus' doctrine, according to which the πάθη are produced by a wrong opinion. Pohlenz was led to this assumption by the fact that he
first considered Antiochus as the source of the third book of Cicero's *Tusculanae*,
where the Chrysippean view is openly supported (see his article in *Hermes* 41
(1906), 338). The casual mention of Antiochus at § 59 does not, however, represent
a sufficient reason to trace this book back to him. Moreover, as Strache has pointed
out (op. cit. 32), the criticism of the Academic Crantor and of the Peripatetics
which appears in it (see especially §§ 12–13, 22, and 71) does not fit in with the
general attitude of Antiochus, who liked to present himself as the restorer, against
Arcesilas' scepticism, of the philosophy of the *antiqui*, i.e. of the Old Academy and
of the Peripatetic school which, in his opinion, did not substantially differ from
each other (*Ac. Post.* i. 37 and 38). Later on, Pohlenz changed his view about the
source of the third book of the *Tusculanae* (see the note S 244 Z 16 in *Die Stoa* ii.
126) but kept on thinking that Antiochus had followed Chrysippus in his doctrine
of πάθος without, however, being able to produce sufficient evidence in support
of his assumption (see *Die Stoa* i. 252).

ETHICS 89

καὶ μανθάνω μὲν οἷα δρᾶν μέλλω κακά,
θυμὸς δὲ κρείσσων τῶν ἐμῶν βουλευμάτων.
(c. 6, vol. v Kühn, p. 408. 6 ff.)[1]

It is important to notice that Clement also, speaking about the conflict between reason and πάθος, quotes the same lines of the *Medea*: τουτέστι τὸ ἔκδοτον γεγενῆσθαι τῷ πάθει· ἡ Μήδεια δὲ καὶ αὐτὴ ὁμοίως ἐπὶ τῆς σκηνῆς βοᾷ·

καὶ μανθάνω μὲν οἷα δρᾶν μέλλω κακά,
θυμὸς δὲ κρείσσων τῶν ἐμῶν βουλευμάτων.
(*Strom*. ii. 63. 3, vol. ii. 147. 3 ff.)

We leave the problem of the occurrence of the same two lines of Euripides' *Medea* in Clement and in Galen aside for the moment, and go back to illustrate the doctrine of πάθος in some exponents of Middle Platonism. Plutarch in his *De Virtute morali* shows, just as Galen does, his polemical attitude towards those Stoics who maintained that πάθος is the product of a wrong judgement of reason (καὶ γὰρ τὸ πάθος εἶναι λόγον πονηρὸν καὶ ἀκόλαστον, ἐκ φαύλης καὶ διημαρτημένης κρίσεως σφοδρότητα καὶ ῥώμην προσλαβούσης, 441 d) and resorts to the partition of the soul into a rational and an irrational part (ἔοικε δὲ λαθεῖν τούτους ἅπαντας ᾗ διττὸς ἡμῶν ὡς ἀληθῶς ἕκαστός ἐστι, 441 d) in order to prove that it is in the latter that the πάθη have their origin (ἕτερον δὲ τὸ παθητικὸν καὶ ἄλογον καὶ πολυπλανὲς καὶ ἄτακτον καὶ ἐξεταστοῦ δεόμενον, 442 a). The πάθη are not, therefore, originated by a wrong opinion, but directly by the bodily conditions, οὐ γὰρ ὀρθότητι δοξῶν οὐδὲ φαυλότητι δήπου ... ἀλλ' αἱ περὶ τὸ αἷμα καὶ τὸ πνεῦμα καὶ τὸ σῶμα δυνάμεις τὰς τῶν παθῶν διαφορὰς ποιοῦσιν, καθάπερ ἐκ ῥίζης τοῦ παθητικοῦ τῆς σαρκὸς ἀναβλαστάνοντος, 451 a,[2] cf. *De Libid. et Aegr.* c. 9 (vii. 10. 9–11 Bern.), τὰ δὲ πάθη πάντα καὶ τὰς ἀσθενείας ὥσπερ ἐκ ῥίζης τῆς σαρκὸς ἀναβλαστάνειν.[3] In these two last passages we meet the same close connection between πάθος and body, which we have noticed in *Strom*. vi. 136. 1 (see p. 86 above). The agreement between Clement and Plutarch appears even more complete, if we

[1] For the quotation in Galen of these two lines of Euripides' *Medea* see also Witt, 81.
[2] Theiler also, *Die Vorbereitung* ..., 88, refers to this passage of Plutarch.
[3] Ziegler also in his article 'Plutarchos', *RE* xxi 1, col. 751, has drawn attention to the presence of Plutarch's doctrine of πάθος in his work *De Libidine et Aegritudine*.

remember that for Plutarch sensations and the animal life are peculiar to the irrational part of the soul and are closely related to the body: ὥσπερ τὸ αἰσθητικὸν ἢ τὸ θρεπτικὸν καὶ τὸ φυτικὸν τῆς ψυχῆς μέρος· ἀλλὰ ταῦτα μὲν ὅλως ἀνήκοα λόγου καὶ κωφὰ τρόπον τινὰ τῆς σαρκὸς ἐκβεβλάστηκε καὶ περὶ τὸ σῶμα ... καταπέφυκε, *De Virt. m.* 442 b. This passage immediately reminds us of what Clement says in *Strom.* vi. 135. 3 about the πνεῦμα σαρκικόν.[1]

The same views can be found in Albinus, who adopts Chrysippus' definition of πάθος but stresses its origin from the irrational part of the soul, denying, at the same time, that it can be the product of a κρίσις: ἔστι τοίνυν πάθος κίνησις ἄλογος ψυχῆς ὡς ἐπὶ κακῷ ἢ ὡς ἐπὶ ἀγαθῷ· ἄλογος μὲν οὖν εἴρηται κίνησις, ὅτι οὐ κρίσεις τὰ πάθη οὐδὲ δόξαι, ἀλλὰ τῶν ἀλόγων τῆς ψυχῆς δυνάμεων κινήσεις· ἐν γὰρ τῷ παθητικῷ τῆς ψυχῆς συνίσταται (*Did.* 185. 22 ff.). Like Plutarch, Albinus draws a sharp line between the λογιστικόν and the παθητικόν and stresses the clash which occurs between them (c. xxiv, pp. 176–7).[2] Moreover, in the same chapter (p. 177), he quotes the same two lines of Euripides' *Medea* which, as we have seen, are quoted both by Galen and by Clement. Immediately afterwards, Albinus quotes two lines of Euripides' *Chrysippus*:

αἲ αἲ τόδ' ἤδη θεῖον ἀνθρώποις κακόν,
ὅταν τις εἰδῇ τἀγαθόν, χρῆται δὲ μή.

These two lines occur in Plutarch, *De Virt. m.* 446 a as well, in a context in which he speaks, exactly as Albinus does, about the clash between πάθος and reason. Immediately before, Plutarch quotes another line of Euripides' *Chrysippus*, γνώμην ἔχοντα μ' ἡ φύσις βιάζεται which is quoted also by Clement, before the two lines of the *Medea*. All these lines occurring in Galen, Clement, Albinus, and Plutarch were originally contained in Chrysippus' work Περὶ παθῶν.[3] But it is not unlikely that Posidonius, in his

[1] The views expounded by Plutarch in *De Virt. m.* 442 b and 451 a (cf. also *De Libid. et Aegr.*, c. 9) most probably go back to Posidonius, as Theiler, op. cit. 88, is inclined to believe: cf. *De Plac. Hipp. et Plat.* v, c. 5, vol. v Kühn, p. 464. 6–7.
[2] See also Witt, 81.
[3] That the lines 1078–9 of Euripides' *Medea* were quoted by Chrysippus is confirmed by Galen (see the quotation of Galen's passage, p. 88 above). Chrysippus was very fond of quotations from Greek poetry: A. Elter, *De Gnomologiorum graecorum historia atque origine* (Bonn, 1893–5), has shown that the late anthologies containing fragments of different Greek poems of the classical period go ultimately back to Chrysippus' work (on this argument see also A. Peretti, 119).

work against Chrysippus, should have quoted the same lines of tragic poetry, in order to prove Chrysippus' contradictions in his doctrine of πάθος. This is exactly what Galen does (see p. 88 above), most probably following the example of Posidonius.¹ Plutarch, Albinus, and Clement may have found the same lines, if not in the original work by Posidonius, in some school-book reproducing his views on the origin of πάθος as well as his polemic against Chrysippus. As both Plutarch and Albinus show, Posidonius' theory of πάθος and his criticism of Chrysippus had become part of the school-Platonism of the first centuries A.D. The presence of this Posidonian doctrine in Middle Platonism may be due to the influence of Antiochus who, most probably, shared the views held by Posidonius and Panaetius on this argument.²

In Neoplatonism, Plotinus holds practically the same views. According to him, the 'real' man is one and the same thing with the rational principle, ἴδιον δέ [sc. νοῦς] ὅτι ἔχει ἕκαστος αὐτὸν ὅλον ἐν ψυχῇ τῇ πρώτῃ, Enn. i. 1. 8, cf. Enn. i. 1. 7, τὸ δὲ ἐντεῦθεν ὁ ἄνθρωπος ὁ ἀληθὴς σχεδόν . . . συνδρόμου γὰρ ὄντος τοῦ ἀνθρώπου τῇ λογικῇ ψυχῇ. The real soul remains therefore impassible, τὴν αἰτίαν τὸ³ ζῆν τῷ συναμφοτέρῳ δοῦσαν ἀνάγκη αὐτὴν ἀπαθῆ εἶναι τῶν παθῶν, Enn. i. 1. 6, cf. Enn. i. 1. 9, ἀτρεμήσει οὖν οὐδὲν ἧττον ἡ ψυχὴ πρὸς ἑαυτὴν καὶ ἐν ἑαυτῇ. Sensations and the πάθη have their origin not in the 'real' soul which, being rational, remains distinct from the body even when it still dwells in it (χωριζομένη δὲ καὶ χωριστῇ καὶ ἐνταῦθα οὔσῃ, Enn. i. 10. 11) but in a compound which is formed by the body and by a kind of reflection of the real soul: τῆς ψυχῆς . . . οὐχ αὐτὴν δούσης τῆς τοιαύτης εἰς τὸ συναμφότερον . . . ἀλλὰ ποιούσης ἐκ τοῦ σώματος τοῦ τοιούτου καί τινος οἷον φωτὸς τοῦ παρ' αὐτῆς δοθέντος τὴν τοῦ ζῴου φύσιν ἕτερόν τι, οὗ τὸ αἰσθάνεσθαι καὶ τὰ ἄλλα ὅσα ζῴου πάθη εἴρηται, Enn. i. 1. 7, cf. Enn. i. 1. 8, φαντάζεται τοῖς σώμασι παρεῖναι ἐλλάμπουσα εἰς αὐτὰ καὶ ζῷα ποιοῦσα οὐκ ἐξ αὐτῆς καὶ σώματος, ἀλλὰ μένουσα μὲν αὐτή, εἴδωλα δὲ αὐτῆς διδοῦσα. This reflection of the soul, which permeates the body and which, together with it, represents the natural seat of sensations and of the πάθη, is the equivalent of Clement's πνεῦμα σαρκικόν or σωματικόν: Plotinus' words ἕτερόν τι, οὗ τὸ αἰσθάνεσθαι καὶ τὰ ἄλλα ὅσα ζῴου

¹ See Witt, 81. ² See footnote 2, p. 87 above.
³ τό is Kirchhoff's emendation; the manuscript tradition has τοῦ.

πάθη εἴρηται, *Enn.* i. 1. 7, recall what Clement says in *Strom.* vi. 136. 1, διὰ τοῦ σωματικοῦ ἄρα πνεύματος αἰσθάνεται ὁ ἄνθρωπος, ἐπιθυμεῖ, ἥδεται, ὀργίζεται, as well as the Plutarchean passages of *De Virt. m.* 451 a and of *De Libid. et Aegr.* 9 quoted above.[1] Philo also agrees with the general doctrine of πάθος which occurs both in Clement and in Middle Platonism. He gives the same definition of πάθος as that which was current in the Old Porch, πᾶν μὲν πάθος ἐπίληπτον, ἐπεὶ καὶ πᾶσα ἄμετρος καὶ πλεονάζουσα ὁρμὴ καὶ τῆς ψυχῆς ἡ ἄλογος καὶ παρὰ φύσιν κίνησις (*De spec. Leg.* iv. 79, vol. v. 227. 5–6),[2] but at the same time makes it clear that the πάθη have their origin in the inferior and irrational parts of the soul, τῷ δὲ ἐπιθυμητικῷ τὸν περὶ τὸ ἧτρον καὶ τὴν κοιλίαν τόπον, ἐνταῦθα γὰρ κατοικεῖ ἐπιθυμία, ὄρεξις ἄλογος (*Leg. Alleg.* iii. 115, vol. i. 139. 4–5), and that they cannot be considered as produced by a judgement of reason, τὸ δὲ ἄλογον αἴσθησίς ἐστι καὶ τὰ ταύτης ἔκγονα πάθη, καὶ μάλιστα εἰ μὴ κρίσεις εἰσὶν ἡμέτεραι (*Leg. Alleg.* ii. 6, vol. i. 91. 20–1). Moreover he also, as Clement, Plutarch, and Plotinus do, brings body, sensations, the ἄλογον, and the πάθη into close connection with one another, as can be seen from *Leg. Alleg.* i. 24 (i. 67. 7–8), *Leg. Alleg.* ii. 50 (i. 100. 11–12), *De Fuga* 91 (iii. 129. 11–13), and *De Somn.* ii. 255 (iii. 299. 16–17).[3]

4. Some scholars have seen a further proof of the strong influence which Stoicism had on Clement in the occurrence, in his writings, of the idea of obedience to the λόγος ὀρθός and to φύσις.[4] But it is especially Pohlenz who, in more recent times, has laid a particularly strong emphasis on the importance which this Stoic doctrine has for Clement's ethics. No modern scholar has felt so deeply the meaning of the Stoic maxim which prescribes that one should live according to nature, the laws of which are identical with those established by the universal Logos: 'Wie

---

[1] On Plotinus' doctrine of πάθος and his dependence on Posidonius see Theiler, *Vorbereitung* . . ., especially pp. 85–9.

[2] On the dependence of the definition of πάθος given by Philo on the Old Porch see W. Völker, *Fortschritt und Vollendung bei Philo von Alexandrien* (*TU* 49), 80.

[3] On Philo's views on πάθος see Völker, op. cit., pp. 79–85, and Pohlenz, *NGA*, phil.-hist. Kl. (1942), 457–9, and *Die Stoa* i. 376. On the agreement between Clement and Philo in their attitude towards ἡδονή see Völker, *Der wahre Gnostiker* . . ., 129.

[4] See, for instance, Merk, 48–9, Daskalakis, 88 ff., and J. Stelzenberger, 169–70 and 261.

den Logos, so hat Klemens auch den zweiten Eckpfeiler der griechischen und insbesondere der stoischen Philosophie, den Physisbegriff . . . organisch in sein theistisches Lehrgebäude einzubauen versucht. Die Physis musste zur Schöpfung des transzendenten Gottes werden; aber Klemens erkannte wenigstens die Gesetzmässigkeit des Naturgeschehens grundsätzlich an, und im griechischen Sinne suchte er auch ihren normativen Character für die Ethik festzuhalten. Die Physis ist also die Norm für das Handeln des Menschen aber nur, weil in ihr der Logos waltet. Das hat in der griechischen Philosophie am klarsten die Stoa erkannt. Sie hat darum das naturgemässe Leben des Menschen in einem folgerichtigen Leben nach dem rechten Logos gefunden, die Beherrschung der Sinnlichkeit durch die Vernunft gefordert, und unter diesem Gesichtspunkt das gesamte Handeln des Menschen durch eine strenge Pflichtenlehre geregelt.'[1] There is no doubt about the fact that the Stoic doctrine of the λόγος ὀρθός and φύσις as a standard for human morals occurs frequently in Clement; it will suffice to refer to such passages as *Paed.* ii. 87. 2 (i. 210. 23), *Paed.* iii. 99. 1 (i. 290. 9), *Paed.* iii. 100. 2 (i. 290. 21–3), *Strom.* i. 182. 1 (ii. 111. 19), *Strom.* ii. 18. 4 (ii. 122. 12–13), *Strom.* iii. 72. 3 (ii. 228. 29).[2] Pohlenz's enthusiasm for what he thinks to be his discovery takes him to such lengths that he seems to forget that in Philo also the identity between φύσις and λόγος ὀρθός is extremely frequent, and has a fundamental importance in his system. Philo completely adopts the Stoic doctrine according to which the laws of nature are the same as the laws of human morals, in so far as they are the product of the universal λόγος ὀρθός. This is the reason why he took up also the Stoic conception of man as a citizen of the universe, who sees in the laws of nature the same ruling principles of his morals. The following instances will suffice to show how deep such a belief was in Philo:

> *Opif. M.* 3 (i. 1. 10–14) : . . . since the universe is in harmony with the law and the law with the universe, the man who observes the law becomes at once a citizen of the universe: he regulates his actions according to the will of nature, which administers the whole universe.

---

[1] *NGA*, phil.-hist. Kl. (1943), 176–7.
[2] See also Pohlenz, art. cit. 140–5, 148, 162–3, and *Die Stoa* i. 418–19 and 421–2.

Opif. M. 143 (i. 41. 21–6): Since every well-ordered state has got a constitution, the citizen of the universe must necessarily follow the constitution adopted by the whole universe; this constitution is represented by the right rational principle of nature, which more exactly is called 'rule' since it is a divine law, according to which what is fitting for each being is distributed.

De Agr. 66 (ii. 108. 20): . . . using as master the law of nature.[1]

De Plant. 49 (ii. 143. 20–1): The best man maintained that to be able to live according to nature represents the aim of happiness.

De Migr. Abr. 128 (ii. 293. 4–5): 'To live according to nature' is the aim which is celebrated by the best philosophers.

De Vita Mos. i. 48 (iv. 131. 12–13): Since he [i.e. Moses] adopts as his sole pattern the right rational principle of nature, which alone is the origin and the source of virtues.

Quod omn. prob. liber sit 160 (vi. 45. 6–7): . . . they will attain a right aim . . . the life according to nature.

As in the case of the definition of νόμος, Pohlenz has not seen that here also Philo must necessarily represent the intermediate link between Clement and Stoicism. And just as in the case of νόμος, Pohlenz, though producing so many instances of the occurrence of the Stoic conception of the λόγος ὀρθός and φύσις in Philo,[2] has failed to observe the close correspondence between the Jew and the Christian. For both nature was bound to become the product of the creation of a transcendent God; for both the universal Logos was no longer simply the immanent Stoic principle, but the link between the transcendent God, the world, and man; for both, moreover, God, through His Son, the Logos, had given His laws both to nature and to man. It seems therefore far more likely that Clement, as a Christian, should have taken the conception of Logos and φύσις as a standard for human morals not directly from the Porch but from Philo, whose philosophy he found so much more akin to his own religious faith.[3]

[1] This passage of Philo should be compared with Clement, *Paed.* ii. 95. 3, τῇ φύσει, ἣν χρὴ διδάσκαλον ἐπιγραφομένους . . .

[2] *NGA*, phil.-hist. Kl. (1942), 462 f.; cf. *Die Stoa* i. 376: 'Er legte den grössten Wert auf den Nachweis, dass das mosaische Gesetz in Einklang mit der Natur stehe.'

[3] I cannot agree with what Pohlenz says about the different ways in which Philo and Clement treated the Greek conceptions of φύσις and λόγος or Greek culture in general: 'Denn Philon bleibt immer der gesetzestreue Jude, der sich die ihm innerlich fremde hellenische Gedankenwelt nur angeeignet hat, um seine Väterreligion mit dem modernen Empfinden in Einklang zu bringen, und sich als

ETHICS

Plutarch also, who usually does not conceal his critical attitude towards the Porch, stresses the Stoic idea of the unity and universality of the law of nature, which is 'one' because it has been established by one and the same God, the ruler of the universe; all men must obey this law and, in this sense, they are citizens of the universe:

De Exil. 601 a–b: οἱ αὐτοὶ νόμοι πᾶσι, ὑφ' ἑνὸς προστάγματος καὶ μιᾶς ἡγεμονίας ... ᾗ χρώμεθα πάντες ἄνθρωποι φύσει πρὸς πάντας ἀνθρώπους ὥσπερ πολίτας.
De Alex. Magni Fort. aut Virt. i. 329 b: ... ἀλλὰ πάντας ἀνθρώπους ἡγώμεθα δημότας καὶ πολίτας, εἷς δὲ βίος ᾖ καὶ κόσμος, ὥσπερ ἀγέλης συννόμου νόμῳ κοινῷ συντρεφομένης.[1]

The doctrine of φύσις and of λόγος ὀρθός as a standard for human morals is combined, in Clement's thought, with the Stoic idea of the fight against the πάθη and, in this way, with the Platonic doctrine of the obedience of the two inferior parts of the soul to the ruling principle of reason. Elements of Stoic ethics are therefore closely mingled with Platonic topics, conceptions, and images, and form together with these a coherent ethical system, the main features of which are to be found again both in Philo and in Middle Platonism. The Platonic λογιστικόν, which is identified with the Stoic λόγος ὀρθός, must, just as in the fourth book of the Republic, keep the θυμοειδές and the ἐπιθυμητικόν under its control.[2] Reason appears very often as the charioteer guiding the two horses of his chariot—which represent the θυμοειδές and the ἐπιθυμητικόν—and preventing them from rearing, or as the helmsman guiding his ship in the right direction.[3] But the only

oberflächliche Natur bei äusserlichen Kompromissen beruhigen mochte. Bei Klemens gehört das griechische Denken ebenso zu seinem Wesen wie das Bedürfnis, sich eine geschlossene Weltanschauung zu bilden' (NGA, phil.-hist. Kl. (1943), 175–6). After a first reading both of Clement and of Philo my personal feeling is that in Clement the idea of obedience to φύσις is not worked out to the same extent as it appears to be in Philo. Nowhere in Clement could I find such passages as De Opif. M. 3 or 143.

[1] On these two passages of Plutarch see also Andresen, Logos u. Nomos, 266.
[2] See, for instance, Rep. iv. 440 b and 440 e about the conflict between the irrational parts of the soul and reason, and 441 e–442 b about the submission of the θυμοειδές and ἐπιθυμητικόν to the λογιστικόν.
[3] Both images have their origin in the Platonic Phaedrus: see 246 b 1–3, καὶ πρῶτον μὲν ἡμῶν ὁ ἄρχων ξυνωρίδος ἡνιοχεῖ, εἶτα τῶν ἵππων ὁ μὲν αὐτῷ καλός τε καὶ ἀγαθὸς καὶ ἐκ τοιούτων, ὁ δὲ ἐξ ἐναντίων τε καὶ ἐναντίος, and 247 c 7–8, ψυχῆς κυβερνήτῃ ... νῷ.

way to achieve this is, in Clement's opinion, to impose a rule over the irrational πάθη, to heal them, since they are the worst disease of the soul. This result can only be attained by the Logos, the divine being which is present all over the universe as well as in the human mind. The different ways in which He manifests Himself—the law of nature, the ten commandments, the κυριακαὶ ἐντολαί of the Old Testament and the teaching of Christ during His stay on earth—have one and the same aim: the healing of the πάθη, and consequently also the restoration of the harmony in the soul. It will be convenient to produce first some evidence for the occurrence of these topics in Clement and then to show how the fundamental idea of this stage of his ethics—namely the stressing of the necessity of imposing the control of reason over the πάθη and the irrational parts of the soul—can be related both to Philo and to Middle Platonism.

(a) On the Logos moderating and healing the πάθη:

Paed. i. 1. 2 (i. 90. 8–9) : The consolatory Logos heals passions.

Paed. i. 3. 1 (i. 91. 3) : The consequence of this is the healing of passions.[1]

Paed. i. 3. 3 (i. 91. 11–13) : As those whose body is ill need a physician, so those whose soul is weak need an educator who is able to heal our passions.

Paed. i. 6. 1 (i. 93. 11–13) : Only the Logos of the Father is the physician who heals the human illness and the holy enchanter of the ill soul.

Paed. i. 6. 2 (i. 93. 18–19) : The physician who heals the whole of mankind heals both the body and the soul of man.

Paed. i. 6. 4 (i. 93. 23–4) : . . . the Logos heals the soul by means of commands and favours.

Paed. i. 51. 1 (i. 120. 21–2) : The Logos . . . heals passions.

Paed. iii. 98. 2 (i. 289. 30–1) : Jesus . . . who heals both our body and our soul.

Strom. i. 159. 3 (ii. 100. 17–19) : Reason is the ruling principle of the passions of the soul, which we master by means of virtue: it impresses self-control, temperance, and piety [upon the soul].

Strom. vi. 136. 1 (ii. 500. 26–7) : The authoritative principle reigns as soon as it succeeds in mastering desires.

---

[1] Exactly the same expression (ἴασις τῶν παθῶν) is used by the Valentinians in the description of the function of Jesus, who is sent out of the *pleroma* of the aeons in order to free Σοφία from passions: see Iren. *Adv. Haer.* i. 4. 5 and *Exc. ex Theod.* 45. The close correspondence between these two passages, which both contain the expression ἴασις τῶν παθῶν, has been pointed out by O. Dibelius, *ZNW* 9 (1908), 231.

Strom. vi. 136. 2 (ii. 500. 27 ff.): The command 'thou shalt not desire' means that thou shalt not be a slave of the fleshly spirit, but command over it.[1]

(*b*) On the Logos as ἡνίοχος and κυβερνήτης:

Protr. 121. 1 (i. 85. 18–21): We must love Christ, the good charioteer of men ... He, after yoking together the two horses which every man possesses, leads the chariot towards immortality.[2]

Paed. iii. 53. 2 (i. 266. 29–34): Luxuriousness drifting into insolence can leap, rear up, and shake off the charioteer, the educator, who, drawing back the reins from afar, leads towards salvation the horses of man, viz. the irrational part of the soul which becomes wild under the effect of pleasures and desires.

Strom. ii. 51. 6 (ii. 141. 5–6): Reason, the authoritative principle, if it remains unshaken and keeps the control of the soul, is called the helmsman.

Strom. v. 52. 5 (ii. 362. 4 ff.): 'He threw into the sea' the beastlike and impulsive passion which is endowed with many legs, namely desire, together with the charioteer who had mounted upon the chariot and abandoned the reins to pleasures ...[3]

Strom. v. 53. 1 (ii. 362. 7–9): Plato also in his treatise 'About the soul' says that both fall down, namely the charioteer and the revolting horse (viz. the irrational element of the soul, which is divided into two parts, courage and desire).[4]

(*c*) On the two tables of stone containing the ten commandments:

Strom. vi. 134. 1 (ii. 499. 28–30): It seems that the commandments

---

[1] The verb ἄρχειν is a very common Platonic term; Plato uses it whenever he comes to speak about the sovereignty of the soul over the body or about the rule of reason over the irrational parts of the soul: see, for instance, *Phaedo* 80 a, *Rep.* iv. 441 e and 442 d.

[2] This passage has been rightly compared by G. W. Butterworth, *CQ* 10 (1916), 202, with Plato, *Phaedrus* 246 b. Clement represents Christ as the ἡνίοχος since for him Christ is the universal Logos who is present also in human reason.

[3] The passage is derived from Philo, *De Agr.* 82–3 (iii. 111. 19 ff.): in both passages the ἡνίοχος represents the man who instead of ruling over his πάθη is overcome by them. The reference given by Stählin to *Leg. Alleg.* ii. 99 is wrong, since whereas in *De Agr.* 82 the ἀναβάτης represents the man who is a slave of passions, in *Leg. Alleg.* ii. 99 the knight (ἱππεύς) falling backwards represents the νοῦς which shakes itself free from the πάθη: the difference between the two images is made clear by Philo himself, who in *Leg. Alleg.* ii. 103 (i. 111. 9–15) points out the opposition between the ἀναβάτης and the ἱππεύς.

[4] The passage is rightly referred by Stählin, app. ad loc., to Plato, *Phaedrus* 247 b 3–6.

are written in a twofold way for two different spirits, namely the authoritative principle and the other which is subordinate to the former.

Strom. vi. 136. 4 (ii. 501. 1–3): It is therefore reasonable to say that the two tables indicate the commandments which, before the coming of the law, were imparted to the two spirits.

As Galen tells us in the fifth book of his *De Placitis Hippocratis et Platonis*, it was Chrysippus who had regarded πάθος as a disease of the soul and pointed out the parallelism existing between the illness of the body and that of the soul[1] and consequently also between the healing of the body and that of the soul.[2] This explains why he called one of his works θεραπευτικὸν τῶν παθῶν βιβλίον.[3] Both Posidonius and Galen, though criticizing Chrysippus' psychology and his theory of the origin of πάθος, had approved and adopted the image of πάθος as a disease of the soul.[4] Clement therefore, when speaking, especially at the beginning of the *Paedagogus*, of the healing of πάθος, expounds a Chrysippean and Posidonian conception.[5] In the use of this Stoic topic he found, however, a predecessor in Philo. The agreement between the two authors is perfect in every respect. Like Clement, Philo regards πάθος as a disease which must be healed by the Logos,[6] resorts to the Platonic images of the ἡνίοχος and κυβερνήτης extremely frequently,[7] stresses the necessity of keeping the two

[1] *De Plac. Hipp. et Plat.* v, c. 2 (vol. v Kühn, p. 438. 6 ff.), cf. p. 438. 14 ff. It should not be forgotten, however, that Plato also regards the πάθη and κακία (i.e. the attempt of the irrational parts of the soul to overthrow the rule of reason) as an illness of the soul: see, for instance, *Rep.* iv. 439 d 1–2, 444 d 13–e 2 and *Timaeus* 86 b 5–7.

[2] *De Plac. Hipp. et Plat.* v, c. 2 (v Kühn, p. 437. 11 ff.).

[3] *De Plac. Hipp. et Plat.* iv, c. 5 (v. 397. 7).

[4] *De Plac. Hipp. et Plat.* v, c. 2 (v. 433. 11 ff.), συμφέρεται μέντοι τῷ Χρυσίππῳ καὶ αὐτὸς [sc. Posidonius] ὡς νοσεῖν τε καὶ λέγειν τὴν ψυχὴν ἅπαντας τοὺς φαύλους. Posidonius was also fond of the image of the charioteer and of the two horses, as can be seen from *De Plac. Hipp. et Plat.* v, c. 5 (v. 466. 19–467. 8) (this passage is quoted also by Schmekel, 272 n. 3).

[5] See, however, also my remarks in footnote 1, above.

[6] See, for instance, *De Post. C.* 46, 72, and 74, *Quod D. sit imm.* 67 and 182, *Leg. Alleg.* ii. 79, iii. 118, 124, 129 and 177, *Quod det. pot. ins. sol.* 146, *De Somn.* i. 69 and 112, *Quaest. in Gen.* ii. 23 and 29, iii. 28 and 30, *De Vita cont.* 2, *Quis rer. div. Her.* 284.

[7] I shall mention only some passages: *Leg. Alleg.* i. 72 and 73, ii. 104, iii. 80, 118, 123, 127, 128, 136, and 137; *De Sacr. Ab. et C.* 49 and 51; *Quod det. pot. ins. sol.* 23 and 141, *Quod D. sit imm.* 129, *De Agr.* 70, 73, 88, and 94. The passage of *De Agr.* 73, ἵπποι μὲν οὖν ἐπιθυμία καὶ θυμός εἰσιν, ὁ μὲν ἄρρην, ἡ δὲ θήλεια, should be compared with Clement, *Strom.* iii. 93. 1 (ii. 238. 29–30), θυμὸν μὲν ἄρρενα

irrational parts of the soul under the strict control of reason,[1] and considers the two tables of stone containing the ten commandments as related to the λογιστικόν and the ἄλογον.[2] The πάθη, in this ethical stage, are not completely eradicated, but kept by the Logos within certain limits, which are also the limits established by nature: εἰ μόναις ταῖς κατὰ φύσιν μεμετρημέναις ὀρέξεσι, μηδὲν ὑπερoριζούσαις τῶν κατὰ φύσιν ἐπὶ τὸ μᾶλλον ἢ παρὰ φύσιν, ἔνθα τὸ ἁμαρτητικὸν φύεται, ἀρκεῖσθαι βουλοίμεθα, *Strom.* ii. 109. 1 (ii. 172. 20–2).[3] No expression suits such ethical views better than the term μετριοπάθεια, which both Clement and Philo employ for this purpose. In *Strom.* ii. 39. 4 (ii. 134. 3–4) Clement, speaking about the φόβος in the Old Testament, maintains that it does not produce ἀπάθεια, but the moderation of passions or μετριοπάθεια. Philo, speaking about Aaron who is able to keep the πάθη under the control of reason (*Leg. Alleg.* iii. 126), says that by doing so he practises μετριοπάθεια: ἀλλ' ὅ γε προκόπτων δεύτερος ὢν Ἀαρὼν μετριοπάθειαν, ὡς ἔφην, ἀσκεῖ (*Leg. Alleg.* iii. 132). It is the kind of μετριοπάθεια at which Plato hints in the *Republic*[4] and which

ὁρμήν, θήλειαν δὲ τὴν ἐπιθυμίαν. In *Phaedrus* 246 b there is no such distinction between the sexes of the two horses. Clement must have found it in Philo, who always shows a strong inclination to consider what is female as something bad, intimately connected with αἴσθησις.

[1] See, for instance, *Leg. Alleg.* i. 41, iii. 116, *De Sacr. Ab. et C.* 80, *De Post. C.* 71, *De Agr.* 17, 58, and 88, *De Plant.* 144, and *De Conf. Ling.* 165.

[2] See *Quis rer. divin. Her.* 167 (iii. 38. 22–39. 2). The dependence of *Strom.* vi. 134. 1 and 136. 4 on this passage of Philo has been observed by Stählin, app. ad loc., and by Heinisch, 273.

[3] It is this kind of ethics that is characteristic of Clement's *Paedagogus*, containing a multitude of prescriptions for the common everyday life (particularly in books II and III): the Christian must always keep the right mean and avoid any excess. The occurrence of the doctrine of virtue as a μεσότης in this work (see p. 64 above) is not accidental. On the *Paedagogus* in general see F. Quatember, especially pp. 42–50, 95–108, and 122–42; and the lively paper by H. I. Marrou, *Entr. Hardt* iii. 183–200. As to the question of the use made by Clement of the Λόγοι of Musonius Rufus in the *Paedagogus* see particularly P. Wendland, *Quaestiones Musonianae* (Berlin, 1886), and *Philo und die kynisch-stoische Diatribe* (Berlin, 1895), 191–200. I only wish to say here that the ideas characteristic of the Cynic-Stoic diatribe were very common during the first two centuries A.D.: they occur very frequently in Philo (see Wendland, *Philo und die kynisch-stoische Diatribe*, 3–67) and in Plutarch's *Moralia*, which Clement probably used in the *Paedagogus* together with the Λόγοι of Musonius (see Stählin, *Register*, 53–5).

[4] See *Rep.* iv. 431 c 5–7. K. Gronau, 254, has drawn attention to two other passages of the *Republic*, namely iv. 423 e 4–5 and x. 619 a 5–6. The underlying idea of this last passage recalls the Aristotelian conception of virtue as μεσότης.

represents the moral standard of the Old Academy,¹ Aristotle
and the Lyceum,² Middle Stoicism,³ and Antiochus.⁴

¹ See *Ac. Post.* i. 38: *cumque perturbationes animi illi ex homine non tollerent naturaque
et condolescere et concupiscere et extimescere et efferri laetitia dicerent, sed ea contraherent
in angustumque deducerent, Ac. Post.* i. 39: *cumque eas perturbationes antiqui naturales esse
dicerent,* and *Ac. Pr.* ii. 135: *mediocritates illi probabant et in omni permotione naturalem
volebant esse quendam modum.* The exponents of the Old Academy also followed the
maxim 'to live according to nature': see *Ac. Post.* i. 19: *ac primam partem illi bene
vivendi a natura repetebant eique parendum esse dicebant neque ulla alia in re nisi in natura
quaerendum esse illud summum bonum quo omnia referrentur, Ac. Pr.* ii. 131: *honeste autem
vivere, fruentem rebus eis, quas primas homini natura conciliet, et vetus Acadaemia censuit,
ut indicant scripta Polemonis quem Antiochus probat maxime,* and the passage of *Strom.* ii.
133. 4 concerning Speusippus: Σπεύσιππός τε . . . τὴν εὐδαιμονίαν φησὶν ἕξιν εἶναι
τελείαν ἐν τοῖς κατὰ φύσιν ἔχουσιν. Antiochus was strongly influenced by this doctrine of the Old Academy, as the passage of *Ac. Pr.* ii. 131 clearly shows.
² Owing to the doctrine of virtue as the right mean between the two extremes.
This is also the idea which underlies Arius Didymus' exposition of Peripatetic
ethics, in Stob. *Ecl.*, vol. ii, p. 116. 19 ff.
³ See Schmekel, 219, on Panaetius (cf. footnote 1 on the same page) and
pp. 272–3 on Posidonius (cf. also footnote 3 on p. 272); Gronau, 254 (on Posidonius); Zeller, iii/1. 586 (on Panaetius); Praechter, *Grundr.* 477 (on Panaetius)
and 480 (on Posidonius); Pohlenz, *Die Stoa* i. 199 and 202 (on Panaetius) and 236
(on Posidonius).
⁴ I think it very likely that Antiochus was in favour of μετριοπάθεια and entirely
agree with Strache on this point (*Ekl.* 31–7). Here also Antiochus must have followed the *antiqui.* The passage of *Ac. Post.* i. 38 which expounds the doctrine of
μετριοπάθεια in the Old Academy can also be regarded as expressing Antiochus'
view. Antiochus considered emotions as quite natural to a certain extent (see
De Fin. v. 62–4) and consequently does not seem to have condemned them as the
Old Porch had done. From *Ac. Pr.* ii. 135–6, however, where Antiochus is reproached
by Cicero for having denied that the *sapiens* can feel any kind of emotion, it
might be inferred that he adopted rather ἀπάθεια than μετριοπάθεια. This is the
interpretation which Pohlenz has given of the passage (see *Hermes* 41 (1906),
338 n. 3, his review of Strache's dissertation on Arius Didymus, *BPhW* 31 (1911),
1499–1500, and *Die Stoa* i. 252). Whereas A. Lüder thinks that it is not possible to
reach a definite conclusion on this question (p. 49), Luck (pp. 48, 50, and 67) and
Witt (*Albinus . . .,* 90) are inclined to share Pohlenz's view. If this view is correct,
it must also be admitted that Antiochus has consciously abandoned the teaching
of the Old Academy, of the Lyceum, and of Middle Stoicism to which he is
usually greatly indebted and of which he aims at being the follower. This seems
to me to be hardly believable. A different interpretation can be given of the passage of *Ac. Pr.* ii. 135. As we have seen (p. 69 above), Antiochus has inherited both
from the Academy and from the Porch the doctrine of the αὐτάρκεια of virtue, the
possession of which makes the wise man happy even in the greatest misfortunes.
In this way, it is very likely that he would have given a picture of the *sapiens*
similar to that given by the Stoics. It was probably such a picture that led Cicero
to believe, in *Ac. Pr.* ii. 135, that Antiochus had adopted the ἀπάθεια of the Old
Porch. Most probably, however, the doctrine of the αὐτάρκεια of virtue did not
contrast, in Antiochus' opinion, with that of the moderation of emotions: the
sapiens can be happy in every circumstance, provided that he succeeds in keeping
the πάθη under the strict control of reason; their complete destruction is not necessary. A very clear instance, in this respect, is provided by Albinus: he openly

This kind of ethics is also characteristic of Middle Platonism. A striking agreement can be observed between such authors as Plutarch, Albinus, Calvisius Taurus, and Maximus of Tyre. For Plutarch the task of reason is not the total destruction, but the moderation of the πάθη:

> De Virt. m. 443 c: For reason . . . does not aim at completely destroying passion (this is neither possible nor good) but imposes a limit and a rule upon it and gives origin to the ethical virtues, which are not based on freedom from emotions but on their moderation and on the right mean.
>
> De Virt. m. 444 b: . . . impulse needs reason in order to be limited, so that passions may be moderated and are not allowed to go beyond or to be inferior to the right measure.
>
> De Virt. m. 444 b–c: This is the role according to nature of the practical reason, to eliminate the lack of measure of passions and the faults.
>
> De Virt. m. 449 b: They call joy, will, and caution innocent emotions and not absence of emotions; in this case, they use the right terms, for the innocent emotion arises when reason does not destroy completely passion, but imposes an order and a rule upon it.
>
> De Virt. m. 451 c: The ethical disposition of the soul takes place when, under the effect of reason, passions and movements are given fairness and moderation.
>
> De sera Num. Vind. 551 c: . . . the divine part of virtue . . . mildness and moderation of emotions.

In order to represent the way in which reason rules over the irrational part of the soul, Plutarch, just like Clement, Philo, and Posidonius, resorts to the image of the charioteer, τὸ παθητικὸν ὥσπερ εὐήνιον θρέμμα καὶ πρᾶον ὁ λογισμὸς ἡνιοχεῖ, De Virt. m. 445 b, cf. 445 c, οἷον ὁ Πλάτων ἐξεικονίζει περὶ τὰ τῆς ψυχῆς ὑποζύγια, τοῦ χείρονος πρὸς τὸ βέλτιον ζυγομαχοῦντος ἅμα καὶ τὸν ἡνίοχον διαταράττοντος.

Albinus considers the μετριοπαθής as the virtuous man who stays in the middle between the ἀμετροπαθής or ὑπερπαθής and the ἀπαθής (Did. 184. 23–4). That he is in favour of μετριοπάθεια can be inferred from the following passages:

rejects ἀπάθεια and declares himself in favour of μετριοπάθεια (see p. 101 below) but, at the same time, adopts the doctrine of the αὐτάρκεια of virtue and resorts to the Platonic and Stoic picture of the *sapiens* who remains happy in every circumstance of his life (see p. 70 above). It naturally follows, from Antiochus' adoption of μετριοπάθεια, that he regarded virtue as a μεσότης (see Strache, *Ekl.* 37).

Did. 184. 27–30: Since moderation of passions is the best thing, and moderation is nothing but the right mean between excess and defect, such virtues are based on the right mean, for they keep us in the middle as far as passions are concerned. *Did.* 182. 12 ff.: Some passions are wild, some others fair; to the latter belong those passions which are natural and necessary in man and suitable for him; this condition persists as long as passions remain moderate.[1]

Taurus also rejects the complete destruction of the πάθη and prefers μετριοπάθεια:

Gellius, *Noct. Att.* i. 26. 11: *nam sicut aliorum omnium, quos Latini philosophi affectus vel affectiones, Graeci πάθη appellant . . . non privationem utilem esse censuit, quam Graeci στέρησιν dicunt, sed mediocritatem, quam μετριότητα illi appellant.*[2]

Maximus of Tyre insists on the idea of the rule of the λόγος over the πάθη which he considers as a disease of the soul,[3] and resorts to the image of the charioteer.[4] That the moral standard is represented for him by μετριοπάθεια can be seen from the following evidence:

Or. i. 19 b (p. 4. 18–20): ξυναρμοζόμενος [sc. ὁ τῶν φιλοσόφων λόγος] τοῖς πάθεσι καὶ πεπαίνων μὲν τὰ σκυθρωπά, συνευφημοῦν δὲ τοῖς φαιδροτέροις.
Or. xxvii. 116 b–117 a (p. 328. 1 ff.): καὶ περὶ ψυχὴν τὴν ἔχουσαν καλῶς . . . σῴζει μὲν ὁ λόγος, σῴζεται δὲ τὰ πάθη . . . καὶ μετρεῖ μὲν ὁ λόγος, μετρεῖται δὲ τὰ πάθη.

The ethics of μετριοπάθεια is to be found in Neoplatonism as well, where it is brought into connection with the first of the four classes of virtues, that of the πολιτικαὶ ἀρεταί. It is interesting to observe that Porphyry, in describing it, resorts to the Stoic idea

[1] With the last sentence of this passage it is worth comparing Clement, *Strom.* ii. 109. 1 (ii. 172. 21), μηδὲν ὑπεροριζούσαις τῶν κατὰ φύσιν ἐπὶ τὸ μᾶλλον ἢ παρὰ φύσιν, ἔνθα τὸ ἁμαρτητικὸν φύεται. Albinus also compares the λόγος to a κυβερνήτης, *Did.* 184. 5–6. The way in which he describes the opposition between reason and πάθος (*Did.* 176. 35 ff., cf. 177. 2–3 οὐδὲ τῶν ἐναντιουμένων . . . περὶ αὐτὸ . . . δυναμένων συστῆναι) reminds us of what Philo says in *Leg. Alleg.* iii. 116 (i. 139. 7–8), ἐπεὶ μάχεται ὁ λόγος τῷ πάθει καὶ ἐν αὐτῷ μένειν οὐ δύναται.
[2] Cf. K. Praechter in his article on Taurus, *RE*, Zweite Reihe, Neunter Halbband, col. 62; see also Moreschini, *ASNSP* 33 (1964), 21 and 23, and *Studi sul 'De dogm. Plat.' di Apuleio*, 95.
[3] See especially the whole section of *Or.* xxii. 116 a (pp. 325. 13–326. 11).
[4] *Or.* i. 23 b (p. 14. 17 ff.).

of the obedience to nature and to the λόγος which we have noticed both in Clement and in Philo: αἱ μὲν οὖν τοῦ πολιτικοῦ ἐν μετριοπαθείᾳ κείμεναι, τῷ ἕπεσθαι καὶ ἀκολουθεῖν τῷ λογισμῷ τοῦ καθήκοντος κατὰ τὰς πράξεις (Sent. xxii. 2, p. 17. 17); ἡ μὲν οὖν κατὰ τὰς πολιτικὰς ἀρετὰς διάθεσις ἐν μετριοπαθείᾳ θεωρεῖται, τέλος ἔχουσα τὸ ζῆν ὡς ἄνθρωπος κατὰ φύσιν (Sent. xxii. 3, p. 19. 3–5). The same view occurs in Plotinus: αἱ μὲν τοίνυν πολιτικαὶ ἀρεταί ... ἀμείνους ποιοῦσιν ὁρίζουσαι καὶ μετροῦσαι τὰς ἐπιθυμίας καὶ ὅλως τὰ πάθη, Enn. i. 2. 2, cf. i. 2. 7, ἡ σωφροσύνη ἐκείνη μετροῦσα (i.e. the σωφροσύνη belonging to the class of the political virtues).

5. The ethics of μετριοπάθεια does not represent for Clement the ideal of perfection. If in the first ethical stage the doctrine of the right mean appears to be sufficient (see Paed. ii. 16. 4, vol. i. 166. 2–4) in so far as it produces the moderation of the πάθη (Strom. ii. 39. 4 and 109. 1), in the higher ethics of the perfect Christian it must be replaced by a stronger ethical rule, the κατόρθωμα: οὕτως καὶ πᾶσα πρᾶξις γνωστικοῦ μὲν κατόρθωμα, τοῦ δὲ ἁπλῶς πιστοῦ μέση πρᾶξις, Strom. vi. 111. 3.[1] This means, as Clement openly maintains, that in order to reach perfection it is necessary to pass from the simple moderation of the πάθη to their complete destruction or, in other words, from μετριοπάθεια to ἀπάθεια: ἡ κατάστασις δὲ ἡ τοιάδε ἀπάθειαν ἐργάζεται, οὐ μετριοπάθειαν (Strom. vi. 74. 1); ὁ τοίνυν μετριοπαθήσας τὰ πρῶτα καὶ εἰς ἀπάθειαν μελετήσας (Strom. vi. 105. 1); ἀπεκδυσάμενος τὰ πάθη ὁ πιστὸς ἡμῶν μέτεισιν ἐπὶ βελτίονα τῆς προτέρας μονήν (Strom. vi. 109. 3). The sharp distinction between two classes of men, which corresponds to the distinction between pistis and gnosis,[2] appears clearly also in the twofold ethical stage μετριοπάθεια / ἀπάθεια.

In Clement's adoption of ἀπάθεια many a scholar has seen a direct influence of Stoic ethics.[3] Nobody has, however, adequately

---

[1] The distinction between κατόρθωμα and μέση πρᾶξις or καθῆκον goes back to Panaetius (see Zeller, iii/1. 586); Philo also, however, seems to know it in so far as he connects both the κατορθώματα and the καθήκοντα with virtues the symbols of which are, according to him, the different trees growing in the garden of Eden: see Leg. Alleg. i. 56 (i. 75. 6–8).   [2] See chapter III, pp. 137 ff. below.
[3] See, for instance, Merk, 67–8; de Faye, 274–313; Daskalakis, 97 ff.; P. Guilloux, RAM 3 (1922), 296; Pohlenz, NGA, phil.-hist. Kl. (1943), 166 ff., and Die Stoa i. 421. Völker, Der wahre Gnostiker ..., 524 ff., thinks on the contrary that ἀπάθεια is simply a term which Clement borrowed from the Porch and filled with a 'Christian meaning': see particularly his criticism of de Faye's view according to which Clement's ἀπάθεια is completely Stoic (p. 525 n. 1).

pointed out the close agreement which exists between Clement, Philo, and Neoplatonism both in the sharp distinction between a lower and a higher ethical stage and in the adoption of the Stoic term ἀπάθεια for the designation of moral perfection.[1] In the third book of his *Legum Allegoriae* Philo draws a sharp line between Aaron, who simply imposes the rule of reason over his πάθη but is unable to destroy them completely, and Moses, who, on the contrary, has achieved their total destruction: 'whereas Aaron . . . having this passion tries to heal it by means of the saving medicines which have been mentioned, Moses, on the contrary, thinks that anger must be entirely cut off from the soul, since he is not satisfied with moderation of passions, but with the complete absence of them' (*Leg. Alleg.* iii. 129); 'but Aaron, making gradual progress in a secondary position, practises, as I have said, the moderation of passions, for he is not able to cut off his breast and his anger' (*Leg. Alleg.* iii. 132); 'because he [i.e. Moses] being perfect, does not aim at mediocrity, nor does he want the simple moderation of passions, but, owing to the abundance of his resources, completely cuts off all passions; on the other hand those ⟨who are satisfied with⟩ mediocrity[2] first make war against passions but soon afterwards come to terms and arrange a truce with them' (*Leg. Alleg.* iii. 134).

In these passages of Philo the difference between a lower and a higher ethical stage is expressed as clearly as in Clement. Particularly striking is the use in both authors of the same *termini technici* μετριοπάθεια / ἀπάθεια. That for Philo, just as for Clement, ἀπάθεια represents moral perfection, can be inferred from the following passages as well:

Leg. Alleg. ii. 100 (i. 110. 28): ἀπάθειαν, τὸ κάλλιστον, καρπώσεται.

Leg. Alleg. ii. 102 (i. 111. 8–9): εἰ γὰρ ἀπάθεια κατάσχῃ τὴν ψυχήν, τελέως εὐδαιμονήσει.

Leg. Alleg. iii. 131 (i. 142. 9 ff.): μοῖραν γὰρ ὁ θεὸς ἔνειμεν ἀρίστην τὸ ἐκτέμνειν τὰ πάθη δύνασθαι. ὁρᾷς πῶς ὁ τέλειος τελείαν ἀπάθειαν ἀεὶ μελετᾷ.

---

[1] Pohlenz, *Die Stoa* i. 397 and 421, has noticed the correspondence between Clement and Porphyry but does not seem to have taken it duly into account. Rather, his remarks sound incidental.

[2] I should like to put a ⟨φρονοῦντες⟩ after οἱ δὲ βραχέως καὶ οὐ μεγάλως: cf., a few lines above, the exact parallel represented by the words βραχὺ καὶ ταπεινὸν οὐδὲν φρονεῖ.

ETHICS 105

Leg. Alleg. iii. 140 (i. 143. 24 f.): ὁ μὲν τέλειος ὅλον ἐκτέμνων τὸν θυμόν . . .
De Prov. i. 56 Aucher: *moderate rem accipit* [sc. *iustus*] *animo passione omni carente minimeque perturbato.*
De Prov. i. 66: *iustus nullam omnino in se patitur passionem.*[1]

In Neoplatonism Plotinus and Porphyry point out, exactly as do Clement and Philo, the distinction between a lower and a higher ethical stage. If the task of the political virtues is, as we have seen, to achieve μετριοπάθεια, the goal of the two higher classes of virtues (namely the cathartic and the theoretical virtues) is the more perfect ἀπάθεια:

Plotinus, *Enn.* i. 2. 3: τὴν δὲ τοιαύτην διάθεσιν τῆς ψυχῆς καθ᾽ ἣν νοεῖ τε καὶ ἀπαθὴς οὕτως ἐστίν . . .
Idem, *Enn.* i. 2. 6: ἡ δὲ ἀνδρεία ἀπάθεια . . .
Idem, *Enn.* i. 2. 7: ἡ δὲ [sc. σωφροσύνη] ὅλως ἀναιροῦσα [sc. τὰ πάθη] . . .
Porphyry, *Sent.* xxii. 3 (p. 19. 6): ἡ δὲ κατὰ τὰς θεωρητικὰς [sc. διάθεσις] ἐν ἀπαθείᾳ.[2]

The adoption of the Stoic ideal of ἀπάθεια naturally leads Clement to resort to Stoic topics in his description of the perfect Christian, as it appears especially in the seventh book of the *Stromateis*. Clement lays a strong emphasis on his being completely satisfied with the permanent possession of *gnosis*, which has destroyed in him any desire or need of external goods,[3] as well as on his total independence from any external event.[4] Some scholars have dwelt at some length on this argument, and it is therefore not necessary to repeat what they have said.[5] I only wish to point

[1] Pohlenz, *NGA*, phil.-hist. Kl. (1942), 460–1, has pointed out the presence of the ideal of ἀπάθεια in Philo, but has not drawn the necessary conclusions from the correspondence between him and Clement.
[2] It must be pointed out that in Plato's system also the distinction between a lower and a higher ethical stage, between μετριοπάθεια and ἀπάθεια, seems to be implied: if the main feature of the ethics of the *Republic* is represented by the moderation of desires and pleasures and by their submission to reason (see the evidence quoted in footnote 4, p. 99 above), in the *Phaedo* the philosopher is represented as being completely free from any emotion and desire: see, for instance, 81 a 6–8, καὶ φόβων καὶ ἀγρίων ἐρώτων . . . ἀπηλλαγμένῃ, and 83 b 5–7, ἡ τοῦ ὡς ἀληθῶς φιλοσόφου ψυχὴ οὕτως ἀπέχεται τῶν ἡδονῶν τε καὶ ἐπιθυμιῶν καὶ λυπῶν καὶ φόβων καθ᾽ ὅσον δύναται.
[3] See, for instance, *Strom.* vii. 18. 2 (iii. 13. 25–14. 1) and vii. 44. 4–5 (iii. 33. 14–17).
[4] *Strom.* vii. 18. 1 (iii. 13. 21–2) and vii. 83. 1 (iii. 59. 12 ff.).
[5] See, for instance, de Faye, 274–313; P. Gouilloux, *RAM* 3 (1922), 288, and Pohlenz, *NGA*, phil.-hist. Kl. (1943), 166–75. G. Bardy, *VSAM* 39 (1934, Suppl.),

out here that such a representation of the γνωστικός is not peculiar to Clement, but is rather due to the Platonizing religious *Stimmung* of the first centuries A.D. The image of the Stoic *sapiens*[1] strongly influenced the pictures which such authors as Philo, Apuleius, and Plotinus gave of the perfect man. Clement's description of the γνωστικός is worth comparing with the analogous descriptions which occur at the end of the first book of Philo's *De Providentia*,[2] in the second book of *De Platone* of Apuleius,[3] and, as Witt has observed, in the fourth book of the first *Ennead* of Plotinus (especially from chapter 4 on) bearing the title Περὶ εὐδαιμονίας.[4]

6. The highest moral ideal is expressed in Clement not only by the term ἀπάθεια, but also by the Platonic formula which occurs in *Theaetetus* 176 b, ὁμοίωσις θεῷ κατὰ τὸ δυνατόν. It represents, in Clement's thought, the true human τέλος.[5] Compared with it, the Stoic formula ἀκολούθως τῇ φύσει ζῆν, which Clement had adopted in the inferior ethics of μετριοπάθεια, is rejected without any hesitation: ἐντεῦθεν οἱ Στωϊκοὶ τὸ ἀκολούθως τῇ φύσει ζῆν τέλος εἶναι ἐδογμάτισαν, τὸν θεὸν εἰς φύσιν μετονομάσαντες ἀπρεπῶς, *Strom*. ii. 101. 1.[6] Just as μετριοπάθεια is no longer sufficient in moral perfection, but must become ἀπάθεια, in the same way the Stoic formula ἀκολούθως τῇ φύσει ζῆν, which fits the lower ethics, appears to be worthless at the higher ethical level, and must therefore be replaced by ὁμοίωσις θεῷ. A similar idea can be

100–1, does not seem to like very much the presence of Stoic features in Clement's description of the γνωστικός: 'Une inquiétude cependant nous prend en lisant ces lignes. N'avons-nous pas trouvé ailleurs des pensées analogues et des philosophes païens n'ont-ils pas parlé à peu près dans les mêmes termes que Clément? . . . Ses conseils rendent un son qui n'est pas exclusivement chrétien.'
[1] Plato also, however, has given a similar picture of the philosopher in the *Phaedo* (see above, p. 105 n. 2); the way in which he describes the δίκαιος in the second book of the *Republic* (ii. 361 e, cf. p. 68 above) should also be taken into account.
[2] See particularly §§ 56, 62, 63, 64, 66, and 69 Aucher. P. Wendland, *Philos' Schrift über die Vorsehung*, 17 f., has pointed out the Stoic origin of the ideas which underlie Philo's description of the *iustus*.
[3] See particularly §§ 248, 249, 250, 252, and 253 Thomas.
[4] See Witt, *CQ* 25 (1931), 203 n. 13.
[5] See Clement's eulogy of the Platonic ὁμοίωσις in *Strom*. ii. 100. 3.
[6] Ἀπρεπῶς is Stählin's correction of the εὐπρεπῶς of L. This correction is absolutely necessary, since Clement could never have said τὸν θεὸν εἰς φύσιν μετονομάσαντες εὐπρεπῶς about the Stoics, against whose materialism he does not conceal his polemical attitude (see chapter I, p. 48 above).

found in Philo and in Plotinus. If in *De Opif. M.* 143 Philo stresses the importance of living according to nature and adopts the Stoic conception of man as a κοσμοπολίτης,[1] on the other hand in *De Gig.* 51 (ii. 53. 14 ff.) he makes it clear that there can be a higher life than that of the obedience to nature, peculiar to the κοσμοπολίτης; such a life consists in the close communion with the world of the ideas, which, in Philo's opinion, are the thoughts of God himself and form all together his Logos:[2] θεοῦ δὲ ἄνθρωποι ἱερεῖς καὶ προφῆται, οἵτινες οὐκ ἠξίωσαν πολιτείας τῆς παρὰ τῷ κόσμῳ τυχεῖν καὶ κοσμοπολῖται γενέσθαι, τὸ δὲ αἰσθητὸν πᾶν ὑπερκύψαντες εἰς τὸν νοητὸν κόσμον μετανέστησαν, κἀκεῖθι ᾤκησαν, ἐγγραφέντες ἀφθάρτων καὶ ἀσωμάτων ἰδεῶν πολιτείᾳ.[3] Plotinus, at the end of his treatise 'About virtues', maintains that the life of the perfect man is no longer the life which is connected with the political virtues, but a higher life, which is that of the gods: καὶ ὅλως ζῶν οὐχὶ τὸν ἀνθρώπου βίον τὸν τοῦ ἀγαθοῦ ὃν ἀξιοῖ ἡ πολιτικὴ ἀρετὴ διαζῆν, ἀλλὰ τοῦτον μὲν καταλιπών, ἄλλον δὲ ἑλόμενος τὸν τῶν θεῶν· πρὸς γὰρ τούτοις ⟨αὐτῷ⟩ . . . ἡ ὁμοίωσις, *Enn.* i. 2. 7. It is exactly the idea contained in these two passages of Philo and of Plotinus that explains Clement's temporary adoption of the Stoic formula and its subsequent rejection.

H. Merki has made a detailed inquiry into the use of the expression ὁμοίωσις θεῷ in Greek philosophy, in Philo, and in the Greek Christian authors up to Gregory of Nyssa.[4] His book represents, without any doubt, a most relevant contribution to the attempts made to define the meaning which this Platonic topic assumes in the works of different authors.[5] Those who wish to know exactly what Clement meant by ὁμοίωσις θεῷ will feel entirely satisfied after reading the pages which Merki has devoted to him.[6] Here I shall confine myself to expounding briefly Merki's conclusions and to drawing attention to some important

---

[1] Cf. p. 94 above. [2] Cf. chapter III, pp. 204–5 below.

[3] Philo also praises the Platonic ὁμοίωσις in extremely warm terms: see *De Fuga et Inv.* 63 and *De Opif. M.* 144 (for further evidence in Philo see Pohlenz's note S 377 Z 39 in *Die Stoa* ii. 184). On the ideal of contemplative life both in Clement and in Philo, which is connected with *gnosis*, we shall have to speak more in detail later on (see chapter III, pp. 163–9 below).

[4] H. Merki, Ὁμοίωσις θεῷ . . . (Freiburg in der Schweiz, 1952).

[5] See W. Jaeger's review of Merki's book in *Gnomon*, 27 (1955), 573–81, republished in his *Scripta Minora* (Roma, 1960), ii. 469–81.

[6] See Merki, 45–60.

108 ETHICS

correspondences between Clement, Philo, and Neoplatonism which, as far as I can see, Merki has not worked out.

The first thing to observe is that Clement is inclined to bring the word ὁμοίωσις which he found in the *Theaetetus* into connection with the ὁμοίωσις of Gen. 1. 26: ποιήσωμεν τὸν ἄνθρωπον κατ' εἰκόνα ἡμετέραν καὶ ὁμοίωσιν. He does not consider the two expressions κατ' εἰκόνα and καθ' ὁμοίωσιν as synonyms: whereas the expression κατ' εἰκόνα means for him that man, when he was created, was given by God a rational faculty which was a copy of the divine Logos, the image of God,[1] the expression καθ' ὁμοίωσιν does not refer, in his opinion, to the natural kinship with God which man has possessed since his creation, but points on the contrary to the moral perfection which man must reach during his life by practising virtue. In other words, whereas the εἰκών is a natural possession of everybody, ὁμοίωσις is achieved by means of personal efforts.[2] That this must have been Clement's view is shown by the passage of *Strom.* ii. 131. 5 (ii. 185. 23–8), where he practically identifies the Platonic ὁμοίωσις with the ὁμοίωσις of Genesis: τοῦτο δὲ [sc. perfection] ἐν ἐπιστήμῃ τοῦ ἀγαθοῦ τίθεται [sc. Plato] καὶ ἐν ἐξομοιώσει τῇ πρὸς τὸν θεόν, ὁμοίωσιν ἀποφαινόμενος "δίκαιον καὶ ὅσιον μετὰ φρονήσεως εἶναι". ἢ οὐχ οὕτως τινὲς τῶν ἡμετέρων[3] τὸ μὲν "κατ' εἰκόνα" εὐθέως κατὰ τὴν γένεσιν εἰληφέναι τὸν ἄνθρωπον, τὸ "καθ' ὁμοίωσιν" δὲ ὕστερον κατὰ τὴν τελείωσιν μέλλειν ἀπολαμβάνειν ἀποδέχονται; Here we cannot speak, as perhaps Völker would, of 'platonische Wortlaut und christlicher Inhalt' or of a 'christliche Umdeutung einer platonischen Formel'; on the contrary, the passage of *Theaetetus* 176 b is used to interpret Genesis 1. 26.[4]

Clement was led to consider ὁμοίωσις θεῷ as a product of human effort by Philo. Although Philo, in *De Opif. M.* 71, seems to regard the expressions κατ' εἰκόνα and καθ' ὁμοίωσιν as synonyms, in so far as he thinks that Moses added the words καθ' ὁμοίωσιν in order to make it clear that human reason was

---

[1] Cf. chapter I, p. 15 above.
[2] On this point see especially the pertinent remarks of A. Mayer, 6–7. Cf. also Merki, 53 n. 3.
[3] The expression τινὲς τῶν ἡμετέρων refers most probably to the Christian teachers of Clement among whom Pantaenus must be included (cf. *Strom.* i. 11. 1–2, vol. ii. 8. 18–9. 3).
[4] On the close relationship between philosophy and interpretation of Scripture see my remarks on pp. 57 ff. above.

the true image of the divine Logos (προσεπεσημήνατο ἐπειπὼν τῷ κατ' εἰκόνα τὸ καθ' ὁμοίωσιν εἰς ἔμφασιν ἀκριβοῦς ἐκμαγείου τρανὸν τύπον ἔχοντος), on the other hand, he lays emphasis on the fact that it depends on man to keep his own reason spotless so that it may always remain the true image of the divine Logos. This is what Philo implies when he says γενόμενος εἰκὼν κατὰ τὸν ἡγεμόνα νοῦν ἐν ψυχῇ, δέον ἀκηλίδωτον τὴν εἰκόνα φυλάξαι καθ' ὅσον οἷόν τε ἦν ἐπακολουθήσαντα ταῖς τοῦ γεννήσαντος ἀρεταῖς, De Virt. 205 (v. 329. 10ff.). In this passage the words καθ' ὅσον οἷόν τε ἦν remind us of the Platonic expression κατὰ τὸ δυνατόν, whereas the sentence δέον ἀκηλίδωτον τὴν εἰκόνα φυλάξαι . . . ἐπακολουθήσαντα ταῖς τοῦ γεννήσαντος ἀρεταῖς clearly hints at the practical realization of ὁμοίωσις θεῷ. Philo here has in mind both the *Theaetetus* and Genesis.

By means of a careful analysis of several passages of Clement Merki has shown what, according to him, makes man ὅμοιος θεῷ: steadfastness (p. 48), absence of emotions (pp. 48–52), purity and contemplation (p. 51), faith, love, and searching for God (p. 52), separation from the sensible things and communion with the intelligible realities (p. 53), gentleness, benevolence, and religiousness (p. 54), forgivingness (p. 55), kindness (p. 55), absence of needs (p. 56), and imitation of Christ (pp. 57–60). Among these topics that of purity and contemplation and that of separation from the sensible things and communion with the intelligible realities are closely related to the idea of *gnosis*, and therefore deserve a more detailed inquiry, which will be attempted in the next chapter.[1] Other topics such as steadfastness (βεβαιότης), religiousness (θεοσέβεια), and kindness (εὐεργεσία) are also characteristic of Philo, as both Merki[2] and Völker[3] have shown.

It is especially the connection between ὁμοίωσις and ἀπάθεια that links Clement both with Philo and with Neoplatonism.

---

[1] See chapter III, pp. 163 ff. below. Jaeger also has pointed out that the close connection between ὁμοίωσις and *gnosis* deserves further investigation: 'Die hier auftauchenden Probleme, die mit dem Entstehen einer christlichen Gnosis bei Clemens zusammenhängen . . . konnten natürlich in diesem lexicalbegriffsgeschichtlichen Zusammenhang nicht zu voller Entfaltung gebracht werden' (review of Merki's book, *Scripta Minora* ii. 475).

[2] See the section which Merki has devoted to Philo, especially pp. 38–44.

[3] See Völker, *Fortschritt und Vollendung bei Philo von Alexandrien* (*TU* 49), 253, 319, and 330 ff.

Since God is, by his own nature, completely ἀπαθής,[1] it also follows that ὁμοίωσις θεῷ means for Clement the total ἀπάθεια, as the following evidence shows:

Strom. ii. 103. 1 (ii. 169. 24–5): ἤ γε μὴν καρτερία καὶ αὐτὴ εἰς τὴν θείαν ὁμοίωσιν βιάζεται, δι᾽ ὑπομονῆς ἀπάθειαν καρπουμένη. *Strom.* iv. 138. 1 (ii. 309. 11–13): οὐκ ἐγκρατὴς οὗτος ἔτι, ἀλλ᾽ ἐν ἕξει γέγονεν ἀπαθείας, σχῆμα θεῖον ἐπενδύσασθαι ἀναμένων. *Strom.* iv. 147. 1 (ii. 313. 14–15): καλοῦ δὲ εἶναι ἄμεινον τὸ διὰ τὴν πρὸς τὸ θεῖον ἐξομοίωσιν ἀπαθῆ καὶ ἐνάρετον γενέσθαι. *Strom.* vii. 13. 3 (iii. 10. 23 f.): ἐξομοιούμενος θεῷ ὁ γνωστικός, τῷ φύσει τὸ ἀπαθὲς κεκτημένῳ. *Strom.* vii. 84. 2 (iii. 60. 5 ff.): ἀπαθείας, καθ᾽ ἢν ἡ τελείωσις, ἐξομοιουμένη θεῷ. *Strom.* vii. 86. 5 (iii. 61. 32–62. 1): μετὰ γνώσεως τὰ πάθη τὰ ψυχικὰ ἀπερρύψασθε, εἰς τὸ ἐξομοιοῦσθαι ὅση δύναμις τῇ ἀγαθότητι τῆς τοῦ θεοῦ προνοίας.[2]

Philo also maintains several times that God is without any need and completely ἀπαθής:[3] this implies that for him as well ὁμοίωσις θεῷ is one and the same thing with ἀπάθεια. The same combination of ἀπάθεια and ὁμοίωσις which we have observed in Clement occurs also in Neoplatonism:

Plotinus, *Enn.* i. 2. 3: τὴν δὲ τοιαύτην διάθεσιν τῆς ψυχῆς, καθ᾽ ἢν νοεῖ τε καὶ ἀπαθὴς οὕτως ἐστίν, εἴ τις ὁμοίωσιν λέγοι πρὸς θεόν, οὐκ ἂν ἁμαρτάνοι.[4]

Idem, *Enn.* i. 2. 6: ἡ δὲ ἀνδρεία ἀπάθεια καθ᾽ ὁμοίωσιν τοῦ πρὸς ὃ βλέπει, ἀπαθὲς ὂν τὴν φύσιν.[5]

---

[1] See, for instance, *Strom.* ii. 40. 1 (ii. 134. 10), ii. 72. 2 (ii. 151. 13), ii. 81. 1 (ii. 155. 15 ff.), iv. 151. 1 (ii. 315. 16 ff.), v. 24. 2 (ii. 341. 2), vi. 73. 6 (ii. 468. 26), vi. 137. 4 (ii. 501. 22–3).

[2] Besides Merki, other scholars also have observed the connection between ὁμοίωσις θεῷ and ἀπάθεια in Clement: see, for instance, G. W. Butterworth, *JTS* 17 (1916), 158–9; O. Faller, *Gregorianum* 6 (1925), 417; Pohlenz, *NGA*, phil.-hist. Kl. (1943), 166; T. Rüther, 66; W. Völker, *Der wahre Gnostiker . . .*, 532–3; J. Wytzes, *VC* 9 (1955), 149; and J. Waszink, *Entretiens Hardt* iii. 167–8. That Clement's views are similar to those of Philo and of Neoplatonism has, however, not been pointed out.

[3] See, for instance, *De Opif. M.* 8, *Leg. Alleg.* iii. 2, iii. 81 and 203, *De Cher.* 44, 46, 86, *De Sacr. Ab. et C.* 101, *Quod det. pot. ins. sol.* 54, 55, 56, *De Post. C.* 4 and 28, *Quod D. sit imm.* 7, 22, 52, 56, *De Plant.* 35.

[4] Merki also, p. 19, refers to this passage of Plotinus.

[5] These words of Plotinus are faithfully reproduced by Porphyry, *Sent.* xxii. 4 (p. 20. 16–18).

Porphyry, *Sent.* xxii (p. 19. 6–7): ἡ δὲ κατὰ τὰς θεωρητικὰς ἐν ἀπαθείᾳ, ἧς τέλος ἡ πρὸς τὸν θεὸν ὁμοίωσις.
Idem, *De Abst.* ii. 43 (172. 18–19): θεῷ ... ὁμοιοῦσθαι, ὃ γίνεται δι' ἀπαθείας.

In this way, it is possible to observe some important correspondences between Clement, Philo, and Neoplatonism: the presence, in all of them, of the twofold ethical stage μετριοπάθεια / ἀπάθεια; the tendency to consider God as completely ἀπαθής; and consequently also the tendency to identify ὁμοίωσις with ἀπάθεια. Clement's ethical ideal resembles much more that of Philo and of Neoplatonism than that of such authors as Plutarch, Taurus, and Albinus who, as far as we can see, do not go beyond the ethics of μετριοπάθεια.[1]

But there are some other implications in Clement's conception of ὁμοίωσις which it is necessary to illustrate. Not only God, but also Christ is ἀπαθής. As he, in the lower ethics, had taught men to heal and moderate their πάθη, in the same way he is here the teacher and model of the perfect ἀπάθεια:

Strom. v. 94. 5 (ii. 388. 14–16): εἰκὼν μὲν γὰρ θεοῦ λόγος θεῖος καὶ βασιλικός, ἄνθρωπος ἀπαθής.
Strom. vi. 71. 2 (ii. 467. 13–15): αὐτὸς δὲ ἀπαξαπλῶς ἀπαθὴς ἦν.
Strom. vii. 7. 2 (iii. 7. 4): τοῦ κυρίου ἀπαθοῦς ἀνάρχως γενομένου.
Strom. vii. 7. 5 (iii. 7. 15–16): εἰς ἕξιν ἀπαθείας ἐπαίδευσεν.
Strom. vii. 72. 1 (iii. 51. 33–4): εἰς μὲν οὖν μόνος ὁ ἀνεπιθύμητος ἐξ ἀρχῆς, ὁ κύριος ὁ φιλάνθρωπος.[2]

It is Christ whom men must try to imitate in order to reach the ὁμοίωσις with the ἀπαθής God: ὥστε ἕνεκά γε τούτων ἐξομοιοῦσθαι βιάζεται τῷ διδασκάλῳ εἰς ἀπάθειαν, *Strom.* vi. 72. 1; ποιότητά τινα κυριακὴν λαβὼν εἰς ἐξομοίωσιν θεοῦ, *Strom.* vi. 150. 3; ὅσοι δὲ ἐξομοιοῦσθαι σπεύδουσιν τῷ ὑπ' αὐτοῦ δεδομένῳ χαρακτῆρι

---

[1] As far as we can see from the extant remains of the Middle Platonists, Apuleius seems to be the only exponent of Middle Platonism who has openly adopted ἀπάθεια instead of μετριοπάθεια: in *De Plat.* ii. 247 he says: *perfecte sapientem esse non posse dicit Plato nisi ... purgata et effaecata animi voluptate.* See also, on this point, C. Moreschini, *Studi sul 'De dogm. Plat.' di Apuleio*, 95.

[2] This role of Christ has been pointed out by some scholars: see, for instance, A. Koch, *ZAM* 7 (1932), 363; Pohlenz, *NGA*, phil.-hist. Kl. (1943), 128: 'dem wahren Seelenarzt, dem Heiland, der über die Metriopathie hinausführt und in der affektlosen Liebe den Weg zur absoluten Apathie, zur Ruhe in Gott und zum wahren Seelenfrieden weist' (cf. *Die Stoa* i. 421); Rüther, 63–79; Völker, 531, and Merki, 57–60. Merki, 50, reproduces in the text the sentence of Pohlenz quoted above without making it clear that it belongs to Pohlenz, and not to him.

112 ETHICS

ἀνεπιθύμητοι . . . γενέσθαι βιάζονται, *Strom.* vii. 72. 1; οὗτος ἡμῖν
εἰκὼν ἦν ἡ ἀκηλίδωτος, τούτῳ παντὶ σθένει πειρατέον ἐξομοιοῦν τὴν
ψυχήν, *Paed.* i. 4. 2.[1] This helps also to understand the meaning
of the following passages:

Strom. iv. 152. 1 (ii. 315. 25–6): εἰς δὲ τὴν ἀπάθειαν θεούμενος ὁ
ἄνθρωπος ἀχράντως μοναδικὸς γίνεται.
Strom. iv. 157. 2 (ii. 318. 5 f.): διὸ καὶ τὸ εἰς αὐτὸν καὶ τὸ δι' αὐτοῦ
πιστεῦσαι μοναδικόν ἐστι γενέσθαι.
Strom. vi. 87. 2 (ii. 475. 16): εἰς μονάδα τελευτώσης τῆς τοῦ δικαίου
προκοπῆς.

It must be remembered that Clement identifies Christ, the Logos,
with the μονάς: both the Logos and the intelligible world which
for him are one and the same thing are called by him μονάς.[2]
Clement, as we shall see later on, found this doctrine in Philo,
who also identifies the intelligible world with the Logos and calls
it μονάς.[3] This is the reason why Clement, when speaking about
the perfection of man, uses such terms as μοναδικός or μονάς:
since Christ, the Logos, is the μονάς, man must become μοναδικός
as well in order to reach the ὁμοίωσις with God. The passages
quoted above reproduce therefore nothing more than the doctrine of ὁμοίωσις from the point of view of the Philonic doctrine,
accepted by Clement.[4]

The whole structure of Clement's ethical system appears to be
deeply influenced by the ethical doctrines of Philo, of Middle
Platonism, and of Neoplatonism. The syncretism of Platonic,
Stoic, and Aristotelian elements which can be observed in the
first four points which have formed the object of our inquiry
is practically the same in Clement, in Philo, in Middle Platonism,

[1] The use of the expression εἰκὼν ἀκηλίδωτος may have been suggested to Clement
by Philo: see the passage of *De Virt.* v. 205 (v. 329. 10 ff.) quoted above (p. 109).
[2] Cf. chapter III, pp. 191 and 207 below. [3] Cf. chapter III, p. 207 below.
[4] Philo also, in describing the highest perfection of man, uses the term μονάς:
see the passages of *Quod D. sit imm.* 11, *De Vita Mos.* ii. 288, and *De spec. Leg.* i. 66
mentioned by Völker, *Der wahre Gnostiker . . .*, 533 n. 1. Völker is right in connect-
ing Clement's passage about the perfect man's becoming μοναδικός with these
passages of Philo. It must, however, be remembered that both in Clement and in
Philo the terms μονάς and μοναδικός hint at the Logos, and not at God, as Völker
seems to believe (pp. 532–3). Both for Clement and for Philo God is above the
μονάς (see chapter III, p. 216 below). That for Clement the term μοναδικός hints
at the Logos is also proved by the fact that the passage of *Strom.* iv. 157. 2 which is
introduced by the causal preposition διό comes immediately after the passage of
Strom. iv. 156. 1–2, where the υἱός is described as πάντα ἕν.

and in Neoplatonism: not only Clement, but also Philo and the exponents of Middle Platonism and of Neoplatonism lay a strong emphasis on the autarky of virtue, on the function of the single cardinal virtues, and on the necessity of moderating desires and passions by submitting the irrational parts of the soul to reason and by obeying the law of nature, established by the Logos. As far as the highest ethical ideal is concerned, however, Clement goes far beyond the limits characteristic of the kind of ethics which seems to have been dominant in Middle Platonism: the simple moderation of passions is for him only a first and inferior ethical stage, a preliminary step towards perfection; perfection itself can only be achieved by means of the total destruction of passions, which alone can enable man to become similar to God. By considering perfection as fully achieved only in the second ethical stage and by identifying the Stoic ideal of ἀπάθεια with the Platonic formula ὁμοίωσις θεῷ he shows a complete agreement both with Philo and with Plotinus and Porphyry (see points 5 and 6 of our inquiry).

And yet there is something which distinguishes Clement from Philo, Middle Platonism, and Neoplatonism. If the fundamental features of Clement's ethical system are also characteristic of Philo and of the exponents of Middle Platonism and of Neo-platonism; if Clement's ethical ideal is also the ideal which appears in the ethics of Philo and of Neoplatonism, the way in which the practical achievement of the moderation of passions and of their destruction takes place is not perfectly identical in Clement on the one hand, and in Philo and in the whole Platonic tradition on the other. During our inquiry we have had occasion to point out that, for Clement, it is Christ, the Logos, who has the task of healing the passions of man, and of guiding him gradually towards perfection by educating him.[1] In other words, according to Clement, human reason alone, though of divine origin, by no means suffices to achieve first the moderation of passions and then their total destruction and moral perfection: the divinity itself, i.e. the Son of God, must help man in his fight against the πάθη, in his efforts to reach ἀπάθεια and ὁμοίωσις θεῷ. For Philo also the divine Logos, the Son of God,[2] accomplishes,

---

[1] See pp. 96–7 and 111 above.
[2] For Philo also the Logos is the son of God: see, for instance, *De Agr.* 51 (ii. 106. 1–2) πρωτόγονον υἱόν.

as we have seen, a most important role in ethics; but even when he is represented as the perpetual source of virtues,[1] he remains still the immanent law of the universe in the Stoic and Platonic sense[2] and consequently is only the ethical norm for man;[3] and when he heals human passions, he is scarcely more than this law and the activity of human reason which is derived from him. For the Christian Clement the Logos, though still accomplishing these functions,[4] does not limit himself to them: he is not simply the impersonal law of φύσις and of ethics, nor does he represent only human reason; being one and the same thing with Christ, his intervention in the human sphere is far more concrete and personal: he teaches, he educates, he guides, he is the παιδαγωγός,[5] both when he is a metaphysical principle and after his descent on the earth, when he acts as a historical person. The λόγος διὰ τοῦ παιδαγωγοῦ παραδιδόμενος of which Clement speaks in *Paed.* iii. 35. 2 is not simply the virtue originated by the universal Logos of the Porch and of Philo:[6] the words διὰ τοῦ παιδαγωγοῦ παραδιδόμενος hint also at the direct and personal intervention of the Son of God.

Also in the case of Plato and of the whole Platonic tradition it is not possible to speak of a direct intervention of the divinity in human ethics. It is true that Plato, in the *Meno*, speaks of ἀρετή as being granted to some men θείᾳ μοίρᾳ;[7] that, in the *Timaeus*, he represents philosophy as coming from heaven;[8] and that, in the *Phaedo*, he gives philosophy the task of freeing the soul from the bonds of the body.[9] But the ἀρετή of the *Meno*

---

[1] See particularly the passage of *De Plant.* 121 (ii. 157. 13–14) quoted on p. 64 above.

[2] Not only for the Porch but also for Plato the universe is endowed with an immanent, rational law which is practically one and the same thing with the world-soul: see the evidence quoted in chapter III, p. 210 below.

[3] See pp. 75–6, 93–4 above.   [4] See pp. 93, 96–7 above.

[5] These functions of Christ appear particularly evident in the *Paedagogus*: see, for instance, *Paed.* iii. 99. 1 (i. 290. 9), πάντα ὁ λόγος ποιεῖ καὶ διδάσκει καὶ παιδαγωγεῖ.

[6] On this passage of the *Paedagogus* see also p. 64 above.

[7] *Meno* 99 e 5–6 and 100 b 2–3. Clement quotes these passages of the *Meno* in *Strom.* v. 83. 2–4 and regards the ἀρετή mentioned in them as hinting at the gnostic virtue of the perfect Christian (cf. p. 66, above and footnote 1 on the same page); he uses both passages also as evidence in support of his views about the esoteric character of *gnosis* (see pp. 144 ff. below).

[8] *Tim.* 47 b 1–2.

[9] *Phaedo* 83 a 2–3, οὕτω παραλαβοῦσα ἡ φιλοσοφία ἔχουσαν αὐτῶν τὴν ψυχὴν ἠρέμα παραμυθεῖται καὶ λύειν ἐπιχειρεῖ.

simply means the 'excellence' and 'ability' of the oracle-mongers, the seers, the poets, and the statesmen, and the expression θεία μοίρα can scarcely mean anything more than the divine inspiration by which these people are filled;[1] philosophy is represented in the *Timaeus* as coming from heaven, since it has its origin in the contemplation of the wonderful order and harmony of the universe which enables man to establish this harmony also in his soul;[2] and the philosophy which in the *Phaedo* frees the soul from the bonds of the body is nothing more than the product of the activity of human φρόνησις. The νοῦς which in the *Timaeus*, in the *Philebus*, and in the tenth book of the *Laws* is represented as the highest metaphysical principle[3] does not support man

[1] *Meno* 99 c 11–d 5.

[2] In the sentence ἐξ ὧν ἐπορισάμεθα φιλοσοφίας γένος (*Tim.* 47 a 7–b 1) the words ἐξ ὧν refer to the contemplation of the order of nature which is described in the immediately preceding clause, νῦν δ' ἡμέρα τε καὶ νὺξ ὀφθεῖσαι... (47 a 4–5). As to the relationship between the harmony of the universe and that of the soul the passage of *Timaeus* 47 b 6–c 4 is particularly important: τὰς ἐν οὐρανῷ τοῦ νοῦ κατιδόντες περιόδους χρησαίμεθα ἐπὶ τὰς περιφορὰς τὰς τῆς ἐν ἡμῖν διανοήσεως, συγγενεῖς ἐκείναις οὔσας, ἀταράκτοις τεταραγμένας, ἐκμαθόντες δὲ καὶ λογισμῶν κατὰ φύσιν ὀρθότητος μετασχόντες, μιμούμενοι τὰς τοῦ θεοῦ πάντως ἀπλανεῖς οὔσας, τὰς ἐν ἡμῖν πεπλανημένας καταστησαίμεθα.

[3] In *Timaeus* 39 e 7 the Demiurge is called νοῦς; moreover, in 29 a 5–6 he is described as 'the best of the causes', ὁ ἄριστος τῶν αἰτίων, and in 37 a 1 as 'the best of the intelligible beings', τῶν νοητῶν ἀεί τε ὄντων ὑπὸ τοῦ ἀρίστου. In my opinion, G. Müller, *Zetemata* 3 (1951), 81–2, is quite right, by taking into account the two passages of *Timaeus* 29 a 5–6 and 37 a 1, in identifying the Demiurge of the *Timaeus* both with the αἰτία of *Philebus* 27 b 1, 27 b 9, and 30 c 5 and with the idea of good which in the *Republic* is placed above the intelligible beings and above οὐσία (*Rep.* vi. 509 a 4–5, 509 b 8–10). In the *Philebus* the highest αἰτία is called νοῦς (30 c 5–7, αἰτία οὐ φαύλη, κοσμοῦσα τε καὶ συντάττουσα... σοφία καὶ νοῦς λεγομένη, cf. 30 e 1, νοῦς ἐστι γένους τις τοῦ πάντων αἰτίου λεχθέντος). In *Laws* x. 897 b 1–2 also the highest principle which imparts rationality to the world-soul is represented as νοῦς: νοῦν μὲν προσλαβοῦσα ἀεὶ θεῖον ὀρθῶς θεὸς οὖσα ὀρθὰ καὶ εὐδαίμονα παιδαγωγεῖ πάντα (I follow here the text of A. Diès, *Platon*, Tome xii, Paris, Les Belles Lettres, 1956). Like the νοῦς-Demiurge of the *Timaeus* and the νοῦς-αἰτία of the *Philebus*, the νοῦς of the tenth book of the *Laws* is not something immanent in the universe and practically identical with the world-soul, as Müller, 84 ff., seems to believe; it remains a transcendent principle, as can be inferred both fromt he expression προσλαβοῦσα of 897 b 1, which points to a distinction between the world-soul and the νοῦς, and from the fact that the circular movement is considered as an 'image' of the movement of the νοῦς and 'similar' to it (897 e 1, 897 e 4–5, 898 a 5–6): Plato always uses the term 'image' when he wants to point out the distinction between the sensible things and the intelligible, transcendent realities. H. Görgemanns, *Zetemata* 25 (1960), 200, is therefore quite right in saying: 'Der Nus tritt also erneut in Erscheinung. Er ist aber nicht einfach eine der zur Seele gehörigen Funktionen, sondern scheint eine von der Seele unabhängige Wesenheit zu sein, die sie hinzunehmen kann oder nicht.' On the substantial identity between the νοῦς-Demiurge of the *Timaeus*, the νοῦς-αἰτία of the

directly in his fight against pleasures and desires, nor does it guide him towards moral perfection; like the Logos of the Porch and of Philo, it is only the cause of the harmony of the universe, which represents also the pattern of human morals.[1] A kind of guardianship of man is allotted to the inferior astral gods, both in the *Timaeus* and in the tenth book of the *Laws*;[2] but this guardianship, as far as the ethical field is concerned, goes scarcely beyond the task of punishing the transgressors of the law.[3] The παιδεία of the Platonic philosopher is not originated by the constant intervention of the divine νοῦς in the human sphere, but it is simply the result of the activity of human φρόνησις: the divinity helps man only in so far as it drops in him that divine element which becomes his reason.[4] These considerations concerning Plato are also valid for the whole Platonic school-tradition up to Neoplatonism.[5] Only some utterances of Maximus of Tyre seem to recall Clement's Christian conceptions.[6]

In Clement's conception of Christ the ideal of ἀπάθεια, which the Old Porch had formulated and which both Philo and Neoplatonism have inherited, assumes a concrete shape: in the role he plays in ethics the synthesis between Christianity and Hellen-

---

Philebus, and the νοῦς of the tenth book of the *Laws*, see R. Hackforth, *CQ* 30 (1936), 4 and 6–7.

[1] On the transcendent νοῦς as cause of the rational order and harmony of the universe see particularly *Philebus* 28 e 2–6, 30 c 5–7, *Timaeus* 30 a 5–6, *Laws* x. 897 b 1–3, 897 c 4–7 (this νοῦς should not be identified with the world-soul, about which see chapter III, p. 210 below; on this important distinction between the transcendent νοῦς and the immanent world-soul in the *Philebus*, *Timaeus*, and *Laws* x see R. Hackforth, *CQ* 30 (1936), 4 and 7). As to the conception according to which the harmony of the universe is the pattern of human morals see the passage of *Timaeus* 47 b 6–c 4 quoted above, p. 115 n. 2. Plato's sentence in *Laws* x. 897 b 2, παιδαγωγεῖ πάντα, to which W. Jaeger, *Early Christianity and Greek Paideia*, 66, draws attention, scarcely implies anything more than this conception (Plato says that the world-soul παιδαγωγεῖ πάντα since it, in his opinion, is the cause of the harmony of the universe which reflects itself also in human morals).

[2] See, for instance, *Timaeus* 41 d 1–3, *Laws* x. 900 c 9–d 1, 902 c 1–2.

[3] See *Laws* x. 904 e 2–905 b 8.

[4] See the passage of *Timaeus* 41 c 7–d 1 quoted in chapter I, footnote 4, p. 23 above.

[5] Plutarch, *De sera Num. Vind.* 550 d–e, expounds the same views about the close relationship between the harmony of the universe and human morals which we have noticed in *Timaeus* 47 b 6–c 4 (cf. footnote 2, p. 115 above): καὶ τὴν ὄψιν αὐτὸς οὗτος ὁ ἀνὴρ [sc. Plato] ἀνάψαι φησὶ τὴν φύσιν ἐν ἡμῖν, ὅπως ὑπὸ θέας τῶν ἐν οὐρανῷ φερομένων καὶ θαύματος ἀσπάζεσθαι καὶ ἀγαπᾶν ἐθιζομένη τὸ εὔσχημον ἡ ψυχὴ καὶ τεταγμένον ἀπεχθάνηται τοῖς ἀναρμόστοις καὶ πλανητοῖς πάθεσι . . . As to Plotinus, see chapter III, p. 171 below.

[6] *Or.* xxxviii. 134 a. This passage is quoted in footnote 2, p. 66 above.

ism appears to be perfect. Christian, and not Greek, is the idea
that the Son of God cooperates in the salvation of the whole
of mankind and is also the teacher and model of moral perfection; on the other hand, typically Greek is the moral ideal
which Clement, under the twofold influence of Philo and of
Neoplatonism, has adopted and applied to the Son of God.

When we pass from the inferior to the higher ethical level represented by ἀπάθεια and by ὁμοίωσις θεῷ we get into the sphere
of *gnosis*. Moral perfection is for Clement the necessary condition
which man must satisfy if he wants to possess *gnosis*: only he who,
with the help of Christ, has become ἀπαθής and ὅμοιος to God
is admitted into the higher knowledge of the divinity or *gnosis*.
The function which Christ accomplishes in the higher ethical
level by enabling man to become ἀπαθής and ὅμοιος to God is
the exact counterpart of the role he plays in the theoretical side
of *gnosis*. To this most important point, which sharply separates
Clement from Philo, Middle Platonism, and Neoplatonism and
brings him into direct connection with Christian Gnosticism, we
shall have occasion to come back in the next chapter.

III

PISTIS, GNOSIS, COSMOLOGY, AND THEOLOGY

1. *The Doctrine of 'Pistis'*

THE most important aspect of Clement's philosophy is represented by the idea of *gnosis*. In order to be able to grasp
its full meaning, we shall have to analyse it in all its various
implications. But since the idea of *gnosis* is, in Clement's thought,
closely connected with that of *pistis*, it is necessary to attempt
first to sketch Clement's theory of *pistis*. Only after this preliminary inquiry will it be possible to pass to the study of *gnosis*.

Clement's theory of *pistis* represents a serious attempt to give
a scientific explanation of the words *pistis* and πιστεύειν which
occur so frequently in the Gospels. Clement was perfectly aware
of the danger represented by a twofold opposition against the
evangelical idea of 'faith' : that of some Greek philosophers, who
strongly criticized the readiness of the Christians to believe in
the sayings of Jesus without trying to give a rational explanation
of them ;[1] and that of the gnostics—especially of those belonging
to the school of Valentine—who sharply distinguished the *pistis*
of the common believers from the higher *gnosis* which, according
to them, was a natural gift bestowed as a privilege only on very

---

[1] Some evidence for the criticism which the Christian *pistis* had met in the
Greek world can be found in two Greek philosophers of the second century A.D.,
namely Galen and Celsus. R. Walzer has collected some statements of Galen on
Jews and Christians : in two of these Galen openly criticizes the inclinations of the
Christians and of the Jews to believe in some undemonstrated laws and to accept
everything on faith (the first of these statements occurs in *De Pulsuum Differentiis* ii.
4, vol. viii, p. 579. 15 Kühn, the second in the treatise against Aristotle's theology
Εἰς τὸ πρῶτον κινοῦν ἀκίνητον which has survived only in an Arabic version : see
Walzer, *Galen on Jews and Christians* (Oxford, 1949), 14–15). Celsus also did not
miss the opportunity of criticizing the Christian idea of *pistis*: see, for instance, i. 9
and vi. 7 b. The close kinship between the criticism of Celsus and that of Galen
has been pointed out by Walzer, op. cit. 53. A hint at the polemic of the Greek
philosophers against *pistis* can also be found in *Strom.* ii. 8. 4 (ii. 117. 8–9), πίστιν
δέ, ἣν διαβάλλουσιν κενὴν καὶ βάρβαρον νομίζοντες Ἕλληνες . . .

few persons, the πνευματικοί.¹ On the other hand, Clement had also to face the dangerous attitude of those Christians who rejected any attempt to give a scientific content to their beliefs and to develop their *pistis* into a higher form of knowledge.² These are the reasons which led Clement to build up his own doctrine of *pistis* and to give an original solution to the problem of its relations with *gnosis*.³

As we shall see presently, Clement, in order to achieve this result, resorted again to the school-philosophy of his time as well as to some ideas characteristic of Philo. He attached the three following meanings to *pistis*:

1. *pistis* is the attitude peculiar to the human mind when it believes in the first principles of demonstration; in more general terms, it also designates any kind of immediate knowledge;
2. *pistis* is the firm conviction which the human mind possesses after reaching the knowledge of something by means of a scientific demonstration;
3. *pistis* may also mean the tendency of the believers to accept the truths contained in the teachings of Scripture without attempting to reach a deeper comprehension of them.⁴

---

¹ See, for instance, *Strom.* ii. 10. 2 (ii. 118. 13–17), οἱ δὲ ἀπὸ Οὐαλεντίνου τὴν μὲν πίστιν τοῖς ἁπλοῖς ἀπονείμαντες ἡμῖν, αὐτοῖς δὲ τὴν γνῶσιν τοῖς φύσει σῳζομένοις κατὰ τὴν τοῦ διαφέροντος πλεονεξίαν σπέρματος ἐνυπάρχειν βούλονται, μακρῷ δὲ κεχωρισμένην πίστεως, ᾗ τὸ πνευματικὸν τοῦ ψυχικοῦ, λέγοντες.

² See *Strom.* i. 43. 1 (ii. 28. 18–20), ἔνιοι δέ . . . μόνην καὶ ψιλὴν πίστιν ἀπαιτοῦσιν. They are obviously the same Christians who are opposed to the study of Greek philosophy (see chapter I, footnote 1, p. 9 above).

³ On this question see also H. Chadwick, *Early Christian Thought . . .*, 51–4, and *The Cambridge History of later Greek and early medieval Philosophy*, 168.

⁴ Several scholars have inquired at some length into the doctrine of *pistis* in Clement and into the problem of its relations with *gnosis*: see, for instance, E. Redepenning, Erste Abt., 152–67; H. Ritter, Erster Theil, 431 ff.; H. Preische, 7–19; Knittel, *TQ* 55 (1873), 171–219 and 363–417; C. Merk, 17–27; E. de Faye, in his book *Clément d'Alexandrie*, 207 ff., and in his essay in *AEHE* (Sect. des sc. relig., 1919), 11–14; M. Daskalakis, 32–43; K. Prümm, *Scholastik* 12 (1937), 17–57 (a detailed analysis of the second book of the *Stromateis*); P. T. Camelot, *Foi et Gnose . . .*, 28–42 and 43–50; W. Völker, 221–254; and H. A. Wolfson, *The Philosophy of the Church Fathers*, 112 and 120–7. Among all these scholars only Merk, Daskalakis, and Wolfson are aware of the presence in Clement of three different meanings of the word *pistis* (Daskalakis, 36, seems, however, to lay emphasis particularly on the second and third meanings). Völker, though admitting that *pistis* in Clement may mean different things (p. 234), falls short of establishing which exactly its meanings are. The question of the mutual relations between these three different meanings has, however, not been thoroughly examined as yet.

The first two meanings concern some definite epistemological questions; the third meaning belongs to the religious sphere. They are, however, closely related to one another.[1] It will be best to examine each of them, together with its philosophical sources,[2] and then to show their mutual relations. In this way, we shall also be able to understand better what Clement exactly thought about *pistis* and about its relations with *gnosis*.

1. The first meaning of *pistis* occurs in the following passage of the *Stromateis*:

> *Strom.* vii. 95. 6 (iii. 67. 25 f.): εἰκότως τοίνυν πίστει περιλαβόντες ἀναπόδεικτον τὴν ἀρχήν...

The idea which underlies this passage is expounded at some length in the so-called eighth book of the *Stromateis*, which contains some material dealing mainly with logic and epistemology.[3] The following passage is particularly worth noticing:

> *Strom.* viii. 6. 7–7. 2 (iii. 83. 16–24): either everything needs a demonstration, or something is *itself trustworthy*. In the first case we, by requiring the demonstration of each demonstration, shall

---

[1] See pp. 137 ff. below.

[2] A better comprehension of Clement's doctrine of *pistis* can only be attained by means of a detailed inquiry into its sources, which has not yet been made. Daskalakis, 33–5, refers to the Stoic and Epicurean doctrine of πρόληψις as well as to the Stoic συγκατάθεσις; Camelot, 29 ff., does not go much beyond the results reached by Daskalakis; Prümm limits himself to mentioning the Stoic doctrine of πρόληψις and of the κοιναὶ ἔννοιαι (p. 23) and to speaking of an 'Einbau der Glaubensdefinition in die stoische Erkenntnislehre' (p. 25) and of an 'Unbeweisbarkeit der obersten Prinzipien . . . ganz im Sinne des Aristoteles '(p. 27). Völker is satisfied with a general assertion: 'Er [i.e. Clement] entlehnt reichlich aus allen philosophischen Systemen, wobei er selbst die Schule Epikurs nicht ausschließt, er sucht Plato und Aristoteles für seine eigene Gedanken nutzbar zu machen' (p. 234).

[3] The view held by T. Zahn, 104–30, according to which the so-called eighth book of the *Stromateis*, the *Excerpta ex Theodoto*, and the *Eclogae propheticae* represent the abridgements made in some later period of the original eighth book of the *Stromateis* as it had been composed by Clement, has been rightly criticized by I. von Arnim, who has pointed out that the material on logic which has come down to us under the heading '*Stromateis*, book VIII' could not form a part of the eighth book of the *Stromateis* which Clement intended to write, but is mainly based on notes taken by Clement himself during his reading of some handbooks of logic (see particularly p. 12). That Arnim's view was the correct one has been proved by Ernst, who has clearly shown that Clement used this material throughout the first seven books of the *Stromateis* (see especially pp. 8–11, 13–15, 24–30, 41–7).

be involved in an infinite regress, and in this way the demonstration itself will be overthrown. In the second case *the things which are themselves trustworthy* will become the principles of demonstrations. The philosophers then admit that the principles of all things are undemonstrated. Consequently, if there is a demonstration, there must necessarily be *something prior to it*, which is trustworthy and which is called 'primary' and undemonstrated. Therefore every demonstration is traced back to an undemonstrated *belief*.

Here Clement (or, more exactly, the author of the handbook which represents his source) says that some demonstrations must be based on undemonstrated principles, which are themselves trustworthy (τὰ ἐξ αὐτῶν πιστά).[1] This is the reason why, at the end of the passage, he calls the first principle *pistis*, ἐπὶ τὴν ἀναπόδεικτον ἄρα πίστιν ἡ πᾶσα ἀπόδειξις ἀνάγεται, Strom. viii. 7. 2 (iii. 83. 23–4), and maintains that by means of *pistis* it is possible to assume the existence of some undemonstrated principle, εἰκότως τοίνυν πίστει περιλαβόντες ἀναπόδεικτον τὴν ἀρχήν, Strom. vii. 95. 6 (iii. 65. 25 f.).

The same conception, expressed in the same terms, occurs also in some definitions of demonstration given by Clement's source:

Strom. viii. 7. 6 (iii. 83. 31 f.): λόγος τοιοῦτος οἷος ἐκ τῶν ἤδη πιστῶν τοῖς οὔπω πιστοῖς ἐκπορίζειν τὴν πίστιν δυνάμενος.

Strom. viii. 8. 1 (iii. 84. 13–14): ἀπόδειξις δέ ἐστιν, ὅταν ἀπὸ τῶν πρώτων τις εἰς τὸ ζητούμενον ἀφικνῆται.

To the existence of an absolute and unconditioned principle in the dialectic process attention had been drawn already by Plato at the end of the sixth book of the *Republic*, μέχρι τοῦ ἀνυποθέτου ἐπὶ τοῦ παντὸς ἀρχὴν ἰών, 511 b 6–7. But it was especially Aristotle who developed this doctrine; like Clement's source, Aristotle maintains that it is impossible to require a demonstration for every demonstration, and that some demonstrations must start from some absolute, undemonstrated, true, and consequently

---

[1] The same idea appears also in *Strom*. ii. 13. 4–14. 1 (ii. 119. 26–32); this passage, as Prümm, 28 n. 18, has pointed out, is closely related to *EN* vi. 1140ᵇ31–1141ᵃ3. On the Aristotelian terminology which occurs in the passage see also the very exact correspondences collected by Früchtel in his note 119. 27–31 (vol. ii of the reprint of Stählin's edition, p. 524). Früchtel rightly observes that Clement's dependence on Aristotle is not direct, but must presuppose the existence of some intermediate source.

also trustworthy principles: it is worth looking at *An. Pr.* 64^b32–6, *An. Post.* 71^b20–3, 72^a7–8, 72^b20–1, 84^a30–3, *Top.* 100^b18–21,[1] *EN* 1140^b31–3.[2]

This doctrine of the absolute ἀρχή, which is regarded by Plato as the end of the dialectic process and which is identified by Aristotle with the trustworthy and undemonstrated principle of demonstration, has, however, become part of the school-tradition.[3] No work dealing with logical and epistemological doctrines could have omitted it.[4] Small wonder, therefore, if it also occurs in Middle Platonism. Albinus, in chapter V of the *Didaskalikos*, describes the process of analysis in these terms:

> *Did.* 157. 9 ff.: ἀναλύσεως δὲ εἴδη ἐστὶν τρία· ἡ μὲν γάρ ἐστιν ἀπὸ τῶν αἰσθητῶν ἐπὶ τὰ πρῶτα νοητὰ ἄνοδος, ἡ δὲ διὰ τῶν δεικνυμένων καὶ ἀποδεικνυμένων ἄνοδος ἐπὶ τὰς ἀναποδείκτους καὶ ἀμέσους προτάσεις, ἡ δὲ ἐξ ὑποθέσεως ἀνιοῦσα ἐπὶ τὰς ἀνυποθέτους ἀρχάς.

Cf. *Did.* 157. 21–2: ἕως ἂν ἔλθωμεν ἐπὶ τὸ πρῶτον καὶ ὁμολογούμενον.

In these two passages of Albinus it is easy to notice the presence both of Platonic and of Aristotelian terms. Whereas the ἀνυπόθετοι ἀρχαί of the first passage remind us of *Rep.* vi. 511 b 6–7, the terms ἀναποδείκτους καὶ ἀμέσους προτάσεις and πρῶτον of the first and second passages are the same terms which occur in the passages of Aristotle quoted above.[5] It is interesting to observe that the definition of analysis given by Clement's source corresponds exactly to the second of the three kinds of analysis described by Albinus:

---

[1] To *An. Post.* 84^a30–3 and *Top.* 100^b18–21 attention has been drawn also by Ernst, 20.

[2] Prümm, 27 n. 18, has been able to mention only this passage of Aristotle. Völker, 235 n. 2, does not produce more evidence, but simply refers to Prümm's footnote; both Prümm and Völker, speaking about the doctrine of the ἀρχαί in Clement, have taken into account only the passage of *Strom.* ii. 13. 4 without mentioning the longer section of *Strom.* viii. 6. 7–7. 2.

[3] It occurs also in Alexander of Aphrodisias, the well-known commentator of Aristotle and a contemporary of Clement: see, for instance, *In Top.*, vol. ii, Pars ii, p. 18. 16 Wallies, and *In Top.*, vol. ii, Pars ii, p. 16. 4–8 Wallies. The reference to the first passage is given also by Ernst, 20.

[4] See, for instance, Galen, *De Meth. med.*, c. 4, vol. x, p. 33. 15–18 Kühn, *Inst. log.* i. 5 (p. 4. 16–18 Kalbfleisch), xvi. 6 (p. 39. 17–19), xvi. 7 (p. 40. 3–4): these references are produced by Ernst, 20. To them it is possible to add *Inst. log.* xvii. 1 (p. 42. 7–8) and xvii. 2 (p. 42. 14–16).

[5] Cf. also the passages of Alexander of Aphrodisias and of Galen to which the two preceding footnotes refer.

Clement, *Strom.* viii. 8. 1 (iii. 84. 9 ff.) : ἕκαστον μὲν γὰρ τῶν ἀποδεικνυμένων διά τινων ἀποδεικνυμένων ἀποδείκνυται, προαποδεδειγμένων κἀκείνων ὑφ᾽ ἑτέρων, ἄχρις ἂν εἰς τὰ ἐξ αὐτῶν πιστὰ ἀναδράμωμεν ... ὅπερ ἀνάλυσις ὀνομάζεται.

Albinus, *Did.* 157. 11 ff. : ἡ δὲ διὰ τῶν δεικνυμένων ἄνοδος ἐπὶ τὰς ἀναποδείκτους καὶ ἀμέσους προτάσεις. Cf. *Did.* 157. 21–2 : ἕως ἂν ἔλθωμεν ἐπὶ τὸ πρῶτον καὶ ὁμολογούμενον.

The Aristotelian terms ἀναποδείκτους καὶ ἀμέσους προτάσεις and πρῶτον used by Albinus correspond exactly to the terms ἀναποδείκτους (or ἀναπόδεικτον) and πρώτων which occur in *Strom.* viii. 7. 1–2 and viii. 8. 1 ; the term ὁμολογούμενον, which occurs in *Did.* 157. 21–2, has practically the same meaning as the terms τὰ ἐξ αὐτῶν πιστά or τὰ ἤδη πιστά used by Clement's source in *Strom.* viii. 7. 1–2, viii. 7. 6, and viii. 8. 1.[1] It is easy to infer, from these close correspondences between Clement's source and Albinus, that the logical doctrines of Aristotelian origin contained in the so-called eighth book of the *Stromateis* come from a school-handbook analogous to that used by Albinus in chapters IV and V of the *Didaskalikos*, in which he expounds some Aristotelian logical doctrines which he does not hesitate to trace back directly to Plato, without any mention of Aristotle. Like many other Stoic and Aristotelian doctrines, the Aristotelian doctrine of the absolute, undemonstrated, and trustworthy principles of demonstration has become a constitutive element of the syncretism characteristic of some schools of Middle Platonism.

Clement's source is inclined to consider as principles of demonstration not only the universal and trustworthy principles of Aristotle, but also what appears evident both to sensation and to mind :

Strom. viii. 7. 3–4 (iii. 83. 24–9) : εἶεν δ᾽ ἂν καὶ ἄλλαι τῶν ἀποδείξεων ἀρχαὶ μετὰ τὴν ἐκ πίστεως πηγήν, τὰ πρὸς αἴσθησίν τε καὶ νόησιν ἐναργῶς φαινόμενα ... τὰ δὲ ἐξ ἑαυτῶν [sc. sensation and mind] γεννώμενα σύνθετα μέν, οὐδὲν δ᾽ ἧττον ἐναργῆ καὶ πιστά ... τῶν πρώτων.

---

[1] The term ὁμολογούμενον occurs also in the definitions of demonstration given by Clement, *Strom.* viii. 5. 1 (iii. 82. 14–15), ἀπόδειξιν ... λόγον εἶναι ... ἐκ τῶν ὁμολογουμένων ἐκπορίζοντα τὴν πίστιν, and by Plutarch, *De Plac. Philos.* 877 c 1 ff., πᾶσα γὰρ ἀπόδειξις καὶ πᾶσα πίστις ἐπιστήμης πρὸς δὲ καὶ πᾶς συλλογισμός ἔκ τινων ὁμολογουμένων τὸ ἀμφισβητούμενον συνάγει. On the presence of Stoic terminology in the definition of demonstration in *Strom.* viii. 5. 1 see footnote 1, p. 132 below.

Strom. viii. 14. 3 (iii. 88. 20–1): ἀρχὴ δὲ τούτων ἁπάντων ἐστὶ τὸ πρὸς αἴσθησίν τε καὶ νόησιν ἐναργές.[1]

The same idea underlies also a passage of the second book of the *Stromateis*:

Strom. ii. 9. 5 (ii. 118. 2–4): Θεόφραστος δὲ τὴν αἴσθησιν ἀρχὴν εἶναι τῆς πίστεώς φησι· ἀπὸ γὰρ ταύτης αἱ ἀρχαὶ πρὸς τὸν λόγον τὸν ἐν ἡμῖν καὶ τὴν διάνοιαν ἐκτείνονται.

Clement can say here that sensation is the source of faith because sense-perceptions are ἐναργεῖς and what possesses ἐνάργεια is πιστόν (cf. *Strom.* viii. 7. 3–4).

Closely connected with this doctrine which considers as principles of demonstration (i.e. of scientific knowledge) what appears evident both to sensation and to mind is the view according to which scientific knowledge is based both on sensations and on mind. The passage of *Strom.* ii. 13. 2 in which this view is expounded shows some very close correspondences with a section of the seventh book of Sextus Empiricus' *Adversus Mathematicos* (§§ 216 ff.) containing an exposition of the epistemological doctrines of the Peripatetic school:

Strom. ii. 13. 2 (ii. 119. 22–3): ἐκ δὲ αἰσθήσεως καὶ τοῦ νοῦ ἡ τῆς ἐπιστήμης συνίσταται οὐσία.

Adv. Math. vii. 226: φαίνεται οὖν ἐκ τῶν εἰρημένων πρῶτα κριτήρια τῆς τῶν πραγμάτων γνώσεως ἥ τε αἴσθησις καὶ ὁ νοῦς, ἡ μὲν ὀργάνου τρόπον ἔχουσα, ἡ δὲ τεχνίτου. . . . οὕτως οὐδὲ ὁ νοῦς χωρὶς αἰσθήσεως δοκιμάσαι πέφυκε τὰ πράγματα.

Strom. ii. 13. 2 (ii. 119. 23–4): κοινὸν δὲ νοῦ καὶ αἰσθήσεως τὸ ἐναργές.

Adv. Math. vii. 218: κοινὸν δὲ ἀμφοτέρων [sc. αἰσθήσεως καὶ νοήσεως] ὡς ἔλεγεν ὁ Θεόφραστος τὸ ἐναργές.[2]

The expression κοινὸν δὲ νοῦ καὶ αἰσθήσεως τὸ ἐναργές which occurs in Clement's passage reminds us at once of the very similar

---

[1] Galen also holds this view in *De Meth. med.* i, c. 5, vol. x, p. 39. 7–9 Kühn (cf. Ernst, 21) and in *Inst. log.* i. 5 (p. 4. 13–15 Kalbfleisch). From the first of these two passages it can be inferred that Galen had expounded this doctrine at some length in his logical work Περὶ ἀποδείξεως ὑπομνήματα. On this huge work by Galen see Walzer, op. cit. 20 and the literature quoted in footnote 2 on the same page. Galen refers to it also in *Inst. log.* xvii. 1 (p. 42. 10 Kalbfleisch).

[2] To this last passage of Sextus Empiricus attention has been drawn by Stählin, app. crit., vol. ii. 119, and by Witt, *Albinus* . . ., 34 n. 4, and 53.

expressions τὰ πρὸς αἴσθησίν τε καὶ νόησιν ἐναργῶς φαινόμενα (*Strom.* viii. 7. 3) and τὸ πρὸς αἴσθησίν τε καὶ νόησιν ἐναργές (*Strom.* viii. 14. 3).

At this point the doubt may arise whether Clement's statements in the four passages quoted above (*Strom.* viii. 7. 3–4, viii. 14. 3, ii. 9. 5, and ii. 13. 2) depend directly on the Peripatetic school-tradition or on some intermediate source. After a first reading of these four passages one would be more inclined to accept the first solution: from the mention of Theophrastus in *Strom.* ii. 9. 5 it could be easily inferred that Clement used either a work by Theophrastus or a Peripatetic school-handbook; and the passages of *Strom.* ii. 13. 2, viii. 7. 3–4, and viii. 14. 3, owing to their close parallelism with *Adv. Math.* vii. 226 and 218, seem also to suggest a direct dependence on the teaching of the Peripatetic philosopher. Yet things are not so simple. It has been shown by R. Hirzel that §§ 141–261 of the seventh book of the *Adversus Mathematicos*, containing an exposition of the epistemology of several philosophical schools (namely of Plato, of the exponents of the Academy, of the Cyrenaics, of the Peripatetics, and of the Stoics), go back to a work by Antiochus of Ascalon which can perhaps be identified with the Κανωνικά mentioned at § 201.[1] Hirzel came to this conclusion by pointing out the striking correspondences between the exposition of Plato's epistemology (§§ 141–4) and that of the Peripatetic school (§§ 216–26) as well as their substantial agreement with the epistemological doctrines of Antiochus. The fundamental idea which underlies the description of the Platonic and Peripatetic epistemology is that scientific knowledge must be considered as the product of sense-perceptions and of the activity of reason.[1] This idea, according to which no knowledge is possible without

---

[1] R. Hirzel, III. Theil, 493–524. For the identification of the work used by Sextus Empiricus with the Κανωνικά see especially p. 493 and pp. 520–1. Hirzel, 493–4, thinks it possible that Antiochus, in his Κανωνικά, had made a detailed survey of the epistemological doctrines of the most important philosophical schools.

[2] See Hirzel, 496–7: 'Der zweite für Antiochos als den Urheber der historischen Darstellung sprechende Grund liegt darin, daß dessen eigentümliche Erkenntnistheorie auch in diesem historischen Abschnitt zum Vorschein kommt. Für Antiochos nun ist characteristisch, daß nach demselben eine Erkenntnis nur vermittelst der Sinne möglich, die Wahrheit aber noch nicht in den Sinneseindrücken gegeben ist, sondern nur vermittelst des Geistes oder der Vernunft, des Logos, daraus gewonnen werden kann, und daß zweitens diese wesentlich stoische Theorie von ihm für die platonisch-aristotelische ausgegeben wurde.'

sense-perceptions, does not agree entirely with the actual epistemology of Plato and Aristotle, but simply reproduces the point
of view of Antiochus.[1] Since, therefore, the passages of *Adv. Math.*
vii. 226 and 218 quoted above can be traced back to Antiochus
and since they show a close correspondence with *Strom.* ii. 13. 2,
viii. 7. 3–4, and viii. 14. 3, it is very likely that these three passages
of Clement as well are dependent on Antiochus.

In this way, even the passage of *Strom.* ii. 9. 5, in spite of its
referring to Theophrastus, can be related to Antiochus. What
Clement says here is not only closely related to *Strom.* ii. 13. 2,
Strom. viii. 7. 3–4, and *Strom.* viii. 14. 3 so as to form together with
these passages a coherent epistemological system, but is also in
perfect agreement with Antiochus' epistemological views, according to which the self-evidence of sense-perceptions represents
the first, fundamental stage for the growth of knowledge and has
a direct influence on reason. The passage of *Strom.* ii. 9. 5 should
be compared with *Ac. Pr.* ii. 19: *ordiamur igitur a sensibus, quorum
ita clara iudicia et certa sunt, Ac. Pr.* ii. 30: *mens enim ipsa, quae
sensuum fons est atque ipse sensus est, naturalem vim habet, quam intendit ad ea, quibus movetur* [sc. sense-perceptions], and *Ac. Post.* i.
30: *quamquam oriretur a sensibus* [sc. *iudicium veritatis*] . . .

---

[1] See Hirzel, 498: 'Aus ihnen [sc. from the sentences of §§ 141–4] namentlich
erhellt, daß wir hier nicht die echte platonische Theorie vor uns haben. Denn
. . . widerspricht ihr . . . die in den angeführten Worten erhaltene, daß unser
Geist auch die Fähigkeit die Sinneseindrücke zu beurtheilen nur den Sinnen ver-
danken oder daß das Denken aus der sinnlichen Wahrnehmung stammen solle
. . . Dagegen können wir eine solche Entstellung von Antiochos erwarten, da
durch die selbe die platonische Lehre seiner eigenen gleich wurde. Denn nach
Antiochos ist ein Denken ohne Begriffe nicht möglich, diese selber aber sind
sämmtlich aus den sinnlichen Wahrnehmungen geschöpft'; and p. 510: 'Dem
entsprechend wird zum Schluß das Verhältnis der beiden Kriterien, der Sinne
und des Geistes, durch eine Vergleichung erläutert, die die Sinne als Werkzeug,
den Geist als den dasselbe benutzenden Künstler bezeichnet. In dieser Darstellung
ist ebenso auffallend das Fehlen einer für die aristotelische Erkenntnistheorie
wichtigen Bestimmung, wonach der νοῦς einer unmittelbaren Erkenntnis fähig,
ein intuitives Vermögen ist, als die Übereinstimmung mit der platonischen Lehre,
wie sie bei Sextos aufgefaßt wird. Daß beides für die Ableitung von Antiochos
spricht, versteht sich von selber.' It may also be worth while to look at Hirzel's
further remarks on pp. 499–520. I shall only draw attention to some passages
in which the emphasis laid on the importance of sense perceptions is particularly
strong: συμπεριλαβὼν αὐτῷ [sc. τῷ λόγῳ] καὶ τὴν δι᾽ αἰσθήσεως ἐνέργειαν (§ 141 on
Plato); συνεργοῦ δεῖται ὁ λόγος τῆς αἰσθήσεως (§ 144 on Plato); οὕτως οὐδὲ ὁ νοῦς
χωρὶς αἰσθήσεως δοκιμάσαι πέφυκε τὰ πράγματα (§ 226 on the Peripatetics); τῆς
φύσεως . . . πρὸς ἐπίγνωσιν τῆς ἀληθείας τὴν αἰσθητικὴν δύναμιν ἀναδούσης (§ 259
on the Stoics); and τὴν . . . φαντασίαν τῆς αἰσθήσεως . . . δι᾽ ἧς τῶν πραγμάτων
ἀντιλαμβάνεται (§ 260, on the Stoics).

Accordingly, it is very likely that Clement would have found the epistemological doctrines which occur in *Strom.* ii. 9. 5, ii. 13. 2, viii. 7. 3–4, and viii. 14. 3 not directly in Theophrastus or in a handbook of the Peripatetic school, but in an exposition of the epistemology of the Peripatetics made by Antiochus or by some exponent of his school.[1] What Antiochus aimed at was to show the substantial agreement between Plato, Aristotle, and their schools and to present himself as the follower of the *antiqui*, i.e. of the exponents of the Old Academy and of the Lyceum.[2] In order to achieve this result, he kept himself close to the epistemological views of the Peripatetics and of the Stoics,[3] made no distinction between Aristotle and Theophrastus, and attributed both to Plato and to Aristotle his own epistemological views (which were also the views of Theophrastus and of the Stoics). The best evidence, in this respect, is provided by §§ 141–261 of the seventh book of the *Adversus Mathematicos* which, as R. Hirzel has pointed out, shows the unmistakable mark of his teaching.

Closely related to the idea of *pistis* as a belief in those principles which appear evident both to sensation and to mind is the definition of *pistis* as συγκατάθεσις which appears in the following passages of Clement:

Strom. ii. 8. 4 (ii. 117. 8–9): πίστις δέ... πρόληψις ἑκούσιός ἐστι, θεοσεβείας συγκατάθεσις.

Strom. ii. 54. 5–55. 1 (ii. 142. 25–9): τὰς δὲ συγκαταθέσεις οὐ μόνον οἱ ἀπὸ Πλάτωνος ἀλλὰ καὶ οἱ ἀπὸ τῆς Στοᾶς ἐφ' ἡμῖν εἶναι λέγουσιν· πᾶσα οὖν δόξα καὶ κρίσις καὶ ὑπόληψις καὶ μάθησις συγκατάθεσίς ἐστιν· ἢ οὐδὲν ἄλλο ἢ πίστις εἴη ἄν.

---

[1] On the dependence of the passages of *Strom.* ii. 13. 2 and viii. 7. 3–4 on Antiochus see also Witt, *Albinus*..., 34, and L. Früchtel, in his review of Witt's book, *BPhW* (1938), coll. 999–1000. As to the dependence on Antiochus of *Strom.* ii. 9. 5, Früchtel, loc. cit., produces no evidence in support of his assumption. A further correspondence can be observed between Clement's source and Antiochus: the passage of *Strom.* viii. 7. 3, εἶεν δ' ἂν καὶ ἄλλαι τῶν ἀποδείξεων ἀρχαί... τὰ πρὸς αἴσθησίν τε καὶ νόησιν ἐναργῶς φαινόμενα, should be compared with Cicero, *De Fin.* iv. 8: *iam argumenti ratione conclusi caput esse faciunt ea, quae perspicua dicunt.* As to the close correspondence between *Strom.* viii. 7. 5, ἔστιν ἥνπερ ἰδίαν λόγου δύναμιν πεφυκυῖαν ἅπαντες ἔχομεν φύσει, and *Ac. Pr.* ii. 30: *mens enim ipsa... naturalem vim habet,* see chapter I, footnote 1, p. 13 above.

[2] On this point see chapter II, footnote 3, p. 100 above.

[3] See footnote 2, p. 125, and footnote 1, p. 126 above. On Antiochus' epistemology see H. Strache, *Ekl.* 7–19, G. Luck, 53–4, and M. Pohlenz, *Die Stoa* i. 249.

Strom. v. 86. 1 (ii. 383. 1): ἤδη δὲ ἡ πίστις εἰ καὶ ἑκούσιος τῆς ψυχῆς συγκατάθεσις . . .

The term συγκατάθεσις had been employed especially by the Stoics: it indicated the positive reaction or 'assent' of mind to the sense-perceptions. A passage of the *Academica Posteriora* of Cicero, belonging to the exposition made by Varro of Zeno's teaching, provides a clear illustration of this doctrine: *sed ad haec, quae visa sunt et quasi accepta sensibus, adsensionem adiungit* [sc. *Zeno*] *animorum, quam esse volt in nobis positam et voluntariam. Visis non omnibus adiungebat fidem, sed eis solum, quae propriam quandam haberent declarationem earum rerum, quae viderentur* (*Ac. Post.* i. 40–1).[1] In this passage *adsensio* (συγκατάθεσις) and *fides* (πίστις) are practically one and the same thing. It would therefore be natural to suppose, as Pohlenz did,[2] a direct influence of Stoicism in the adoption of the Stoic term συγκατάθεσις. It must, however, not be forgotten that here Varro is speaking from the standpoint of Antiochus;[3] that Antiochus himself adopted the Stoic doctrine of συγκατάθεσις and connected it with *pistis* can also be seen from the following evidence:

Ac. Pr. ii. 37: *simul illud aperiebatur, comprehendi multa et percipi sensibus, quod fieri sine adsensione non potest.*

Ac. Pr. ii. 38: . . . *sic non potest* [sc. *animal*] *obiectam rem perspicuam non approbare.*

Ac. Pr. ii. 38: *qui enim quid percipit, adsentitur statim.*

Ac. Pr. ii. 39: *omninoque ante videri aliquid quam agamus necesse est, eique, quod visum sit, adsentiatur.*[4]

De Finibus iv. 9: *denuntiant, ut neque sensuum fidem sine ratione nec rationes sine sensibus exquiramus atque ut eorum alterum ab altero ne separemus.*[5]

The sense of the sentence of the last passage, *neque sensuum fidem sine ratione . . . exquiramus*, is that it is reason that must ultimately decide whether to believe or not in sense-perceptions. That such a decision is expressed by an assent of mind (*adsensio*, συγκατάθεσις) is clearly shown by the passages of the *Academica Priora* quoted

---

[1] On the Stoic doctrine of συγκατάθεσις see also J. S. Reid's footnote 20, p. 223 in his commentary of the *Academica* of Cicero (London, 1885).

[2] *NGA*, phil.-hist. Kl. (1943), 150.   [3] See Witt, 29 n. 1, and also 34.

[4] On the change of construction in this passage see Reid, footnote 15, p. 225.

[5] On the dependence of this passage of *De Finibus* on Antiochus see Witt, 29 and 50.

above. The identification of *pistis* (*fides*) with συγκατάθεσις (*adsensio*) is therefore characteristic of Antiochus and it is very likely that, in this case as well, he would have had some influence on Clement. That Clement knew that some exponents of the Academy had adopted the Stoic doctrine of συγκατάθεσις is shown by the passage of *Strom.* ii. 54. 5 (ii. 142. 25–6), τὰς δὲ συγκαταθέσεις οὐ μόνον οἱ ἀπὸ Πλάτωνος ἀλλὰ καὶ οἱ ἀπὸ τῆς Στοᾶς ἐφ' ἡμῖν εἶναι λέγουσιν. The words οἱ ἀπὸ Πλάτωνος refer most probably to Antiochus and his followers; moreover, the emphasis laid on the agreement between the Academy and the Porch reminds us of the general attitude of Antiochus, who, as we have seen, did his best to point out the correspondence existing between the different philosophical schools. Accordingly, some doubt may arise about the statement made by H. A. Wolfson: 'He [sc. Clement] is the first to combine the Aristotelian term faith with the Stoic term assent.'[1]

An analogous conclusion can be drawn from the definition of *pistis* as a preconception (πρόληψις). Clement approves Epicurus' statement according to which *pistis* is a preconception of mind: ναὶ μὴν καὶ ὁ Ἐπίκουρος ... πρόληψιν εἶναι διανοίας τὴν πίστιν ὑπολαμβάνει· πρόληψιν δὲ ἀποδίδωσιν ἐπιβολὴν ἐπί τι ἐναργὲς καὶ ἐπὶ τὴν ἐναργῆ τοῦ πράγματος ἔννοιαν (*Strom.* ii. 16. 3, vol. ii. 121. 8–12 = fr. 255 Usener, p. 187. 29). Later on he himself defines *pistis* as a πρόληψις: καὶ ἡ μὲν πίστις ὑπόληψις ἑκούσιος καὶ πρόληψις εὐγνώμονος πρὸ καταλήψεως, *Strom.* ii. 28. 1 (ii. 128. 1–2). For Epicurus knowledge is based on sense-perceptions, which, according to him, are always true: τὴν φαντασίαν, ἣν καὶ ἐνάργειαν καλεῖ, διὰ παντὸς ἀληθῆ φησιν ὑπάρχειν (Sext. Emp. *Adv. Math.* vii. 203, = fr. 247 Usener, p. 179. 20–1). The preconception (πρόληψις) is, in Epicurus' view, nothing else than an application of mind to the clearness of sense-perceptions, ἐπιβολὴ ἐπί τι ἐναργές (see the passage of Clement quoted above). Consequently for Epicurus any preconception is the direct product of sense-perceptions.[2]

It may at a first glance be surprising to find, in a passage of Clement, the acceptance of a view of the 'atheistic' Epicurus,

---

[1] *The Philosophy of the Church Fathers* i. 120.
[2] See also *Vita Epic.*, c. 33, τὴν δὲ πρόληψιν λέγουσιν ... μνήμην τοῦ πολλάκις ἔξωθεν φανέντος, and C. Bailey's note on this passage, p. 415 of his commentary (*Epicurus. The extant Remains*, Oxford, 1926).

whom he does not hesitate to attack elsewhere.¹ Such a surprise
is, however, bound to vanish as soon as we remember that the
Epicurean doctrine of πρόληψις is in perfect agreement with
the views of the Stoics, who considered sense-perceptions as the
basis of every knowledge and as the first cause of what they too
called προλήψεις.² This was also the view of Antiochus, as can be
seen from *Ac. Pr.* ii. 30: *mens enim ipsa, quae sensuum fons est, atque
ipse sensus est, naturalem vim habet quam intendit ad ea, quibus movetur;
itaque alia visa sic adripit, ut eis statim utatur, alia quasi recondit,
e quibus memoria oritur. Cetera similitudinibus construit, ex quibus
efficiuntur notitiae rerum, quas Graeci tum ἐννοίας tum προλήψεις
vocant.* There can be therefore only one reason why Clement
accepts the Epicurean doctrine of πρόληψις: he found it in agreement with his own epistemological views which, as we have seen,
he had inherited from the school-teaching deriving from Antiochus. It is important to observe that, after mentioning Epicurus'
doctrine, Clement maintains that a preconception is transformed
into knowledge by instruction, ὁ μαθὼν δὲ ἤδη κατάληψιν ποιεῖ τὴν
πρόληψιν, *Strom.* ii. 17. 1 (ii. 121. 14–15), and that it is prior to
knowledge, πρόληψις . . . πρὸ καταλήψεως, *Strom.* ii. 28. 1 (ii. 128.
1–2). This is not in agreement with Epicurus' views, according to
which πρόληψις is itself knowledge, τὴν δὲ πρόληψιν λέγουσιν οἱονεὶ
κατάληψιν ἢ δόξαν ὀρθὴν ἢ ἔννοιαν ἐναποκειμένην, *Vita Epic.* 33.
On the other hand, Clement's statements show a perfect agreement with the teaching of Antiochus, who thought that it was
the rational activity of mind that had the task of transforming the
product of sense-perceptions (πρόληψις) into knowledge (κατά-
ληψις): *eo* [sc. to sense-perceptions] *cum accessit ratio argumentique
conclusio rerumque innumerabilium multitudo tum et perceptio eorum omnium
apparet et eadem ratio perfecta his gradibus ad sapientiam pervenit. Ad
rerum igitur scientiam vitaeque constantiam aptissima cum sit mens hominis,
amplectitur maxime cognitionem et istam κατάληψιν quam, ut dixi,
verbum e verbo exprimentes comprehensionem dicemus* (*Ac. Pr.* ii. 30–1).

¹ Völker, 236 n. 4, cannot refrain from expressing his wonder: 'Clemens beruft
sich ausdrücklich auf Epikur, und ich finde es bezeichnend, daß er sich nicht
scheut auf die Autorität dieses auch von ihm abgelehnten Philosophers u. U. zu
stützen.' On Clement's polemic against Epicurus see chapter I, p. 45 above.
Even in this passage Clement does not miss the opportunity of criticizing Epicurus:
before mentioning his definition of *pistis* as πρόληψις he says ὁ μάλιστα τῆς ἀληθείας
προτιμήσας τὴν ἡδονήν, *Strom.* ii. 16. 3 (ii. 121. 9).
² See Reid's footnote 5 on *Ac. Pr.* ii. 30, p. 213, with all the material concerning
the Stoics.

While mentioning and approving Epicurus' definition of *pistis* as πρόληψις, Clement had therefore the teaching of Antiochus still floating in his mind. I think it very probable, although I cannot prove it directly, that Clement, just as in the case of the reference to Theophrastus (*Strom.* ii. 9. 5), took the Epicurean doctrine of πρόληψις not directly from Epicurus' writings, but from a school handbook reproducing the epistemological teaching of Antiochus. It should not be forgotten that Antiochus seems to have devoted part of one of his writings to the exposition of the Epicurean doctrine of knowledge, as can be inferred from the section of *Adv. Math.* vii. 203–16, belonging to that part of the seventh book of the *Adversus Mathematicos* which, according to Hirzel, can be traced back to him.[1]

To sum up. According to its first meaning, the term *pistis* indicates in Clement (*a*) the acceptance of the first, undemonstrated principles of demonstration; (*b*) the acceptance also, as principles of demonstration, of what appears evident both to reason and to mind, and, in this way, (*c*) also any kind of immediate knowledge based on sense-perceptions and expressed by such terms as 'assent' or 'preconception'. The doctrine of the acceptance of the first and undemonstrated principles had been formulated by Plato and developed by Aristotle; it has, however, come down to Clement not directly from Aristotle, but from a school-tradition which also appears in the *Didaskalikos* of Albinus. The doctrine of the acceptance of what appears evident to sensation and, in more general terms, of sense-perceptions as origin of immediate knowledge is quoted in the name of Theophrastus; most probably, however, Clement has received it not from the Peripatetic school, but from the school-teaching going back to Antiochus. The definitions of *pistis* as συγκατάθεσις or πρόληψις which both refer to immediate knowledge produced by sense-perceptions can also be traced back to Antiochus.[2]

[1] The scholars (for instance Camelot, 29, Völker, 236, and Wolfson, *The Philosophy* . . . i. 121) who have mentioned Clement's passage referring to Epicurus, i.e. *Strom.* ii. 16. 3, have not thought of the possibility that Clement's dependence on Epicurus is based on an intermediate source.

[2] Philo does not possess such a complicated doctrine of *pistis* as Clement (on some analogies in the use of the terms *pistis* and πιστεύειν between them see the references given by Völker, 248, especially nn. 2 and 5). His epistemological views are, however, the same as those of Antiochus. Like Antiochus, Philo maintains that knowledge is the product of the combined activity of sensations and mind, *Leg. Alleg.* i. 29 (i. 68. 15–21) and ii. 40 (i. 98. 14–16). There are, moreover, some very close

2. It is peculiar to the scientific demonstration to attain a trustworthy conclusion. The term *pistis* designates therefore also the firm belief of reason in the truth of the conclusion of demonstration. This is the ideas which underlies some definitions of demonstration given by Clement in the so-called eighth book of the *Stromateis*:

Strom. viii. 5. 1 (iii. 82. 12–14): ὡσαύτως δὲ καὶ τὴν ἀπόδειξιν πάντες ἄνθρωποι ὁμολογήσαιεν ἂν λόγον εἶναι τοῖς ἀμφισβητουμένοις ἐκ τῶν ὁμολογουμένων ἐκπορίζοντα τὴν πίστιν.[1] Cf. Strom. ii. 48. 1 (ii. 138. 18–20).[2]

Strom. viii. 5. 3 (iii. 82. 16–17): κυριώτατα μὲν οὖν ἀπόδειξις λέγεται ἡ τὴν ἐπιστημονικὴν πίστιν ἐντιθεῖσα ταῖς τῶν μανθανόντων ψυχαῖς. Cf. Strom. ii. 49. 3 (ii. 139. 5–7).[3]

Strom. viii. 7. 6 (iii. 83. 31–3): ἐὰν οὖν τις εὑρεθῇ λόγος τοιοῦτος οἷος ἐκ τῶν ἤδη πιστῶν τοῖς οὔπω πιστοῖς ἐκπορίζεσθαι τὴν πίστιν δυνάμενος, αὐτὸν τοῦτον εἶναι φήσομεν οὐσίαν ἀποδείξεως. Cf. Strom. vii. 98. 3 (iii. 69. 22–4).[4]

parallels between the Jewish author and Antiochus: in *Leg. Alleg.* i. 29 Philo compares the νοῦς to a τεχνίτης, just as Antiochus seems to have done, Sext. Emp. *Adv. Math.* vii. 226; Philo clearly maintains that the νοῦς must be considered as the source of sensations, since it is the principle which imparts life to them (*Leg. Alleg.* i. 29, vol. i. 68. 18–19; ii. 41, vol. i. 98. 23; and ii. 45, vol. i. 99. 12 f.): the same things had been said by Antiochus, Cic. *Ac. Pr.* ii. 30, *mens enim ipsa, quae sensuum fons est . . . naturalem vim habet*; Philo is inclined to consider sensations as potentially existing in mind, *Leg. Alleg.* ii. 45 (i. 99. 8–12): Antiochus had held the same view, as can be seen from *Ac. Pr.* ii. 30: *mens . . . quae . . . ipse sensus est* (on this Antiochean doctrine and its sources see Strache, *Ekl.* 12 and 28, and Reid's footnote 1 concerning *Ac. Pr.* ii. 30, p. 212). It must not be forgotten that Antiochus remained in Alexandria for some time (*Ac. Pr.* ii. 11) and probably lectured there. Eudorus of Alexandria, a disciple of Antiochus, has most probably played a role of mediator between Antiochus and Philo: after P. Boyancé, who had hinted at the possibility of a close relationship between Antiochus, Eudorus, and Philo, *REG* 72 (1959), 378–9, W. Theiler has recently drawn attention to some very close correspondences between Philo and Eudorus: see *Parusia, Festgabe für I. Hirschberger*, 204–15.

[1] The terminology of this definition of demonstration shows a Stoic influence, as can be seen from *SVF* ii. 226 (cf. Ernst, 16, and Witt, 33 n. 5). A similar definition of demonstration was given by Antiochus: *itaque argumenti conclusio, quae est graece* ἀπόδειξις, *ita definitur: ratio quae ex rebus perceptis ad id, quod non percipiebatur, adducit*, *Ac. Pr.* ii. 26 (the reference to this passage is given by Witt, 33 n. 7; see also Ernst, 16). Ernst is right in pointing out (p. 19) the correspondence between the definition of demonstration given by Clement and the definition of syllogism given by Alexander of Aphrodisias, *In An. Pr.* 25b32, vol. ii, pars i, pp. 43. 8–9 and 44. 14–15 Wallies.

[2] The correspondence between these two passages of Clement has been shown by Ernst, 24, and by Stählin, app. crit., vols. ii. 138 and iii. 82.

[3] On the correspondence between *Strom.* viii. 5. 3 and ii. 49. 2 see Ernst, 27.

[4] On the correspondence between *Strom.* viii. 7. 6 and vii. 98. 3 see Ernst, 28 (cf. Stählin, app., vol. iii. 69 and 83).

These passages explain why, in the second book of the *Stromateis*, Clement, referring to Aristotle, says: Ἀριστοτέλης δὲ τὸ ἑπόμενον τῇ ἐπιστήμῃ κρῖμα, ὡς ἀληθὲς τόδε τι, πίστιν εἶναί φησι (*Strom.* ii. 15. 5, vol. ii. 120. 25–6). That the peculiar character of scientific knowledge (i.e. of the knowledge attained by means of demonstration) is represented by the firm belief of mind (*pistis*) in its truth is an idea which frequently occurs in Aristotle, as can be seen from *Top.* 103ᵇ7,[1] 131ᵃ23,[2] *An. Pr.* 68ᵇ12, 68ᵇ13–14, *An. Post.* 72ᵃ25–6, 72ᵃ30–1, 72ᵃ35–6, *EN* 1139ᵇ33–4,[3] *Rhet.* 1355ᵃ5–6,[4] and 1377ᵇ23.[5]

The *pistis* produced by demonstration possesses, however, for Clement a scientific character only if the demonstration itself is scientific. As there are some demonstrations which may be called scientific, and some others which on the contrary belong to the sphere of opinion (δόξα), in the same way there are two kinds of *pistis*, the one scientific, the other based simply on opinion. Such a distinction appears in the following passages of the *Stromateis*:

Strom. ii. 48. 1 (ii. 138. 20–4): πίστεως δ' οὔσης διττῆς, τῆς μὲν ἐπιστημονικῆς, τῆς δὲ δοξαστικῆς, οὐθὲν κωλύει ἀπόδειξιν ὀνομάζειν διττήν, τὴν μὲν ἐπιστημονικήν, τὴν δὲ δοξαστικήν, ἐπεὶ καὶ ἡ γνῶσις καὶ ἡ πρόγνωσις διττὴ λέγεται, ἡ μὲν ἀπηκριβωμένην

---

[1] Wolfson also, *The Philosophy* ..., 114 n. 12, refers to this passage.

[2] This reference is given also by L. Früchtel, note 120. 25, vol. ii. 525 of the reprint of Stählin's edition.

[3] On this passage of Aristotle see also Früchtel, loc. cit.

[4] This passage of Aristotle, together with that of *EN* 1139ᵇ33–4, should be compared with Clement, *Strom.* ii. 15. 5, Ἀριστοτέλης δὲ τὸ ἑπόμενον τῇ ἐπιστήμῃ κρῖμα ὡς ἀληθὲς τόδε τι πίστιν εἶναί φησι. Clement seems also to be inclined to consider *pistis* as a vehement assumption, as can be inferred from *Strom.* ii. 16. 1, ὑποκρίνεται δὲ τὴν πίστιν ἡ εἰκασία, ἀσθενὴς οὖσα ὑπόληψις. This passage finds its counterpart in Aristotle, *Top.* 126ᵇ18, ἡ πίστις ὑπόληψις σφοδρά (cf. Stählin, app. crit., vol. ii. 120; Witt, 33 n. 13; and Wolfson, *The Philosophy* ... 113 n. 3) and *Top.* 126ᵇ25–6, ὁμοίως δὲ καὶ ἡ πίστις παρέσται τῇ ὑπολήψει, εἴπερ σφοδρότης ὑπολήψεώς ἐστιν, ὥστε ἡ ὑπόληψις πιστεύσει. Even here, however, Clement's dependence on Aristotle is not direct, but must be based on some intermediate source, probably the school-book containing some Peripatetic material on logic which he also consulted when he wrote down the notes forming the so-called eighth book of the *Stromateis*. Like *pistis* in its strictly epistemological sense, the term ὑπόληψις assumes in Clement a twofold meaning: it may refer to *pistis* as a product of demonstration, as in the passage *Strom.* ii. 16, 1 quoted above, and it may also refer to *pistis* as immediate knowledge, as in the passage of *Strom.* ii. 28. 1 (ii. 128. 1–2), where it appears together with πρόληψις: καὶ ἡ μὲν πίστις ὑπόληψις ἑκούσιος καὶ πρόληψις ... πρὸ καταλήψεως.

[5] The same idea of *pistis* occurs also in Alexander of Aphrodisias: see, for instance, *In An. Pr.* Prooemium (vol. ii, p. 4. 23–5 Wallies), *In An. Pr.* 25ᵇ32 (ii. 43. 6–9, 43. 10–12, 44. 6–8), *In An. Pr.* 26ᵇ31 (ii. 68. 20–1), *In Top.* 103ᵇ2 (vol. ii. 62. 6–7).

ἔχουσα τὴν ἑαυτῆς φύσιν, ἡ δὲ ἐλλιπῆ. Cf. *Strom.* viii. 5. 2–3 (iii. 82. 14–18).[1]

The distinction between *pistis* and ἀπόδειξις ἐπιστημονική and δοξαστική which Clement points out in these two passages is based on the distinction drawn by Aristotle between the scientific syllogism on the one hand and the dialectical and rhetorical syllogisms on the other. Whereas the scientific syllogism or demonstration (see *An. Pr.* 71ᵇ18, ἀπόδειξιν δὲ λέγω συλλογισμὸν ἐπιστημονικόν) is based on premisses which are primary and true, the two other kinds of syllogism start from premisses which belong to the sphere of δόξα. The distinction between scientific and dialectical syllogism appears in *Top.* 100ᵃ27–30, ἀπόδειξις μὲν οὖν ἐστιν, ὅταν ἐξ ἀληθῶν καὶ πρώτων ὁ συλλογισμὸς ᾖ . . . διαλεκτικὸς δὲ συλλογισμὸς ὁ ἐξ ἐνδόξων συλλογιζόμενος,[2] cf. *An. Pr.* 46ᵃ9–10, εἰς δὲ τοὺς διαλεκτικοὺς συλλογισμοὺς ἐκ τῶν παρὰ φύσιν προτάσεων.[3] The dialectical syllogism is called by Aristotle also ἐπιχείρημα, *Top.* 162ᵃ15–16.[4] Also the rhetorical way of arguing (ἀπόδειξις ῥητορική) is based, just as the dialectical syllogism is, on premisses which are only probable: ἐνθύμημα δέ ἐστι συλλογισμὸς ἐξ εἰκότων ἢ σημείων . . . τὸ μὲν εἰκός ἐστι πρότασις ἔνδοξος, *An. Pr.* 27ᵃ1; cf. *Rhet.* 1355ᵃ6–7, ἔστι δ' ἀπόδειξις ῥητορικὴ ἐνθύμημα, and ibid. 1355ᵃ8–9, τὸ δ' ἐνθύμημα συλλογισμός τις.[5] All this substantially agrees with what Clement says in *Strom.* ii. 49. 2, ἡ δὲ δοξαστικὴ ἀπόδειξις πρὸς τῶν ῥητορικῶν γινομένη ἐπιχειρημάτων ἢ καὶ διαλεκτικῶν συλλογισμῶν and in *Strom.* viii. 7. 8 (iii. 84. 4–7), εἰ δ' ἐξ ἐνδόξων μόνων [sc. ἄρξαιτό τις] οὐ μὴν πρώτων γε . . . συλλογιεῖται μέν, οὐ μὴν ἐπιστημονικήν γε ποιήσεται τὴν ἀπόδειξιν; cf. *Strom.* viii. 6. 2 (iii. 83. 1–3).

All these Aristotelian doctrines have, however, become part of the philosophical syncretism of the first centuries A.D. and occur therefore also in Middle Platonism. Plutarch also, like Aristotle

---

[1] The correspondence between *Strom.* ii. 48. 1 and viii. 5. 2–3 has been pointed out by Ernst, 24. The πρόγνωσις which is mentioned in both passages of Clement refers obviously to the acceptance of the premises of demonstration. If these premises are true, the πρόγνωσις will be ἐπιστημονική, if they are only probable and based on δόξα the πρόγνωσις will be ἐλπιστική or δοξαστική.

[2] The reference to this passage of the *Topics* is given also by Ernst, 17 and 19.

[3] On this passage of the *Prior Analytics* see also Witt, 45 n. 7.

[4] On this passage of the *Topics* see also Witt, loc. cit. Witt's reference to *Parva Nat.* 451ᵃ19 is inapplicable.

[5] The distinction between ἐπιστήμη and δόξα is made clear by Aristotle himself: see the section 88ᵇ30–89ᵇ6 (= chap. 33) of the first book of the *Posterior Analytics*.

and Clement, connects *pistis* with scientific knowledge and demonstration: this is the only possible meaning of the expression πᾶσα γὰρ ἀπόδειξις καὶ πᾶσα πίστις ἐπιστήμης in *De Plac.* *Philos.* 877 c 1, which should be compared with *Strom.* ii. 15. 5 (ii. 120. 25–6) τὸ ἑπόμενον τῇ ἐπιστήμῃ κρῖμα ὡς ἀληθὲς τόδε τι πίστιν εἶναι. Albinus adopts the Aristotelian distinction between scientific demonstration, dialectical syllogism, and rhetorical syllogism which we have observed in Clement and which is the origin of his conception of the twofold *pistis*, i.e. of the πίστις ἐπιστημονική and δοξαστική: in *Did.* 153. 27 ff. he says τὸ συλλογιστικόν, τοῦτο δὲ εἰς τὸ ἀποδεικτικὸν [sc. διαιρεῖται] ὅπερ ἐστὶ περὶ τὸν ἀναγκαῖον συλλογισμόν,[1] καὶ εἰς τὸ ἐπιχειρηματικόν, ὃ θεωρεῖται περὶ τὸν ἔνδοξον συλλογισμόν, καὶ τρίτον εἰς τὸ ῥητορικόν, ὅπερ ἐστὶ περὶ τὸ ἐνθύμημα, ὃ καλεῖται ἀτελὴς συλλογισμός. This passage of Albinus, in which the influence of Aristotelian terminology is particularly evident, derives most probably from a school-book containing Peripatetic doctrines.[2] From an analogous school-book Clement took the notes which appear in the passages of *Strom.* viii. 5. 2–3, 7, 7–8 and of which he made use in some sections of the other books of his *Stromateis*.[3] Here we have, needless to say, a case analogous to that we have observed when dealing with the doctrine of the ἀναπόδεικτοι ἀρχαί (see p. 123 above).

Since *pistis* is the direct product of scientific demonstration, it is also one and the same thing with scientific knowledge or gnosis: ἡ γὰρ ἀνωτάτω ἀπόδειξις ... πίστιν ἐντίθησι ... ἥτις ἂν εἴη γνῶσις, *Strom.* ii. 49. 3 (ii. 139. 5–8). But Clement goes even beyond this assertion: since scientific knowledge can only exist if reason possesses a firm conviction (*pistis*) about its truth (τὸ ἑπόμενον τῇ ἐπιστήμῃ κρῖμα ὡς ἀληθὲς τόδε τι πίστιν εἶναι, *Strom.* ii. 15. 5, vol. ii. 120. 25–6), *pistis* can be regarded as something higher than ἐπιστήμη: κυριώτερον οὖν τῆς ἐπιστήμης ἡ πίστις καὶ

[1] Cf. Aristotle, *An. Post.* 73ᵃ24, ἐξ ἀναγκαίων ἄρα συλλογισμός ἐστιν ἀπόδειξις. This reference is given by Witt, 45 n. 6. His further reference to *An. Post.* 81ᵃ38 f. is wrong.
[2] Witt, 45, thinks it possible that even here Albinus has been influenced by the teaching of Antiochus. He draws attention to the passage of *Ac. Post.* i. 32 where the distinction between logic and rhetoric is pointed out (this passage is quoted by him, pp. 45–6, but the exact reference is missing).
[3] An influence of the teaching of Antiochus on the distinction between demonstration and syllogism which occurs in *Strom.* viii. 7. 8 (iii. 84. 4–7) is, however, also possible. Witt, 33 n. 10, refers to Cicero, *De Fin.* v. 9: *non modo probabili argumentatione sed etiam necessaria ... ratione.*

ἔστιν αὐτῆς κριτήριον, *Strom.* ii. 15. 5 (ii. 120. 26–7). In this way, Clement's *pistis* plays a far more important role in epistemology than the Platonic *pistis* which, as we can see from the *Republic* and the *Timaeus*, is confined, together with εἰκασία, to the inferior stage of knowledge, namely to the knowledge of γένεσις which is sharply distinguished from that of οὐσία.[1]

3. Clement often uses the term *pistis* in a strictly religious sense: it indicates then the attitude of some Christians, who take what is said by Scripture as true, but do not bother to inquire about it.[2] Such a meaning appears in the following passages of the *Stromateis*:

Strom. vii. 55. 2 (iii. 40. 22–5): πίστις μὲν οὖν ἐνδιάθετόν ἐστιν ἀγαθόν, καὶ ἄνευ τοῦ ζητεῖν τὸν θεὸν ὁμολογοῦσα εἶναι τοῦτον καὶ δοξάζουσα ὡς ὄντα.

Strom. vii. 57. 3 (iii. 42. 4): τῶν διὰ πίστεως παρειλημμένων.

Strom. vii. 95. 9 (iii. 68. 2): οἱ μὲν ἀπογευσάμενοι μόνον τῶν γραφῶν πιστοί.

This is the ψιλή or κοινὴ πίστις which is mentioned in other passages as well: see *Strom.* i. 43. 1 (ii. 28. 30), *Strom.* iv. 100. 6 (ii. 293. 2), *Strom.* v. 9. 2 (ii. 331. 19), *Strom.* v. 11. 1 (ii. 332. 27), *Strom.* v. 26. 1 (ii. 342. 2), *Strom.* v. 53. 3 (ii. 362. 16). This *pistis*, though representing the base (θεμέλιος) of the Christian life[3] and being sufficient for salvation,[4] is nevertheless, in Clement's

[1] See *Rep.* vi. 511 d 6–e 2, vii. 533 e 7–534 a 5, *Timaeus* 29 c 3. To these passages of Plato is related Albinus, *Did.* 154. 23 ff., ὧν ὁ μὲν περὶ τὰ νοητὰ ἐπιστήμη τέ ἐστι καὶ ἐπιστημονικὸς λόγος, ὁ δὲ περὶ τὰ αἰσθητὰ δοξαστικός τε καὶ δόξα. The antithesis between the λόγος ἐπιστημονικός and δοξαστικός which appears here must not lead us to establish a parallel with the distinction drawn by Clement between the πίστις ἐπιστημονική and δοξαστική: in Albinus the terms ἐπιστημονικός and δοξαστικός are used in Platonic sense (the one being referred to the νοητά, the other to the αἰσθητά), whereas in Clement the same terms reproduce an Aristotelian doctrine. On this point Albinus could not agree with the teaching of Antiochus, who regarded αἴσθησις as the source of any knowledge (see Witt, 53). On the correspondence between Albinus' epistemology and that of Antiochus apart from this important difference see Witt, 53 ff.

[2] Cf. Merk, 18: 'Der Glaube nimmt die Überlieferung der Schrift ohne Prüfung für wahr an.'

[3] *Strom.* ii. 31. 3 (ii. 129. 26–30), v. 2. 5 (ii. 327. 10), v. 26. 1 (ii. 342. 2–3), and *Strom.* vii. 55. 5 (iii. 41. 1). It is important to point out that the expression ψιλὴ πίστις which Clement uses in the passages of *Strom.* i. 43. 1, v. 9. 2, and v. 53. 3 quoted above is also Valentinian: see, for instance, Iren. *Adv. Haer.* i. 6. 1 (i. 53. 7), πίστεως ψιλῆς.

[4] See, for instance, *Strom.* ii. 11. 2 (ii. 119. 2), v. 9. 2 (ii. 331. 19–20), and v. 18. 3 (ii. 337. 27).

thought, still far from being perfect. Clement lays a strong emphasis on the necessity of developing this simple *pistis* into a higher form of knowledge, which he calls *gnosis*:

> *Strom.* v. 5. 2 (ii. 328. 27–9): We know that the research which accompanies faith and which builds the magnificent knowledge of the truth on the base represented by faith, is the best.
> *Strom.* v. 11. 1 (ii. 332. 27–333. 1): We maintain that faith must not remain lazy and isolated, but must make progress together with research.
> *Strom.* vii. 95. 9 (iii. 68. 2–4): Those who take simply a taste of Scriptures possess only faith, those who go further on succeed in discerning exactly the truth: they are the gnostics.

What Clement says in these passages becomes clearer as soon as one realizes that for him the full comprehension of the Christian teaching cannot be attained by means of the simple acceptance of the literal meaning of Scripture, but requires a particular study and interpretation of it: '. . . it is not good to listen to what is said simply with our flesh: we must search after and apprehend the hidden meaning by means of an adequate study and comprehension', *Quis Div. salv.* 5. 2 (iii. 163. 16–20), cf. *Quis Div. salv.* 5. 4 (iii. 163. 29–31), 'it is not good to listen with our ears superficially: it is necessary to apply our mind to the spirit of the saviour and to the secret part of his thought.'[1] The ζήτησις of which Clement speaks is therefore nothing but the attempt to disclose the hidden and higher meaning of Scripture.

At this point it must be observed that Clement combines the religious *pistis* (i.e. the acceptance of Scripture) with the epistemological *pistis* (i.e. the acceptance of the principle of demonstration and of its result). If, by means of an act of faith, it must be admitted that what is said by Scripture, being inspired by God, is true, the main problem still consists in determining *in what sense* Scripture is true, i.e. which meaning must be

---

[1] Clement's words δεῖ . . . μὴ σαρκίνως ἀκροᾶσθαι τῶν λεγομένων and οὐκ ἐπιπολαίως δέχεσθαι ταῖς ἀκοαῖς προσῆκεν hint most probably at the same people about whom he speaks in the first book of the *Stromateis*, namely those Christians who are quite satisfied with the ψιλὴ πίστις and suspect anything which, at a first glance, appears extraneous to it (see *Strom.* i. 43. 1). To *Quis Div. salv.* 5. 2 and 5. 4 are closely related the passages of *Strom.* vi. 126. 1 (ii. 495. 18–21), vi. 126. 2 (ii. 495. 22–4), and vi. 129. 4 (ii. 497. 15–19) which will be quoted in the section on *gnosis* (see pp. 145–6 below).

attached to the words of Scripture which the Christian accepts as true. Accordingly, the accepted truth of Scripture becomes the ἀρχή of demonstration; the study and interpretation of Scripture becomes the scientific demonstration; and the inner meaning which is disclosed at the end of this study becomes the conclusion of demonstration which, as we have seen, is also trustworthy and, in so far as it is trustworthy, represents scientific knowledge. In other words, the interpretation of Scripture aims at disclosing its inner meaning exactly as demonstration aims at inferring the still unknown conclusion from the true and self-evident premisses. That the content of Scripture becomes the ἀρχή of demonstration is shown by the comparison between *Strom.* vii. 96. 1, ἀπ' αὐτῶν περὶ αὐτῶν τῶν γραφῶν ἀποδεικνύντες (cf. also *Strom.* vii. 93. 1, πρὶν ἂν τὴν ἀπόδειξιν ἀπ' αὐτῶν λάβωμεν τῶν γραφῶν), and *Strom.* vii. 96. 5, πίστει περιλαβόντες ἀναπόδεικτον τὴν ἀρχὴν ἐκ περιουσίας καὶ τὰς ἀποδείξεις παρ' αὐτῆς τῆς ἀρχῆς περὶ τῆς ἀρχῆς λαβόντες. The close parallelism which exists between the sentences ἀπ' αὐτῶν περὶ αὐτῶν τῶν γραφῶν ἀποδεικνύντες and ἀποδείξεις παρ' αὐτῆς τῆς ἀρχῆς περὶ τῆς ἀρχῆς λαβόντες proves that Scripture is regarded by Clement both as the starting-point or principle of demonstration and as the object of demonstration itself. This is the only possible explanation which can be given of the words ἀποδείξεις παρ' αὐτῆς τῆς ἀρχῆς περὶ τῆς ἀρχῆς λαβόντες. That demonstration consists in a study and interpretation of Scripture which aims at disclosing its inner meaning and consequently at producing also scientific knowledge is shown by *Strom.* ii. 49. 3 (ii. 139. 5–8), ἡ γὰρ ἀνωτάτω ἀπόδειξις, ἣν ᾐνιξάμεθα ἐπιστημονικήν, πίστιν ἐντίθησι διὰ τῆς τῶν γραφῶν παραθέσεώς τε καὶ διοίξεως ταῖς τῶν μανθάνειν ὀρεγομένων ψυχαῖς, ἥτις ἂν εἴη γνῶσις. This is also the idea which is implied in *Strom.* v. 18. 3 (ii. 337. 25–7), ἐνέχυρον γὰρ τῆς ἀληθείας τὴν ἀπόδειξιν ἀπαιτοῦσιν οἱ πολλοὶ οὐκ ἀρκούμενοι ψιλῇ τῇ ἐκ πίστεως σωτηρίᾳ, and *Strom.* vii. 57. 3 (iii. 42. 4–7), ἡ γνῶσις δὲ ἀπόδειξις τῶν διὰ πίστεως παρειλημμένων ἰσχυρὰ καὶ βέβαιος, διὰ τῆς κυριακῆς διδασκαλίας ἐποικοδομένη τῇ πίστει, εἰς τὸ ἀμετάπτωτον καὶ μετ' ἐπιστήμης καταληπτὸν παραπέμπουσα.

If we now keep in mind the inclination of Clement to identify the acceptance of the principle of demonstration with the religious *pistis*, and the demonstration itself with the interpretation of Scripture, we shall also be in the position to understand better why he likes to call *pistis* the basis (θεμέλιος) of gnosis[1] and why he insists on the inseparability of these two ideas (οὔθ᾽ ἡ γνῶσις ἄνευ πίστεως οὔθ᾽ ἡ πίστις ἄνευ γνώσεως, Strom. v. 1. 3, vol. ii. 326. 9). As the trustworthy ἀρχή is the basis on which both demonstration and scientific knowledge must rest, in the same way the acceptance of the truth of Scripture is the preliminary condition of the existence of its interpretation and consequently also of gnosis; and as in demonstration there is a necessary link between its premisses and its conclusions, in the same way the acceptance of Scripture must necessarily lead to the discovery of its hidden implications.

An analogous interpretation can be given of the passage of Strom. v. 2. 3–5 (ii. 327. 7–14) in which Clement, quoting a sentence of St. Paul, Rom. 1: 17, speaks of a twofold pistis: "δικαιοσύνη δὲ θεοῦ ἐν ταὐτῷ ἀποκαλύπτεται ἐκ πίστεως εἰς πίστιν." φαίνεται οὖν ὁ ἀπόστολος διττὴν καταγγέλλων πίστιν, μᾶλλον δὲ μίαν, αὔξησιν καὶ τελείωσιν ἐπιδεχομένην· ἡ μὲν γὰρ κοινὴ πίστις καθάπερ θεμέλιος ὑπόκειται, ἡ δὲ ἐξαίρετος ἐποικοδομένη συντελειοῦται τῷ πιστῷ καὶ συναπαρτίζεται αὐτῇ ἐκ μαθήσεως περιγινομένη. Whereas the κοινὴ πίστις is the acceptance of Scripture which, as we have seen, is also the principle of demonstration, the ἐξαίρετος πίστις is the pistis which is one and the same thing with the scientific knowledge produced by demonstration (or study of Scripture): in other words, it is the ἐπιστημονικὴ πίστις which is identical with gnosis (cf. Strom. ii. 49. 3, ἡ γὰρ ἀνωτάτω ἀπόδειξις . . . πίστιν ἐντίθησι . . . ἥτις ἂν εἴη γνῶσις).[2] With these ideas expounded in Strom. v. 2. 3–5 is closely connected the sentence of Strom. ii. 16. 2 (ii. 121. 7–8), πιστὴ τοίνυν ἡ γνῶσις, γνωστὴ δὲ ἡ πίστις. The result of demonstration (gnosis), in so far as it possesses the ἐπιστημονικὴ πίστις, is called by Clement trustworthy (πιστή); on the other hand, the expression γνωστὴ

[1] See the references given in footnote 3, p. 136 above, and also the passage of Strom. v. 5. 2 on p.137 above.

[2] Merk thinks that the distinction between the two πίστεις which appears in Strom. v. 2. 3–5 can be identified with the distinction between πίστις ἐπιστημονική and δοξαστική (p. 19). Such identification is wrong. The distinction between πίστις ἐπιστημονική and δοξαστική is based on the nature of the premisses of demonstration, which can either be true or belong to the sphere of δόξα (see p. 133 above), whereas the distinction between the κοινὴ πίστις and the ἐξαίρετος πίστις corresponds to the distinction between the principle of the scientific demonstration and its conclusion. Moreover, there can be no relation between the κοινὴ πίστις of Strom. v. 2. 3–5 and the δοξαστικὴ πίστις: Scripture as a principle of scientific demonstration cannot be regarded as one of those ἀρχαί which are only probable, but not necessarily true.

δὲ ἡ πίστις hints at the development of the κοινὴ πίστις (the principle of demonstration) into *gnosis*.[1]

There is, however, some reason why Clement stresses the necessity of developing the simple *pistis* into a higher form of knowledge. We have already seen (p. 138 above) that such a development is based on a special interpretation of Scripture, namely on the discovery of its inner meaning. Clement is here under the direct influence of Philo. In his work *De Vita contemplativa* Philo, speaking about the Θεραπευταὶ who, according to him, possess a higher knowledge of God in so far as they dedicate themselves completely to the contemplative life, makes it clear that they are not satisfied with the acceptance of the letter of Scripture, but aim also at penetrating more deeply into it, in order to grasp its inner meaning: 'when they study the sacred Scriptures they cultivate their ancestral philosophy, since they regard the words which express them as symbols of a hidden nature, which reveals itself in covert meanings', *De Vita cont.* 28 (vi. 53. 10–13), cf. *De Vita cont.* 78 (vi. 67. 1–9), 'the interpretations of the holy Scriptures aim at the covert meaning and are made possible by allegory; in the eyes of these people, the whole Mosaic legislation is like an animal: its body is represented by the written prescriptions, its soul by the inner meaning which is kept hidden by the words and is invisible. Owing especially to this meaning the rational soul begins to contemplate the realities which are akin to it: using the words like a mirror, it sees the extraordinary beauty of the thoughts which are reflected in them, discloses the symbols, and brings forward the inner meanings in their purity for those who, starting from a small allusion, are able to contemplate the invisible realities by means of the visible things.' These two passages of Philo practically expound the ideas which we have noticed in the passages of Clement's *Quis Dives salvetur* quoted above (p. 137).[2] The conclusion we

---

[1] Völker, 236–7, rightly observes: 'Als Sinn von «πιστὴ τοίνυν ἡ γνῶσις» ergäbe sich also die uns bereits geläufige Erkenntnis, daß in der ἐπιστήμη die πίστις enthalten sei. Für die Deutung von «γνωστὴ δὲ ἡ πίστις» ist ii. 17. 1, ii. 121. 14 f. wichtig: ὁ μαθὼν δὲ ἤδη κατάληψιν ποιεῖ τὴν πρόληψιν, d. h. aus der Vorstellung wird ein fester Begriff, eine deutliche und klare Anschauung, ein Wissen. Die πίστις wird ins Bereich der ἐπιστήμη erhoben.' On the development of *pistis* into *gnosis* see also de Faye's pertinent remarks in his paper in *AEHE* (Section des sciences religieuses, 1919), 11–14.

[2] The allegorical interpretation of Scripture of which Philo speaks in these passages is the same interpretation as that which he uses throughout his writings. On

can draw from such correspondences is that Clement was able to stress the difference between the simple *pistis* and *gnosis* because he found already formed in Philo the idea of the presence of an inner meaning in Scripture. He adopted this idea of Philo, and applied it to his own doctrine of *pistis* as acceptance both of the principle of demonstration and of its conclusion, which he had taken from one of the several handbooks on logic circulating in the philosophical schools of his time.

If the conclusions we have reached are right, we can safely maintain that Clement's conception of *pistis* and of its relations with *gnosis* is a perfectly coherent doctrine. There is no contradiction between the passage of *Strom.* ii. 15. 5 (ii. 120. 26–7), κυριώτερον οὖν τῆς ἐπιστήμης ἡ πίστις καὶ ἔστιν αὐτῆς κριτήριον, on the one hand, and such passages as *Strom.* vi. 109. 2 (ii. 486. 21), πλέον δέ ἐστι τοῦ πιστεῦσαι τὸ γνῶναι, *Strom.* vi. 164. 3 (ii. 516. 23–4), ἐπὶ τὴν ἀκρότητα τῆς πίστεως χωρήσας, τὴν γνῶσιν αὐτήν, *Strom.* vi. 165. 1 (ii. 517. 3–4), τὴν γνῶσιν . . . τελείωσιν οὖσαν τῆς πίστεως, and *Strom.* vii. 55. 2 (iii. 44. 24–5), διὰ ταύτης [sc. τῆς γνώσεως] τελειοῦται ἡ πίστις, ὡς τελείου τοῦ πιστοῦ ταύτῃ μόνως γινομένου, on the other. We can appreciate the perfect coherence of Clement's thought if we are aware of what he means by *pistis*. Whereas in *Strom.* ii. 15. 5 the *pistis* which is κυριώτερον τῆς ἐπιστήμης is the ἐπιστημονικὴ πίστις which is the result of demonstration and practically one and the same thing with *gnosis* (see p. 135 above), in the passages of *Strom.* vi. 109. 2, vi. 164. 3, vi. 165. 1, and vii. 55. 2 the term *pistis* hints at the ψιλὴ πίστις or acceptance of the letter of Scripture which must be developed into *gnosis*.

Such a doctrine of *pistis* enabled Clement to give his own answer to the Greek philosophers, to the followers of Valentine, and also to the *simpliciores*. By regarding *pistis* as the acceptance of the principle of scientific demonstration and as immediate knowledge, he made it clear that, since any kind of knowledge must ultimately be based on some undemonstrated principle, there was no sufficient reason for the opposition of the Greek philosophers against the Christian idea of faith;[1] by pointing

Philo's general views about the right way of interpreting Scripture see H. Leisegang's article 'Philo', *RE* 39 Halbband, coll. 36–9, and H. A. Wolfson, *Philo* i. 55 ff.

[1] The passage of *Strom.* ii. 16. 4 (ii. 119. 26 ff.), εἰ δέ τις λέγοι τὴν ἐπιστήμην ἀποδεικτικὴν εἶναι μετὰ λόγου, ἀκουσάτω ὅτι καὶ αἱ ἀρχαὶ ἀναπόδεικτοι, shows us

out the necessary link between *pistis* (i.e. the acceptance of the principle of demonstration) and *gnosis* (the result of demonstration itself) and by identifying *gnosis* with the scientific *pistis* he showed to the Valentinians that there was no antithesis between *pistis* and *gnosis*; by stressing the necessity of developing the simple *pistis* into *gnosis* by means of scientific demonstration (i.e. by means of interpretation of Scripture) he provided the *simpliciores* with the possibility of reaching a better comprehension of their own religious doctrines. It will be the purpose of the following section to establish which is the actual meaning of Clement's *gnosis* in all its implications.

2. *The Idea of 'Gnosis'*

Our examination of Clement's views on *pistis* and on its relations with *gnosis* has made clear the role which he attributes to the latter. As we have seen it indicates, first of all, a deeper comprehension and knowledge of the Christian doctrines which must be achieved by means of a particular interpretation or 'demonstration' of Scripture. Only in this way is it possible, in Clement's opinion, to reach that contemplation of the highest divinity which he calls also *gnosis* and which represents the ultimate aim of his Christian philosophy.

In Clement's conception of *gnosis* it is possible to distinguish two different stages. *Gnosis* can already be attained by man to some extent during his stay on earth; but it reaches its climax after the death of the body, when the soul of the γνωστικός is allowed to fly back to its original place where, after becoming a god, it can enjoy, in a complete and perpetual rest, the contemplation of the highest divinity 'face to face', together with the other θεοί.

The underlying ideas of both these stages of *gnosis* cannot be fully appreciated without taking their manifold relations with the cultural milieu of Egypt in the second and third centuries A.D. duly into account. The Platonic tradition, the Jewish-Alexandrine philosophy, and the heretical Christian Gnosticism which was

both the objection of the Greek philosophers against the Christian *pistis* and the answer which Clement gives to them. This has been rightly pointed out by Völker, 235.

so flourishing in Egypt during the first centuries of our era[1] combine together in Clement's conception of *gnosis* and influence it even in its minutest details: they are actually both the features and the colours of a complex picture which, however, gives the impression of unity and intimate coherence to the observer.

To these constitutive elements of Clement's *gnosis* modern scholars have generally paid almost no attention,[2] the only two partial exceptions being represented by J. Daniélou and E. Baert.[3] The present section aims therefore at studying Clement's *gnosis* by examining, first of all, its cultural background. Our analysis will dwell particularly on the following points:

1. esotericism; symbolism of Scripture; the secret tradition;
2. the role of the Logos as source and teacher of *gnosis*;
3. the ideal of contemplative life, in close connection with the idea of separation from the sensible world and of communion with the intelligible realities;
4. the role of the encyclical disciplines and of philosophy in the building of *gnosis*;
5. the allegorical interpretation of the Jewish tabernacle and of the entry of the High Priest into the Holy of Holies;
6. the *Himmelsreise* of the 'gnostic' soul and its deification.

The first four points deal with the first stage of *gnosis*, i.e. with the *gnosis* which man can obtain during his earthly life; the sixth point is concerned with the second stage of *gnosis*, i.e. with the

---

[1] Some important exponents of Gnosticism such as Basilides, Carpocrates, and Valentine hailed from Egypt and studied or taught in Alexandria: see O. Bardenhewer, *Erster Band*, 347 and 358; most probably, Christianity came into Egypt first under the form of Gnosticism: see, on this argument, W. Bauer, 52 ff., H. Lietzmann, ii. 283 ff., and W. Till, *LPP* 4 (1949), 230.

[2] This is true of P. T. Camelot, *Foi et gnose...*, 69–133; of J. Lebreton, *RSR* 18 (1928), 457–88; of G. Békés, *SA* 14 (Romae, 1942); of J. Moingt, *RSR* 37 (1950), 195–251, 398–421, 537–64, and 38 (1951), 82–118; and of W. Völker, 301–21, 321–32, 334–64, 381–403, and 403–45.

[3] J. Daniélou, *Message évangélique...*, 407–25, and *EJ* 21 (1962), 199–215; E. Baert, *FZPhTh* 12 (1965), 460–80. On these works we shall have to speak more in detail later on. A. Wlosok, *AHAW*, phil.-hist. Kl. (1960), 143–79, has not examined the *gnosis* of the Christian who has reached perfection (i.e. the *gnosis* of which Clement speaks in the *Stromateis*) but only the 'preliminary' *gnosis*, i.e. the way in which Clement describes baptism and the conversion of the heathens to Christianity; she has rightly drawn attention to some interesting correspondences between Clement, the Jewish-Alexandrine philosophy, and Hermetism in this respect.

gnosis which the soul possesses after its separation from the body; the fifth point can be related to both stages of *gnosis*.

1. It is peculiar to the higher *gnosis* to possess an esoteric character. Its doctrines cannot be revealed to anybody, but must on the contrary be reserved to very few people, namely to those who have proved themselves worthy of apprehending them. The distinction between the ψιλὴ πίστις and *gnosis* is also the distinction between those who are not allowed to approach the most sacred doctrines and those few who are admitted to this knowledge. Clement lays a very strong emphasis on this idea, which can be regarded as the *leitmotiv* of the *Stromateis*. 'He who is still blind and obtuse, who possesses neither capacity of understanding nor the fearless and penetrating insight peculiar to the soul longing for contemplation . . . is like a person attending the sacred rites without being initiated or one taking part in a holy dance without being educated; being still impure and unworthy of the pure truth, and also devoid of harmony and of order and material, he must still stay out of the divine choir';[1] 'only those who are often in contact with them [i.e. with the writings of the barbarian philosophy] and, in their faith and in their whole life, have produced sufficient evidence of their fitness, shall possess according to them [i.e. the writings of the barbarian philosophy] the real philosophy and the true theology.'[2] In order to find further support for his view, Clement quotes also passages of the *Republic*,[3] the *Theaetetus*,[4] and the *Epinomis*,[5] and also a passage of the forged letter of Lysis to Hipparchus: 'Nor must one communicate the treasures of wisdom to those whose soul is unclean even in a dream; it is not allowed to hand over what is attained by means of such hard struggles to the first person one meets with or to expound the mysteries of the word to those who are uninitiated.'[6] Clement glances at the most important Greek philosophical schools in order to prove that what he has been saying

---

[1] *Strom.* v. 19. 2–3 (ii. 338. 22–6).   [2] *Strom.* v. 56. 3 (ii. 364. 8–11).
[3] *Strom.* v. 17. 4 (ii. 337. 10–11) (*Rep.* vi. 494 a).
[4] *Strom.* v. 33. 5 (ii. 348. 4–7) (*Theaet.* 155 e).
[5] *Strom.* v. 7. 6 (ii. 330. 8–12) (*Epinom.* 973 e).
[6] *Strom.* v. 57. 2 (ii. 364. 24–7). The complete text of this letter can be found in Iamblichus, *De Vita Pyth.* 75–8 (pp. 42. 23–45. 16 Dübner). On the forgery see W. Theiler in his review of Delatte's book, *Études sur la littérature pythagoricienne*, in *Gnomon* 2 (1926), 149.

so far is right: if the Pythagoreans, the Platonists, the Epicureans, the Stoics, and the Aristotelians agreed in keeping the most important of their doctrines hidden and in giving, in this way, an esoteric character to their philosophical systems, is there not more reason to keep the true philosophy out of the reach of common people?[1] This idea underlies Clement's interpretation of the evangelical passage Matt. 22: 14, πολλοὶ γὰρ κλητοί, ὀλίγοι δὲ ἐκλεκτοί, and leads him to bring it into connection with Socrates' words in *Phaedo* 69 c, ναρθηκοφόροι μὲν πολλοί, βάκχοι δέ τε παῦροι.[2] In the same way Clement interprets also Matt. 10: 26, οὐδὲν κρυπτὸν ὃ οὐ φανερωθήσεται, οὐδὲ κεκαλυμμένον ὃ οὐκ ἀποκαλυφθήσεται: he makes it clear that this sentence hints only at those who show themselves capable of understanding in a certain way what is revealed to them, τῷ κρυπτῶς ἐπαΐοντι τὸ κρυπτὸν φανερωθήσεσθαι διὰ τοῦδε προεθέσπισεν τοῦ λογίου, καὶ τῷ παρακεκαλυμμένως τὰ παραδιδόμενα οἵῳ τε παραλαμβάνειν δηλωθήσεται τὸ κεκαλυμμένον ὡς ἡ ἀλήθεια, καὶ τὸ πολλοῖς κρυπτὸν τοῦτο τοῖς ὀλίγοις φανερὸν γενήσεται, Strom. i. 13. 3 (ii. 10. 6–10). That for Clement the doctrines of *gnosis* represent something hidden, which only very few people are allowed to know, is also proved by the following evidence:

Strom. v. 35. 5 (ii. 349. 18–350. 2): the objects which are recorded to stay on the holy ark symbolize what is within the intelligible world, which is hidden and closed to the many.

Strom. v. 80. 3 (ii. 379. 8–10): the prophet indicates that the holy, really mystical speech concerning the ungenerated principle and its powers must remain hidden.

Strom. vi. 70. 2 (ii. 466. 30–1): the gnostic about whom I speak comprehends what seems to be incomprehensible to other people.

Strom. vi. 116. 1 (ii. 490. 17–18): . . . teaching that the holy doctrines are hidden.

Strom. vi. 124. 5 (ii. 494. 26–7): . . . in a hidden way and in mystery: according to the allegorical interpretation, such things are said into the ear.[3]

Strom. vi. 126. 1–2 (ii. 495. 18–24): Scripture keeps its meaning hidden for several reasons: first, that we may be disposed to search and always sit up over the discovery of the saving words,

---

[1] See Strom. v. 58. 1–5 (ii. 365. 6–17).
[2] See Strom. v. 17. 4–5 (ii. 337. 10–13) and cf. Strom. i. 92. 3 (ii. 59. 13–15).
[3] These words represent Clement's own interpretation of the sentence of Matt. 10: 27, ὃ δὲ ἀκούετε εἰς τὸ οὖς.

secondly because it is not suitable for everybody to understand . . .
therefore the holy mysteries are hidden in parables and kept
safe for the selected men and for those who, coming from *pistis*,
are admitted into *gnosis*.
Strom. vi. 129. 4 (ii. 497. 16–19): Since the truth does not belong
to everybody, it is kept hidden in several ways: it illuminates
only those people who are initiated in *gnosis*, namely those who,
being moved by love, search after it.

The secret character of the doctrines of *gnosis* explains why
Clement often calls them μυστήρια, represents the study and
apprehension of them as a process of initiation (μυεῖσθαι), and
considers those who have attained the knowledge of the higher
truth as μύσται. He is very fond of these terms, and resorts to
them whenever he comes to speak about *gnosis*: it is worth looking
at such passages as *Strom.* i. 13. 1 (ii. 9. 24–10. 1), i. 13. 4 (ii. 10.
11–12), i. 15. 3 (ii. 11. 21), i. 32. 3 (ii. 21. 14–15), i. 32. 4 (ii. 21.
21–3), i. 176. 2 (ii. 108. 27–9), iv. 3. 1 (ii. 249. 8),[1] iv. 109. 2
(ii. 296. 11–12),[2] v. 61. 1 (ii. 367. 14–15), v. 90. 3 (ii. 385. 21–3),
vi. 95. 1 (ii. 479. 18–19), vi. 102. 1 (ii. 483. 10–12), vi. 126. 2
(ii. 495. 23–4), vi. 127. 5 (ii. 496. 20–2), vii. 4. 3 (iii. 5. 10–
11), vii. 6. 1 (iii. 6. 8), vii. 97. 4 (iii. 68. 8–9), *Quis Div. salv.*
36. 1 (iii. 183. 21–2), 37. 1 (iii. 183. 31–2), *Ecl. Proph.* 35. 1
(iii. 147. 17).[3]

---

[1] On the exact meaning of this expression (cf. also *Strom.* v. 71. 1) see p. 190
below.

[2] On the μυστήρια of the ἑβδομάς and ὀγδοάς see pp. 184 and 185 below.

[3] Völker, 312, is therefore wrong in maintaining that 'Clemens macht von ihr
[viz. the tendency to stress the esotericism of *gnosis*] freilich nur selten Gebrauch'.
It must be remembered that the use of mystery terms in the *Stromateis* cannot be
compared with the occurrence of the same terms at the end of the *Protrepticus*.
Here Clement represents Christianity as a mystery religion to which he wants to
convert all his pagan readers and, for this purpose, makes free use of the vocabulary
characteristic of the Greek mysteries (see, for instance, *Protr.* 119. 1, vol. i. 84. 4 ff.,
and 120. 1, vol. i. 84. 23 ff.). The apologetic tendency of these passages is something
different from the esotericism which is characteristic of the *gnosis* of the *Stromateis*.
This circumstance, to which A. Wlosok, *AHAW*, phil.-hist. Kl. (1960), 152–4,
has paid no attention, has been rightly pointed out by H. G. Marsh, *JTS* 37
(1936), 70: 'We must not forget that there are two Clements, the Alexandrine
philosopher and the Christian evangelist. The former defended the restriction of
esoteric truth, the latter knew that the gospel for the salvation of mankind must
be proclaimed to all.' Camelot, op. cit. 87–8, translates Marsh's words almost
literally: 'C'est bien ici que l'on perçoit qu'il y a deux Cléments, le didascale
chrétien et le philosophe alexandrin: le premier sait bien que l'évangile du salut
doit être prêché à tous, et c'est lui qui parlait dans le *Protreptique*; le second réserve
à une élite le trésor caché de la verité.'

The term μυστήριον occurs in three parallel passages of the
Synoptics (Matt. 13: 11, Mark 4: 11, and Luke 8: 10): Christ
speaks either of the 'mysteries of God' (Mark: 4 11 and Luke
8: 10) or of the 'mysteries of the kingdom of heaven' (Matt.
13: 11).[1] Clement does not hesitate to bring these 'mysteries' into
connection with the secret doctrines of *gnosis*: it is not without
any reason that he quotes the sentence of Matt. 13: 11, ὑμῖν
δέδοται γνῶναι τὰ μυστήρια τῆς βασιλείας τῶν οὐρανῶν in a context
in which he lays a strong emphasis on the esotericism of *gnosis*
(*Strom.* v. 80. 6, vol. ii. 379. 18). In the same way he interprets
St. Paul's use of the terms μυστήριον and σοφία. After maintaining
that 'the sacred and mystic speech concerning the ungenerated
principle and its powers must be kept hidden' (*Strom.* v. 80. 3)
he goes on to quote the well-known passage of the first epistle to
the Corinthians in which St. Paul seems to reserve the revelation
of σοφία to the τέλειοι (1 Cor. 2: 6–7, σοφίαν δὲ λαλοῦμεν ἐν τοῖς
τελείοις . . . λαλοῦμεν θεοῦ σοφίαν ἐν μυστηρίῳ, τὴν ἀποκεκρυμ-
μένην, *Strom.* v. 80. 4).[2] Clement wants to find his own esoteric
conception of *gnosis* also in other passages of St. Paul's epistles
in which the apostle uses the term μυστήριον,[3] and interprets them
accordingly. In *Strom.* v. 60. 1, after quoting the passage of Eph.
3: 3–5, he adds his own comment, ἔστι γάρ τις τελείων μάθησις.
A few lines below, he quotes the passage of Col. 1: 25–7 (*Strom.*
v. 61. 3) and distinguishes the μυστήριον τὸ ἀποκεκρυμμένον . . . ὃ
νῦν ἐφανερώθη τοῖς ἁγίοις αὐτοῦ from the πλοῦτος τῆς δόξης τοῦ
μυστηρίου: according to him, whereas the former hints at the
secret tradition of *gnosis*, which the Lord revealed to some of his

---

[1] Cf. H. von Soden, *ZNW* 12 (1911), 191, and D. Deden, *ETL* 13 (1936),
426–7.

[2] I have not been convinced by Deden's attempt (pp. 413–14) to deny the
presence of any esotericism in chapters 2 and 3 of the first Epistle to the Corinthians. That in this epistle St. Paul hints at the distinction between less perfect
and more perfect Christians is also clear from the passage 3: 1 ff., κἀγώ, ὦ ἀδελφοί,
οὐκ ἠδυνήθην ὑμῖν λαλῆσαι ὡς πνευματικοῖς, ἀλλ᾿ ὡς σαρκίνοις, ὡς νηπίοις ἐν Χριστῷ,
γάλα ὑμᾶς ἐπότισα, οὐ βρῶμα. The passage of 1 Cor. 2. 6 f. is quoted by Clement
also in *Strom.* v. 65. 5 together with 3. 1 ff. (see *Strom.* v. 66. 1). Clement stresses
of course the esotericism of both passages and interprets them according to his
own esoteric views: see *Strom.* v. 65. 4 (ii. 370. 4–5), τὴν προφητικὴν καὶ ὄντως
ἀρχαίαν σῴζων ἐπίκρυψιν, and *Strom.* v. 66. 1 (ii. 370. 15–17), where the γάλα and
the βρῶμα which are mentioned in 1 Cor. 3: 1 ff. are interpreted by him as referring
the former to the first element of the Christian faith, the latter to the higher *gnosis*.

[3] See especially Rom. 16: 25–6, Col. 1: 25–7, Eph. 1: 9, 3: 3–5, and 3: 9, and
cf. K. Prümm, *ZKT* 61 (1937), 395–6.

apostles and which they transmitted to their successors, the latter represents the simple *pistis*.[1]

The reason why Clement was led to lay such a strong emphasis on the esoteric character of *gnosis* and to give an esoteric interpretation to the passages of the Gospels and of St. Paul containing the term μυστήριον is not far to seek. The idea that the highest doctrines (namely the doctrines concerning the highest divinity, the origin of the world and of man, and the destiny of the human soul after the death of the body) represent a *secretum arcanum* which can be revealed only to very few initiated is characteristic of the Jewish-Alexandrine philosophy, of Middle Platonism, of Neoplatonism, and also of the heretical Christian Gnosticism which Clement knew very well and which in some sense he wanted to emulate. Already in the Wisdom of Solomon the doctrines concerning the essence and the origin of the divine σοφία are represented as μυστήρια and connected with *gnosis*: τί δέ ἐστι σοφία καὶ πῶς ἐγένετο, ἀπαγγελῶ καὶ οὐκ ἀποκρύψω ὑμῖν μυστήρια, ἀλλ' ἀπ' ἀρχῆς γενέσεως ἐξιχνιάσω καὶ θήσω εἰς τὸ ἐμφανὲς τὴν γνῶσιν αὐτῆς, 6: 22; cf. 2: 22, καὶ οὐκ ἔγνωσαν μυστήρια θεοῦ.[2] But it is in Philo that the use of the language of the mysteries is particularly clear. Like Clement, Philo resorts to mystery terms extremely frequently in order to represent the secret character of his theological doctrines and stresses the necessity of keeping them hidden from the multitude. The following passages are particularly worth noticing:

> *Leg. Alleg.* ii. 57 (i. 101. 24–5): Not everybody must be allowed to contemplate the secrets of God.
>
> *Leg. Alleg.* iii. 3 (i. 113. 17): The souls which are prepared to search after the invisible mysteries of God . . .
>
> *Leg. Alleg.* iii. 27 (i. 119. 10–12): Which soul succeeded in hiding and in destroying vice, except that to which God revealed

---

[1] *Strom.* v. 61. 1 (ii. 367. 14–19). On the interpretation which Clement gives of Col. 1: 25–7 see also Marsh, 66 and 70, Prümm, 400, and Camelot, op. cit. 86. A further proof of Clement's inclination to give an esoteric interpretation of St. Paul is provided by his particular predilection for the sentence of 1 Cor. 8: 7, ἀλλ' οὐκ ἐν πᾶσι ἡ γνῶσις: in *Strom.* iv. 97. 1 after quoting it he adds his own remark, ἡ ἐν ὀλίγοις παραδιδομένη; in *Strom.* v. 17. 1 he connects it with *Rep.* vi. 494 a, *Phaed.* 69 c, and Matt. 22: 14; in *Strom.* v. 61. 3 he again quotes it in order to explain his interpretation of Col. 2: 2 f.

[2] The references to these two passages of the Wisdom of Solomon are given by Deden, 428. Some other passages from the Book of Daniel, the Book of Enoch, the Apocalypse of Ezra, and the Apocalypse of Baruch, quoted by Deden, 429–32, are also worth noticing.

himself, namely that which he deemed worthy of the secret mysteries?

Leg. Alleg. iii. 219 (i. 162. 4–5) : Open your ears, you initiated, and listen to the holy initiations.

De Cher. 42 (i. 180. 15–16) : We teach the divine initiations to those initiated who are worthy of the most holy initiations.

De Cher. 48 (i. 181. 19–21) : Receive these doctrines as really holy mysteries in your souls, you initiated whose ears are purified, and do not reveal them to any uninitiated, but control and keep this treasure in yourselves.

De Cher. 49 (i. 182. 2–3) : I was initiated in the great mysteries by Moses, who is dear to God.

De Sacr. Ab. et C. 60 (i. 226. 11–12) : That it [sc. the soul] after being initiated may not be prepared to reveal the mysteries of the perfect initiations to anybody.

De Sacr. Ab. et C. 60 (i. 226. 14–15) : Because the holy speech concerning the ungenerated principle and its powers must remain hidden.[1]

Quod D. sit imm. 61 (ii. 70. 12–13) : . . . being initiated in the uncorrupt mysteries concerning the supreme being.

De Somn. i. 164 (iii. 240. 5–7) : Until you, leading us towards the hidden splendour of the holy doctrines, show us the invisible beauties which are closed to the uninitiated.

De Somn. i. 191 (iii. 246. 11–12) : [The holy Logos] recalls also many ineffable doctrines, which nobody among the uninitiated is allowed to know.

De Somn. i. 226 (iii. 253. 13) : [The holy Logos] . . . has mottled us with the secret doctrines of the true philosophy.

De Vita cont. 25 (vi. 52. 15) : They are initiated in the mysteries of the wise life.

Quaest. in Gen. iv. 8 (Suppl., vol. i. 282 Loeb) : . . . not because knowledge and understanding of the wisdom of the Father and His two highest powers are hidden from many . . . .[2]

Plato also had described the knowledge of the idea of beauty as τὰ τέλεα καὶ ἐποπτικά (*Symp.* 210 a) and represented the

---

[1] Clement has copied this passage of Philo in *Strom.* v. 80. 3 (ii. 379. 8–10).

[2] On Philo's predilection for the language of the mysteries see also P. Ziegert, *TStK* 67 (1894), Heft 4, 706–32; R. Reitzenstein, 65 and 427 ff.; and H. A. Wolfson, *Philo* i. 43–54. As to the view held by E. R. Goodenough in his book *By Light, Light* (and before him by F. C. Conybeare, *Philo about the contemplative Life,* 303), according to which Philo's use of mystery terms is due to the existence of actual mystery cults in the Jewish community of Alexandria, see A. D. Nock's criticism in his review of Goodenough's book, *Gnomon* 13 (1937), 156–65.

contemplation of the ὑπερουράνιος τόπος as the result of a process
of initiation (ἐτελοῦντο τῶν τελετῶν ἣν θέμις λέγειν μακαριωτάτην,
Phaedr. 250 b, cf. 250 e, μυούμενοί τε καὶ ἐποπτεύοντες);[1] he had
also held the view that the highest doctrines could not be communicated to everybody.[2] The same inclination to stress the
esoteric character of the highest doctrines occurs in Middle
Platonism and in Neoplatonism. Plutarch, referring to the passage of *Symp.* 210 a, approves Plato's use of the term ἐποπτικόν
for the designation of the highest part of philosophy, namely
theology (*De Is. et Os.* 382 d); he represents the knowledge of the
highest divinity as a τελετή (καὶ θιγόντες ἀληθῶς τῆς περὶ αὐτὸ
καθαρᾶς ἀληθείας οἷον ἐν τελετῇ τέλος ἔχειν φιλοσοφίας νομίζουσι,
De Is. et Os. 382 d, cf. *Quaest. Conv.* viii. 2, 718 c–d, τὴν νοητὴν καὶ
ἀΐδιον φύσιν, ἧς θέα τέλος ἐστὶ φιλοσοφίας οἷον ἐποπτεία τελετῆς,
and *De Def. Orac.* 422 e, ἐκείνης ὄνειρον εἶναι τῆς ἐποπτείας καὶ
τελετῆς), and makes it clear that such a knowledge cannot be
revealed to everybody (τὸ μὴ φατὸν μηδὲ ὁρατὸν ἀνθρώποις κάλλος,
De Is. et Osir. 383 a). Albinus, after paraphrasing Plato's famous
words in *Timaeus* 28 c, maintains that he had allowed only a few
select disciples to listen to the exposition of the highest doctrines
(πάνυ γοῦν ὀλίγοις τῶν γνωρίμων καὶ τοῖς γε προκριθεῖσι τῆς περὶ
τοῦ ἀγαθοῦ ἀκροάσεως μετέδωκε, *Did.* 179. 33–4) and uses the
term μυεῖσθαι in connection with the study of the theoretical
part of philosophy (εἰ μέλλει τὰ μείζω μυεῖσθαι μαθήματα, *Did.*
182. 8). The same views are held in Neoplatonism by Plotinus:
τοῦτο δὴ ἐθέλον δηλοῦν τὸ τῶν μυστηρίων τῶνδε ἐπίταγμα, τὸ μὴ
ἐκφέρειν εἰς μὴ μεμυημένους, ὡς οὐκ ἔκφορον ἐκεῖνο ὂν ἀπεῖπε
δηλοῦν πρὸς ἄλλον τὸ θεῖον, ὅτῳ μὴ καὶ αὐτῷ ἰδεῖν εὐτύχηται, *Enn.*
vi. 9. 11.

The same ideas can be found among the Christian Gnostics.
Like Clement, they claim to possess a higher teaching—the true
gnosis—which cannot be revealed to everybody and must be kept
hidden and reserved for a few initiated: for them also, therefore,
gnosis is a 'mystery'. This is one of the fundamental features of
all gnostic systems. Some passages of Hippolytus' *Refutatio* (on
the Naassenes and on the gnostic Justin) and of Irenaeus' *Ad-*

[1] Clement most probably had these passages of Plato in mind in *Strom.* i. 176. 2
(see p. 146 above) as Stählin, app. crit. ad loc., rightly points out. The passage of
Phaedrus 250 b–c is quoted in *Strom.* v. 138. 3.
[2] See for instance *Theaet.* 155 e, *Timaeus* 28 c, and *Epist.* vii. 341 c. On Clement's
quotations of these passages of Plato see p. 144 above and chapter I, p. 42 above.

versus Haereses (on the Valentinians) are very instructive in this respect:

Hippolytus, *Ref.* v. 8. 26 (iii. 93. 27–8): ταῦτά ἐστι, φησί, τὰ ἄρρητα ὑπὸ πάντων λεγόμενα μυστήρια.

Ref. v. 8. 26 (iii. 94. 2–3): καὶ ταῦτα, φησίν, ἐστὶ τὰ τοῦ πνεύματος ἄρρητα μυστήρια, ἃ ἡμεῖς ἴσμεν μόνοι.

Ref. v. 8. 27 (iii. 94. 5–6): πάνυ γάρ, φησί, δύσκολόν ἐστι παραδέξασθαι καὶ λαβεῖν τὸ μέγα τοῦτο καὶ ἄρρητον μυστήριον.

Ref. v. 27. 2 (iii. 133. 1–2): ὀμνύω ... τηρῆσαι τὰ μυστήρια ταῦτα καὶ ἐξειπεῖν μηδενί (about Justin).

Irenaeus, *Adv. Haer.* I, preface (i. 4. 9–10): ... τὰ τερατώδη καὶ βαθέα μυστήρια, ἃ οὐ πάντες χωροῦσιν, ἐπεὶ μὴ πάντες τὸν ἐγκέφαλον ἐξεπτύκασιν.

Adv. Haer. i. 1. 3 (i. 12–13. 1): καὶ ταῦτ᾽ εἶναι τὰ μεγάλα καὶ θαυμαστὰ καὶ ἀπόρρητα μυστήρια.

Adv. Haer. i. 4. 2 (i. 36, 13–14): ἀλλὰ ἀνακεχωρηκότα καὶ τερατώδη καὶ βαθέα μυστήρια.

Adv. Haer. i. 6. 1 (i. 53. 3–5): οἱ πνευματικοὶ ἄνθρωποι, οἱ τὴν τελείαν γνῶσιν ἔχοντες περὶ θεοῦ καὶ τῆς Ἀχαμώθ· μεμνημένους δὲ μυστήρια εἶναι τούτους ὑποτίθενται.

In the writings of Nag-Hammadi[1] the esotericism of the higher *gnosis* is also strongly emphasized. In the Letter of James, the first treatise of the so-called codex Jung,[2] James begs his addressee to refrain from communicating to many people the content of the letter which the Saviour did not reveal indistinctly to all his apostles.[3] The Gospel of Thomas[4] presents itself at the opening

[1] For some general information about the discovery of Nag-Hammadi and the documents themselves see especially H. C. Puech and J. Doresse, *CAIBL* (1948), 87–95, Togo Mina, *VC* 2 (1948), 129–36, J. Doresse, *VC* 2 (1948), 137–60, *CAIBL* (1949), 176–80, and *BAB* (1949), 435–49, J. Doresse and Togo Mina, *VC* 3 (1949), 129–41, J. Doresse, *BAB* (1950), 432–9, H. C. Puech, *Coptic Studies in Honour of W. E. Crum* (Boston, Mass., 1950), 91–154, J. Doresse, *Les Livres secrets des gnostiques d'Égypte* i. 133–56, and A. D. Nock, *JTS* 9 (1958), 314–24. Two complete lists of the Coptic manuscripts and of the writings which are contained in each of them are given by Puech, *Coptic Studies in honour of W. E. Crum*, 101–10, and by Doresse, *Les Livres secrets des gnostiques d'Égypte* i. 165–7.

[2] See H. C. Puech and G. Quispel, *VC* 8 (1954), 3; the Codex Jung (which is now in Zürich) is manuscript II of the list of Puech (art. cit. 104) and XIII of the list of Doresse (op. cit. 167).

[3] See H. C. Puech and G. Quispel, *VC* 8 (1954), 8.

[4] This gospel is contained in manuscript III of the list of Puech (art. cit. 104) and X of the list of Doresse (op. cit. 167). An edition of the Coptic text of the Gospel and an English translation of it can be found in *The Gospel according to Thomas. Coptic Text established and translated by A. Guillaumont, H. C. Puech, G. Quispel, W. Till and Yassah Abd al Masih* (Leiden–London, 1959).

as 'the secret words' of Jesus and contains the saying 'I tell
my mysteries to those who are worthy of my mysteries'.¹ The
Gospel of Philip² insists on the secret and mysterious character
of *gnosis*, which must not be divulged, and consequently also on
the sharp distinction between those who possess it and ordinary
people:

101. 4–5 (p. 29): And he separated his own . . .

102. 5–8 (p. 30): One single name they did not utter in the world,
the name which the Father gave to the Son, which is above all
things, which is the name of the Father.

102. 10–12 (p. 30): This name those who have it know indeed,
but they do not speak of it.

103. 22 (p. 31): But only a few who see it reap it.

130. 17 ff. (p. 58): To these [i.e. to the friends of the bridegroom
and to the sons of the bridegroom] is given to enter every day
into the bridal chamber. But the others . . . let them be nourished
from the crumbs that fall from the table like the dogs.

132. 22 (p. 60): . . . but the bridal chamber is hidden.

133. 12–13 (p. 61): . . . in order that we might go in to the secrets of
the truth.

133. 18–19 (p. 61): . . . the perfect things are open to us, and the
hidden things of the truth.

The Gospel of Truth represents *gnosis* as a hidden mystery which
has been revealed to the perfect men;³ and in the Apocryphon of
John⁴ Jesus says to John:

---

¹ The esoteric character of the gospel has rightly been stressed by Y. Janssens,
Muséon 75 (1962), 304.

² This gospel is contained in the manuscript which contains the Gospel of
Thomas, viz. manuscript III of the list of Puech (art. cit. 104) and X of the
list of Doresse (op. cit., 167). It has been translated into English by R. McL. Wilson (London, 1962). The edition of the Coptic text and a German translation
of it have been published by W. C. Till, *Das Evangelium nach Philippos* (Berlin,
1963); in quoting it I follow Wilson's translation.

³ Gospel of Truth 18. 11–16. This gospel, which is contained in the codex Jung,
has been edited by M. Malinine, H. C. Puech, and G. Quispel (Zürich, 1956);
this edition contains also a French, German, and English translation of the Coptic
text.

⁴ This work is contained in a papyrus of Berlin as well as in three papyri of
Nag-Hammadi (codex I of the lists of Puech, art. cit. 102–3, and of Doresse,
op. cit. 165, codex III of the list of Puech, art. cit. 104–5 [= Doresse X, op.
cit. 167], and codex VIII of the list of Puech, art. cit. 107 [= Doresse II, op.
cit. 165]). The version of the papyrus of Berlin has been edited and translated
by W. C. Till, *TU* 60 (Berlin, 1955) (I follow this edition in my quotations);
the three versions of Nag-Hammadi have been edited and translated into German
by M. Krause and P. Labib, *Abh. des deutschen archäol. Inst. Kairo*, Band I (1962).

22. 11–17 (p. 85 Till) : Listen to what I am going to tell thee today, that thou mayst tell it to those who possess the same spirit as thou, who belong to the unwavering race of the perfect man, and to those who are able to understand it.[1]

64. 17–65. 1 (pp. 170–1 Till) : Thou hast contemplated important things, which are very difficult to reveal to others, except to those who belong to the unwavering race.[2]

75. 15–20 (p. 191 Till) : I tell thee this that thou mayst write it down and transmit it secretly to those who possess the same spirit as thou.[3]

At the opening of the longer version of the same apocryphon contained in manuscripts II and IV of Nag-Hammadi,[4] we read :

Codex II. 1. 1–4 (p. 109 Krause–Labib) : And he, namely Jesus Christ, revealed these secrets which are hidden in the silence and taught them to John.[5]

The *Pistis-Sophia* and the Books of Jeu also expound the same views : the *Pistis-Sophia* calls the *gnosis* of the highest divinity 'first mystery' ;[6] and the opening of the first Book of Jeu runs : 'This is the book of the knowledge of the invisible God which is

It must be remembered that M. Krause and P. Labib adopt different numbers for the manuscripts : in their edition codex III (see pp. 17–20) is codex I of Puech and Doresse, codex II (pp. 13–17) is codex III of Puech and X of Doresse, and codex IV (pp. 21–2) is codex VIII of Puech and II of Doresse. Codex III of Krause–Labib (= Puech I, Doresse I) and the papyrus of Berlin contain a shorter version of the apocryphon, whereas manuscripts II (= Puech III, Doresse X) and IV (= Puech VIII, Doresse II) contain a longer version : see M. Krause–P. Labib, 3. A critical edition and an English translation of the version of codex II Krause–Labib (= Puech III, Doresse X) have been published by S. Giversen, *Acta theologica Danica* v (Copenhagen, 1963).

[1] Cf. codex II Krause–Labib, 2. 22–5 (p. 113 of their edition).
[2] Cf. codex II Krause–Labib, 25. 20–3 (pp. 180–1).
[3] Cf. codex II Krause–Labib, 31. 29–31 (p. 198).
[4] See footnote 4, p. 152 above.
[5] Cf. codex IV, 1. 1–3 (p. 201). This passage is not present in the version of the papyrus of Berlin. I quote it according to the edition of Krause–Labib.
[6] A German translation of *Pistis-Sophia* can be found in *Koptisch-gnostische Schriften herausgegeben von C. Schmidt* (Die griech. christl. Schriftst. der ersten drei Jahrh.), 2. Auflage bearbeitet von W. C. Till (Berlin, 1954) ; an English version has been made by H. R. S. Mead (London, 1924). The expression 'first mystery' which I refer to occurs in chapter I, p. 1. 5 Schmidt. Although the first three books of the *Pistis-Sophia* must be traced back to the second half of the third century A.D. (see Till, op. cit., preface, p. xxiv) and are therefore later than Clement, they can nevertheless be quoted in order to illustrate one of the fundamental features of the gnostic systems, namely the esotericism.

revealed by means of the hidden mysteries which show the select race the way leading in rest to the life of the Father.'[1]

Clement has therefore, in common with the Jewish-Alexandrine philosophy, with Middle Platonism and Neoplatonism, and also with Gnosticism, the tendency to use mystery terms to describe the esoteric character of *gnosis.* This seems to suggest a literary dependence of Clement on this tradition rather than a direct influence of the ancient Greek mysteries upon him.[2]

Clement's inclination to stress the esotericism of *gnosis* explains why he regards Scripture as veiled by symbols which have to be disclosed by means of an allegorical interpretation. According to him, both the Old and the New Testaments were purposely written in symbols so that the truth might be kept hidden from the multitude and revealed only to a few initiated.[3] Here again Clement shows how closely he depends on the Alexandrine tradition going back to Philo. Philo also had regarded the letter of Scripture as a symbol covering an inner truth;[4] his literary output is nothing but an attempt to provide the 'initiated' reader with an extensive commentary on the Pentateuch, based on allegorical interpretation of it. Clement most probably did the same thing—applying Philo's allegorical method also to the New Testament—in his lost work Ὑποτυπώσεις. The importance which he attributes to the interpretation of Scripture, which alone, in his thought, can enable man to pass from *pistis* to *gnosis,*[5]

---

[1] A German version of the Books of Jeu is contained in the same volume which contains the *Pistis-Sophia* (see the preceding footnote). The Books of Jeu were written most probably at the beginning of the third century A.D. (see Till, op. cit., p. xxxii).

[2] Bratke, *TStK* 60 (1887), 647–708, is the most important supporter of the view that Clement was directly influenced by the Greek mysteries. Although it cannot be denied that Clement had a very detailed knowledge of them, as can be seen from the *Protrepticus,* his literary dependence on Philo, on Middle Platonism, and on the gnostic literature especially in the *Stromateis* must also be taken into account. P. Ziegert, 725 ff., and R. C. Hanson, 54–5, have rightly pointed out the influence which Philo had on Clement in this respect. Völker, 312 n. 2, is wrong in maintaining that 'Man darf m. E. der Mysteriensprache weder bei Philo noch bei Clemens irgendwelche Bedeutung beilegen'. He does not seem to have understood that the use made by Philo and Clement of mystery terms has a particular aim: the stressing of the esoteric character of *gnosis.*

[3] See especially the whole section of *Strom.* vi. 126. 1–127. 4 (ii. 495. 18–496. 20). On Clement's tendency to stress the symbolical meaning of Scripture see also C. Mondésert, *RSR* 26. 158–80, and *Clément d'Alexandrie. Introduction à l'étude de sa pensée religieuse . . .*, 131–52.

[4] See p. 140 above.　　　　　　　　　　[5] See pp. 138–9 above.

finds its explanation in his conception of *gnosis* and of Scripture, which he has inherited from his Alexandrine predecessor.

The esoteric character of Clement's *gnosis* enables us also to understand why he insists on the existence of a 'secret' or 'gnostic' tradition different from the ordinary Christian tradition. Christ— Clement says—spoke in parables in order to prevent his teaching from being divulged[1] and communicated secret doctrines to those few among his disciples who were worthy of apprehending them (αὐτίκα οὐ πολλοῖς ἀπεκάλυψεν ἃ μὴ πολλῶν ἦν, ὀλίγοις δέ, οἷς προσήκειν ἠπίστατο, τοῖς οἵοις τε ἐκδέξασθαι καὶ τυπωθῆναι πρὸς αὐτά, *Strom*. i. 13. 2, vol. ii. 10. 1–3). This view is confirmed by what Clement himself says in a letter rediscovered only recently, in which he draws attention to the existence of a secret version of the Gospel of Mark.[2] According to Clement, the apostles transmitted this system of secret doctrines which they had received from Christ to their successors and, in this way, gave origin to a γνωστικὴ παράδοσις which has come down also to Clement.[3] The object of this tradition is represented, in Clement's view, by the theological and cosmological doctrines of *gnosis* or, more exactly, by a method of allegorical interpretation aiming at finding such doctrines in the Old and in the New Testament. Clement himself brings the 'ecclesiastical canon' into direct connection with the interpretation of Scripture which was taught by Christ and preserved by his successors.[4]

In recent times J. Daniélou has tried to find an explanation for the presence of this conception in Clement by tracing it back to the apocalyptic Jewish-Christian literature of the first and second centuries A.D. (in other words, to what he calls 'Judéo-Christianisme').[5] He has drawn attention particularly to the Epistle of the Twelve Apostles,[6] to the Letter of James, and to the

---

[1] *Strom*. vi. 124. 6 (ii. 494. 30–2), οὔτε ὁ σωτὴρ αὐτὸς ἁπλῶς οὕτως, ὡς τοῖς ἐπιτυχοῦσιν εὐάλωτα εἶναι, τὰ θεῖα μυστήρια ἀπεφθέγξατο, ἀλλ᾽ ἐν παραβολαῖς διελέξατο. Cf. Matt. 13: 11–13 and 13: 34 (this last passage is quoted by Clement in *Strom*. vi. 125. 1), Mark 4: 11–12, and Luke 8: 10.

[2] See W. Jaeger, *Early Christianity and Greek Paideia*, 56–7 and 132 n. 22.

[3] *Strom*. i. 11. 3 (ii. 9. 4–8), *Strom*. v. 61. 1 (ii. 367. 14–16), *Strom*. vi. 61. 1 (ii. 462. 18–21), and *Strom*. vi. 61. 3 (ii. 462. 28–30).

[4] *Strom*. vi. 125. 2 (ii. 495. 3–5) and *Strom*. vi. 131. 4–5 (ii. 498. 12–17). See also Bratke, art. cit. 674, Camelot, *Foi et gnose* . . ., 94, Völker, 364, and Hanson, 57 and 58.   [5] J. Daniélou, *EJ* 21 (1962), 199–215.

[6] This epistle has come down to us in an Ethiopic and in a Coptic version; both versions have been edited and translated into German by C. Schmidt and J. Wainberg, *TU* 43 (Leipzig, 1919).

Acts of John.[1] If it must be admitted that two passages of the Epistle of the Twelve Apostles contain doctrines which can be regarded as 'gnostic'—in the first Christ says 'I shall reveal to you what happens on the earth and in heaven',[2] the second describes his descent through the seven heavens[3]—it must nevertheless be pointed out that the general trend of this work is far from the strict esotericism which, as we have seen, is characteristic of Clement's *gnosis*: in the Epistle Christ never insists on the necessity of keeping his teaching hidden from the multitude. As to the Letter of James,[4] it seems difficult to trace it back to a non-heretical Christian community of Egypt as Daniélou, following van Unnik, does:[5] the strict esotericism which characterizes it and the emphasis laid on the function of *gnosis*, which alone imparts life to those who possess it, seem rather to suggest a Valentinian origin.[6] The Acts of John[7] contain only one passage which seems to recall Clement's conception of a special teaching of Christ: at § 97 Christ is represented in the act of explaining the mystery of the cross to John. Here also, however, we are still far from Clement's conception of the γνωστικὴ παράδοσις as a system of secret doctrines concerning the explanation of Scripture which was revealed by Christ to a few disciples and trans-

---

[1] See Daniélou, art. cit., especially pp. 202–3 and 205–6.

[2] See chapter 12 of the Ethiopic version, op. cit. 44, and chapter V of the Coptic version, op. cit. 45; cf. Daniélou, art. cit. 202.

[3] See chapter 13 of the Ethiopic version (op. cit. 44, 46, 48, 50) and chapters V and VI of the Coptic version (op. cit. 45, 47, 49, 51); cf. Daniélou, art. cit. 205.

[4] On this letter see p. 151 above.

[5] See Daniélou, art. cit. 202, and cf. W. C. Van Unnik, *VC* 9 (1956), 149–56.

[6] I have not been convinced by Van Unnik's attempt to deny the gnostic origin of the letter; H. C. Puech and G. Quispel, *VC* 8 (1954), 1–51, have pointed out its Valentinian character (see what they say especially on pp. 9, 15, 20–1). A. Orbe, *AG* 83 (Romae, 1956), 199–200, though avoiding taking a definite position on the problem of the origin of the letter, does not exclude the possibility that it goes back to a particular group of Valentinians who were in favour of martyrdom. [The edition of the Coptic text of the Letter of James has recently come out: *Epistula Jacobi apocrypha*, ed. M. Malinine, H. C. Puech, G. Quispel, W. Till, R. Kasser, adiuvantibus R. McL. Wilson, Jan Zandee (Zürich u. Stuttgart, 1968). Like the *Gospel of Truth*, it is furnished with French, English, and German translations. I was glad to see, reading the preface, that H. C. Puech is still strongly inclined to see in it a gnostic work (see especially p. xxxv)].

[7] They have been edited by M. Bonnet (*Acta Apostolorum apocrypha*, ediderunt R. A. Lipsius et M. Bonnet, Lipsiae, 1898); these Acts of John should not be confounded with the *Acta Iohannis* recounted by Prochorus and edited by T. Zahn (Erlangen, 1880).

mitted by them to their successors. Actually neither the Epistle of the Twelve Apostles nor the Acts of John provide us with convincing evidence in support of Daniélou's thesis concerning the existence of the conception of an esoteric *gnosis* and of a secret tradition in the Jewish-Christian apocalyptic and apocryphal literature of the first two centuries A.D. If we want to explain the presence in Clement of such a conception we must look somewhere else: we must again resort to Gnosticism. The parallels which it provides with Clement's doctrine of the γνωστικὴ παράδοσις are really striking.

According to Irenaeus, the followers of Valentine maintained that the Lord had spoken in parables in order to keep *gnosis* hidden (ταῦτα δὲ φανερῶς μὲν μὴ εἰρῆσθαι διὰ τὸ μὴ πάντας χωρεῖν τὴν γνῶσιν, μυστηριώδως δὲ ὑπὸ Σωτῆρος διὰ παραβολῶν μεμηνύσθαι, *Adv. Haer.* i. 3. 1, vol. i. 24. 10–25. 1). This passage of Irenaeus reminds us at once of a parallel statement of Clement in *Strom.* vi. 124. 6 (ii. 494. 30–2), οὔτε ὁ Σωτὴρ ἁπλῶς οὕτως, ὡς τοῖς ἐπιτυχοῦσιν εὐάλωτα εἶναι, τὰ θεῖα μυστήρια ἀπεφθέγξατο, ἀλλ' ἐν παραβολαῖς διελέξατο. According to another gnostic sect, that of the Carpocratians, Jesus used to have secret talks with his disciples in order to explain *gnosis* to them and allowed them to transmit these secret doctrines to those who would prove themselves worthy of apprehending them: . . . τὸν Ἰησοῦν λέγοντες ἐν μυστηρίῳ τοῖς μαθηταῖς αὐτοῦ καὶ ἀποστόλοις κατ' ἰδίαν λελαληκέναι, καὶ αὐτοὺς ἀξιῶσαι . . . ταῦτα παραδιδόναι, *Adv. Haer.* i. 25. 5 (i. 209. 10–210. 2). The view which occurs in this passage is practically the same as that which Clement expounds in *Strom.* i. 13. 2 (ii. 10. 1–3), αὐτίκα οὐ πολλοῖς ἀπεκάλυψεν ἃ μὴ πολλῶν ἦν, ὀλίγοις δέ, οἷς προσήκειν ἠπίστατο τοῖς οἵοις τε ἐκδέξασθαι καὶ τυπωθῆναι πρὸς αὐτά.[1] What Irenaeus says about the Carpocratians in the passage quoted above is confirmed by Clement himself: in his letter[2] Clement admits that a secret tradition does exist, and that the sect of the Carpocratians had succeeded in knowing it, but had interpolated many errors into it.[3] It is important to notice that Clement does not reject at all the Carpocratian conception of the secret tradition but, on the contrary, accepts it entirely, limiting himself to expressing some reservations

---

[1] This passage of Clement should be compared also with the passages 22. 11–17 and 75. 15–20 of the Apocryphon of John quoted above: see p. 153.
[2] See footnote 2, p. 155 above.　　　　　　[3] See W. Jaeger, op. cit. 56–7.

on its content. The conception of the secret, esoteric tradition of *gnosis* is the same both in Clement and in Gnosticism.

2. The esoteric knowledge of the highest divinity can be revealed only by the Son. Just as in ethics the Logos acts both as a metaphysical principle and as a historical person,[1] so also in *gnosis* he has the same dual role. 'God, being undemonstrated, is not the object of science, but the Son is wisdom, science, truth, and whatever is kindred with these things', says Clement in *Strom.* iv. 156. 1 (ii. 317. 21–3). That the knowledge of the highest divinity can be attained only by means of the Logos, the second hypostasis, is shown also by the following evidence:

Strom. i. 97. 2 (ii. 62. 17): ἡ δὲ εὕρεσις [sc. ἀληθείας] δι' υἱοῦ.

Strom. ii. 45. 7 (ii. 137. 11–12): θεραπεύων τὸν τῶν ὅλων θεὸν διὰ τοῦ ἀρχιερέως λόγου, δι' οὗ καθορᾶται τὰ κατ' ἀλήθειαν καλὰ καὶ δίκαια.

Strom. v. 12. 3 (ii. 334. 8): ὅτι δι' υἱοῦ ὁ πατὴρ γνωρίζεται.

Strom. vii. 2. 2 (iii. 6 f.): παρ' οὗ ἐκμανθάνειν ἔστιν τὸ ἐπέκεινα αἴτιον, τὸν πατέρα τῶν ὅλων.

Strom. vii. 13. 2 (iii. 10. 7–8): προσομιλεῖν τῷ θεῷ διὰ τοῦ μεγάλου ἀρχιερέως.

Strom. vii. 16. 6 (iii. 12. 20–2): οὗτος ὁ τῷ ὄντι μονογενής . . . ἐναποσφραγιζόμενος τῷ γνωστικῷ τὴν τελείαν θεωρίαν.

This function of the Logos in *gnosis* explains why Clement sometimes calls him 'teacher' and describes his activity in *gnosis* as a 'teaching': particularly important in this respect are the passages *Strom.* iv. 162. 5 (ii. 320. 19–20), v. 1. 3 (ii. 326. 10–11), v. 1. 4 (ii. 326. 13), vi. 122. 1 (ii. 493. 6–7), vi. 123. 1 (ii. 493. 30–1).

Considered as the source of *gnosis* the Logos is also the μέγας ἀρχιερεύς: like the High Priest,[2] the Logos also possesses the full knowledge of the first principle. Clement sometimes applies the term μέγας ἀρχιερεύς to the Logos.[3]

How can the Logos be the transmitter of *gnosis* when he is still only a metaphysical principle? We have already pointed out, in the first chapter, that, according to Clement, he, as πνεῦμα or λόγος σπερματικός, is the source both of philosophy and of the

---

[1] See chapter II, pp. 113 ff. above.   [2] See pp. 173 ff. below.
[3] *Strom.* ii. 45. 7, ii. 134. 2, vi. 153. 4, vii. 9. 2, vii. 13. 2.

prophecy of the Old Testament:[1] in this way he enables some distinguished men—namely the Greek philosophers and the prophets—to reach some knowledge of the highest divinity. Almost every scholar of Clement has noticed that Greek philosophy and the Old Testament actually represent, according to the Alexandrine theologian, two parallel covenants which, in God's plans, are to prepare the 'Christian message';[2] we have, on our side, added that this Christian message, the 'true philosophy', must be identified with the higher, esoteric gnosis, i.e. with that gnosis which the Logos, after becoming a man, revealed completely to a few select people by explaining to them the exact way of interpreting Scripture.[3]

After becoming a historical person also the Logos is therefore the source of gnosis. In the previous section we have noticed what a strong emphasis Clement lays on the doctrine of the secret tradition. Here we must only add that Clement, in a fragment of the Ὑποτυπώσεις preserved by Eusebius, makes it clear that Christ revealed gnosis to some of his disciples also after his resurrection: Ἰακώβῳ τῷ δικαίῳ καὶ Ἰωάννῃ καὶ Πέτρῳ μετὰ τὴν ἀνάστασιν παρέδωκεν τὴν γνῶσιν ὁ κύριος..., Hypotypos. fr. 13 (vol. iii. 199. 21 ff.). For Clement Christ is, first of all, a gnostic teacher who has come down to the earth in order to lead a few selected persons to the higher gnosis of his father, by educating them to the perfect ἀπάθεια[4] and by teaching them secret doctrines based on the allegorical interpretation of Scripture. This is what Clement means by salvation.[5] The idea of Christ as a redeemer of the whole of mankind by means of his sacrifice is replaced, in Clement's philosophical system, by the esoteric idea of gnosis.[6] The wood of the cross becomes, in this way, the indispensable transmitter of gnosis: ἐπεὶ μηδὲ ἄνευ τοῦ ξύλου εἰς γνῶσιν ἡμῖν ἀφῖκται, Strom. v. 72. 3 (ii. 375. 3–4).

The doctrine of the metaphysical Logos as source of the knowledge of the highest divinity is present already in Philo who,

---

[1] See chapter I, p. 16 above.
[2] See chapter I, footnote 1, p. 11 above.
[3] See chapter I, p. 56 above.   [4] See chapter II, pp. 111–12 above.
[5] Strom. iv. 136. 5 (ii. 308. 30). In this passage, however, Clement makes it clear that if gnosis and σωτηρία were separated, the γνωστικός would not hesitate to choose gnosis.
[6] I completely agree, on this point, with V. Courdaveaux, RHR 25 (1892), 303–8. Courdaveaux hints also at the influence which Gnosticism had on Clement (p. 291) without, however, examining this problem in detail.

by his identification of the metaphysical Logos with the wisdom
of God,[1] is led to consider the former as the source of any human
wisdom and of the higher, esoteric knowledge:

De Fuga et Inv. 97 (iii. 130. 16–131. 1): πρὸς τὸν ἀνωτάτω λόγον
θεῖον, ὃς σοφίας ἐστὶ πηγή.
De Fuga et Inv. 137 (iii. 139. 4): ... λόγον θεῖον, ἀφ᾽ οὗ πᾶσαι
παιδεῖαι καὶ σοφίαι ῥέουσιν ἀένναοι.[2]
De Somn. i. 191 (iii. 246. 7–12): ὁ ἱερὸς λόγος ... πολλὰ καὶ τῶν
ἀρρήτων ἀναφέρει ὧν οὐδένα τῶν ἀτελέστων ἐπακοῦσαι θέμις.

Like Clement, Philo sometimes calls the Logos μέγας ἀρχιερεύς.[3]
But it is especially in Gnosticism that the idea of the only-
begotten Son, the second hypostasis, and of the historical person
of Jesus as sources and transmitters of gnosis[4] assumes a particular
relevance: it represents actually, together with the tendency to
stress the esotericism of gnosis, one of its characteristic features.
Already in the New Testament it had been said 'nobody knows
the Father except the Son and those to whom the Son wants to
reveal him' (Matt. 11: 27, cf. Luke 10: 22) and 'the only-begotten

---

[1] See p. 209 below.
[2] This passage should be compared with De Plant. 121 (see p. 64 above) and
De Somn. ii. 221 (see p. 20 above). The three passages contain similar images: the
Logos is compared either to a source (De Fuga et Inv. 137, De Plant. 121) or to
a stream (De Somn. ii. 221). It must also not be forgotten that Philo compares
philosophy to a shower (see pp. 19–20 above).
[3] See, for instance, De Migr. Abr. 102, De Fuga et Inv. 108, De Somn. i. 215.
[4] It must be remembered that in the Valentinian system the only-begotten Son
is not identical with Jesus: the only-begotten Son is the first emanation of the
Father, i.e. the second hypostasis which is formed by the couple νοῦς / ἀλήθεια
(Irenaeus, Adv. Haer. i. 1. 1, vol. i. 9. 7–9; i. 1. 2, vol. i. 10. 10–11; Exc. ex Theod.
6. 3 and 7. 1), whereas Jesus (who is called also 'Saviour' and 'Paraclete') is the
Being which the Aeons send out of the pleroma in order to help Sophia, the fallen
Aeon: see Exc. 23. 1, 23. 2, 43. 2, and Irenaeus, Adv. Haer. i. 4. 4 (i. 38. 8–11)
(the parallelism between the two last passages has been pointed out by O. Dibelius,
ZNW 9 (1908), 231). It is he who frees Sophia from passions, gives origin to
matter and to the sensible things (Exc. 45–6, cf. Iren. Adv. Haer. i. 4. 5, vol.
i, pp. 39–40), and comes down to the earth (Exc. 59–60). The distinction
between the only-begotten Son and Jesus is pointed out in Exc. 7. 3, ὁ δὲ ἐνταῦθα
ὀφθεὶς οὐκέτι "μονογενὴς" ἀλλ᾽ "ὡς μονογενής". The following sentences of Exc.
7. 3–4, stressing the identity between the Being which has come down on the
earth and the Being which remains in the heavenly world, must be understood as
Clement's own remarks, as F. Sagnard, Extraits de Théodote, footnote 4, pp. 67–71,
rightly points out. On this distinction between the only-begotten Son and the
Saviour it is also worth looking at the figures in Sagnard's book La Gnose valentinienne
..., 145, 317, 318, and 339 (see also p. 561, 'Mais ce fils n'est pas descendu lui-
même').

Son who is in the womb of the Father explained Him' (John 1: 18). The heretical gnostics regarded these gospel passages as in keeping with their own views,[1] and found therefore in them the best support for their theory of the transmission of the esoteric *gnosis* by means of a divine being. Theodotus, the exponent of the eastern branch of the Valentinian school, regarded the only-begotten Son as the Being which the Father emanated in order to reveal himself to all other Aeons and, therefore, also as the source of the *gnosis* of the Father: ἄγνωστος οὖν ὁ Πατὴρ ὤν, ἠθέλησεν γνωσθῆναι τοῖς Αἰῶσι· καὶ διὰ τῆς ἐνθυμήσεως τῆς ἑαυτοῦ ... πνεῦμα γνώσεως οὔσης ἐν γνώσει προέβαλε τὸν Μονογενῆ. γέγονεν οὖν καὶ ὁ ἀπὸ γνώσεως ... προελθὼν γνῶσις, τουτέστι ὁ υἱός, ὅτι "δι᾿ υἱοῦ ὁ πατὴρ ἐγνώσθη", *Exc. ex Theod.* 7. 1.[2] The same conception underlies the interpretation which Gnosticism gives of the activity of Jesus on the earth: Jesus came down to the earth in order to teach a few selected people the *gnosis* of the unknown Father. In the hymn of the Naassenes Jesus, being about to descend into the material world, says μυστήρια πάντα δ᾿ ἀνοίξω, μορφὰς δὲ θεῶν ἐπιδείξω· τὰ κεκρυμμένα τῆς ἁγίας ὁδοῦ, γνῶσιν καλέσας, παραδώσω, Hippolytus, *Ref.* v. 10. 2 (iii. 103. 19–104. 3); the Valentinians maintained that Jesus had been born from Mary when the time of the revelation of the mysteries had come, ὁπότε οὖν ἔδει ἀρθῆναι τὸ κάλυμμα καὶ ὀφθῆναι ταῦτα τὰ μυστήρια, γεγένηται ὁ Ἰησοῦς διὰ Μαρίας τῆς παρθένου, Hippolytus, *Ref.* vi. 35. 3 (iii. 164. 17–18); the author of the Gospel of Philip says that Jesus 'revealed the great bridal chamber', i.e. *gnosis*, 119. 7–9 (p. 47);[3] in the Gospel of Truth the following passages are particularly worth noticing:

p. 16. 32–4: ... the grace of knowing from the Father of Truth him through the power of the Verb.
p. 18. 12–21: The Gospel ... which he revealed to the perfect, thanks to the clemency of the Father, as a hidden mystery, he,

---

[1] R. M. Grant, *Gnosticism and early Christianity*, 152, rightly observes about Matt. 11: 27: 'It stands on the borderline between apocalyptic and gnostic thought.'
[2] Stählin, app. crit., vol. iii. 108, R. P. Casey, *The Excerpta ex Theodoto . . .*, 44, and F. Sagnard, *Extraits de Théodote*, 69, rightly bring the sentence δι᾿ υἱοῦ ὁ πατὴρ ἐγνώσθη into connection with the three gospel passages Matt. 11: 27, Luke 10: 22, and John 1: 18.
[3] In the Valentinian system the 'bridal chamber' (νυμφών) is one and the same thing with the *pleroma* of the Aeons: see footnote 3, p. 178 below

Jesus, the Christ. He enlightened them and indicated a path for them; and the path is the truth which he taught them.

p. 38. 23–4: . . . but he reveals himself through a Son.

p. 40. 30–3: he sent him in order that he might speak about the place and about his place of repose from which he had come forth.

p. 41. 4 ff.: He will speak about the place from which each one has come and the region from which he has received his essential being.

According to this Gospel, the Christ 'nailed to a cross of wood . . . became a fruit of the Gnosis of the Father' (p. 18. 24–6). This passage reminds us at once of what Clement says in *Strom.* v. 72. 3 about the symbolical meaning of the wood of the cross.[1]

The same conception of Jesus as revealer of *gnosis* appears also in the Apocryphon of John, in the Wisdom of Jesus Christ,[2] and in the first Book of Jeu:

Apocryphon of John 22. 2–9 (p. 85 Till): I have come down in order to reveal to thee what happens, what happened, and what will happen, that thou mayst know the invisible as well as the visible realities, and in order to teach thee the perfect man.[3]

Wisdom of Jesus Christ 87. 13–15 (p. 215 Till): I have come out of the being which has no limit in order to teach you all things.

Ibid. 102. 1–6 (p. 245): I am he who has come out . . . in order to teach you all this.

First Book of Jeu, chapter 1 (p. 257. 14–16 Schmidt): . . . in the doctrine . . . which Jesus, the living Being, taught to his apostles.

The idea, which we have met in Clement, that Jesus transmitted *gnosis* to a few disciples after his resurrection is also very common in Gnosticism: in such writings as the Letter of James, the Apocryphon of John, the Gospel of Mary,[4] the Wisdom of Jesus Christ, and the Pistis-Sophia Jesus imparts his esoteric teaching after his resurrection.

Both in Clement and in Gnosticism we notice, therefore, the same pattern: God, the supreme Being, is unknown, and it is

[1] This correspondence between Clement and the Gospel of Truth has been rightly pointed out by Daniélou, *TU* 79 (Berlin, 1961), 52.

[2] This gnostic work preserved in a Coptic version has been edited and translated into German by W. Till, *TU* 60 (Berlin, 1955), 195–295.

[3] Cf. codex II. 2. 16–20, pp. 112–13 Krause–Labib.

[4] The extant parts of the Gospel of Mary have been edited and translated into German by W. Till, op. cit. 63–79. On this gospel see also Till's article *ΕΥΑΓ-ΓΕΛΙΟΝ ΚΑΤΑ ΜΑΡΙΑΜ, LPP* 1 (1946), 260–5.

possible to reach some knowledge of him only by means of a revealer, namely Jesus, who imparts an esoteric teaching to his
apostles and, in this way, gives rise to a secret tradition.[1] Nothing
can illustrate this pattern better than the words of Ph. Vielhauer:
'Diese Offenbarung und Erkenntnis bringt ein Offenbarer, meist
Jesus, der vom Himmel gekommen ist und als Präexistenter über
die Geheimnisse der oberen Welt Bescheid weiß. Häufig ist es
der Auferstandene, der seine Jünger in geheimer Belehrung unter-
richtet, sie so zu Empfängern der rettenden Gnosis macht und
sie mit deren schriftlichen Weitergabe beauftragt.'[2]

3. If, from the ethical point of view, *gnosis* can be attained by
means of ἀπάθεια, which, as we have seen, represents the higher
ethical level,[3] from the theoretical point of view it mainly consists in the ideal of the contemplative life. The higher knowledge
which the γνωστικός possesses is nothing but a contemplation
of the intelligible world. The idea of *gnosis* appears therefore
often in connection with, and is sometimes also expressed by,
such terms as θεωρία, ἐποπτεία, θέα. The evidence which it is
possible to produce is extremely rich: see particularly the passages of *Strom.* i. 15. 2 (ii. 11. 13–14), i. 166. 2 (ii. 104. 1–2),
ii. 46. 1 (ii. 137. 14–15), ii. 47. 4 (ii. 138. 11–13), ii. 77. 4 (ii. 153.
19), iv. 40. 1 (ii. 266. 5–9),[4] iv. 136. 2 (ii. 308. 22–3), iv. 136. 4
(ii. 308. 26–7), iv. 152. 3 (ii. 315. 31–316. 2), iv. 155. 2–3 (ii.

[1] E. Baert, *FZPhTh* 12 (1965), 478, has noticed the similarity between Clement's
views on the role of the Son in the transmission of *gnosis* and those of the Valentinians, but the scanty evidence he produces does not enable us to realize the
extent of the agreement between Clement and Gnosticism on this most important
point.

[2] Ph. Vielhauer, *Beiheft* 30 *zur ZNW* (1964), 282. It is also worth remembering
what A. von Harnack says, *Lehrb. der Dogmengesch.*, Erster Band, 644–5: 'Der
Logos ist wesentlich . . . der Lehrer, aber in Christus ist er zugleich der Hierurge,
und die Güter, die er spendet, sind ein System von heiligen Weihen, an denen die
Möglichkeit, sich zu höherer Erkenntnis und göttlichem Leben zu erheben, allein
haftet. Tritt hier schon die Verwandtschaft des Clemens mit gnostischen Lehrern,
namentlich mit den Valentinianern, bestimmt hervor, so lässt sie sich auch in
der ganzen Fassung der Aufgabe (das Christentum als Theologie), in der Bestimmung des Formalprinzipes (einschliesslich des Recurses auf Geheimtradition . . .)
und in der Lösung der Probleme nachweisen.' E. Fascher, *TU* 77 (Berlin, 1961),
193–207, though drawing attention to the function of the Logos as teacher (see
especially pp. 199 ff.), does not touch the problem of the relationship between
Clement and Gnosticism.

[3] See chapter II, pp. 103–6 above.

[4] This passage shows the close connection between the ethical and the theoretical
aspect of *gnosis*: ἀπάθεια and θεωρία cannot be separated from each other.

317. 10–14),[1] v. 1. 5 (ii. 326. 19–20), v. 66. 2 (ii. 370. 15–16),[2] v. 67. 3 (ii. 371. 4–5), vi. 61. 2 (ii. 462. 24), vi. 61. 3 (ii. 462. 31–463. 1), vi. 69. 3 (ii. 466. 24), vi. 75. 1 (ii. 469. 5–6), vi. 98. 3 (ii. 481. 15–16), vi. 102. 1–2 (ii. 483. 6–12), vii. 10. 3 (iii. 9. 9–11), vii. 44. 6 (iii. 33. 22–4), vii. 44. 7 (iii. 33. 26), vii. 46. 4 (iii. 34. 26–7), vii. 49. 4 (iii. 37. 7), vii. 61. 1 (iii. 44. 13), vii. 83. 3 (iii. 59. 24–5), vii. 102. 2 (iii. 72. 7–8).[3]

The only way to achieve this contemplation of the intelligible world is, according to Clement, the separation from sensible things and, first of all, from the body. Clement insists on the necessity, for the perfect Christian, of freeing the soul—or, more exactly, its rational part—from the bonds of the body, which is regarded as a prison. This process, by means of which the γνωστικός is able to contemplate the transcendent ideas, is a 'purification'. That this must have been Clement's thought is shown by the following passages:

> Strom. iv. 141. 1 (ii. 313. 25–7): The natural affection for the intelligible realities enables the gnostic man to detach himself from sensible things: in keeping with the knowledge he possesses, he is able to choose the good between beautiful things.
>
> Strom. iv. 152. 3 (ii. 316. 1–2): By means of his absolute purification he contemplates the holy God in a holy way.
>
> Strom. iv. 155. 4 (ii. 317. 15–18): When the soul, after surpassing the material world, is alone and in close communion with the ideas, the gnostic man, like the 'chief' of the Theaetetus, becomes an angel and stays with Christ, being absorbed in contemplation.
>
> Strom. v. 14. 2 (ii. 335. 6–10): In the Phaedrus also [Plato] maintains that only the soul which is alone is able to partake of the genuine wisdom which is superior to any human power, when love enables it to fly from the earth towards heaven.
>
> Strom. v. 19. 4 (ii. 339. 4–7): Plato also thought that he who is impure must not be allowed to touch pure things . . . the mysteries also are not revealed freely to chance persons, but only after some purifications and previous instructions.

[1] Clement has here in mind the beginning of the Sophist, where Socrates calls the stranger who is introduced to him θεός (see Sophist 216 a).

[2] Clement is here explaining what, according to him, is the meaning of 1 Cor. 3. 1 ff. See also footnote 2, p. 147 above.

[3] On Clement's use of the term θεωρία for the designation of gnosis see also Völker, 316 ff. and 403 f. He has, however, quoted only some of Clement's passages. The pages which E. Fascher has devoted to Clement's use of the term ἐποπτεία in his article 'Epoptie', Reallex. für Ant. und Christentum (see especially pp. 980–2), are also worth reading.

Strom. v. 67. 3 (ii. 371. 4–5) : . . . that they may contemplate the divinity . . . after detaching themselves from sensible things.

Strom. vi. 86. 1 (ii. 474. 25–6) : . . . in keeping with the gift of comprehension, which leads us . . . from sensible to intelligible things.

Strom. vii. 27. 6 (iii. 20. 12–16) : We say that the souls must be purified in advance . . . for even before the revelation of mysteries those who are going to be initiated are required to submit themselves to some purifications.[1]

Strom. vii. 40. 1–2 (iii. 30. 22–7) : Trying to detach our body from the earth by means of reason and to elevate our 'soul endowed with wings' by means of the desire of higher things, we do our best to haste towards the sacred realities and to despise the fleshly bond : for we know that the gnostic man is prepared to put into practice the separation from the whole sensible world exactly as the Jews did with Egypt . . .[2]

The intelligible realities obviously cannot be known and contemplated by anything corporeal. The γνωστικός can contemplate them only by means of the divine element dwelling in him, namely the νοῦς. This idea occurs in such passages as *Strom.* i. 71. 1 (ii. 45. 17–18), v. 16. 1 (ii. 336. 1), v. 67. 2 (ii. 370. 29–371. 2), v. 67. 3 (ii. 371. 4–5), v. 73. 1 (ii. 375. 14–15).

The identification of *gnosis* with contemplation, the stressing of the necessity of fleeing away from the sensible world, and the tendency to regard the νοῦς as that part of man which alone can enable him to contemplate the intelligible world are the three elements which connect Clement's ideal of the contemplative life with the Platonic tradition and with Philo. These ideas are already clear in Plato. Plato very often uses such terms as ὁρᾶν, θεᾶσθαι, and θεωρεῖν in order to describe the contemplation of the transcendent ideas : it is worth looking, for instance, at *Phaedo* 66 d 7, 66 e 1–2, 83 b 4, 84 a 7–b 1, *Sympos.* 211 d 1–2, 211 d 8–e 1, 211 e 3–4, 212 a 1–2, *Phaedrus* 247 c 1–2, 247 d 3, 247 d 4, 247 d 5–e 2, 249 e 4–5, *Rep.* vi. 486 a 8–9, vi. 511 c 5–6, vii. 517 b 4–5, vii. 517 d 4–5, vii. 519 c 10, vii. 525 a 1, ix. 582 c 7–8.[3] Moreover, like Clement, Plato considers the purification of

---

[1] This passage reminds us of *Strom.* v. 19. 4 (ii. 339. 4–7).

[2] Egypt is both for Clement and for Philo the symbol of the body. On the allegorical interpretation of this word in Philo, Clement, and other Patristic writers see the paper by U. Treu, *TU* 79 (Berlin, 1961), 191–211.

[3] On the importance of the contemplative life in Plato see A. J. Festugière, *Contemplation et vie contemplative selon Platon*, especially pp. 77–249, and W. Jaeger,

the soul—or, in other words, the separation of the soul from the sensible world and, first of all, from sensations and from the body —as the preliminary condition which makes contemplation itself possible and maintains that the function of contemplating the ideas is peculiar to the νοῦς. The *Phaedo* is the dialogue in which these ideas especially occur: see, for instance, *Phaedo* 65 a 1–2,[1] 65 c 8–9, 65 c 11–12,[2] 66 a 3–6,[3] 67 a 3–6, 67 b 2,[4] 67 c 5–d 2,[5] 65 e 6–66 a 3,[6] 79 a 2–3 and also *Phaedrus* 247 c 6–87 and *Rep.* vi. 511 a 1. Plato directly influenced Clement, who, in some of the passages of the *Stromateis* quoted above, has his words still in his mind.[8]

In Middle Platonism, and in Neoplatonism also, the wisdom which the philosopher possesses is one and the same thing with the contemplation of the intelligible world and depends on the separation of reason from sensible things. Justin tells us that the aim of the Platonism of his time was the contemplation of incorporeal ideas: καί με ᾖρει σφόδρα ἡ τῶν ἀσωμάτων νόησις, καὶ ἡ θεωρία τῶν ἰδεῶν ἀνεπτέρου μοι τὴν φρόνησιν (*Dial.*, c. 2, vol. ii. 10. 1–2). Justin's words are confirmed by Plutarch, Albinus, and Maximus of Tyre. Plutarch regards the contemplation of intelligible things as the τέλος of philosophy (*Quaest. Conv.* viii.

'On the Origin and Cycle of the philosophical Ideal of Life', Appendix II of the English translation of his *Aristoteles* made by R. Robinson (Oxford, 1948), 2nd ed., 430–1. Völker quotes only *Rep.* iv. 486 a (p. 318), *Rep.* vii. 517 d, and *Phaedrus* 247 d (p. 403 n. 2). Aristotle also, following Plato, considered θεωρία as the highest form of life, and praised it both in his early and in his later works: see, for instance, *Protr.* fr. 6 Walzer (on the eulogy of the contemplative life in the *Protrepticus* see especially W. Jaeger, *Aristoteles*, 81 ff. [pp. 80 ff. in the English translation], and his essay quoted above, p. 431); *Met.* 1072ᵇ24 (cf. Zeller ii/2. 615 footnote); *EN* x. 1177ᵇ19–24 (cf. Zeller, p. 614 n. 1) and 1178ᵇ28–30 (cf. Zeller, p. 615 footnote). On the relationship between the *Protrepticus* and the tenth book of the *Nicomachean Ethics* see Jaeger, op. cit. 74 and 79 (pp. 73 and 78 in the English translation).

[1] Cf. Festugière, op. cit. 87 n. 7.   [2] Cf. Festugière, op. cit. 88 n. 3.
[3] Cf. Festugière, op. cit. 72 n. 1 and 88 n. 15.
[4] Cf. Festugière, op. cit. 72 n. 1 and 123 n. 2.
[5] Cf. Festugière, op. cit. 71 n. 2.
[6] Cf. Festugière, op. cit. 72 n. 1.   [7] Cf. Festugière, op. cit. 107 n. 3.
[8] Apart from *Strom.* iv. 155. 2–3 (see footnote 1, p. 164 above) Clement refers directly to Plato in *Strom.* v. 14. 2 and v. 19. 4 (see p. 164 above). In *Strom.* v. 14. 2 Clement is probably thinking of *Phaedrus* 249 c, διὸ δὴ δικαίως μόνη πτεροῦται ἡ τοῦ φιλοσόφου διάνοια; in *Strom.* v. 19. 4 he reproduces the sentence of *Phaedo* 67 b. As to the passage of *Strom.* v. 67. 2, it is directly dependent on *Phaedo* 65 e–66 a (see Stählin's apparatus). It goes without saying that both for Plato and for Clement contemplation is closely connected with φρόνησις, which for both of them is not only a practical but also a theoretical virtue (see chapter II, pp. 72 ff. above).

2. 718 d). Albinus maintains that philosophy consists mainly in the separation of the soul from the body, which takes place when man turns his attention to the knowledge of intelligible realities and of the truth, φιλοσοφία ἐστὶν ὄρεξις σοφίας, ἢ λύσις καὶ περιαγωγὴ ψυχῆς ἀπὸ σώματος, ἐπὶ τὰ νοητὰ ἡμῶν τρεπομένων καὶ τὰ κατ' ἀλήθειαν ὄντα, Did. 152. 4–6, cf. 152. 9ff., πεφυκέναι δὲ τοῦτον [sc. τὸν φιλόσοφον] χρὴ πρῶτον μὲν πρὸς τὰ μαθήματα, ὅσα δύναται προσοικειοῦν καὶ προσάγειν αὐτὸν τῇ γνώσει τῆς νοητῆς οὐσίας; according to him, the theoretical part of philosophy aims, first of all, at knowing the truth, τοῦ μὲν θεωρητικοῦ τὸ κεφάλαιον ἐν τῇ γνώσει τῆς ἀληθείας κεῖται, Did. 152. 28f. His eulogy of the contemplative life has some striking similarities with some passages of Clement, as can be seen from the following comparison:

Albinus, Did. 153. 18–20: πρέπει ...τῷ φιλοσόφῳ μηδαμῶς τῆς θεωρίας ἀπολείπεσθαι, ἀλλ' ἀεὶ ταύτην τρέφειν καὶ αὔξειν.	Clem. Strom. vii. 46. 4 (iii. 34. 26–7): κορυφαῖος δ' ἤδη ὁ γνωστικὸς θεωρίαν εὔχεται αὔξειν καὶ παραμένειν.
	Cf. Strom. vi. 61. 3 (ii. 462. 31–463. 1): ἐντεῦθεν δὲ ἄρα γνῶσιν εἴτε σοφίαν συνασκηθῆναι χρὴ εἰς ἕξιν θεωρίας ἀΐδιον καὶ ἀναλλοίωτον.

The same topics occur in Maximus of Tyre. It will suffice to draw attention to such passages as Or. x. 53 a (113. 16–18),[1] x. 56 a–b (126. 8 ff.),[2] Or. xi. 60 a (140. 14ff.),[3] xi. 60 a (140. 1–5), and xi. 60 a (140. 11).

In Neoplatonism Plotinus draws a sharp distinction between the inferior virtues which he calls political and those virtues the task of which is to purify the soul and to detach it from the body: πῶς οὖν λέγωμεν αὐτὰς καθάρσεις ...; ἢ ἐπειδὴ κακὴ μέν ἐστιν ἡ ψυχὴ συμπεφυρμένη τῷ σώματι καὶ ὁμοιοπαθὴς γινομένη αὐτῷ καὶ πάντα συνδοξάζουσα, εἴη ἂν ἀγαθὴ καὶ ἀρετὴν ἔχουσα εἰ μήτε συνδοξάζοι ἀλλὰ μόνη ἐνεργοῖ· ὅπερ ἐστὶ νοεῖν τε καὶ φρονεῖν· μήτε ὁμοιοπαθὴς εἴη· ὅπερ ἐστὶ σωφρονεῖν· μήτε φοβοῖτο ἀφισταμένη τοῦ σώματος· ὅπερ ἐστὶ ἀνδρίζεσθαι, Enn. i. 2. 3, cf. Enn. i. 2. 5, τοῦτο

---

[1] Cf. Phaedo 66 a, ἀπαλλαγεὶς ὅτι μάλιστα ... σύμπαντος τοῦ σώματος ὡς ταράττοντος.

[2] Cf. Phaedo 67 a, ἐὰν ὅτι μάλιστα μηδὲν ὁμιλῶμεν τῷ σώματι.

[3] Cf. Phaedo 65 e, μήτε τὴν ὄψιν παρατιθέμενος ἐν τῷ διανοεῖσθαι μήτε τινὰ ἄλλην αἴσθησιν ἐφέλκων μηδεμίαν μετὰ τοῦ λογισμοῦ.

δέ ἐστι μάλιστα . . . τὸ χωρίζειν ἀπὸ σώματος πόσον δυνατόν. The natural result of this purification is that the soul turns itself towards the Good and contemplates it: δεῖ οὖν καθηραμένην συνεῖναι. συνέσται δὲ ἐπιστραφεῖσα . . . τοῦτ᾽ οὖν ἡ ἀρετὴ αὐτῆς; ἢ τὸ γιγνόμενον αὐτῇ ἐκ τῆς ἐπιστροφῆς. τί οὖν τοῦτο; θέα καὶ τύπος τοῦ ὀφθέντος, Enn. i. 2. 4, cf. Enn. i. 6. 9, οὐδὲ τὸ καλὸν ἂν ἴδοι ἡ ψυχὴ μὴ καλὴ γενομένη. γενέσθω δὲ πρῶτον θεοειδὴς πᾶς καὶ καλὸς πᾶς, εἰ μέλλει θεάσασθαι θεόν τε καὶ καλόν. Porphyry also connects contemplation with the cathartic virtues: αἱ δὲ τοῦ πρὸς θεωρίαν προκόπτοντος θεωρητικοῦ ἐν ἀποστάσει κεῖνται τῶν ἐντεῦθεν. διὸ καὶ καθάρσεις αὗται λέγονται, ἐν ἀποχῇ θεωρούμεναι τῶν μετὰ τοῦ σώματος πράξεων καὶ συμπαθειῶν πρὸς αὐτό. αὗται μὲν γὰρ τῆς ψυχῆς ἀφισταμένης πρὸς τὸ ὄντως ὄν, Sent. xxxii. 3 (p. 18. 5–9 Mommert).

Philo completely agrees with Clement and with the Platonic tradition. He considers contemplation as the τέλος of man, ψυχῇ ἀπολέμῳ καὶ ὀξυδορκούσῃ τέλος προτεθειμένη τὸν θεωρητικὸν καὶ εἰρηναῖον βίον, De Somn. ii. 250 (iii. 298. 84–5),[1] and as the highest part of philosophy, τῷ θεωρητικῷ μέρει τῆς φιλοσοφίας, ὃ δὴ κάλλιστον καὶ θειότατόν ἐστι, De Vita cont. 67 (vi. 64. 3–4). So, to describe the knowledge of the intelligible realities, he resorts to such terms as θεωρία, θέα, θεωρεῖν, ὅρασις, ὁρατικός, ὁρᾶν: as in Clement and in the Platonic tradition, they become in Philo the technical terms for the designation of *gnosis* and occur extremely frequently in his writings.[2] He also maintains that contemplation can be attained only by means of separation from sensible things and from sensations: 'when ⟨mind⟩ is captured by some philosophical doctrine and is directed by it, it follows it and forgets completely whatever is connected with the corporeal weight. Even as sensations obstruct the exact contemplation of the intelligible reality, those who are fond of this contemplation do their best to neutralize their attack; they shut their eyes and their ears, check the impulses coming from the other sensations, and deem it right to spend some time in lone-

---

[1] Cf. Clement, *Strom.* vi. 61. 2, καὶ δὴ καὶ εἰ ἔστι τέλος τοῦ σοφοῦ ἡ θεωρία.

[2] I shall mention only some passages: *De Plant.* 36 (ii. 140. 27), *De Ebr.* 107 (ii. 191. 9–10), *De Sobr.* 3 (ii. 215. 18–19), *Quod D. sit imm.* 151 (ii. 88. 17), *De Conf. Ling.* 97 (ii. 247. 15–16), *De Migr. Abr.* 169 (ii. 301. 16–17), *De Abr.* 162 (iv. 37. 9), *De spec. Leg.* i. 288 (v. 69. 16–17), *De Praem. et Poen.* 46 (v. 346. 11–12), *De Vita cont.* 11 (vi. 49. 1–2). On the connection between *gnosis* and contemplation in Philo see also R. Reitzenstein, 317–18.

liness and darkness, that no sensible object may bedim the eye of the soul, which God allowed to contemplate the intelligible things', *De Migr. Abr.* 191 (ii. 305. 20 ff.).[1]

4. An important part in the building of *gnosis* is played by the encyclical disciplines, particularly by dialectic, astronomy, and geometry. The main function of dialectic is to lead the γνωστικός to the knowledge of the intelligible things, as is shown by the passages *Strom.* i. 176. 3 (ii. 108. 30–109. 1), *Strom.* i. 177. 1 (ii. 109. 6–9), *Strom.* vi. 80. 4 (ii. 471. 30–472. 1). If dialectic enables the γνωστικός to reach the contemplation of the intelligible realities, astronomy helps him to achieve the separation from material things and to pass from the contemplation of the sensible world to the contemplation of what is beyond it. Man is led to contemplate heaven by his own physical constitution, through which he can stand upright: τὴν κατασκευὴν τοῦ ἀνθρώπου ὀρθὴν πρὸς τὴν οὐρανοῦ θέαν γενομένην, *Strom.* iv. 163. 1 (ii. 320. 22–3). The γνωστικός himself does not reject this contemplation: τοῦ γνωστικοῦ . . . τὴν οὐρανοῦ καὶ τῶν θείων θέαν ἐπανῃρημένου, *Strom.* iv. 169. 1 (ii. 323. 14–15); he knows that, by contemplating the harmony and the order of the universe, his soul will free itself from any contact with earth (ἔκ τε αὖ τῆς ἀστρονομίας γῆθεν αἰωρούμενος τῷ νῷ συνυψωθήσεται οὐρανῷ καὶ τῇ περιφορᾷ συμπεριπολήσει, ἱστορῶν ἀεὶ τὰ θεῖα καὶ τὴν πρὸς ἄλληλα συμφωνίαν, *Strom.* vi. 80. 3, vol. ii. 471. 27–30) and approach the power of the creator (αὕτη γὰρ [sc. astronomy] μετὰ τὴν τῶν μεταρσίων ἱστορίαν περί τε τοῦ σχήματος τοῦ παντὸς καὶ φορᾶς οὐρανοῦ τῆς τε τῶν ἄστρων κινήσεως πλησιαίτερον τῇ κτιζούσῃ δυνάμει προσάγει τὴν ψυχήν, *Strom.* vi. 90. 3, vol. ii. 477. 8–11). It was by the contemplation of heaven that Abraham was led to the knowledge

[1] Other passages of Philo are also worth noticing in this respect: see, for instance, *Quod det. pot. ins. sol.* 158 (i. 294. 7–8), *De Gig.* 61 (ii. 53. 24 ff.), *De Plant.* 25 (ii. 138. 24–139. 3), *De Plant.* 64 (ii. 146. 13–14), *De Ebr.* 69 (ii. 182. 19–22), *De Ebr.* 99 (ii. 189. 12–14), *De Ebr.* 124 (ii. 194. 16–18), *De Ebr.* 152 (ii. 199. 15–19), *De Migr. Abr.* 13 (ii. 271. 2–4). The same ideas (viz. connection between θέα and *gnosis* and separation from the sensible things) occur also in the *Corpus Hermeticum*: see, for instance, *Poim.* 1 (vol. i. 7. 7–8 Nock–Festugière), *CH* vii. 3 (i. 82. 3–4 and 9), x. 4 (i. 114. 19–20 and 115. 1), x. 5 (i. 115. 7), x. 5 (i. 115. 11), x. 6 (i. 115. 15–16). On the use of the terms θέα, θεᾶσθαι, and so on for the designation of *gnosis* in the *Corpus Hermeticum* see especially J. Kroll, *Die Lehren des Hermes Trismegistos*, in the section 'Gnosis: die Termini für den Begriff und ihr technischer Sinn', 350–4.

170   PISTIS, GNOSIS, COSMOLOGY, AND THEOLOGY

of God, ὕστερον δὲ ἀναβλέψας εἰς τὸν οὐρανόν . . . ἐπιγνοὺς θεὸν κρείττονα τῆς ποιήσεως καὶ πάσης τῆς ἐν αὐτῇ τάξεως, προσλαμβάνει . . . τὴν γνῶσιν τοῦ ἑνὸς καὶ μόνου θεοῦ, *Strom.* v. 8. 6 (ii. 333. 4–8),[1] cf. *Strom.* vi. 80. 3 (ii. 471. 29–30), ἀφ᾽ ὧν ὁρμώμενος Ἀβραὰμ εἰς τὴν τοῦ κτίσαντος ὑπεξανέβη γνῶσιν, and *Strom.* i. 31. 2 (ii. 20. 9–10), Ἀβραάμ, ἐκ τῆς τῶν οὐρανίων θέας μετιὼν εἰς τὴν κατὰ θεὸν πίστιν. The task of leading man away from sensible things is allotted also to geometry (ἐπὶ τὰ νοητὰ μετατίθησι ἀπὸ τῶν αἰσθητῶν, *Strom.* vi. 90. 4, vol. ii. 477. 18–19), since it is mainly concerned with objects which do not undergo any change, ἐν δὲ τῇ γεωμετρικῇ οὐσίαν αὐτὴν ἐφ᾽ ἑαυτῆς θεωρῶν καὶ ἐθιζόμενος . . . νοεῖν καὶ οὐσίαν ἀμετάβλητον, ἑτέραν τῶνδε τῶν σωμάτων οὖσαν, *Strom.* vi. 80. 2, vol. ii. 471. 24–7).[1]

The way in which Clement appreciates the encyclical disciplines is in perfect agreement with the Platonic tradition. Already Plato, in the seventh book of the *Republic*, had specified the role of each discipline. According to him, dialectic enables the human mind to know the first principle, ἡ διαλεκτικὴ μέθοδος μόνη ταύτῃ πορεύεται . . . ἐπ᾽ αὐτὴν τὴν ἀρχὴν ἵνα βεβαιώσηται καὶ . . . τὸ τῆς ψυχῆς ὄμμα . . . ἠρέμα ἕλκει καὶ ἄγει ἄνω, *Rep.* vii. 533 c–d.[3] As to astronomy, Plato makes it clear that it must not be studied for its own sake, but in order to reach the knowledge of what lies beyond the sensible world: τῇ περὶ τὸν οὐρανὸν ποικιλίᾳ παραδείγμασι χρηστέον τῆς περὶ ἐκεῖνα μαθήσεως ἕνεκα, *Rep.* vii. 529 d.[4] It is the contemplation of the order of the universe that produces religious faith in man: δύ᾽ ἐστὸν τὼ περὶ θεὸν ἄγοντε εἰς

[1] On Clement's dependence on Philo in the section of *Strom.* v. 8. 5–6 dealing with Abraham (Abraham's original name was Ἀβράμ, which became Ἀβραάμ with the addition of an α only after he reached the knowledge of God) see the references given by Stählin, app. crit., vol. ii. 331, and Heinisch, 192–3.

[2] On Clement's appreciation of the encyclical disciplines see also W. Wagner, *Wert und Verwertung der griechischen Bildung* . . ., E. de Faye, AEHE (*Section des sciences religieuses*, 1919), 1–10, J. Lebreton, RSR 18 (1928), 485–6, P. T. Camelot, RSR 21 (1931), 38–66, and W. Völker, 334–8. Clement's dependence on the Platonic tradition has, however, not been sufficiently stressed by these scholars. Lebreton does not seem to like Clement's predilection for the encyclical disciplines: 'Tout cela s'accorde mal avec l'Évangile' (art. cit. 485); 'ici encore, l'idéal chrétien est perdu de vue . . . En face de cette mystique, encore imparfaitement dégagée du paganisme, on aime redire à Saint Paul, mystique admirable' (art. cit. 486).

[3] See also *Politicus* 287 a, διαλεκτικωτέρους καὶ τῆς τῶν ὅλων λόγῳ δηλώσεως εὑρετικωτέρους. Clement was probably thinking of this passage of Plato in *Strom.* i. 176. 3 (see Stählin, app. crit., vol. ii. 108).

[4] Cf. A. J. Festugière, *La Révélation* . . ., ii. 132–3.

πίστιν . . . ἐν δὲ τὸ περὶ τὴν φοράν, ὡς ἔχει τάξεως, ἄστρων τε καὶ ὅσων ἄλλων ἐγκρατὴς νοῦς ἐστιν τὸ πᾶν διακεκοσμηκώς, *Laws* xii. 966 d–e.[1] Geometry also helps to lead the mind of the philosopher to the knowledge of the truth and contributes to its elevation, ὁλκὸν ἄρα, ὦ γενναῖε, ψυχῆς πρὸς ἀλήθειαν εἴη ἂν καὶ ἀπεργαστικὸν φιλοσόφου διανοίας πρὸς τὸ ἄνω σχεῖν, *Rep.* vii. 527 b. Like Clement, Plato maintains that the objects of geometry do not undergo any change or corruption, ὡς τοῦ ἀεὶ ὄντος γνώσεως, ἀλλ' οὐ τοῦ ποτέ τι γιγνομένου καὶ ἀπολλυμένου . . . τοῦ γὰρ ἀεὶ ὄντος ἡ γεωμετρικὴ γνῶσίς ἐστι, *Rep.* vii. 527 b.

The same views can be found in Philo, in Middle Platonism, in Neoplatonism, and in the *Corpus Hermeticum*. The idea that the human mind, by contemplating the wonderful order and harmony of the universe, is able to go beyond it and to attain some knowledge of its creator occurs in Philo's writings very frequently.[2] What Albinus says on the function of dialectic, astronomy, and geometry entirely agrees with the corresponding statements of Clement and of Plato. Dialectic leads to the knowledge of first principles and of divine things (*Did.* 162. 8–10 and 17–18); astronomy enables man to pass from the sensible to the intelligible world and to attain some knowledge of the δημιουργός (*Did.* 162. 22–8 and 30–2); geometry is concerned with what does not undergo any change and contributes to the knowledge of the Good (*Did.* 161. 16–20). Plotinus allots to dialectic and contemplation of heaven the same role as that which appears in Plato, Albinus, and Clement.[3] As to the *Corpus Hermeticum*, it will suffice to say that in the fifth treatise Hermes tells Tat that the best

---

[1] The passage of *Timaeus* 90 a–b is also worth noticing: ἐκεῖθεν γάρ, ὅθεν ἡ πρώτη τῆς ψυχῆς γένεσις ἔφυ, τὸ θεῖον τὴν κεφαλὴν καὶ ῥίζαν ἡμῶν ἀνακρεμαννὺν ὀρθοῖ πᾶν τὸ σῶμα. The human mind, by turning the head towards heaven, enables the whole human body to stand upright. As we have seen (p. 169 above) a similar idea is expounded by Clement in *Strom.* iv. 163. 1 (ii. 320. 22–3). On the whole section of *Timaeus* 90 a–d see Festugière, ii. 133–4.

[2] See, for instance, *Opif. M.* 70–1 (i. 23. 14–24. 5), *Leg. Alleg.* iii. 84 (i. 131. 20–4), iii. 97 (i. 134. 27–9), and iii. 99 (i. 135. 3–11), *Quod det. pot. ins. sol.* 89 (i. 278. 21–5), *De Post. C.* 167 (ii. 37. 7–9), *De Plant.* 20 (ii. 138. 1–2) and 22 (ii. 138. 6–12), *Quis Rer. divin. Her.* 79 (iii. 19. 1–3) and 98 (iii. 23. 3–6), *De Mut. Nom.* 76 (iii. 170. 11–13) and 179–80 (iii. 187. 18–22), *De spec. Leg.* i. 34 (v. 9. 7–14), and *Quaest. in Gen.* ii. 34. On the presence in Philo of this idea see also Festugière, op. cit. ii. 558–65.

[3] See *Enn.* i. 3. 4 (i. 64. 9–12) on dialectic; and *Enn.* ii. 9. 16 (ii. 134. 49–135. 55) on the contemplation of heaven: ἀργὸς δὲ τίς οὕτως ἔσται τὴν γνώμην καὶ εἰς οὐδὲν ἄλλο κινήσεται, ὥστε ὁρῶν σύμπαντα μὲν τὰ ἐν αἰσθητῷ κάλλη, σύμπασαν δὲ

way to reach some knowledge of God is to contemplate heaven: 'If you want to see him, think of the sun, think of the orbit of the moon, think of the order of the stars. Who is he who keeps this order?'[1] 'There is somebody . . . who is the creator and the Lord of all these things.'[2]

According to Clement, there is a close relationship between the encyclical disciplines, philosophy, and *gnosis*. Since dialectic, astronomy, and geometry can free man from sensible things and enable him to approach τὰ νοητά,[3] they also prepare him for the apprehension of philosophy.[4] Philosophy itself is, in Clement's thought, a kind of preparation for *gnosis*: we have already noticed, in the first chapter, that this conception of Clement finds its explanation in the fact that philosophy is for him closely connected with the interpretation of Scripture on which the acquisition of *gnosis* ultimately depends and, in history, is given the task of preparing the Christian message.[5]

With the help of the encyclical disciplines and of philosophy the Christian is able to attain *gnosis* or, in other words, to contemplate intelligible ideas. In this way, he 'attempts to be a god', μελετᾷ εἶναι θεός, *Strom.* vi. 113. 3 (ii. 488. 27). More exactly he, being the perfect image of his teacher, the divine Logos, is already a god: τελέως ἐκτελεῖται κατ' εἰκόνα τοῦ διδασκάλου ἐν σαρκὶ περιπολῶν θεός, *Strom.* vii. 101. 4 (iii. 71. 20–1). This means that not only through ἀπάθεια, but also through *gnosis* and θεωρία the perfect Christian attains ὁμοίωσις θεῷ:[6] both for the γνωστικός and for the highest divinity the main activity consists ἐν τῷ ἀεὶ νοεῖν.[7] Θεωρία and *gnosis* play there-

---

συμμετρίαν, καὶ τὴν μεγάλην εὐταξίαν ταύτην καὶ τὸ ἐμφαινόμενον ἐν τοῖς ἄστροις εἶδος καὶ πόρρωθεν οὖσιν, οὐκ ἐντεῦθεν ἐνθυμεῖται, καὶ σέβας αὐτὸ λαμβάνει, οἷα ἀφ' οἵων; On the last passage of Plotinus see also Festugière, op. cit. ii. 142.

[1] *CH* v. 3 (i. 61. 8–10).

[2] *CH* v. 4 (i. 61. 22–3). The presence in the *Corpus Hermeticum* of the idea that the contemplation of the universe leads to the knowledge of God has been pointed out especially by Festugière, op. cit. ii. 55 ff.

[3] *Strom.* i. 93. 5 (ii. 60. 10–11).

[4] *Strom.* i. 30. 1 (ii. 19. 22) and vi. 91. 1 (ii. 477. 20).

[5] See chapter I, pp. 56–9 above.

[6] A similar view is held by Plotinus. He who has succeeded in purifying his soul and has consequently reached contemplation is a god: ἀλλ' ἡ σπουδὴ οὐκ ἔξω ἁμαρτίας εἶναι ἀλλὰ θεὸς εἶναι, *Enn.* i. 2. 6 (i. 57. 2–3), cf. ibid. (i. 57. 6 and 11–13).

[7] It must be remembered that Clement's God is not above the νοῦς as the 'one' of Plotinus: see pp. 222–3 below.

fore, in the theoretical field, the role which ἀπάθεια is given in ethics.

If we consider the results we have reached in points 2, 3, and 4 of our inquiry into Clement's idea of *gnosis*, we cannot help noticing a combination of Platonic and gnostic ideas, namely the idea of the contemplation of the transcendent, intelligible world and of the role of the encyclical disciplines on the one hand and the idea that Christ is the teacher and the transmitter of esoteric doctrines on the other. In other words: for Clement *gnosis* consists mainly in the Platonic ideal of the contemplative life; but the necessary condition which makes this contemplation possible is represented by the esoteric teaching of Christ. We are, therefore, faced with a fact which shows a close parallelism with what we have observed at the end of the chapter on ethics:[1] in both cases a Greek ideal (ἀπάθεια and ὁμοίωσις θεῷ in ethics, contemplation of the intelligible world in *gnosis*) finds its concrete realization only in the gnostic idea of the intervention of Christ, who is the teacher both of moral perfection and of the secret doctrines concerning the highest divinity, the heavenly world and the origin of the material world. If we now keep in mind the close connection which for Clement exists between moral perfection and *gnosis*—the perfect man is for him the γνωστικός—we can also adequately appreciate the intimate coherence of his thought as well as the perfect balance between the Greek and the Gnostic elements on which it rests.

5. In order to round off the picture of Clement's *gnosis* something must now be said about the interpretation he gives of the Jewish tabernacle and of the entry of the High Priest into the Holy of Holies as well as on the *Himmelsreise* of the 'gnostic' soul after the death of the body. The allegorical interpretation of the Jewish tabernacle and of the High Priest occupies the sixth chapter of the fifth book of the *Stromateis*. A detailed analysis of this chapter has been made by C. Mondésert in his book on Clement,[2] and its substantial dependence on Philo (especially on the second book of *De Vita Mosis*) has been acknowledged both by Heinisch[3] and by Stählin.[4] I shall here limit myself to

---

[1] See pp. 112–17 above.   [2] *Clément d'Alexandrie . . .*, 172–82.
[3] *Der Einfluß Philos . . .*, 233–9 (on the High Priest) and 240–9 (on the tabernacle).   [4] See app. crit., vol. ii. 347–53.

drawing attention to some points of Clement's interpretation of the Jewish tabernacle, which gives us a clear idea of the way in which he interprets Scripture and to pointing out the close connections between Clement and Gnosticism in the representation he gives of the Entry of the High Priest into the Holy of Holies.

(*a*) The first five pillars of the tabernacle (Exod. 26. 37) are the symbols of the five senses; the covering which is stretched before them symbolizes the sensible world, in so far as it is variegated with blue, purple, scarlet, and linen, which represent the four elements (*Strom.* v. 32. 3 and 33. 3–5). Both the pillars and the covering must keep ordinary people back in the surrounding space, without allowing them to go further on, into the part of the tabernacle which is reserved for the priests. The ordinary people represent the uninitiated, those who believe only in the five material senses (see 33. 3–6).

(*b*) In the intermediate space between the external covering (κάλυμμα) and the internal veil (παραπέτασμα) there is the altar of incense (Exod. 30: 1 ff.): it is the symbol of the earth, which is situated in the middle of the universe (33. 1–2).

(*c*) The candlestick which is placed to the south of the altar of incense (Exod. 25: 30 ff., 26: 35) is the symbol of the seven planets which perform their revolutions towards the south (34. 8–9).[1]

(*d*) The internal veil is placed at the entrance into the Holy of Holies (Exod. 26: 32). The four pillars symbolize the four covenants as well as the mystic name of four letters, Jave, the meaning of which is 'He who is and shall be' (34. 4–6). Here is the boundary between the sensible and the intelligible world; only he who has become High Priest can enter the intelligible world and attain the *gnosis* of the ineffable principle, which is above every name (34. 7).

(*e*) The holy ark which is placed beyond the veil[2] is the symbol of the intelligible world, which is hidden and closed to the many (35. 5 and 36. 3).[3]

---

[1] On the following interpretations which Clement gives of the candlestick and of its lights (they are brought into connection with Christ and with the seven first-created angels, *Strom.* v. 35. 1) see Heinisch, 247–8 and Daniélou, *Message évangélique* . . ., 221–2.

[2] Clement does not say this openly, but cf. Philo, *De Vita Mos.* ii. 95, ἡ δὲ κιβωτὸς ἐν ἀδύτῳ καὶ ἀβάτῳ τῶν καταπετασμάτων εἴσω.

[3] In the several interpretations which Clement gives of the two Cherubin standing on the lid of the ark he depends on Philo. The identification of them with the

(*f*) The robe of the High Priest symbolizes the sensible world (37. 1–39. 2).[1] Up to this point Clement, generally following Philo, bases his interpretation mainly on the Platonic distinction between the sensible and the intelligible world. But what he says about the entry of the High Priest into the Holy of Holies and about the *gnosis* he enjoys after his entry cannot be explained by resorting simply to Philo and to Platonism: 'The High Priest, taking off his consecrated robe . . . washes himself and puts on the other tunic—a Holy of Holies one, so to speak—which is to accompany him into the adytum. In my opinion, he exhibits the Levite and the Gnostic as the chief of the other priests, who are bathed in water and clothed in faith alone, and who are given their own abode; but he, distinguishing the objects of the intellect from the things of sense and rising above the other priests, hastens towards the entrance of the intelligible world. He is purified from the things here below not by water, as formerly when he was enrolled in the tribe of Levi, but by the gnostic word. Being purified in his whole heart, having also improved his moral behaviour to the highest possible pitch, having risen beyond the common priests up to a yet higher level, being quite sanctified both in word and in life, having put on the bright array of glory, and received the ineffable inheritance of that spiritual and perfect man which no eye ever saw and no ear ever heard and no human heart ever received, he is filled with insatiable contemplation face to face.'[2]

This passage of the *Stromateis* reminds us at once of paragraph 27 of the *Excerpta ex Theodoto*, in which the entry of the High Priest into the Holy of Holies is brought into direct connection

eighth heaven and with the intelligible world (*Strom.* v. 36. 3) shows also the influence of the Jewish author: Philo identifies the two Cherubin with the two highest powers of God which form his Logos (*De Cher.* 27–8 and *De Vita Mos.* ii. 97) and the Logos himself with the νοητὸς κόσμος (see pp. 204–5 below). The connection between *Strom.* v. 36. 3 and *De Vita Mos.* ii. 97 has been shown by Heinisch, who has, however, not quoted *De Cher.* 27–8. Neither Stählin nor Früchtel has drawn attention to Philo in order to explain Clement's last interpretation of the two Cherubin.

[1] It must be remembered that Clement refers the name which is engraved on the plate of the High Priest to the divine Logos (*Strom.* v. 38. 6–7). He combines Philo with passages of the New Testament: see the references given by Heinisch, op. cit. 239 and by Stählin, app. crit., vol. ii. 353.

[2] *Strom.* v. 39. 3–40. 1 (ii. 353. 7–24). I have mainly followed the English translation by the Rev. W. Wilson (Ante-Nicene Christian Library), Edinburgh, 1869, but I have modified it in some points.

with the entry of the gnostic soul into the heavenly world and with its deification: 'The priest on entering within the second veil removed the plate at the altar of incense, and entered himself in silence with the name engraved upon his heart, indicating the laying aside of the body which has become pure like the golden plate and bright through the purification of the soul and on which was stamped the lustre of piety, by which he was recognized by the Principalities and Powers as having put on the Name. Now he discards his body, the plate which has become light, within the second veil, that is, in the rational sphere, the second complete veil of the universe, at the altar of incense, that is, near the angels who are the ministers of the prayers carried aloft. Now the soul, stripped by the power of him who has knowledge, as if it had become a body of the power, passes into the spiritual realm and becomes now truly rational and high priestly, so that it might now be animated, so to speak, directly by the Logos, just as the archangels become the high-priests of the angels and the first-created the high-priests of the archangels. But how can there be a correction produced by Scripture and apprehension for the soul which has become pure, when it is granted to see God "face to face"? Thus, having transcended the angelic teaching and the Name taught in Scripture, it comes to the knowledge and comprehension of the facts. It is no longer a bride but has become a Logos and rests with the bridegroom together with the first-called and first-created, who are friends by love, sons by instruction and obedience, and brothers by community of origin. So that it belonged to the dispensation to wear the plate and to continue the pursuit of knowledge, but the work of power was that man becomes the bearer of God, being controlled directly by the Lord and becoming, as it were, his body.'[1]

The scholars who have examined or translated this paragraph of the *Excerpta* have regarded it as belonging to Clement.[2] The

---

[1] This is R. P. Casey's translation, *The Excerpta ex Theodoto*..., 61–3; in 27. 1 I have, however, followed the text of F. Sagnard, *Extraits de Théodote*, 114, δεικνὺς τὴν ἀπόθεσιν ⟨τοῦ σώματος⟩ τοῦ καθάπερ πετάλου χρυσοῦ καθαροῦ γενομένου καὶ κούφου διὰ τὴν κάθαρσιν τῆς ψυχῆς, ἐν ᾧ...; in 27. 2 I have translated παρὰ τοὺς... ἀγγέλους 'near the angels'; and in 27. 4 I have modified Casey's translation of the sentence of 27. 4, ποῦ δὲ ἔτι γραφῆς καὶ μαθήσεως κατόρθωμα τῇ ψυχῇ ἐκείνῃ τῇ καθαρᾷ γενομένη ὅπου καὶ ἀξιοῦται "πρόσωπον πρὸς πρόσωπον" θεὸν ὁρᾶν;

[2] O. Dibelius, *ZNW* 9 (1908), 245–6; R. P. Casey, op. cit. 9–10; F. Sagnard, *La Gnose valentinienne*..., 521 and footnote 2 on the same page, and *Extraits*

paragraph contains, however, some ideas which fit much better
the way of thinking of a gnostic author. First, the rather obscure
sentences of 27. 1, ⟨τοῦ σώματος⟩ τοῦ καθάπερ πετάλου χρυσοῦ
καθαροῦ γενομένου . . . ἐν ᾧ ἐγκεχάρακτο τὸ γάνωμα τῆς θεοσεβείας
δι᾽ οὗ ταῖς Ἀρχαῖς καὶ ταῖς Ἐξουσίαις ἐγινώσκετο, and of 27. 5,
ὑπερβᾶσα τὸ ὄνομα τὸ διδασκόμενον ἐγγράφως, can only be explained satisfactorily if we remember the doctrine of the Ophites
concerning the constitution of the sensible world and the *Himmelsreise* of the 'gnostic' soul: according to the Ophites, each of the
seven heavens of the sensible world is allotted to an archon
who is given one of the names of the God of the Old Testament
(the archontes are Ἰαλδαβαώθ, Ἰάω, Σαβαώθ, Ἀδωναῖος, Ἀσταφαῖος,
Αἰωλαιός, Ὡραῖος) ; the 'gnostic' soul finds in each heaven its
way closed by an archon and in order to be able to pass to the
superior heaven it must pronounce a formula and show the
archon a kind of 'free pass'.[1] In our paragraph this 'free pass' is
represented by the golden plate of the High Priest, which symbolizes the purity of the soul's 'body'. In this way the sentence
of 27. 1 quoted above can be interpreted as hinting at the fact
that the 'Archontes' and the 'Powers'[2] let the soul go through
the heavens after seeing the 'free pass'; and the sentence of 27. 5
can be interpreted as referring to the leaving behind (ὑπερβᾶσα)
of the archontes who are given the names of the God of the Old
Testament (τὸ ὄνομα τὸ διδασκόμενον ἐγγράφως), as well as to
the Valentinian doctrine which allots the seven heavens to the
Demiurge, the Biblical God.[3] Secondly, if in our paragraph the
entry of the High Priest into the Holy of Holies does not symbolize
the *gnosis* which the perfect man enjoys upon the earth, but the

---

de Théodote, 11, 13, and 116, 'Belle élévation de Clément sur la montée de
l'âme jusqu'à la vision face à face'; A. Orbe, *AG* 113 (Romae, 1961), 559–62;
E. Baert, *FZPhTh* 12 (1965), 468–9, A. Méhat, *Étude sur les Stromates de Clément
d'Alexandrie*, 465.

[1] See Origen, *Contra Celsum* VI, chap. XXXI (vol. ii. 100–2), and cf. W. Anz,
TU 15. 11–13, and A. Recheis, 142–4. An analogous list of seven archontes—
who are allotted to the seven heavens—is contained in the Apocryphon of John
41. 17–42. 7 (pp. 123–5 Till). The close correspondence between Origen and the
Apocryphon of John has been pointed out by R. M. Grant, *Gnosticism and early
Christianity*, 47–8. As to the origin of the name Ialdabaoth, R. M. Grant, *VC* 11
(1957), 149, thinks it derived from Yahweh Elohe Zebaoth, 'Yahweh God of hosts'.

[2] It is interesting to notice that the terms Ἀρχαῖς . . . Ἐξουσίαις in *Exc.* 27. 1
correspond to the terms ἄρχων and ἐξουσίαν which occur in Origen, *Contra Celsum*
VI, chap. XXXI (ii. 101. 7 and 10).

[3] Iren. *Adv. Haer.* i. 5. 3 (ii. 44. 1–3) and i. 5. 4 (i. 48. 6–8).

Himmelsreise of the soul and its entry into the heavenly world, it is difficult to regard the σῶμα of 27. 1 and 27. 2—represented by the golden plate—as the material body: the soul cannot lay aside the material body first in the intelligible world (ἀποτίθεται ... ἐν τῷ νοητῷ κόσμῳ, 27. 2). It is far more likely that the 'body' mentioned in 27. 1 and 27. 2 refers to the less perfect element of the human soul, i.e. to that 'psychical' part of it which, according to the Valentinians, the πνευματικοί lay aside in the eighth heaven, before entering the divine *pleroma*.[1] Thirdly, the idea of the marriage of the soul which appears in the words οὐκέτι νύμφη ἀλλ᾽ ἤδη λόγος γενομένη καὶ παρὰ τῷ νυμφίῳ καταλύουσα[2] reminds us of the Valentinian doctrine of the marriage of the souls of the πνευματικοί with the angels or λόγοι,[3] as well as of

---

[1] *Exc.* 64, ἀποθέμενα τὰ πνευματικὰ τὰς ψυχάς; Iren. *Adv. Haer.* i. 7. 1 (i. 59. 1–2), ἀποδυσαμένους τὰς ψυχάς, and i. 7. 5 (i. 65. 9–10), τῶν ψυχῶν αὐτῶν κατ᾽ ἀνάγκην ἐν μεσότητι μετὰ τοῦ δημιουργοῦ ἀναπαυσαμένων εἰς τὸ παντελές; it must be noticed that the author of *Exc.* 27 calls 'body' the 'psychical' part of the πνευματικός and 'soul' the 'pneumatical' element. His tendency to call 'body' what envelops the superior element appears also in the sentence of 27. 3, ἡ ψυχὴ ... οἷον σῶμα τῆς δυνάμεως γενομένη.

[2] I myself prefer to read γενομένη and καταλύουσα instead of γενόμενος and καταλύων accepted by all editors (Stählin, Casey, Sagnard) since the subject is always ψυχή.

[3] The Valentinians called the angels also λόγοι (see *Exc.* 25. 1, τὸν ἄγγελον ὡρίσαντο οἱ ἀπὸ Οὐαλεντίνου λόγον ἀπαγγελίαν ἔχοντα τοῦ ὄντος and cf. Hippol. *Ref.* vi. 34. 3, vol. iii. 163. 2, ... λόγους, οἵτινές εἰσιν ἄγγελοι ἐπουράνιοι). As to the marriage between the pneumatical souls and the angels see especially *Exc.* 21. 2, τὰ θηλυκὰ δὲ ἀπανδρωθέντα ἑνοῦται τοῖς ἀγγέλοις καὶ εἰς πλήρωμα χωρεῖ, *Exc.* 64, τὰ πνευματικὰ ... κομιζόμενα καὶ αὐτὰ τοὺς νυμφίους τοὺς ἀγγέλους ἑαυτῶν εἰς τὸν νυμφῶνα ἐντὸς τοῦ ὅρου εἰσίασι ... αἰῶνες νοεροὶ γενόμενα, Iren. *Adv. Haer.* i. 7. 1 (i. 54. 1–4), τοὺς δὲ πνευματικοὺς ... πνεύματα νοερὰ γενομένους ... νύμφας ἀποδοθήσεσθαι τοῖς περὶ τὸν Σωτῆρα ἀγγέλοις cf. i. 7. 5 (i. 65. 5–9) and Gospel of Philip 130. 23–4 (p. 58), bridegrooms and brides belong to the bridal chamber (with the passages of the *Excerpta* and of Irenaeus it is worth comparing *Poim.* 26, καὶ αὐτοὶ εἰς δυνάμεις ἑαυτοὺς παραδιδόασι, καὶ δυνάμεις γενόμενοι ἐν θεῷ γίνονται). I do not think that Dibelius, p. 245, is right in saying 'so ist das nicht die valentinianische Vorstellung von den Pneumatikern, die sich mit ihrem Syzygos-Engel verbinden ...'; in my opinion, the term λόγος of *Exc.* 27. 5 hints at the angel: the angels, as we have seen, are also called λόγοι (Casey is quite right in translating 'has become a Logos', p. 61). After the marriage the pneumatical soul becomes one and the same thing with the angel or λόγος (see *Exc.* 22. 3, ἐγειρόμεθα οὖν ἡμεῖς, ἰσάγγελοι τοῖς ἄρρεσιν ἀποκατασταθέντες ... εἰς ἕνωσιν; F. Sagnard, *Extr. de Théod.*, 101 n. 5, rightly observes 'on en arrive à une identité personnelle, à l'unité d'une seule personne'). The expression λόγος γενομένη of *Exc.* 27. 5 should be compared with *Exc.* 21. 3, ἀπανδρωθέντα ἑνοῦται τοῖς ἀγγέλοις, with *Exc.* 22. 3, ἰσάγγελοι τοῖς ἄρρεσιν ἀποκατασταθέντες, with *Exc.* 64, αἰῶνες νοεροὶ γενόμενα, with Iren. *Adv. Haer.* i. 7. 1, πνεύματα νοερὰ γενομένους, and with *Poim.* 26, δυνάμεις γενόμενοι. The terms λόγοι, ἄγγελοι, αἰῶνες, δυνάμεις are practically equivalent in Gnosticism.

the gnostic doctrine according to which the *pleroma* is the 'bridal chamber'.[1] Fourthly, the words of 27. 6, ἀδελφοὶ δὲ διὰ τὸ τῆς γενέσεως κοινόν, referring to the relationship between the first-created angels and the Logos,[2] seem to reflect the Valentinian doctrine of the 'pneumatical' origin both of Jesus and of the angels.[3] Fifthly, the terms φίλων . . . υἱῶν which in 27. 5 are applied to the πρωτόκτιστοι, remind us that the author of the Gospel of Philip applies the same terms to those who possess *gnosis*.[4] Sixthly, the deification of the soul expressed by the words ἤδη λόγος γενομένη of 27. 5 is perfectly in keeping with some parallel statements of the Gospel of Philip, in which deification is considered either as the necessary condition for the possession of *gnosis* or as its natural consequence.[5] Accordingly, it is far more likely that this paragraph of the *Excerpta* belongs to a gnostic writer (perhaps to Theodotus himself) rather than to Clement.[6]

If paragraph 27 of the *Excerpta* goes back to a gnostic source, we possess a first, important piece of evidence about the presence in Gnosticism of the allegorical interpretation of the Holy of Holies and of the entrance of the High Priest into it. Two other pieces of evidence are represented by a fragment of Heracleon

---

[1] See Iren. *Adv. Haer.* i. 7. 1 (i. 58. 11–59. 1), and cf. *Exc.* 64.

[2] Cf. Sagnard, *Extr. de Théod.* 11 : ' "Elus" et "Anges" sont *amis, fils* et *frères* du Logos.'

[3] See, for instance, *Exc.* 35. 1, ὁ Ἰησοῦς . . . τοὺς ἀγγέλους τοῦ διαφέροντος σπέρματος συνήγαγεν ἑαυτῷ.

[4] Gospel of Philip 130. 17 ff. (p. 58) : 'to these (i.e. to the friend of the bridegroom and to the sons of the bridegroom) is given to enter every day into the bridal chamber.'

[5] Gospel of Philip 109. 20–2 (p. 37) : 'it is not possible for anyone to see anything of those that are established unless he becomes like them' ; 109. 27–32 (p. 37) : 'but thou didst see something of that place and thou didst become these : thou didst see the Spirit, and thou didst become Spirit. Thou didst see Christ, thou didst become Christ. Thou didst see the Father, thou shalt become Father' ; 126. 33–127. 5 (pp. 54–5) : 'if thou become Spirit the Spirit will be joined to thee. If thou become Logos, it is the Logos which will mix with thee. If thou become light, it is the light which will consort with thee. If thou become one of those who belong above, those who belong above will find their rest in thee.'

[6] If paragraph 27 does not belong to Clement but to a gnostic author, the same can be said about paragraphs 10–15 of the *Excerpta* (the close connection between §§ 10–15 and § 27 has been observed by P. Collomp, *RPh* 37 (1913), 19 ff., and by W. Bousset, *Jüdisch-christlicher Schulbetrieb* . . ., 157 ff.). The materialistic conception of the angels which appears in §§ 10–15 does not agree with Clement's tendency to regard the higher beings as incorporeal: both Casey (op. cit. 14–15) and Sagnard (*Extr. de Théod.* 12–15), who are inclined to attribute §§ 10–15 to Clement, are aware of this difficulty.

and by the Gospel of Philip. Heracleon identifies the Holy of Holies with the *pleroma* which only the πνευματικοί are allowed to enter and the front hall of the tabernacle, which is reserved to the Levites, with the space outside the *pleroma* which is the dwelling-place of the ψυχικοί: ἡγεῖται γὰρ τὰ μὲν ἅγια τῶν ἁγίων εἶναι τὸ ἱερόν, εἰς ἃ μόνος ὁ ἀρχιερεὺς εἰσῄει, ἔνθα . . . τοὺς πνευματικοὺς χωρεῖν· τὰ δὲ τοῦ προνάου, ὅπου καὶ οἱ Λευῖται, σύμβολον εἶναι τῶν ἔξω τοῦ πληρώματος ψυχικῶν εὑρισκομένων ἐν σωτηρίᾳ, fr. 13 Völker.[1] The author of the Gospel of Philip calls the Holy of Holies 'bridal chamber',[2] thus hinting at the Valentinian idea of the marriage between the πνευματικοί and the angels or λόγοι in the *pleroma*,[3] and calls those who possess *gnosis* 'friends and sons of the bridegroom'.[4]

We can now understand better the underlying ideas of the passage *Strom.* v. 39. 3–40. 1 translated above. When Clement wrote it, he had still in mind paragraph 27 of the *Excerpta* as well as other passages of gnostic writings dealing with the topic of the entry of the High Priest into the Holy of Holies. The sharp distinction drawn by Clement between the High Priest and the common priests—it symbolizes the distinction between the 'gnostic' man and the common believers[5]—finds its exact counterpart in the distinction between the Holy of Holies and the front hall which is present in fr. 13 of Heracleon; the emphasis laid on the purification of the High Priest (i.e. of the soul which possesses *gnosis*) is equally strong in Clement

---

[1] A. Orbe, *AG* 113. 563 ff., and E. Baert, *FZPhTh* 12 (1965), 468–9, have rightly drawn attention to this passage of Heracleon.

[2] Gospel of Philip 117. 24–5 (p. 45): 'the Holy of Holies one is the bridal chamber' and 132. 21–3 (p. 60): 'but the bridal chamber is hidden. It is the Holy of holies one.'

[3] Gospel of Philip 130. 23–4 (p. 58): 'bridegrooms and brides belong to the bridal chamber.'

[4] Gospel of Philip 130. 16–17 (p. 58).

[5] *Strom.* v. 39. 4 (ii. 353. 12–15). Cf. Heinisch, 232–3: 'Der Vorrang, den der Hohepriester vor dem gewöhnlichen Priester besitzt, ist für Clemens der Anlaß, den ersten als Symbol des Gnostikers, den letzteren als Symbol des Pistikers auf-zufassen. Wie der Priester im Vorhof der rituellen Waschung sich unterzieht und die heilige Kleidung anlegt, so empfängt der Christ die Taufe und bekleidet sich mit dem Glauben. Wie aber der Hohepriester die hl. Schar der Priester weit überragt, so steht der Gnostiker viel höher als die Menge der gewöhnlichen Gläubigen. Er zieht ja den hohenpriestlichen Prachtornat an . . . d. i. er begnügt sich nicht mit der sinnlichen Erfahrung, sondern eignet sich auch die Wissenschaft an, welche ihn allein befähigt, das Allerheiligste zu betreten, nähmlich zu tieferer Erkenntnis Gottes vorzudringen.'

and in *Exc.* 27;[1] the connection between the enjoyment of *gnosis* and the entry of the High Priest into the Holy of Holies can be observed both in Clement and in *Exc.* 27;[2] and the terms 'son' and 'friend', which Clement applies to the High Priest, occur, as we have seen, both in *Exc.* 27 and in the Gospel of Philip.[3] A further correspondence between Clement and Gnosticism can be observed. In order to describe the *gnosis* which the High Priest enjoys in the Holy of Holies Clement resorts in *Strom.* v. 40. 1 to 1 Cor. 2: 9, ἣν ὀφθαλμὸς οὐκ εἶδεν καὶ οὓς οὐκ ἤκουσεν καὶ ἐπὶ καρδίαν ἀνθρώπου οὐκ ἀνέβη; as E. Baert has pointed out, the same passage of St. Paul was used by the gnostic Justin for the description of the object of *gnosis*.[4]

Clement's representation of the entry of the High Priest into the Holy of Holies goes far beyond the sphere of Platonism and of Philo: it plunges directly into Gnosticism. Actually only Gnosticism can enable us to appreciate it fully.

6. During our examination of *Exc.* 27 we have had the opportunity to touch the question of the ascent of the gnostic soul through the heavens and of its final deification. This topic characteristic of *Exc.* 27 is adopted, with some variations, also by Clement, since it occurs in some passages of the *Stromateis* and of the *Eclogae propheticae.*

Some modern scholars—namely W. Bousset, G. Békés, A. Recheis, J. Daniélou, E. Baert, and A. Méhat—have inquired into this second stage of Clement's *gnosis*.[5] Recheis, Daniélou, and Méhat especially have carefully analysed all Clement's passages dealing with the *gnosis* which the gnostic soul enjoys after

[1] *Strom.* v. 40. 1 (ii. 353. 17–18), καθαρὸς μὲν ⟨οὖν⟩ τὴν καρδίαν πᾶσαν; *Exc.* 27. 1, δεικνὺς τὴν ἀπόθεσιν ⟨τοῦ σώματος⟩ τοῦ καθάπερ πετάλου χρυσοῦ καθαροῦ γενομένου καὶ κούφου διὰ τὴν κάθαρσιν τῆς ψυχῆς.
[2] *Strom.* v. 40. 1 (ii. 353. 24), ἐμπίμπλαται τῆς ἀκορέστου θεωρίας; cf. *Exc.* 27. 5, ἐπὶ τὴν γνῶσιν καὶ κατάληψιν τῶν πραγμάτων ἔρχεται.
[3] See footnote 4, p. 180 above. It is far too simple to say 'Les termes frère, ami et fils expriment l'amour et la communauté qu'il y a entre le gnostique et le Christ' (Baert, art. cit. 471). Baert has not noticed that these terms as well come from Gnosticism.
[4] See Hippolytus, *Ref.* v. 24. 1 (iii. 125. 25–6) and v. 27. 2 (iii. 133. 4–5), and cf. Baert, art. cit. 462 and footnote 47 on the same page.
[5] W. Bousset, *ARW* 4 (1901), 148–9; G. Békés, *SA* 14 (Romae, 1942), 73–88; A. Recheis, pp. 56–73 and 147–51; J. Daniélou, *Message évangélique...*, 407–25, and *EJ* 21 (1962), 207–11; E. Baert, *FZPhTh* 12 (1965), 462–74; A. Méhat, *Étude sur les Stromates...*, 456–75.

its separation from the body and with its ascent up to the dignity of the highest angels. There is therefore no need to quote again these passages and to repeat what has already been said by these scholars. It will, instead, be better to concentrate our attention on a point which has not been sufficiently examined by them, namely on the close kinship between Clement's views on the *Himmelsreise* of the soul and those characteristic of Gnosticism and Platonism.

In order to find a satisfactory solution for the problem of the determination of the cultural background of Clement's conception of the *Himmelsreise* both W. Bousset and J. Daniélou have brought it into connection with the Jewish and Christian apocalyptic literature.[1] If it must be admitted that the general conception of the soul which goes through the heavens and enjoys the vision of God and of the heavenly world is fundamentally the same both in Clement and in these products of late Judaism and of early Christianity, there are, however, some features in Clement's picture of the *Himmelsreise* which cannot be adequately explained without resorting to Gnosticism and to Platonism.

Clement believes in the existence of angels who watch the ascent of the souls through the heavens (τοῖς ἐφεστῶσι τῇ ἀνόδῳ ἀγγέλοις, *Strom.* iv. 116. 2, vol. ii. 299. 19); their main task consists in stopping the ascent of the souls which are not yet completely detached from the material things and not yet free from passions and in letting go through and praising those souls which, on the contrary, are completely free from anything material and possess *gnosis*: τοὺς μὲν γὰρ ἐπαγομένους τινὰ τῶν κοσμικῶν κατέχουσιν οἱ τὸ τέλος ἀπαιτοῦντες τοῖς σφετέροις βαρουμένους πάθεσι, τὸν δὲ γυμνὸν τῶν ὑποπιπτόντων τῷ τέλει, πλήρη δὲ γνώσεως καὶ τῆς ἐξ ἔργων δικαιοσύνης συνευχόμενοι παραπέμπουσι, τὸν ἄνδρα σὺν καὶ τῷ ἔργῳ μακαρίσαντες, *Strom.* iv. 117. 2 (ii. 299. 24–8). In order to be able to continue its ascent the soul must

[1] See Bousset, art. cit. 138–54. Bousset quotes Enoch I and II (pp. 138–40), the Testaments of the twelve Patriarchs (p. 140), the Ascension of Isaiah (pp. 140–1), the Apocalypse of Baruch (pp. 141–2), the Apocalypse of Sophonias (p. 142), the Apocalypse of Abraham (p. 143), the Apocalypse of Moses (p. 143), St. Paul, 2 Cor. 12: 2 (pp. 143–4), the Apocalypse of Ezra, and the Life of Joseph (p. 150) and, like Daniélou (op. cit. 407–25 and art. cit. 207–11) connects Clement with this kind of literature (pp. 148–9). Daniélou does not quote Bousset's article, which anticipates most of his conclusions. Méhat also, op. cit. 463, draws attention to the relationship between Clement's *Himmelsreise* and the Jewish apocalypses.

PISTIS, GNOSIS, COSMOLOGY, AND THEOLOGY 183

show these angels or powers a kind of 'free pass' or 'identity token' (σύμβολον) represented by its purity and by the justice of its actions upon the earth: σύμβολον ἅγιον τὸν χαρακτῆρα τῆς δικαιοσύνης τὸν φωτεινὸν ἐπιδεικνύμενος τοῖς ἐφεστῶσι τῇ ἀνόδῳ ἀγγέλοις ... τὴν ποιότητα τῆς διαθέσεως τὴν ἐπικειμένην τῇ ψυχῇ κατ᾽ ἐπιχώρησιν τοῦ ἁγίου πνεύματος γεγανωμένῃ, *Strom.* iv. 116. 2 (ii. 299. 18–21), cf. *Strom.* vii. 83. 1 (iii. 59. 14 ff.), οὐδὲ αἰσχύνεται ἀποθανεῖν, εὐσυνείδητος ὢν ταῖς ἐξουσίαις ὀφθῆναι, πάντας ὡς ἔπος εἰπεῖν τοὺς τῆς ψυχῆς ἀποκεκαθαρμένος σπίλους.[1]

Here we are in the realm of Gnosticism. What Clement says in these passages reminds us at once of the doctrine of the *Himmelsreise* of the Ophites,[2] of the Gnostic Apocalypse of Paul contained in a papyrus of Nag-Hammadi,[3] and of the sentence of *Exc.* 27. 1, ⟨τοῦ σώματος⟩ τοῦ καθάπερ πετάλου χρυσοῦ καθαροῦ γενομένου καὶ κούφου διὰ τὴν κάθαρσιν τῆς ψυχῆς, ἐν ᾧ ἐγκεχάρακτο τὸ γάνωμα τῆς θεοσεβείας, δι᾽ οὗ ταῖς Ἀρχαῖς καὶ ταῖς Ἐξουσίαις ἐγινώσκετο.[4] The only difference between Clement and Gnosticism consists in the fact that whereas in Gnosticism the archontes are generally evil powers under the jurisdiction of Jaldabaoth, the inferior Demiurge of the material world,[5] Clement considers them as good angels who have received from God the task of watching the ascent of the souls: he, as an orthodox Christian, could not regard the sensible world and the seven heavens as the creation of an inferior Demiurge who was inly hostile to the

---

[1] On the presence of this topic in Clement see especially A. Recheis, 147–50; Recheis rightly calls these angels 'customers' (see for instance p. 148).

[2] See p. 177 above and footnote 1 on the same page.

[3] This apocalypse has been edited and translated into German by A. Böhlig and P. Labib, *Wiss. Zeitschr. der Martin-Luther Univ. Halle Wittenberg* (1963); codex V of Böhlig–Labib corresponds to codex III of the list of Doresse (p. 165) and to codex VII of the list of Puech (pp. 106–7). The apocalypse describes Paul's ascent through the heaven (see 24. 6–7, p. 26); in the seventh heaven an archon under the guise of an old man tries to prevent Paul from going up to the eighth heaven (see especially 23. 19–22, p. 25).

[4] The term γάνωμα of *Exc.* 27 is parallel to the γεγανωμένη of *Strom.* iv. 116. 2; the term ἐξουσίαι occurs both in *Exc.* 27 and in *Strom.* vii. 83. 1. The fact that this topic of *Exc.* 27 is adopted by Clement also should not lead us to attribute paragraph 27 of the *Excerpta* to him: as we have seen (pp. 177 ff. above) it contains also other topics (such as the tendency to apply the names of the Biblical God to the angels, the laying aside of the soul's 'body' at the entry of the bridal chamber, the marriage between the soul and the angel or λόγος) which are characteristic of Gnosticism.

[5] See, for instance, Apocryphon of John 41: 12–14 (p. 123 Till) and cf. codex II Krause–Labib 11. 4–5 (p. 139).

spiritual world of the *pleroma*, but only as the product of the creative activity of the divine Logos.

In *Strom.* vii. 57. 5 (iii. 42. 11–14) Clement maintains that he who becomes perfect during his life upon the earth (μετὰ γοῦν τὴν ἐν σαρκὶ τελευταίαν προκοπήν) hastes towards the court of the Father and the abode of the Lord (εἰς τὴν πατρῴαν αὐλὴν ἐπὶ τὴν κυριακὴν . . . ἐπείγεται μονήν), going through the holy *hebdomas* (διὰ τῆς ἁγίας ἑβδομάδος). This passage finds its natural integration in *Strom.* vi. 108. 1 (ii. 486. 6–9), in which Clement maintains that perfect men do not remain in the *hebdomas* but inherit the benefits of the *ogdoas* and enjoy the pure vision produced by insatiable contemplation: οἱ μὴ καταμένοντες ἐν ἑβδομάδι ἀναπαύσεως, ἀγαθοεργίᾳ δὲ θείας ἐξομοιώσεως εἰς ὀγδοατικῆς εὐεργεσίας κληρονομίαν ὑπερκύψαντες ἀκορέστου θεωρίας εἰλικρινεῖ ἐποπτείᾳ προσανέχοντες. In both passages the *ogdoas* is regarded as the dwelling-place of the perfect man: explicitly in *Strom.* vi. 108. 1 and by way of implication in *Strom.* vii. 57. 5. The terms ἑβδομάς and ὀγδοάς have for Clement a double meaning: they symbolize the former the seven heavens, the seventh heaven, and the seventh day of the week, namely the Jewish Sabbath, the latter the eighth heaven of the fixed stars and the Christian Sunday, the eighth day commemorating the resurrection of the Lord.[1] This is the reason why Clement, in *Strom.* vii. 57. 5, hints at the *ogdoas* by using the expression κυριακὴ μονή. Both passages describe, in Clement's thought, both the ascent of the gnostic soul through the seven inferior heavens up to the eighth heaven and its sanctification on the eighth day.

In the gnostic system of Valentine it is possible to find exactly the same ideas. Hippolytus, *Ref.* vi. 32. 9 (iii. 161. 17–18) tells us that according to the Valentinians the soul which has become immortal ἦλθεν εἰς ὀγδοάδα. But particularly important is *Exc. ex Theod.* 63: the πνευματικοί are allotted to the eighth heaven or

---

[1] See Recheis, pp. 150–1: 'Die Hebdomas ist in der Gnosis der Herrschaftsbereich der sieben Fürsten, nämlich die sieben Planetensphären. Darüber breitet sich die Ogdoas, der Fixsternhimmel, der Ort der Ruhe. Die Gnosis wandelt damit die frühchristliche Symbolik der Achtzahl um. Der Sonntag, der Tag der Auferstehung Christi, der achte Tag, ist dem Christen Symbol der künftigen Welt, der künftigen Ruhe. Statt der eschatologischen Typologie entwickelt die Gnosis eine kosmologische Symbolik: statt des historischen Ablaufs eine Hierarchie übereinander gelagerter Sphären', and Sagnard, *Extr. de Théod.*, 185 n. 2: 'Cette Ogdoade est aussi le jour du Seigneur (κυριακή), celui de la Résurrection, le huitième (lendemain de sabbat).'

ὀγδοάς which is called also κυριακή,[1] whereas those who possess the simple faith must remain with the Demiurge in the seventh heaven or ἑβδομάς.[2] In *Exc.* 63 the distinction between a higher and a lower abode (ὀγδοάς–ἑβδομάς) is expressed as clearly as in *Strom.* vi. 108. 1 : actually it is the underlying idea of *Exc.* 63 that enables us to understand what Clement says in *Strom.* vi. 108. 1 in all its implications.[3] The terms ἑβδομάς, ὀγδοάς, and κυριακή possess in the Valentinian system the meanings which they have in Clement.[4]

In the Wisdom of Jesus Christ also the *ogdoas* is represented as the abode reserved for those who possess *gnosis* : 'he who recognizes the Son of man by means of his knowledge and his love . . . will stay together with those who are in the *ogdoas*', 124. 1–9 (p. 289).

The gnostic souls after their *Himmelsreise* surpass the dignity of the angels and of the archangels and reach that of the first-created angels, namely the πρωτόκτιστοι : οἱ τελειωθέντες εἰσὶν ἐξ ἀνθρώπων, ἀγγέλων, ἀρχαγγέλων εἰς τὴν πρωτόκτιστον τῶν ἀγγέλων φύσιν, *Ecl. Proph.* 57. 4 (iii. 154. 6–8).[5] This idea is practically the same idea as that which occurs in paragraph 27 of the *Excerpta*, which, as we have seen, goes back to a gnostic source : καταλύουσα μετὰ τῶν πρωτοκλήτων καὶ πρωτοκτίστων, *Exc.* 27. 5.

[1] *Exc.* 63. 1, ἡ μὲν οὖν τῶν πνευματικῶν ἀνάπαυσις ἐν κυριακῇ, ἐν ᾽Ογδοάδι, ἣ κυριακὴ ὀνομάζεται. The idea that the souls of the perfect man go up to the eighth heaven occurs also in the *Corpus Hermeticum* : see *Poim.* 26 (i. 16. 5), γίνεται ἐπὶ τὴν ὀγδοατικὴν φύσιν, and *CH* xiii. 15 (ii. 206. 16–18), τὴν διὰ τοῦ ὕμνου εὐλογίαν ἣν ἔφης ἐπὶ τὴν ὀγδοάδα γενομένου σου ἀκοῦσαι τῶν δυνάμεων. On the presence of this idea in the *Corpus Hermeticum* see J. Kroll, 296–308, R. Reitzenstein, 50, and A. J. Festugière, *Révélation* . . . iii. 130 ff. There is a striking similarity between the eschatological conceptions of the *Corpus Hermeticum* and those characteristic of the Valentinian system. In *Poim.* 26 the souls, after reaching the ὀγδοάς, meet the divine δυνάμεις, become δυνάμεις themselves, and step inside God : καὶ αὐτοὶ εἰς δυνάμεις ἑαυτοὺς παραδιδόασι, καὶ δυνάμεις γενόμενοι ἐν θεῷ γίνονται. In the Valentinian system (*Exc.* 63–4) the gnostic souls celebrate their wedding with the angels in the ὀγδοάς and then enter together with them into the divine *pleroma*.

[2] *Exc.* 63. 1, αἱ δὲ ἄλλαι πισταὶ ψυχαὶ παρὰ τῷ Δημιουργῷ ; the dwelling-place of the Demiurge is the seventh heaven : see Iren. *Adv. Haer.* i. 5. 4 (i. 48. 6–8), τὸν Δημιουργὸν δὲ εἰς τὸν ἐπουράνιον τόπον, τουτέστι ἐν τῇ ἑβδομάδι.

[3] The close analogy between *Strom.* vi. 108. 1 and *Exc.* 63 has unfortunately escaped E. Baert, who, speaking of *Strom.* vi. 108. 1, refers only to Hippolytus, *Ref.* vi. 32. 9 (p. 465). Baert quotes *Exc.* 63 only to explain the term κυριακή of *Strom.* vii. 57. 5 (see p. 467).

[4] It should not be forgotten, however, that for the Valentinians the term ὀγδοάς indicates also the first four couples of Aeons : on this last meaning see F. Sagnard, *La Gnose valentinienne* . . ., 301 ff.

[5] On the doctrines contained in *Ecl. Proph.* 57 see especially Recheis, 71–2, and J. Daniélou, *Message évangélique* . . ., 421, and *EJ* 21 (1962), 208.

After reaching this dignity, the gnostic soul is very near the Saviour (τῶν ὑπὸ τῷ Σωτῆρι πρώτων τεταγμένων γενησόμενοι, *Strom.* vii. 56. 7): it is in close communion with him, since he and the seven πρωτόκτιστοι represent two entities which cannot be separated from each other.[1] The contemplation 'face to face' which the soul then enjoys (πρόσωπον πρὸς πρόσωπον ἐπιστημονικῶς τὸν θεὸν ἐποπτεύειν, *Strom.* vii. 57. 1) is the contemplation described in *Exc.* 27. 4, ἀξιοῦται πρόσωπον πρὸς πρόσωπον θεὸν ὁρᾶν, and 27. 5, ἐπὶ τὴν γνῶσιν καὶ κατάληψιν τῶν πραγμάτων ἔρχεται; it represents the climax of the contemplation of the intelligible ideas which was granted to the γνωστικός upon the earth and which already enabled him to become an angel and to reach Christ: ὅταν γὰρ ψυχὴ γενέσεως ὑπεξαναβᾶσα καθ' ἑαυτήν τε ᾖ καὶ ὁμιλῇ τοῖς εἴδεσιν ... οἷος ἄγγελος ἤδη γενόμενος σὺν Χριστῷ ἔσται, *Strom.* iv. 155. 4. It must not be forgotten that for Clement Christ, the Logos, represents the totality of the ideas.[2] In Clement's conception of the contemplation 'face to face' and of the close communion with the πρωτόκτιστοι and with Christ Gnostic and Platonic elements blend together in a harmonious unity.

The same blending of Gnostic and Platonic conceptions can be observed also in the use of the term θεοί which Clement applies to the souls which have reached the highest dignity:

Strom. vii. 13. 1 (iii. 10. 8–9): αἱ μακάριαι θεῶν οἰκήσεις.

Strom. vii. 56. 3 (iii. 41. 16–17): τὴν ἐσομένην ἡμῖν κατὰ τὸν θεὸν μετὰ θεῶν δίαιταν.

---

[1] Clement represents the divine wisdom (which for him is identical with the Logos, see pp. 208–9 below) as 'first created', τῆς σοφίας τῆς πρωτοκτίστου τῷ θεῷ, *Strom.* v. 89. 4 (ii. 385. 4–5), and defines both the seven πρωτόκτιστοι and the Logos as 'first-born': see *Strom.* vi. 143. 1 (ii. 504. 18–19) and *Strom.* vi. 58. 1 (ii. 461. 9). Moreover, explaining the mystery of the transfiguration of Jesus in *Strom.* vi. 140. 3 (ii. 503. 9–17), he identifies him with the numbers six, seven, and eight (on the exact meaning of this passage of the *Stromateis* and on its dependence on the gnostic Marcus see A. Delatte, *BEHE* (1915), 237–45); and in *Strom.* vii. 5. 6 (iii. 6. 3–4) he represents the Logos as the chief of all angels. It is therefore very likely that Clement believed in the existence of a very close relationship between the Logos and the seven πρωτόκτιστοι (they are very near God, see *Ecl. Proph.* 57. 1, vol. iii. 153. 26–7). On the πρωτόκτιστοι see also F. Andres, *RQ* 34 (1926), 135–6. As to Clement's speculations on the numbers and his dependence upon Philo in this respect see the material collected by J. D. Phrankoules, Θεολογία 13 (1935), 5–21.

[2] See p. 204 below. The ὀγδοάς, which is the dwelling-place of gnostic souls (see p. 184 above), is very near the intelligible world represented by the Logos: see *Strom.* iv. 159. 2 (ii. 318. 31–319. 1), ἡ ἀπλανὴς χώρα ἡ πλησιάζουσα τῷ νοητῷ κόσμῳ.

Strom. vii. 56. 6 (iii. 41. 23–5) : καὶ θεοὶ τὴν προσηγορίαν κέκληνται, σύνθρονοι τῶν ἄλλων θεῶν, τῶν ὑπὸ τῷ Σωτῆρι πρώτων τεταγμένων, γενησόμενοι.

It is likely that Clement had in mind the Scriptural passage of Ps. 81: 6, ἐγὼ εἶπα· Θεοί ἐστε καὶ υἱοὶ ὑψίστου πάντες. But had not Plato said, in the tenth book of the *Laws*, that the soul which has mingled with the divine virtue becomes one and the same thing with it, enters a holy way, and hastens towards a better place?[1] This Platonic idea of the deification of the soul after the death of the body occurs also in Middle Platonism.[2] Moreover, Clement's term θεοί should be compared with *Poimandres* 26 (i. 16. 11–13), δυνάμεις γενόμενοι ἐν θεῷ γίνονται. τοῦτό ἐστι τὸ ἀγαθὸν τέλος τοῖς γνῶσιν ἐσχηκόσι, θεωθῆναι, with *Exc. ex Theod.* 27. 5, λόγος γενομένη, and 64, αἰῶνες νοεροὶ γενόμενα, and with Irenaeus, *Adv. Haer.* i. 7. 1, πνεύματα νοερὰ γενομένους. The orthodox Clement has not borrowed from heretical Gnosticism the idea of the wedding between the souls and the angels in the divine *pleroma*, but has retained the typically Gnostic and Platonic idea of the deification of the perfect soul. The Platonic ideal of ὁμοίωσις θεῷ can be attained to some extent on the earth by means of ἀπάθεια and contemplation,[3] but finds its complete realization at the end of the *Himmelsreise*.

The direct consequence of *gnosis* and of contemplation 'face to face' is the rest (ἀνάπαυσις). The three following passages are particularly worth noticing:

Paed. i. 29. 3 (i. 107. 25–6) : The highest expression of *gnosis* is rest.
Strom. vii. 57. 1 (iii. 41. 26–31) : *Gnosis* therefore leads man easily towards what is kindred with the soul, divine and holy, and by means of its own light enables him to go through the various mystical levels until it delivers him to the supreme place of repose: it supposes that he whose heart is pure must contemplate God 'face to face' in a way which is in keeping with science and comprehension.
Strom. vii. 68. 5 (iii. 49. 18–20) : The soul after becoming completely spiritual and reaching what is kindred with it remains in the spiritual assembly, in the rest of God.

---

[1] *Laws* x. 904 d, ὁπόταν μὲν ἀρετῇ θείᾳ προσμείξασα γίγνηται διαφερόντως τοιαύτη, διαφέροντα καὶ μετέβαλεν τόπον, ἁγίαν ὁδὸν μετακομισθεῖσα εἰς ἀμείνω τινὰ τόπον ἕτερον.
[2] See Apuleius, *De Plat.* ii. 249 (123. 18–21), nam vinculis liberata corporeis sapientis anima remigrat ad deos et . . . deorum se condicioni conciliat, and ii. 255 (127. 19–20), deorum choreis semideumque permixtam.   [3] See p. 172 above.

The close relationship between *gnosis* and rest is also characteristic of Gnosticism, as can be seen from the following evidence:

Exc. ex Theod. 63. 1 : ἡ μὲν οὖν τῶν πνευματικῶν ἀνάπαυσις ἐν κυριακῇ, ἐν ὀγδοάδι.[1]

Apocryphon of John, Codex II, 26. 31 (p. 184 Krause–Labib): They are brought into the repose of the Aeons.

Gospel of Mary 17. 4–5 (p. 75 Till): In this moment I reach the repose.

Gospel of Philip 119. 13–15 (p. 47): ... and it is fitting for each one of the disciples to enter into his rest.

Gospel of Truth 24. 16–19: ... and cease their strivings in search of the Father reposing in him.

Ibid. 40. 30–3: He sent him in order that he might speak about the Place and about his place of repose from which he had come forth.

Ibid. 41. 28–9: They reach his head which is repose for them.

Ibid. 42. 32: They repose.

Wisdom of Jesus Christ 123. 2–6 (p. 287 Till): He who recognizes the Father by means of his holy knowledge will go to the Father and will obtain rest in the unbegotten Father.[2]

In the idea of the *Himmelsreise* Clement is directly influenced also by Philo. In *Strom.* ii. 51. 1–3 (ii. 140. 1–11) he praises the number ten as the perfect number and identifies it with the highest divinity: as the number ten comes after the first nine numbers, in the same way the soul can reach the highest divinity after surpassing the nine parts into which the sensible world is divided, namely the region of the earth, the seven inferior heavens, and the eighth heaven of the fixed stars; only when the αἰσθητὸς κόσμος is left behind is it possible to reach the *gnosis* of the first principle which is beyond it. Clement connects his eulogy of the number ten with the Pascha, which, according to him, is the symbol of the liberation of the soul from the bonds of the body, represented by Egypt.[3] As Stählin has shown,[4] this section of the *Stromateis* is

---

[1] According to the Valentinians the 'psychical' men also enjoy their rest in the eighth heaven, in which they dwell after the πνευματικοί have entered with the angels into the divine *pleroma*: see Iren. *Adv. Haer.* i. 7. 1, τάς τε τῶν δικαίων ψυχὰς ἀναπαύεσθαι καὶ αὐτὰς ἐν τῷ τῆς Μεσότητος τόπῳ.

[2] The connection between *gnosis* and rest occurs also in the Gospel of Thomas: Ph. Vielhauer discusses sayings 60, 50, and 51 of this gospel in his essay in Beiheft 30 zur ZNW (1964) (especially pp. 293–7). Further material on ἀνάπαυσις has been collected by Vielhauer in this article.

[3] On the presence of this allegory in Clement see also p. 165 above and footnote 2 on the same page.   [4] See app. crit., vol. ii. 140.

directly dependent on Philo, *De Congr. Er. Gr.* 103–6. Here we are again in the sphere of Platonism. The idea of the contemplation of what is beyond heaven has its origin in Plato[1] and occurs also in such authors of Middle Platonism as Albinus and Maximus of Tyre.[2]

3. *The Origin of the World*

According to Clement, the study of theology must come after the study of nature (φυσικὴ θεωρία, φυσιολογία), an important part of which is represented by the problem of the origin of the world. In *Strom.* i. 15. 2 (ii. 11. 14–17) Clement maintains that the study of *gnosis* must be prepared by that of the origin of the world and of nature: ἢ [sc. ἐποπτικὴ θεωρία γνώσεως] προβήσεται ἡμῖν . . . ἀπὸ τῆς τοῦ κόσμου γενέσεως προιοῦσιν, τὰ ἀναγκαίως ἔχοντα προδιαληφθῆναι τῆς φυσικῆς θεωρίας προπαρατιθεμένη. These words are confirmed by the opening of the fourth book of the *Stromateis*, where Clement sets forth the plans for his future literary activity. He expresses the intention to write, after finishing the *Stromateis*,[3] a further work dealing both with the problem of the origin of the world and with theology.[4] The part on the

---

[1] *Phaedrus* 247 c, αἱ δὲ θεωροῦσι τὰ ἔξω τοῦ οὐρανοῦ.

[2] Albinus, *Did.* 180. 18–19, συμπεριπολούσας καὶ τὸ τῆς ἀληθείας πεδίον θεωμένας, and Maximus of Tyre, *Or.* xi. 60 b (141. 8–13), τέλος δὲ τῆς ὁδοῦ οὐχ ὁ οὐρανὸς οὐδὲ τὰ ἐν τῷ οὐρανῷ σώματα . . . ἀλλὰ καὶ τούτων ἐπέκεινα ἐλθεῖν δεῖ, καὶ ὑπερκύψαι τοῦ οὐρανοῦ ἐπὶ τὸν ἀληθῆ τόπον καὶ τὴν ἐκεῖ γαλήνην.

[3] See *Strom.* iv. 2. 1 (ii. 248. 15–16) and *Strom.* iv. 3. 1 (ii. 249. 4–5).

[4] *Strom.* iv. 3. 1 (ii. 249. 4–8). I agree with E. de Faye (*Clément d'Alexandrie*, 87–121), who has demonstrated that the *Stromateis* cannot represent the λόγος διδασκαλικός of which Clement speaks at the beginning of the *Paedagogus* (2. 1, vol. i. 90. 22–4) and that he intended to write, after the *Stromateis*, a further work on the higher *gnosis*, namely the λόγος διδασκαλικός. C. Heussi's attempt to identify the λόγος διδασκαλικός with the *Stromateis* (*ZWTh* 45 (1902), 465–512) has been rightly criticized by de Faye in appendix II of his book (pp. 340–50). Heussi's thesis has been recently taken up by A. Méhat, who is also inclined to see in the *Stromateis* the λόγος διδασκαλικός (see his article in *TU* 64 (1957), 357, and his book *Étude sur les Stromates* . . ., especially pp. 504, 505–7, and 530). I do not think that this view can be accepted. The *Stromateis*, though dealing in many sections with *gnosis*, never examine in detail such arguments as cosmology or theology, which represent the content of the higher *gnosis* and which would fit in very well with the λόγος διδασκαλικός, but rather touch them *en passant*. On the other hand, Clement allots these arguments to a subsequent work (see *Strom.* iv. 3. 1 and also the references collected by de Faye, op. cit. 340–50). As to J. Munck's theory (pp. 109 ff.) (according to which Clement had planned to write two different trilogies, the first represented by the *Protrepticus*, the *Paedagogus*, and the

origin of the world must, in his opinion, precede that on theology:
ἡ γοῦν κατὰ τὸν τῆς ἀληθείας κανόνα γνωστικῆς παραδόσεως φυσιολογία, μᾶλλον δὲ ἐποπτεία, ἐκ τοῦ περὶ κοσμογονίας ἤρτηται λόγου,
ἐνθένδε ἀναβαίνουσα ἐπὶ τὸ θεολογικὸν εἶδος. ὅθεν εἰκότως τὴν
ἀρχὴν τῆς παραδόσεως ἀπὸ τῆς προφητευθείσης ποιησόμεθα γενέσεως (Strom. iv. 3. 2–3, vol. ii. 249. 11–15). It is the study on the
origin of the world that represents the μικρὰ μυστήρια which
must precede the μεγάλα μυστήρια or theology.[1] Unfortunately
we do not possess a systematic account of Clement's views on the
origin of the world: he probably never wrote the work at which
he hints at the beginning of the fourth book of the Stromateis.[2]
There are, however, in the Stromateis, a few scattered passages
which can enable us to reconstruct his thought on this question.[3]

The starting-point of Clement's speculations on the origin of
the world is of course represented by the beginning of Genesis.

λόγος διδασκαλικός, the second by the Stromateis, a second work dealing with
φυσιολογία, and a third work on theology), see Völker's criticism, p. 29 n. 3.
    [1] Strom. iv. 3. 1 (ii. 249. 8), τὰ μικρὰ πρὸ τῶν μεγάλων μυηθέντες μυστηρίων, cf.
Strom. i. 15. 3 (i. 11. 21), ἀγὼν καὶ προαγὼν καὶ μυστήρια τὰ πρὸ μυστηρίων, and
Strom. v. 71. 1 (ii. 374. 1–3). C. Bigg, 92 n., is not quite right in identifying the
μικρὰ μυστήρια with the teaching of the Paedagogus. The Paedagogus does not deal
with the study of gnosis, to which the μικρὰ μυστήρια also belong. In the meaning
which Clement attaches to the expressions μικρὰ μυστήρια and μεγάλα μυστήρια
he is most probably under the influence of Philo, who had identified the μικρὰ
μυστήρια with the indirect knowledge of God, i.e. with that knowledge which
man receives from his works and the μεγάλα μυστήρια with the direct knowledge of
him. This is the idea which underlies the passage of Leg. Alleg. iii. 100 (i. 135.
13–16): see Wolfson, Philo i. 47. Clement's sentence τὰ μικρὰ πρὸ τῶν μεγάλων μυηθέν-
τες μυστηρίων, Strom. iv. 3. 1 (ii. 249. 8), is also worth comparing with Albinus, Did.
182. 8, εἰ μέλλει τὰ μείζω μνεῖσθαι μαθήματα, and with Plato, Gorgias 497 c 3–4.
    [2] Clement may have dealt in detail with the question of the origin of the world
also in his lost work Ὑποτυπώσεις, in which he most probably gave an allegorical
interpretation also of Genesis.
    [3] To Clement's views on the origin of the world modern scholars have paid
almost no attention. E. W. Möller, 506–35, does not examine Clement's dependence upon Philo and Middle Platonism in the question of the origin of the
world. A. de La Barre, DThC iii, col. 155, limits himself to saying: 'La doctrine
de Clément sur la création est généralement correcte en dépit de quelques ré-
miniscences ou imitations platoniciennes ou philoniennes' (de La Barre's further
remark, 'Clément veut trouver dans Platon la doctrine de la création ἐκ μὴ ὄντος',
needs a deeper investigation on the meaning of the expression μὴ ὄν, which does
not hint at the creatio ex nihilo: see p. 195 below). H. F. Weiss, TU 97, does not
say much more than 'Bei Clemens Alexandrinus dagegen begegnen noch Spuren
der Weltbildungstheorien der griechisch-hellenistischen Überlieferung' (p. 154).
The close relationship between Clement and Philo has been pointed out only by
Heinisch, 154–5, 157–8, and 159; however, he has not examined the close agreement between Clement, Philo, and Middle Platonism.

He does not, however, limit himself to paraphrasing the sacred book, but interprets it in a particular way. Here again Philo is his teacher and model. The interpretation of Genesis which the Jewish author gives in *De Opificio Mundi*, in the first book of *Legum Allegoriarum*, and in *De Aeternitate Mundi* is practically the same interpretation as that which we find in chapter XIV of the fifth, as well as in some sections of the sixth book of the *Stromateis*. Clement's adoption of the Philonic interpretation of Genesis shows also how closely his views on the origin of the world are related to those of some exponents of the school-Platonism of his time.

The points on which the agreement between Clement, Philo, and some exponents of Middle Platonism is particularly evident are the following:

1. the distinction between the intelligible and the sensible world, based on the Platonic doctrine of the ideas as patterns of the sensible things;
2. the doctrine of matter;
3. the doctrine according to which the universe was generated, but not in time.

1. In *Strom.* v. 94. 5 (ii. 388. 2–5) Clement quotes the passage Gen. I. 1–3, ἐν ἀρχῇ ἐποίησεν ὁ θεὸς τὸν οὐρανὸν καὶ τὴν γῆν· ἡ δὲ γῆ ἦν ἀόρατος ... καὶ εἶπεν ὁ θεός· γενηθήτω φῶς, καὶ ἐγένετο φῶς. According to him, the οὐρανός, the γῆ, and the φῶς which are mentioned in this passage of Genesis are not the sensible heaven, the sensible earth, and the sensible light, but only their intelligible patterns; in other words, they represent the κόσμος νοητός. Before quoting the words of Genesis he says: ἐν τῇ μονάδι[1] συνίστησιν οὐρανὸν ἀόρατον καὶ γῆν ἀειδῆ καὶ φῶς νοητόν (*Strom.* v. 94. 5, vol. ii. 388. 1–2). In this exegesis of the Biblical passage he follows Philo very closely: Philo also had represented the heaven, the earth, and the light of the beginning of Genesis as intelligible ideas, πρῶτον οὖν ὁ ποιῶν ἐποίησεν οὐρανὸν ἀσώματον καὶ γῆν ἀόρατον ... καὶ ἐπὶ πᾶσιν ... φωτός [sc. ἀσώματον οὐσίαν], *Opif. M.* 29 (i. 9. 4 ff.).

Both for Clement and for Philo Genesis deals with the origin of the sensible world only from 1. 6 on. The στερέωμα which is

[1] On the identity between the μονάς, the intelligible world, and the Logos both in Clement and in Philo see p. 207 below.

192   PISTIS, GNOSIS, COSMOLOGY, AND THEOLOGY

mentioned in Gen. 1 : 6 hints, according to them, at the corporeal world which is στερεόν by its own nature: ἐν δὲ τῇ κοσμογονίᾳ τῇ αἰσθητῇ στερεὸν οὐρανὸν δημιουργεῖ (τὸ δὲ στερεὸν αἰσθητόν) γῆν τε ὁρατὴν καὶ φῶς βλεπόμενον, Strom. v. 94. 1 (ii. 388. 5–6), cf. Philo, De Opif. M. 36 (i. 11. 7 f.), καὶ πρῶτον αὐτοῦ [sc. the sensible world] τῶν μερῶν . . . ἐποίει τὸν οὐρανὸν ὁ δημιουργός, ὃν ἐτύμως στερέωμα προσηγόρευσεν ἅτε σωματικὸν ὄντα· τὸ γὰρ σῶμα φύσει στερεόν. εἰκότως οὖν . . . τὸν αἰσθητὸν καὶ σωματοειδῆ τοῦτο στερέωμα ἐκάλεσεν.

Clement follows Philo also in the theory according to which the sensible world is nothing but an image (εἰκών) of the intelligible world, which is its model and pattern: κόσμον τε αὖθις τὸν μὲν νοητὸν οἶδεν ἡ βάρβαρος φιλοσοφία, τὸν δὲ αἰσθητόν, τὸν μὲν ἀρχέτυπον, τὸν δὲ εἰκόνα τοῦ καλουμένου παραδείγματος, Strom. v. 93. 4 (ii. 387. 21–3). This idea represents a fundamental element in Philo's philosophical system. It clearly appears in such passages as Opif. M. 16 (i. 4. 21–5. 6), Opif. M. 36 (i. 11. 6), Opif. M. 129 (i. 44. 19–20), Quis rer. divin. Her. 280 (iii. 64. 5–7), De Plant. 50 (ii. 143. 24–144. 1), De Ebr. 133 (ii. 196. 2–3), and De Conf. Ling. 172 (ii. 262. 13–14). In these passages Philo simply reproduces the Platonic doctrine according to which the sensible world was formed after the pattern of an intelligible reality. The Timaeus represents the starting-point of Philo's interpretation of Genesis. The Jewish author adopts not only Plato's doctrine, but also his vocabulary: such terms as παράδειγμα, ἀρχέτυπον, μίμημα, εἰκών, νοητόν, ὁρατόν show a clear Platonic origin.[1] This is the reason why Philo—and consequently also Clement—agree with the teaching of Middle Platonism. Plutarch, Albinus, and Apuleius clearly maintain that the sensible world was formed after the pattern with the intelligible and use the same Platonic terminology as that which occurs both in Philo and in Clement.[2]

[1] See Timaeus 28 a–b, 28 c, 29 a–b, 30 c, 30 d, 31 a, 48 e; on the dependence of Philo on the Timaeus in his theory of the origin of the world see especially the dissertation by J. Horowitz, Das platonische νοητὸν ζῷον und der philonische κόσμος νοητός, reprinted, with some additions, under the title Untersuchungen über Philons und Platons Lehre von der Weltschöpfung (Marburg, 1900).

[2] Plutarch, De Anim. Procr. in Tim. 1013 c, εἰκασίᾳ τοῦ νοητοῦ μορφωθὲν εὐθὺς ἁπτὸν καὶ ὁρατόν ἐστι, and 1023 c, τῆς ἰδέας ὡς παραδείγματος, De Is. et Osir. 373 a, ἃς ἀπ' αὐτοῦ [sc. τοῦ νοητοῦ] τὸ αἰσθητὸν καὶ σωματικὸν εἰκόνας ἐκμάττεται καὶ λόγους καὶ ὁμοιότητας ἀναλαμβάνει, 373 b, εἰκόνα τοῦ νοητοῦ κόσμου τὸν αἰσθητὸν γεννᾷ; Albinus, Did. 167. 5–11; and Apuleius, De Plat. i. 192–9.

2. The evidence we possess justifies the assumption that Clement believed in the existence of a matter prior to the origin of the world. He must have held this view in his lost work Ὑποτυπώσεις, which is strongly criticized by Photius also for this reason: ὕλην τε γὰρ ἄχρονον . . . διδάσκει (vol. iii. 202. 10–11). What Clement says in the Stromateis does not contradict the doctrine which he expounded in the Ὑποτυπώσεις, but, on the contrary, provides us with a more complete picture of his views on this question. In Strom. v. 89. 5–6, answering an objection put forward by some opponents, who had reminded him that the Stoics, Plato, andAristotle had regarded matter as one of the first principles, he maintains that matter had been described by these philosophers as originally devoid of any quality and defined by Plato as μὴ ὄν (Strom. v. 89. 6). Clement does not criticize these philosophers at all but, on the contrary, seems to share their views completely.[1]

The doctrine of matter as ἄποιος and ἀσχημάτιστος connects Clement closely both with the Platonic tradition and with the Jewish-Alexandrine philosophy. Following the teaching of Aristotle and of Antiochus, who had identified the ὑποδοχή of which Plato speaks in the Timaeus with matter and considered matter itself as originally devoid of any form,[2] such exponents

---

[1] Clement brings the doctrine of matter formulated by the Greek philosophers into direct connection with Gen. 1 : 2, ἡ δὲ γῆ ἦν ἀόρατος καὶ ἀκατασκεύαστος (Strom. v. 90. 1). I think that H. A. Wolfson, The Classical Tradition (1966), 413–14, goes too far when he says about Clement: 'There were others who either found Plato to be uncertain as to the origin of the pre-existent matter or found him to be vacillating from one opinion to another as to its origin. Thus, to begin with, there is Clement of Alexandria . . .' Clement does not seem to find Plato to be 'uncertain' or 'vacillating' as to the problem of the origin of matter; on the contrary, he does not hesitate to attribute to Plato the view that matter is μὴ ὄν and cannot be regarded as a real ἀρχή (see Strom. v. 89. 6–7).

[2] In the Timaeus Plato had spoken of a receptacle (ὑποδοχή) in which all sensible things come into existence (see especially Timaeus 49 e–50 a, 50 b–c, 50 d–e) and had defined it as formless (50 d–e), difficult to know (51 b 1), apprehensible only by means of a sort of bastard reasoning (52 b 2), and hardly believable (52 b 2). Most probably this receptacle scarcely meant for him anything more than the empty space (on this question see especially C. Bäumker, Das Problem der Materie . . ., 177–88). Aristotle identified the ὑποδοχή of the Timaeus with matter (Phys. iv. 209ᵇ11–13, διὸ καὶ Πλάτων τὴν ὕλην καὶ τὴν χώραν ταὐτό φησιν εἶναι ἐν τῷ Τιμαίῳ· τὸ γὰρ μεταληπτικὸν καὶ τὴν χώραν ἐν καὶ ταὐτόν, De Caelo iii. 306ᵇ18–19, μάλιστα γὰρ ἂν οὕτω δύναιτο, ῥυθμίζεσθαι [sc. τὸ ὑποκείμενον] καθάπερ ἐν τῷ Τιμαίῳ γέγραπται τὸ πανδεχές: cf. E. Zeller, ii/1. 722 n. and 727, ii/2. 322 n. 1, and Weiss, 30 n. 3) and laid emphasis on the fact that matter itself was devoid of any form (De Caelo iii. 306ᵇ17, ἀειδὲς καὶ ἄμορφον δεῖ τὸ ὑποκείμενον εἶναι, cf. Phys. i. 191ᵃ8–12, ὡς γὰρ

of Middle Platonism as Plutarch, Albinus, Apuleius, and the
authors of the sources of the third book of Diogenes Laertius
and of Hippolytus regarded matter as eternal and as originally
devoid of any quality and form.¹ The same doctrine can also be
found in the Wisdom of Solomon,² in Philo,³ and in Justin.⁴

πρὸς ἀνδριάντα χαλκὸς ... τὸ ἄμορφον ἔχει πρὶν λαβεῖν τὴν μορφήν, οὕτως αὕτη
[sc. ἡ ὑποκειμένη φύσις] πρὸς οὐσίαν ἔχει καὶ τόδε τι καὶ τὸ ὄν). Aristotle's identification of the Platonic ὑποδοχή with matter was inherited by Antiochus, who also
considered matter as devoid of any form and quality: sed subiectam putant omnibus
sine ulla specie atque carentem omni illa qualitate ... materiam quandam ... quae tota
omnia accipere possit omnibusque modis mutari, Cic. Ac. Post. i. 27. For the Stoics also
matter was ἄποιος (see SVF i. 85 = i. 493 and also C. Bäumker, op. cit. 331–2
and footnote 1 on p. 332).
    ¹ Plutarch, De An. Procr. in Tim. 1015 d (vi. 163. 10–11), ὁ γὰρ Πλάτων μητέρα
μὲν καὶ τιθήνην καλεῖ τὴν ὕλην, 1024 c (vi. 173. 2–3), χώραν τε γὰρ καλεῖ τὴν ὕλην
ὥσπερ ἕδραν ἔστιν ὅτε καὶ ὑποδοχήν, 1014 b (vi. 159. 13–15), τὴν δ' οὐσίαν καὶ
ὕλην ἐξ ἧς γέγονεν οὐ γενομένην ἀλλ' ὑποκειμένην ἀεὶ τῷ δημιουργῷ, ibid. (vi. 159.
22–3), ἄμορφον μὲν καὶ ἀσύστατον τὸ σωματικόν..., 1014f. (vi. 161. 12–14), τὸ
τὴν ὕλην ἀεὶ μὲν ἄμορφον καὶ ἀσχημάτιστον ὑπ' αὐτοῦ λέγεσθαι καὶ πάσης ποιότητος
καὶ δυνάμεως οἰκείας ἔρημον, De Plac. Philos. 882 c (v. 286. 17–18), Ἀριστοτέλης
καὶ Πλάτων τὴν ὕλην ... ἄμορφον ἀνείδεον ἀσχημάτιστον ἄποιον; Albinus, Did.
162. 25 ff. and 163. 3–7; Apuleius, De Plat. i. 191, materiam vero improcreabilem
incorruptamque commemorat, inabsolutam, informem, nulla specie nec qualitatis significatione
distinctam ... figurationis qualitate viduatam (I follow the text proposed by Sinko,
De Apuleii et Albini ..., 133, who rightly refers to matter the words from inabsolutam
up to distinctam, which in the MSS. appear connected with the ideas); Diog. Laert.
iii. 69 (i. 149. 13–14); Hippol. Ref. i. 19. 3 (iii. 19. 14–20. 1). For all these exponents of Middle Platonism the Platonic ὑποδοχή is not simply the empty space:
see Bäumker, op. cit. 373–4. To the correspondence between Clement and Albinus
in the description of matter attention has been drawn by Früchtel, BPhW 57
(1937), 592 (see also the reprint of Stählin's edition, app. crit., p. 385).
    ² Wisdom of Solomon 11 : 17, κτίσασα τὸν κόσμον ἐξ ἀμόρφου ὕλης. Cf. J. Drum-
mond, i. 225, and H. F. Weiss, 34.
    ³ See, for instance, De Fuga et Inv. 9 (iii. 112. 2) and De spec. Leg. i. 328 (v. 79. 14)
(see also Bäumker, op. cit. 381 n. 5). The only evidence we possess in favour of
the thesis of the presence in Philo of the idea of the creation of matter is represented
by two passages of his work De Providentia: a Greek fragment preserved by Eusebius,
Praep. Ev. vii. 21 (i. 403. 20 ff. Mras) begins with the words περὶ δὲ τοῦ ποσοῦ τῆς
οὐσίας, εἰ γέγονε ὄντως; and in De Prov. ii. 49 Aucher we read quia non solum creare
et edere materiam proprium est providentiae. But as far as we can see from the other
works of Philo which have come down to us, he seems to be far from the Biblical
conception of God as creator ex nihilo and to consider him only as a demiurge who
makes the world out of a pre-existent and formless matter. This is the interpretation of Philo's idea of creation which is commonly accepted by modern scholars:
see, for instance, A. F. Daehne, Geschichtliche Darstellung ..., 328 ff.; C. Siegfried,
232 ff.; H. Soulier, 22 ff.; J. Drummond, i. 297–310; C. Bäumker, op. cit., 384;
E. Zeller, iii. 2. 436; P. Heinisch, 152; E. Bréhier, 80–2; E. Frank, 75 n. 10;
and H. F. Weiss, especially pp. 31–3. Only in De Somn. i. 76 (ἃ πρότερον οὐκ ἦν,
ἐποίησεν, οὐ δημιουργὸς μόνον ἀλλὰ καὶ κτίστης αὐτὸς ὤν) does Philo seem to have
some awareness of the difference between the Biblical idea of creation and the
Greek idea of the Demiurge. It can, however, hardly be inferred from the word

[For note 4 see opposite]

As to the definition of matter as μὴ ὄν to which Clement draws attention in *Strom.* v. 89. 6, it should not lead us to believe that the Alexandrine theologian denied the existence of an original matter and supported the theory of the *creatio ex nihilo*. On the contrary, such definition brings him into close connection with Neopythagoreanism and Neoplatonism. Already Aristotle, by regarding matter as originally formless,[1] had opposed it to οὐσία and to ὄν.[2] This Aristotelian conception was inherited and developed by such exponents of Neopythagoreanism as Moderatus and Numenius and by Plotinus: according to them, since a real being (οὐσία, ὄν) must contain an εἶδος in itself, it necessarily follows that what is devoid of any εἶδος cannot be regarded as a real being, and is therefore μὴ ὄν. Simplicius, *in Phys.* 231. 4–5, reports the view of the Neopythagorean Moderatus (first

κτίστης that Philo believed in the *creatio ex nihilo*: as we have seen (see the preceding footnote) in the Wisdom of Solomon the term κτίζειν is used in connection with matter (see also H. Weiss's pertinent remarks on the use of the terms κτίζειν and κτίστης in Philo, pp. 55–6); and as to the sentence ἃ πρότερον οὐκ ἦν, ἐποίησεν, it can refer both to the origin of the intelligible world, i.e. of the ideas (this is Weiss's opinion, p. 57), and to the origin of sensible things (which are composed of matter and ideas): there is no reason to believe that it refers to matter itself (Bäumker, op. cit. 382 n. 1, rightly observes: 'Das Nichtsein bezieht sich also nicht auf die der Weltbildung voraufgehende Materie als derer Eigenschaft, sondern auf die vor ihrer Bildung noch nicht bestehenden bestimmten Dinge'). The recent attempt made by H. A. Wolfson (*Philo* i. 308 ff.) to prove the existence in Philo of the idea of the *creatio ex nihilo* does not seem to me to be convincing. Wolfson bases his thesis on three arguments: (1) from the passage of *Opif. M.* 29 which deals with the origin of the ideas of the four elements he infers—in my opinion, wrongly—that also the four material elements were created; (2) from the creation of the idea of void which is also mentioned in the same passage he infers the creation of the Platonic ὑποδοχή: but Philo nowhere identifies the idea of void with the ὑποδοχή of the *Timaeus* and with matter; (3) as to the passage of *De Conf. Ling.* 136, in which God is represented as the origin of σώματα and of χώρα, he interprets the word σώματα as meaning 'matter' and again identifies χώρα with the Platonic ὑποδοχή. But both these interpretations are wrong: Philo never uses σῶμα (which for him is a compound of ὕλη and εἶδος) in the sense of 'matter', and nowhere identifies the χώρα generated by God (which for him is the Logos: see *De Somn.* i. 62–3) with the Platonic ὑποδοχή and with matter.

⁴ *Apol.* i. 10, καὶ πάντα τὴν ἀρχὴν ἀγαθὸν ὄντα δημιουργῆσαι αὐτὸν ἐξ ἀμόρφου ὕλης, and i. 59, ὕλην ἄμορφον οὖσαν στρέψαντα τὸν θεὸν κόσμον ποιῆσαι. These two passages demonstrate that Wolfson's view, according to which Justin believed in the creation of matter, cannot be accepted (*The Classical Tradition* (1966), 412–13). On Justin's dependence on Middle Platonism in this respect see C. Andresen, *ZNW* 44 (1952/3), 164–5, and also H. F. Weiss, 147.

---

¹ See the passages of *De Caelo* iii. 306ᵇ17 and of *Phys.* i. 191ᵃ8–12 quoted in footnote 2, p. 193 above.
² See the passage of *Phys.* i. 191ᵃ8–12 quoted in footnote 2, p. 193 above.

century A.D.), who had described the matter which is present in sensible objects as σκίασμα τοῦ μὴ ὄντος: the μὴ ὄν is obviously the ὕλη in general.[1] Like Aristotle, Numenius opposes ὕλη to οὐσία.[2] As to Plotinus, he practically identifies ὕλη with μὴ ὄν.[3] Referring to the ὑποδοχή of the *Timaeus*, he maintains that matter can be known by the human mind only by means of analysis; what remains at the end of this process κατ' ἀφαίρεσιν can hardly be perceived, and does not belong to the class of real beings.[4] Accordingly, the expression μὴ ὄν simply means for Plotinus 'non-real being': it does not imply that Plotinus did not believe in the existence of an original matter.[5] Clement's use of the expression μὴ ὄν in connection with matter reflects a view which was current in Neopythagoreanism and Neoplatonism.[6]

---

[1] As to the attribution of the passage of Simplicius, *in Phys*. 230. 34 ff., to Moderatus see E. R. Dodds, *CQ* 22 (1928), 137–8.

[2] See Proclus, *in Tim*. 299 c (196. 16 Diehl), τὴν μὲν οὐσίαν ἔχουσιν ἀμιγῆ πρὸς τὴν ὕλην . . . ὡς οἱ περὶ Νουμήνιον λέγουσιν.

[3] *Enn*. ii. 4. 10, ἐκ θατέρου οὐκ ἀληθοῦς . . . ἔξω τῶν ὄντων . . . ἐν τῷ μὴ ὄντι (these three expressions all refer to matter). It goes without saying that for Plotinus ὕλη is ἄποιος (*Enn*. i. 4. 8), οὐδὲ σχῆμα (i. 4. 8), πάντων ἔρημος (i. 4. 8), τὸ ἄμορφόν and οὐ . . . εἶδος (i. 4. 10). Cf. Simplicius, *in Phys*. 230. 26, ἀπορρέον εἰς τὸ μὴ ὄν, and 230. 29, ἀποφεύγουσαν αὐτὴν ἀπὸ τοῦ ὄντος. Plutarch (*De An. Procr. in Tim*. 1014 b) and Philo (*De spec. Leg*. i. 328) do not share this view: though admitting that ὕλη is ἄμορφος and ἄποιος, they regard it as οὐσία; in this respect, they are under the direct influence of the Porch. On the identification between ὕλη and οὐσία in the Porch see, for instance, *SVF* i. 85 (= i. 493) and also Bäumker, op. cit. 338: 'Die Materie ist nicht eine Substanz, sondern als oberste, alles befassende Gattung ist sie die Substanz.'

[4] See the whole paragraph of *Enn*. ii. 4. 10 and cf. the whole passage of Simplicius, *in Phys*. 226. 17–227. 22.

[5] Plotinus maintains quite openly that matter does exist: εἰ δέ τις τὴν ὕλην μή φησιν εἶναι, δεικτέον αὐτῷ ἐκ τῶν περὶ ὕλης λόγων τὴν ἀνάγκην τῆς ὑποστάσεως αὐτῆς, *Enn*. i. 8. 15. To this passage of Plotinus attention has been drawn by A. H. Armstrong, *TU* 80 (Berlin, 1962), 427.

[6] V. Ermoni, *JTS* 5 (1904), 123, is therefore wrong in maintaining that 'matter and bodies . . . were created by God'. H. F. Weiss, 154 n. 5, has fallen short of observing the close connection between Clement, Neopythagoreanism, and Neoplatonism in the definition of matter as μὴ ὄν. It is interesting to notice that Plotinus' conception of matter is, in some way, analogous to the conception of the highest divinity which is characteristic of Plotinus himself, of the *Corpus Hermeticum*, of Basilides, and of Ps.-Dionysius Areopagita. The first principle, being without any quality, is beyond real beings: it is either ἐπέκεινα τῆς οὐσίας (*Enn*. v. 4. 1; v. 4. 2) or ἀνουσίαστος (*CH* ii. 5, cf. xii. 1 and vi. 4) or even οὐκ ὤν (Basilides in Hippol. *Ref*. vii. 21, ὁ οὐκ ὢν θεός; the text can be found also in Völker, *Quellen zur Geschichte der christlichen Gnosis*, 47; cf. J. H. Waszink, *Basilides*, *RACh* i. 1221). Ps.-Dionysius Areopagita defines the highest divinity both as μὴ ὄν and as πάσης οὐσίας ἐπέκεινα, the latter expression being for him an explanation of the former (αὐτὸ δὲ μὴ ὄν, ὡς πάσης οὐσίας ἐπέκεινα, *De div. Nom*., PG 3. 588 B 13–14). As

3. In *Strom.* v. 92. 1 Clement maintains that the Greek philosophers had taken from Moses the idea that the universe had a beginning; he himself is openly in favour of this view and, in order to support it, quotes a passage of the *Timaeus* (*Strom.* v. 92. 2).[1] In this way, he agrees with Philo who had also maintained that Plato, in the *Timaeus*, had regarded the universe as γενητός and that, a long time before, Moses had expounded the same doctrine in Genesis.[2] Both Clement and Philo are in agreement with such exponents of Middle Platonism as Plutarch, Atticus, and the author of the source of the third book of Diogenes Laertius.[3] The opposite view—i.e. that according to which the world had no beginning and was ungenerated—was held by other exponents of the school-Platonism, namely Apuleius,[4] Albinus,[5] Celsus,[6] and Taurus.[7] These philosophers practically adopted the

in the case of matter, the definition of God as ἀνουσίαστος, οὐκ ὤν, or μὴ ὄν does not imply the denial of his existence, but simply the fact that he cannot be considered as a 'real being' since he is beyond (or above) οὐσία.

¹ *Tim.* 28 b, πότερον ἦν, ἀρχὴν ἔχων γενέσεως οὐδεμίαν, ἢ γέγονεν, ἀπ' ἀρχῆς τινος ἀρξάμενος; γέγονεν.

² *De Aet. M.* 15, βέλτιον δὲ καὶ ἀληθέστερον ὑπονοεῖν τὸ πρότερον [i.e. what is said in *De Aet. M.* 13, γενητὸν δὲ καὶ ἄφθαρτόν φασι ὑπὸ Πλάτωνος ἐν Τιμαίῳ δηλοῦσθαι], and 19, μακροῖς δὲ χρόνοις πρότερον ὁ τῶν Ἰουδαίων νομοθέτης Μωυσῆς γενητὸν καὶ ἄφθαρτον ἔφη τὸν κόσμον; see also *De Decal.* 58. In *De Prov.* i. 7 Philo seems, however, to have held the view that the universe is eternal: *deus enim non prius intellegere coepit quam agere: nec unquam tempus fuit, quando non ageret ... itaque semper intellegendo facit et sensibilibus principium existentiae praebet.* In this sense the passage is interpreted by Bousset, *Jüdisch-christlicher Schulbetrieb ...,* 144. I do not think that Wendland is right in his attempt to find the idea of the *creatio ex nihilo* in these words of Philo (*Philos Schrift über die Vorsehung,* 5 n. 1).

³ Plutarch, *De An. Procr. in Tim.* 1014 a (vi. 159. 10–12) (cf. Proclus, *in Tim.* i. 381. 26–8 Diehl); Plutarch wrote also a work Περὶ τοῦ γεγονέναι κατὰ Πλάτωνα τὸν κόσμον which is now lost and in which he defended the literal interpretation of *Tim.* 28 b, cf. Praechter, *Grundr. der Gesch. der Philos.,* 537); Atticus in Eusebius, *Praep. Ev.* xv. 6. 7 (ii. 360. 19–20 Mras) (cf. also Proclus, *in Tim.* i. 381. 26–8); Diog. Laert. iii. 71 (i. 150. 5). On this argument see particularly C. Andresen, *ZNW* (1952/3), 163 and footnote 23 on the same page, and *Logos u. Nomos,* 280–3; R. Walzer, *Galeni Compendium Timaei Platonis,* 10–11 (Walzer points out the agreement between the interpretation of *Tim.* 28 b given by Galen, Plutarch, and Atticus with that given by Alexander of Aphrodisias); C. Moreschini, *ASNSP,* Serie II, xxxiii (1964), 34–6, and Ph. Merlan, 63 and 76.

⁴ *De Plat.* i. 198.

⁵ *Did.* 169, 26–30. See also Merlan, 68.

⁶ i. 19. 4–8 and iv. 79 d (cf. Andresen, *Logos u. Nomos,* 80–2). Moreschini is therefore wrong in maintaining, art. cit. 36: 'Quanto a Celso, le sue dottrine cosmologiche l'avvicinano assai al gruppo di Plutarco e di Attico.'

⁷ See Taurus in Iohannes Philoponus, *De Aet. M.* vi. 21 (i. 187. 10–12 Rabe), τοῖς μὲν δυναμένοις καὶ ἄλλως κατανοῆσαι τοῦτο ἠρέμα ὑποδηλοῖ, ὅτι ἀγένητος ὁ κόσμος κατὰ χρόνον, and vi. 8 (i. 147. 11–13), ... ὅτι πρότερον οὐκ ὢν ὕστερον

Aristotelian view of the origin of the world[1] and generally kept themselves close to the allegorical interpretation of the passage of *Timaeus* 28 b which had been given in the Old Academy by Xenocrates and Crantor.[2] An intermediate position between these two opposite views was occupied by the author of the source used by Hippolytus in his exposition of the Platonic philosophy: according to him, the world can be regarded both as ungenerated, since it is formed by matter which is coeternal with God, and as generated, since it is a σῶμα which had its origin when the ideas gave shape to the formless matter.[3]

Although Clement makes it clear that the universe was generated and had a beginning, on the other hand he lays

ἐγένετο, οὐκέτι [i.e. λεγέτω γενητὸν τὸν κόσμον] (on this point see also Merlan, 63). Taurus maintains that it is possible to say that the universe has been generated only in two senses: (*a*) because its parts undergo a perpetual change, and have an origin and an end (Ioh. Phil. *De Aet. M.* vi. 8, vol. i. 146. 20–2; the same view is attributed by Philo, *De Aet. M.* 14, to those interpreters of Plato who regard the universe as generated, ἢ διὰ τὸ ἐν γενέσει καὶ μεταβολῇ τὰ μέρη θεωρεῖσθαι); (*b*) because its existence depends on God, exactly as the light of the moon is originated by the sun (Ioh. Phil. *De Aet. M.* vi. 8, vol. i. 147. 5–9). Taurus did not hesitate to change into εἰ the ἢ of the sentence of *Timaeus* 27 c, ἢ καὶ ἀγενές ἐστιν: see Ioh. Phil. *De Aet. M.* vi. 21 (i. 186. 17–22) and cf. C. Andresen, *Logos u. Nomos*, 278. A survey of the views of those Middle Platonists who regarded the universe as ungenerated can also be found in C. Bäumker, *PhM* 23 (1887), 518; in Andresen, *Logos u. Nomos*, 276–8; and in Moreschini, art. cit. 31–4.

[1] *De Caelo* ii. 283ᵇ26–30; cf. also Philo, *De Aet. M.* 10, Ἀριστοτέλης δέ ... ἀγένητον καὶ ἄφθαρτον ἔφη τὸν κόσμον εἶναι. On this Aristotelian doctrine see also E. Zeller, 'Die Lehre des Aristoteles von der Ewigkeit der Welt', *Vorträge und Abhandlungen* iii. 1–36.

[2] According to Xenocrates and Crantor Plato did not think of a real generation of the world but spoke of a 'generation' only to make himself understood: see Xenocrates, fr. 54 Heinze (διδασκαλίας χάριν) and Plutarch, *De An. Procr. in Tim.* 1013 a–b (θεωρίας ἕνεκα), and cf. A. E. Taylor, 67–8. Theophrastus, following Aristotle, says that according to Plato the universe was generated; immediately afterwards, however, practically adopting the view of Xenocrates and Crantor, he adds that perhaps Plato said this only σαφηνείας χάριν (on the interpretation given by Aristotle and Theophrastus of *Tim.* 28 b see especially Ioh. Phil. *De Aet. M.* vi. 8, p. 145. 15–24). To the allegorical interpretation given by Xenocrates, Crantor, and Theophrastus of *Tim.* 28 b attention has been drawn by C. Bäumker, *PhM* 23 (1887), 514–17 (cf. also Moreschini, art. cit. 29–30). Crantor maintained also that Plato spoke of an origin of the world because the world was dependent on a cause: see Procl. *in Tim.* i. 277. 8 Diehl. This interpretation of *Tim.* 28 b is the one which we have met in Taurus, Ioh. Phil. *De Aet. M.* vi. 8 (i. 147. 5–9): see footnote 7, p. 197 above. On the dependence on the allegorical interpretation of *Tim.* 28 b given by Xenocrates and Crantor of those Middle Platonists who regarded the universe as ungenerated see especially Andresen, *Logos u. Nomos*, 278, and Moreschini, art. cit. 34. Atticus polemizes against such an interpretation of *Timaeus* 28 b: see Eusebius, *Praep. Ev.* xv. 6. 4 (ii. 360. 6–7 Mras).

[3] See Hippol. *Ref.* i. 19 (iii. 20. 2–6) and cf. H. F. Weiss, 20 n. 2.

emphasis on the fact that its origin did not take place in time[1] and that consequently the account of Genesis about the seven days of creation must not be interpreted literally:[2] according to him, the origin of time is closely dependent on the origin of the world and is not prior to it.[3] In this point also Clement depends upon Philo, who had expounded the same ideas in *De Opif. M.* 26–8 and in *Leg. Alleg.* i. 2 and 20.[4]

4. The Doctrine of the Logos

Clement's Logos plays an important role in ethics, in *gnosis*, and in metaphysics. We have already had occasion to speak of the function which the Logos accomplishes in ethics and in *gnosis* both as a metaphysical principle and as a historical person.[5] Here we shall therefore limit our inquiry to the strictly metaphysical aspect of the Logos.

Clement's doctrine of the Logos has been much studied, and its dependence on Philo has generally been acknowledged.[6] That

---

[1] *Strom.* vi. 145. 4 (ii. 506. 14–16), ἵνα τοίνυν γενητὸν εἶναι τὸν κόσμον διδαχθῶμεν, μὴ ἐν χρόνῳ δὲ ποιεῖν τὸν θεὸν ὑπολάβωμεν . . . In this passage Clement interprets the words ὅτε ἐγένετο of Genesis 2. 4 in the sense that the origin of the world did not take place at a determined time: τὸ μὲν γὰρ ὅτε ἐγένετο ἀόριστον ἐκφορὰν καὶ ἄχρονον μηνύει, *Strom.* vi. 145. 5 (ii. 506. 18–19).

[2] See especially *Strom.* vi. 142. 2–3 (ii. 504. 7–15).

[3] *Strom.* vi. 142. 4 (ii. 504. 15–16), πῶς δ' ἂν ἐν χρόνῳ γένοιτο κτίσις, συγγενομένου τοῖς οὖσι καὶ τοῦ χρόνου;

[4] *Leg. Alleg.* 2, εὔηθες πάνυ τὸ οἴεσθαι ἐξ ἡμέραις ἢ καθόλου χρόνῳ γεγονέναι τὸν κόσμον . . . λέγοιτ' ἂν οὖν ὀρθῶς, ὅτι οὐκ ἐν χρόνῳ γέγονεν κόσμος. Like Clement, Philo maintains that the words ὅτε ἐγένετο of Gen. 2: 4 indicate that the origin of the world did not take place at a determined time: ἵνα δὲ μὴ καθ' ὡρισμένας χρόνων περιόδους ὑπολάβῃς τὸ θεῖόν τι ποιεῖν . . . ἐπιφέρει τὸ "ὅτε ἐγένετο" τὸ πότε κατὰ περιγραφὴν οὐ διορίζων, *Leg. Alleg.* i. 20. On these correspondences between Philo and Clement see also Heinisch, 155–6 and 157–8. For Philo also the origin of time is closely connected with the origin of the world since for him time is produced by the movement of the sun and of heaven: see *Leg. Alleg.* i. 2 and *Opif. M.* 26 (accordingly, Philo must not have attached to the χρόνος of *De Decal.* 58— ἦν ποτε χρόνος ὅτε οὐκ ἦν—the strictly technical sense which appears in *Leg. Alleg.* i. 2). On Philo's doctrine of time and on its dependence on Stoicism and on the *Timaeus* see particularly H. Leisegang, *BGPhM* 13 (1913), Heft 4, pp. 11–14.

[5] See pp. 113–17 and pp. 158–63 above.

[6] Many a scholar has pointed out the great similarity between Clement's conceptions of the Logos and of the highest divinity and those of Philo. See, for instance, P. Hofstede de Groot, 40 and 47; E. Redepenning, Erste Abt., 103, 112, and 115–16; E. Vacherot, Tom. I. 253–4; H. Preische, 35 and 37 n. 75; C. Merk, 28–53; J. B. Mayor, in his introduction to the English translation of the seventh book of the *Stromateis* made by J. A. Hort, p. xxxviii; M. Dods, 58; A. Aall,

Clement's Logos, however, as a metaphysical principle, undergoes three different stages of existence and that each of these stages cannot be fully understood without taking the Jewish-Alexandrine philosophy, Middle Platonism, and Neoplatonism duly into account has escaped the majority of modern scholars.[1]

Geschichte der Logosidee in der christlichen Literatur, 396–425; E. de Faye, Clément d'Alex., 230 ff. and 248 ff.; M. Daskalakis, 43–50 and 51–60; P. Heinisch, 127–8, 129–31, 134, 141–3, 146, 148–51 (the most accurate and precise inquiry which has ever been made on the exact correspondences, in the single passages, between Clement and Philo); C. Bigg, 91–9; J. Patrick, 65 and 106–7; R. B. Tollinton, i. 335, 337–8, and 353; R. P. Casey, HThR 18 (1925), 39–41, who rightly stresses the role which Philo played in the formation of Christian Platonism (p. 45), without, however, working out this true premiss throughout his article; C. A. Bernouilli, in his introduction to the German translation of the Stromateis made by F. Overbeck (Basel, 1936), 84 and 114; G. Békés, SA 14. 31–2 and 53–4; M. Pohlenz, NGA, phil.-hist. Kl. (1943), 156–7, who, however, limits his inquiry to the doctrine of God's transcendence in Clement, without touching his 'Logoslehre' which, according to him, is entirely Stoic; and H. A. Wolfson, The Philosophy of the Church Fathers, 204–17 and 266–70, who is concerned mainly with the doctrine of the Logos. It is interesting to notice that both H. Ritter and H. Laemmer, though admitting Clement's dependence on Philo in the doctrine of the highest divinity, deny, at the same time, any dependence of Clement on the Jewish author in the doctrine of the Logos: see Ritter, 442 and 447, and Laemmer, 56–7.

[1] Only T. Zahn, 144–5, R. P. Casey, JTS 25 (1924), 43–56, and H. A. Wolfson, The Philosophy of the Church Fathers, 204–17 and 269, have shown, beyond any doubt, that it is necessary to distinguish in Clement the Logos which is the reason of God from the Logos which was generated by him as a distinct being and which became his Son and the second hypostasis. The passage in which this distinction between two λόγοι clearly appears is the well-known fragment of the Ὑποτυπώσεις preserved by Photius, Bibl. Cod. 109 (see Stählin's edition of Clement, vol. iii. 202. 16–22). T. Zahn, op. cit. 144, has rightly shown that the sentence οὐχ οὗτός ἐστιν ὁ σὰρξ γενόμενος refers to the πατρικῷ λόγῳ which immediately precedes and that the words οὐδὲ μὴν ὁ πατρῷος λόγος are nothing but an explanation of the idea contained in the sentence ἀλλ' οὐχ οὗτός ἐστιν ὁ σὰρξ γενόμενος. Photius' statement μᾶλλον δὲ οὐδὲν ἐκεῖνον is based, according to Zahn (p. 144), on a misunderstanding of Clement's text, in so far as he seems to have related the words ἀλλ' οὐχ οὗτός ἐστιν ὁ σὰρξ γενόμενος not to the πατρικῷ λόγῳ but to the υἱός. H. A. Wolfson, 211, is therefore quite right in translating Clement's fragment as follows: 'The Son is called Logos, being of the same name with the paternal Logos, but it is not this latter that became incarnate. Nor, indeed, is it the paternal Logos, but a certain power of God, an emanation, as it were, of His Logos, that has become nous and pervaded the hearts of men.' Only at the beginning of the Latin translation made by Cassiodorus of a commentary on the first epistle of St. John (Stählin, vol. iii. 209–10) does Clement seem to be openly in favour of the single-stage theory or, in other words, of the theory of the eternal generation of the Logos. But the reliability of this Latin translation is rather scanty, since Cassiodorus himself admits that he did not hesitate to change the original Greek text in order to purge it of errors (... sed aliqua incaute locutus est, quae nos ita transferri fecimus in Latinum, ut exclusis quibusdam offendiculis purificata doctrina eius securior potuisset hauriri; this text of Cassiodorus is quoted by Zahn, op. cit. 134 n. 2). On this

The present section aims therefore at drawing attention to the close connections which exist between these three different stages of Clement's Logos and the corresponding metaphysical principles of the Jewish-Alexandrine philosophy, of Middle Platonism, and of Neoplatonism.

The Logos is, first of all, the mind of God which contains his thoughts; at this stage, he is still identical with God. In the second stage, he becomes a separate hypostasis, distinct from the first principle; in this stage, he represents the immanent law of the universe or, in other words, the world-soul. Let us examine each of these three stages.

That, in the first stage of its existence, the Logos is one and the same thing with the mind of God which contains his thoughts or ideas is clearly implied in the following passages:

Strom. iv. 155. 2 (ii. 317. 11): νοῦς δὲ χώρα ἰδεῶν, νοῦς δὲ ὁ θεός.
Strom. v. 73. 3 (ii. 375. 18–19): δυσάλωτος γὰρ ἡ χώρα τοῦ θεοῦ, ἣν χώραν ἰδεῶν ὁ Πλάτων κέκληκεν.

In both these passages the ideas appear as still comprehended in the mind of God, which is regarded as their χώρα. Clement is here directly dependent on Philo. In *De Cher.* 49 the Jewish author had described God as ἀσωμάτων ἰδεῶν ἀσώματος χώρα;[1] and in *De Opif. M.* 20 he had drawn a comparison between God and the architect who intends to build a new town: as the architect has the town which he wants to build in his mind first, in the same way God has in his mind the intelligible universe; the world consisting of the ideas cannot therefore be comprehended by anything else but by the mind of God (οὐδ' ὁ ἐκ τῶν ἰδεῶν κόσμος ἄλλον ἂν ἔχοι τόπον ἢ τὸν θεῖον λόγον). In this passage the θεῖος λόγος, as H. A. Wolfson has rightly pointed out,[2] is nothing but the reason or mind of God.

point see also Wolfson, 216. As to the other passages of Clement which are usually quoted in order to demonstrate that the Alexandrine theologian did believe in the single-stage theory and in the eternal generation of the Logos (one of the most recent supporters of this view is P. B. Pade, who aims at showing that Clement's Logos is not subordinated to God, but identical with him, pp. 148–60) see Wolfson's pertinent criticism, pp. 204–7. Both Casey, art. cit. 48, 50, and 51, and Wolfson, 208, have rightly pointed out the agreement between Clement, Tatian, Athenagoras, and Theophilus of Antiochia in the doctrine of the twofold Logos.

[1] Both Stählin, app. crit., vol. ii. 317, and Wolfson, op. cit. 210 and 267, have observed this important correspondence between Clement and Philo.
[2] *Philo* i. 230.

Clement clearly maintains that the ideas are the result of the act of thinking of God or, in other words, his thoughts: ἡ δὲ ἰδέα ἐννόημα τοῦ θεοῦ, *Strom.* v. 16. 3 (iii. 336. 8). Philo also had held the same view: in *De Opif. M.* 17–19 he had said that, as the architect, before building the material town, has in his mind first the intelligible patterns of each of its parts (ὥσπερ ἐν κηρῷ τῇ ἑαυτοῦ ψυχῇ τοὺς ἑκάστων δεξάμενος τύπους, *Opif. M.* 18), in the same way God, in order to give origin to the universe, conceived first its intelligible pattern: ἐνενόησε πρότερον τοὺς τύπους αὐτῆς, *Opif. M.* 19. The τύποι which are mentioned here are nothing but the intelligible ideas which are the models of the sensible things. Already in Philo, therefore, the ideas appear as the thoughts of the highest divinity.

The definition of the ideas as thoughts of God is also characteristic of Middle Platonism: it occurs in Albinus, Atticus, Plutarch, and the author of the source used by Hippolytus, as can be seen from the following evidence:

Albinus, *Did.* 163. 12–13: ἔστι δὲ ἡ ἰδέα ὡς μὲν πρὸς θεὸν νόησις αὐτοῦ...

Ibid. 163. 27–8: εἶναι γὰρ τὰς ἰδέας νοήσεις θεοῦ αἰωνίους τε καὶ αὐτοτελεῖς.

Ibid. 163. 29–30: εἴτε γὰρ νοῦς ὁ θεὸς ὑπάρχει... ἔστιν αὐτῷ νοήματα, καὶ ταῦτα αἰώνιά τε καὶ ἄτρεπτα.

Ibid. 164. 27: καὶ αὕτη ἐνέργεια αὐτοῦ ἰδέα ὑπάρχει.

Atticus in Eusebius, *Praep. Ev.* xv. 13. 5 (ii. 377. 13–14 Mras = fr. ix Baudry): τὰ τοῦ θεοῦ νοήματα πρεσβύτερα τῶν πραγμάτων, τὰ τῶν γενομένων παραδείγματα.[1]

Plutarch, *De Plac. Philos.* 882 d (v. 287. 5–7): Σωκράτης καὶ Πλάτων χωριστὰς τῆς ὕλης οὐσίας τὰς ἰδέας ὑπολαμβάνουσιν, ἐν τοῖς νοήμασι καὶ φαντασίαις τοῦ θεοῦ, τουτέστι τοῦ νοῦ, ὑφεστώσας.[2]

Hippol., *Ref.* i. 19. 2 (iii. 9. 10–11): τὸ δὲ παράδειγμα τὴν διάνοιαν τοῦ θεοῦ εἶναι, ὃ καὶ ἰδέαν καλεῖ.[3]

---

[1] The correspondence between Clement and Albinus in the doctrine of the ideas as the thoughts of God has been noticed also by L. Früchtel, *BPhW* 57 (1937), 591 (see also the apparatus of the reprint of Stählin's edition, ii. 336). To the presence of the same doctrine in Atticus attention has been drawn by A. N. M. Rich, *Mnemosyne*, Series IV, 7 (1954), 125 and 129.

[2] I prefer to read ὑπολαμβάνουσι instead of ὑπολαμβάνει, which Bernardakis accepts in his text. As to ὑπολαμβάνουσι see Bernardakis, app. crit., v. 287. This passage demonstrates that R. M. Jones, *CPh* 21 (1926), 325, is wrong in maintaining: 'Plutarch... never calls the ideas the thoughts of God.'

[3] On the presence of this doctrine also in Chalcidius and in Seneca, *Ep.* 65 see the references produced by W. Theiler, *Die Vorbereitung...*, 15–16. Theiler,

In Neoplatonism Plotinus holds practically the same view. According to him the metaphysical νοῦς, with its thought, is the source of the existence of the ideas, which can exist only in it:

Enn. v. 1. 4 (27): ὁ μὲν νοῦς κατὰ τὸ νοεῖν ὑφιστὰς τὸ ὄν.

Enn. v. 9. 5 (12–13): ἢ δῆλον ὅτι νοῦς ὢν ὄντως νοεῖ τὰ ὄντα καὶ ὑφίστησιν.

Enn. v. 9. 8 (12): ἐγκεῖσθαι δεῖ τίθεσθαι ἐν τῷ νοοῦντι τὰ ὄντα.[1]

If, in the first stage, the Logos is identical with the mind of God and also with the ideas which are its thoughts and which are still immanent in it (*Strom.* v. 16. 3, ἡ δὲ ἰδέα ἐννόημα τοῦ θεοῦ, ὅπερ οἱ βάρβαροι λόγον εἰρήκασι τοῦ θεοῦ),[2] in the second stage of its

by taking into account the passage of Cicero, *Orator* 8 and Varro's allegorical interpretation of Minerva in St. Augustine, *De Civ. D.* 7. 28 (op. cit. 18–19) is inclined (op. cit. 39–40) to trace this doctrine back to Antiochus of Ascalon (Theiler's thesis is accepted also by J. H. Loenen, *Mnemos.*, Series IV, 10 (1957), 44–5, and by Ph. Merlan, 55). The view according to which the ideas are the thoughts of God may, however, be older than Antiochus and go back to the Old Academy. In *Timaeus* 39 e Plato had represented the Demiurge as a νοῦς in the act of contemplating the ideas: νοῦς ἐνούσας ἰδέας τῷ ὅ ἐστιν ζῷον . . . καθορᾷ. It must not have been difficult for Xenocrates to bring this passage of the *Timaeus* into connection with the passage of Aristotle, *Met. Λ* 1074ᵇ33–5 in which the highest divinity is represented in the act of contemplating itself, i.e. its own thoughts: αὐτὸν ἄρα νοεῖ . . . καὶ ἔστιν ἡ νόησις νοήσεως νόησις. Accordingly, the ideas, which in *Timaeus* 39 e represent the object of the contemplation of the νοῦς, could be easily identified by Xenocrates, under the influence of Aristotle, *Met. Λ* 1074ᵇ33–5, with the νόησις of God (to this problem attention has rightly been drawn by R. M. Jones, *CPh* 21 (1926), 324–5). Moreover, it must not be forgotten that Xenocrates identified the ideas with numbers (fr. 34 Heinze, p. 171) and the πρῶτος θεός with the νοῦς and the μονάς (fr. 15 Heinze, pp. 164–5; see, on this question, also A. N. M. Rich, *Mnemos.*, Series IV, 7 (1954), 126). It is therefore very likely that Xenocrates would have considered the ideas as produced by the νοῦς exactly as the numbers are produced by the μονάς (Heinze, p. 51, rightly observes: 'jedenfalls bot die letzte Gestalt der platonischen Lehre Anlaß genug dazu, das ἕν in Wahrheit als den alleinigen Schöpfer alles seienden, auch der Ideen, anzusehen').

[1] It should not be forgotten that Plotinus stresses the total identity between the νοῦς and the ideas: see, for instance, *Enn.* v. 1. 4 (31), ἀλλὰ δύο ὄντα τοῦτο τὸ ἕν ὁμοῦ νοῦς καὶ ὄν, v. 3. 5 (26–7), ἐν ἄρα οὕτω νοῦς καὶ τὸ νοητὸν καὶ τὸ ὄν, v. 4. 2 (45–6), νοῦς δὴ καὶ ὄν ταὐτόν, v. 9. 6 (1), νοῦς μὲν δὴ ἔστω τὰ ὄντα, and v. 9. 8 (16–17), μία μὲν οὖν φύσις τότε ὄν ὅ τε νοῦς (cf. Aristotle, *Met. Λ* 1072ᵇ21, ταὐτὸν νοῦς καὶ νοητόν).

[2] Clement most probably had in mind here the passage of Philo, *De Opif. M.* 20, οὐδ' ὁ ἐκ τῶν ἰδεῶν κόσμος ἄλλον ἂν ἔχοι τόπον ἢ τὸν θεῖον λόγον in which the θεῖος λόγος is obviously the mind of God (see p. 201 above). The λόγος τοῦ θεοῦ of this passage of Clement is therefore one and the same thing with the πατρικὸς λόγος of the fragment of the Ὑποτυπώσεις quoted by Photius (Stählin, vol. iii. 202). This λόγος of the Father is also identical with the νοῦς of *Strom.* iv. 155. 2, νοῦς δὲ χώρα ἰδεῶν, νοῦς δὲ ὁ θεός. Since in *Strom.* v. 16. 3 the idea is identified with the

existence it 'comes out' of the divine mind and becomes a distinct being, which is the author of the creation of the sensible world. As H. A. Wolfson has shown, this is clearly implied in the sentence of *Strom.* v. 16. 5 (ii. 336. 12–13), προελθὼν δὲ ὁ λόγος δημιουργίας αἴτιος.[1] In this second stage, the Logos is represented by Clement: (a) as the totality of the ideas or powers of God which, all together, form the κόσμος νοητός and, in connection with this topic, also as μονάς; (b) as the principle (ἀρχή) of everything which has been created, in so far as it is the intelligible pattern of the sensible world; (c) as the wisdom (σοφία) of God.[2]

(a) That the Logos is identical with the totality of the ideas or powers of God is shown by the passage of *Strom.* iv. 156. 1–2 (ii. 317. 24–318. 2): 'all the powers of the divine spirit, gathered into one, complete the same thing, namely the Son; he does not call up the thought of powers exhibited singly. The Son is neither absolutely one as unity nor many as divisible, but one as all is one. Hence he is all. He is the circle of all powers being bound and united in one point.'[3]

Clement found already formed in Philo the doctrine of the Logos as the totality of the powers which are identical with the ideas. That in Philo the Logos, the intelligible world, the ideas and the powers of God are one and the same thing can be seen from the following evidence:

λόγος of the Father, it is easy to infer that Clement believed in the identity between the Logos in the first stage of its existence, the mind of God, and the ideas, exactly as Plotinus believed in the identity between the ideas and the divine νοῦς (see the preceding footnote).

[1] As to the προελθών of *Strom.* v. 16. 2 H. A. Wolfson, *The Philosophy of the Church Fathers*, 208, rightly observes: 'προελθών is a technical term used by the apologists to describe the act of generation by which the Logos emerges from the first stage of its existence and enters upon its second stage when it becomes a distinct personal being. Tatian and Athenagoras use the term προελθών, Justin uses the term ἐλθών.' Wolfson's interpretation is adopted by A. Orbe, *AG* 100. 606.

[2] In this stage of its existence the Logos is also represented as the image (εἰκών) of God; on the presence in Clement of this idea and on its dependence on Philo see chapter I, pp. 15 and 21 above.

[3] I have adopted Bigg's translation, p. 93; I have, however, changed the rendering of the words εἰς ἓν εἰλουμένων and have followed the interpretation given by F. H. Colson of ἀπαρέμφατος in *JTS* 22 (1921), 156–9 (see particularly p. 158). This passage should be compared with the other of *Strom.* vii. 5. 6 (iii. 6. 3–4) in which the Logos is represented as the chief of the hosts of the angels: τούτῳ πᾶσα ὑποτέτακται στρατιὰ ἀγγέλων τε καὶ θεῶν. Like Philo, Clement may have believed in the identity between the angels, the ideas, and the powers of God; on the identity between the angels, the ideas, and the powers in Philo see especially Bigg, 37 and footnote 1 on the same page.

Opif. M. 24 (i. 7. 12–13): οὐδὲν ἂν ἕτερον εἴποι τὸν νοητὸν κόσμον εἶναι ἢ θεοῦ λόγον ἤδη κοσμοποιοῦντος.

Opif. M. 25 (i. 8. 2–3): ἡ ἀρχέτυπος σφραγίς, ὅν φαμεν νοητὸν εἶναι κόσμον, αὐτὸς ἂν εἴη ὁ θεοῦ λόγος.

De Sacr. Ab. et C. 83 (i. 236. 11–12): λόγος ποίκιλμα ὢν ἐκ μυρίων ἰδεῶν.

De Conf. Ling. 172 (ii. 262. 12–14): διὰ τούτων τῶν δυνάμεων ὁ ἀσώματος καὶ νοητὸς ἐπάγη κόσμος, τὸ τοῦ φαινομένου τοῦδε ἀρχέτυπον, ἰδέαις ἀοράτοις συσταθείς.

De Somn. i. 62 (iii. 218. 12–13): ὁ θεῖος λόγος, ὃν ἐκπεπλήρωκεν ὅλον δι᾽ ὅλων ἀσωμάτοις δυνάμεσιν αὐτὸς ὁ θεός.[1]

There are, however, some further implications in Clement's passage quoted above. Clement describes the Logos as the unity which comprehends everything in itself (πάντα ἕν). This idea immediately reminds us of the second hypothesis of Plato's *Parmenides* as well as of some statements of Plotinus about the metaphysical νοῦς. The following correspondences are particularly worth noticing:

Clement, *Strom.* iv. 156. 2: ἀλλ᾽ ὡς πάντα ἕν. ἔνθα καὶ πάντα.

Plot., *Enn.* v. 3. 11 (20–1): καὶ γὰρ αὖ νοῦ ἐντὸς τὰ πάντα.

Id., *Enn.* v. 4. 2 (40–1): τὸ δὲ ἤδη πάντα. εἰ δὲ τοῦτο τὰ πάντα . . .

Id., *Enn.* v. 9. 6 (1–2): νοῦς μὲν δὴ ἔστω τὰ ὄντα . . . ὡς αὐτὸν ἔχων καὶ ἐν ὢν αὐτοῖς.

Id., *Enn.* v. 9. 6 (8–10): ὁ νοῦς ἐστιν ὁμοῦ πάντα . . . ὁ δὲ πᾶς νοῦς περιέχει ⟨πάντα⟩ ὥσπερ γένος εἴδη καὶ ὥσπερ ὅλον μέρη.

Id., *Enn.* v. 9. 8 (3–4): καὶ ὅλος μὲν ὁ νοῦς τὰ πάντα εἴδη.

Plato, *Parmenides* 145 c 1–3: καὶ μὴν τά γε πάντα μέρη τὰ αὑτοῦ τὸ ἕν ἐστι, καὶ οὔτε τι πλέον οὔτε ἔλαττον ἢ πάντα.

Ibid., 145 c 4–5: εἰ ἄρα πάντα τὰ μέρη ἐν ὅλῳ τυγχάνει ὄντα, ἔστι τά τε πάντα τὸ ἕν καὶ αὐτὸ τὸ ὅλον . . .

The similarity between Clement's Logos in the second stage of its existence, the Plotinian νοῦς, and the doctrine of the 'One'

---

[1] On Philo's doctrine of the Logos see especially A. F. Daehne, *Gesch. Darst. der jüdisch-alexandr. Religionsphilos.*, 202–46, A. F. Gfrörer, i. 176–326, C. Siegfried, 219–29, H. Soulier, 63–154, J. Drummond, ii. 156–73, E. Zeller, iii/2. 418–34, A. Aall, *Geschichte der Logosidee in der griechischen Philosophie*, 184–231, P. Heinisch, 137–9, 142–4, and 149, C. Bigg, 36–46, E. Bréhier, 89–121 and 152–7, M. Pohlenz, *NGA*, phil.-hist. Kl. (1942), 445–50, and H. A. Wolfson, *Philo* i. 204–89.

as it appears in the second hypothesis of the *Parmenides* can be easily explained, if we assume that Clement was under the influence of a Neopythagorean interpretation of Plato's *Parmenides* analogous to that on which Plotinus' doctrine of the νοῦς is based. E. R. Dodds has shown that the Neopythagorean schools of the first centuries A.D. distinguished two kinds of 'one': the first, absolutely transcendent 'one', and the second 'one', which is the principle of all things and contains everything in itself; they related the former to the 'one' of the first hypothesis of the *Parmenides* and the latter to the 'one' of the second hypothesis of the same dialogue.[1]

A further correspondence can be observed between *Strom.* iv. 156. 2 and *Enn.* v. 9. 6. Clement compares the Logos to a circle, since 'all the powers are bound and united in one point'. The divine powers are thus represented as the radii of the circle, which all meet in its centre. Plotinus, in order to explain the way in which the divine νοῦς comprehends the totality of the ideas in itself, compares the νοῦς to a seed and to the centre of a circle: in the seed all the faculties of the future being are still undivided, since it is like the centre in which all the generative principles meet (ἐν γὰρ τῷ ὅλῳ ἀδιάκριτα πάντα, καὶ οἱ λόγοι ὥσπερ ἐν ἑνὶ κέντρῳ). The image of the centre of the circle, which represents the meeting-point of all the radii, is exactly the same both in Clement and in Plotinus.[2] About three centuries later,

---

[1] See the paper by E. R. Dodds, *CQ* 22 (1928), 129–42. Both A. F. Daehne, *De γνώσει Clementis Alexandrini* . . ., 95 ff., and R. E. Witt, *CQ* 25 (1931), 201–2, have noticed the similarity between Clement's Logos and Plotinus' νοῦς, but have not pointed out their dependence on the second hypothesis of Plato's *Parmenides*. E. F. Osborn, though mentioning the two different conceptions of the 'One' in the first two hypotheses of Plato's *Parmenides* (pp. 17–18) and hinting at the correspondence between Clement's conception of the Logos as it appears in *Strom.* iv. 156. 1–2 and the Plotinian νοῦς (p. 41 and footnote 11 on the same page), falls short of establishing, in the section which he devotes to Clement's Logos (pp. 38–44), exact parallels between Clement and Plotinus and of pointing out the importance which the Neopythagorean interpretation of the second hypothesis of the *Parmenides* had for their conception of the second hypostasis. It should not be forgotten that Plato also maintains that the intelligible world is 'one': see *Timaeus* 31 a, ἕνα, εἴπερ κατὰ τὸ παράδειγμα δεδημιουργημένος ἔσται, and cf. Albinus, *Did.* 167 33–4, καὶ μονογενῆ τὸν κόσμον ἐποίησε κατὰ τὸν ἀριθμὸν τῇ ἰδέᾳ εἰκασμένον μιᾷ οὔσῃ.

[2] As to the comparison drawn by Daehne (op. cit. 96–7) and by Stählin (app. crit., vol. ii. 318) between *Strom.* iv. 156. 2 and *Enn.* v. 1. 7 see Früchtel's note 318, p. 532 of the reprint of Stählin's edition. I myself think that Clement in *Strom.* iv. 156. 2 resorted to the image of the κύκλος only because the centre of the circle is the meeting-point of all the radii; it is not necessary to assume that, in this con-

the same image will be employed for the same purposes by Ps.-
Dionysius Areopagita: καὶ ἐν κέντρῳ πᾶσαι αἱ τοῦ κύκλου γραμ-
μαὶ κατὰ μίαν ἕνωσιν συνυφεστήκασι· καὶ πάσας ἔχει τὸ σημεῖον ἐν
ἑαυτῷ τὰς εὐθείας ἑνοειδῶς ἡνωμένας πρός τε ἀλλήλας καὶ πρὸς
τὴν μίαν ἀρχὴν ἀφ' ἧς προῆλθον, καὶ ἐν αὐτῷ μὲν τῷ κέντρῳ παν-
τελῶς ἥνωνται, De div. Nom. v. 6 (PG 3. 821. 1–6). It is quite
possible, although it cannot be proved directly, that the common
source of these parallelisms between the Logos of Clement and the
νοῦς of Plotinus is represented by Ammonius Saccas: Ammonius
may have adopted the Neopythagorean interpretation of the
'one' of the second hypothesis of the *Parmenides* and resorted to
the image of the circle in order to illustrate the relationship
between the νοῦς and the ideas.

We can now understand why Clement is inclined to identify
the νοητὸς κόσμος with the μονάς: since the Logos, as second
hypostasis, is the unity which comprehends everything in itself,
the intelligible world, which is identical with the Logos, can
also be defined as μονάς (see *Strom.* v. 93. 4, καὶ τὸν μὲν ἀνατίθησι
μονάδι, ὡς ἂν νοητόν). Philo also, in identifying the νοητὸς κόσμος
and consequently the Logos with the μονάς (*Opif. M.* 15 and 35),
has most probably been influenced by the Neopythagorean
speculations on the 'one'. Both for Clement and for Philo the
μονάς is identical with the Logos: as we shall see, both of them
place the highest divinity above the μονάς itself.[1]

(b) Since the Logos contains all the ideas or powers of God
in himself, and since the ideas are the models or patterns after
which the sensible things are formed, the Logos can be considered as the principle (ἀρχή) of everything which has been
created, or as the instrument of God used in the creation of the
world. This idea is clearly implied in *Strom.* v. 38. 7 (ii. 353. 1–3),
ἡ τῶν ὅλων ἀρχή, ἥτις ἀπεικόνισται μὲν ἐκ θεοῦ τοῦ ἀοράτου, πρώτη
καὶ πρὸ αἰώνων, τετύπωκεν δὲ καὶ μεθ' ἑαυτὴν τὰ πάντα γεννώμενα,
cf. *Strom.* vi. 58. 1 (ii. 461. 6–8), ἐν δὲ καὶ τὸ προγεννηθέν, δι' οὗ
"τὰ πάντα ἐγένετο, καὶ χωρὶς αὐτοῦ ἐγένετο οὐδὲ ἕν". The quotation,
in this last passage, of the beginning of St. John's gospel proves
how strongly Clement is inclined to connect St. John's doctrine

---

nection, he thought of the circular movement of the νοῦς (see, for instance, Plato,
Timaeus 34 a, *Laws* x. 898 a, Philo, *De Gig.* 8, Albinus, *Did.* 168. 4–5, and Plotinus,
Enn. ii. 2. 1, διὰ τί κύκλῳ φορεῖται; ὅτι νοῦν μιμεῖται).

[1] See p. 216 below.

of the Logos with his own conception of the Logos as κόσμος νοητός and τύπος of the sensible things. Here also Clement is under the direct influence of Philo who, having considered the Logos as pattern of the sensible world, had also represented it as the ἀρχή of everything and as God's instrument in the creation of the world.[1]

A further point of contact between Clement and Philo is represented by the interpretation which both of them give of the words ᾗ ἡμέρᾳ of Gen. 2:4; according to them, these words hint at the divine Logos, the principle of creation: see Strom. vi. 145. 5 (ii. 506. 19–21) and cf. Philo, Leg. Alleg. i. 19 and 21.

(c) Clement identifies the Logos as second hypostasis with the divine wisdom, the first of the beings created by God and his adviser: τοῦ υἱοῦ πρὸ καταβολῆς κόσμου συμβούλου γενομένου τοῦ πατρός, αὕτη γὰρ ἦν ἡ σοφία . . . δύναμις γὰρ τοῦ θεοῦ ὁ υἱός, ἅτε πρὸ πάντων τῶν γενομένων ἀρχικώτατος λόγος τοῦ πατρὸς καὶ σοφία αὐτοῦ, Strom. vii. 7. 4 (iii. 7. 9–13), cf. Strom. v. 89. 4 (ii. 385. 4), σοφίας τῆς πρωτοκτίστου.[2] The idea that the divine wisdom is the adviser of God and the first of the created beings is characteristic of the Jewish-Alexandrine philosophy prior to Philo: in Ecclesiasticus 1:4 σοφία is represented as the first-created being, προτέρα πάντων ἔκτισται σοφία; in Prov. 8:22 the divine wisdom says about itself κύριος ἔκτισέν με ἀρχὴν ὁδῶν αὐτοῦ εἰς ἔργα αὐτοῦ; and in the Wisdom of Solomon it assists God during

---

[1] See Leg. Alleg. i. 19 (i. 65. 21–2) and De Conf. Ling. 146 (ii. 257. 4) on the Logos as the ἀρχή of everything; Leg. Alleg. iii. 96 (i. 134. 18–19), De Cher. 127 (i. 200. 10), De Sacr. Ab. et C. 8 (i. 205. 10–11), Quod D. sit imm. 57 (ii. 69. 18), De Fuga et Inv. 95 (iii. 130. 7), De Prov. i. 23 Aucher on the Logos as instrument of God in the creation of the world. By the definition of the Logos as ἀρχή Clement interpret the words ἐν ἀρχῇ at the beginning of Genesis as hinting at the Logos (Strom. vi. 58. 1, vol. ii. 461. 8–10). Such an interpretation is not present in Philo, who, in De Opif. M. 26–7, though quoting the beginning of Genesis, simply points out that the expression ἐν ἀρχῇ must not be understood as hinting at a determined time in which the creation took place. Clement may have been influenced by Philo's identification of the Logos with the ἀρχή as Heinisch, 148, is inclined to believe; I wish, however, to draw attention to the fact that an analogous interpretation is given by the Valentinians of the expression ἐν ἀρχῇ which occurs at the opening of St. John's gospel: they identified the word ἀρχή with the υἱὸς μονογενής (Exc. ex Theod. 6. 1–2). The identification of the Logos as second hypostasis with the ἀρχή of everything occurs also in Justin, who, like Clement and Philo, defines the Logos as ἀρχή: see Dial. 61 (p. 212. 16–17 Otto) and 62 (p. 220. 4–5).

[2] This passage of Clement is in keeping with what Photius tells us about Clement's conception of the Logos in his work Ὑποτυπώσεις: καὶ τὸν υἱὸν εἰς κτίσμα κατάγει (see Stählin, vol. iii. 202. 12).

creation, καὶ μετὰ σοῦ ἡ σοφία ἡ εἰδυῖα τὰ ἔργα σου καὶ παροῦσα ὅτε ἐποίεις τὸν κόσμον, 9:9. The Philonic conception of the Logos as instrument of God in the creation of the world is, to a certain extent, anticipated in this passage of the Wisdom of Solomon.[1] As to the identification of the divine wisdom with the Logos, Philo is Clement's model: for the Jewish author the divine wisdom and the Logos are one and the same thing, ἡ [sc. σοφία] δέ ἐστι θεοῦ λόγος, Leg. Alleg. i. 65 (i. 78. 2). Moreover, like Clement, Philo is inclined to regard the Logos as the first-born (or created) being:

De Abr. 51 (i. 106. 1–2): τὸν ὀρθὸν αὐτοῦ λόγον καὶ πρωτόγονον υἱόν.
De Conf. Ling. 46 (ii. 257. 2–3): τὸν πρωτόγονον αὐτοῦ λόγον.
De Somn. i. 215 (iii. 13–14): ὁ πρωτόγονος αὐτοῦ θεῖος λόγος.

Justin also had identified the Logos with the divine wisdom, Dial. 61 (ii. 212. 18–19), ποτὲ δὲ υἱός, ποτὲ δὲ σοφία [sc. καλεῖται], cf. Dial. 61 (ii. 214. 11), καὶ λόγος καὶ σοφία, and considered it as the first-created being, which was generated by God when he decided to create the world, Apol. i. 23 (i. 72. 6), cf. Apol. ii. 6 (i. 212. 11–13; 214. 1), Dial. 61 (ii. 214. 9–216. 1 ff.) and 62 (ii. 220. 1–6). The agreement between the Jewish-Alexandrine philosophy and the two Christian Platonists is therefore absolute in this respect.[2]

The Logos is not only the transcendent νοητὸς κόσμος which is the model of the sensible world. In the third stage of its existence it is immanent in the universe: it represents then the supreme Weltvernunft, the anima mundi, or, in other words, the law and the harmony of the universe, the power which holds it together, administers it and penetrates into it from one extremity to the other. This idea appears in the following passages:

Protr. 5. 2 (i. 6. 7–9): ἔρεισμα τῶν ὅλων καὶ ἁρμονία τῶν πάντων, ἀπὸ τῶν μέσων ἐπὶ τὰ πέρατα καὶ ἀπὸ τῶν ἄκρων ἐπὶ τὰ μέσα διαταθὲν ἡρμόσατο τόδε τὸ πᾶν.
Strom. v. 104. 4 (ii. 396. 16): τοῦ διοικοῦντος λόγου . . . τὰ σύμπαντα.

---

[1] The same conceptions appear also in St. Paul, Col. 1:15–18, ὅς ἐστιν εἰκὼν τοῦ θεοῦ τοῦ ἀοράτου, πρωτότοκος πάσης κτίσεως, ὅτι ἐν αὐτῷ ἐκτίσθη τὰ πάντα . . . τὰ πάντα δι᾽ αὐτοῦ καὶ εἰς αὐτὸν ἔκτισται . . . καὶ αὐτός ἐστιν πρὸ πάντων . . . On the dependence of the ideas expressed in these sentences on the Jewish-Alexandrine philosophy see especially H. Hegermann, TU 82 (Berlin, 1961), 93–9.
[2] The dependence of Justin's conception of the Logos on the Jewish-Alexandrine philosophy has been rightly pointed out by Heinisch, 145–6 and 147–8.

210 PISTIS, GNOSIS, COSMOLOGY, AND THEOLOGY

Strom. vii. 5. 4 (iii. 5. 22 ff.): αὕτη ἡ μεγίστη ὑπεροχή, ᾗ τὰ πάντα διατάσσεται κατὰ τὸ θέλημα τοῦ πατρὸς καὶ τὸ πᾶν ἄριστα οἰακίζει... ὁ υἱὸς τοῦ θεοῦ... πάντῃ ὢν πάντοτε. *Strom.* vii. 9. 2 (iii. 8. 14–15):... τὸν πρῶτον διοικητὴν τῶν ὅλων ἐκ θελήματος πατρὸς κυβερνῶντα.

Being the law of the universe, the Logos also comprehends it in himself:

Strom. ii. 5. 4 (ii. 115. 23–4): ἐγγυτάτω δὲ δυνάμει, ᾗ τὰ πάντα ἐγκεκόλπισται.[1]

The idea that the Logos is the supreme law of the universe and the power which stretches from its centre up to its extreme boundaries and from these back again to the centre had been a fundamental doctrine of the Porch.[2] Pohlenz was therefore inclined to consider Clement as directly dependent on Stoicism in his conception of the Logos as the universal *Weltvernunft*.[3] It must, however, be observed that Plato also had considered the rational world-soul as stretching from the centre up to the extreme boundaries of the sensible world[4] and as the cause of its order and harmony,[5] and that, owing to the combined influence of Plato and of the Porch, exactly the same conceptions occur both in the Jewish-Alexandrine philosophy and in Middle Platonism. In the Wisdom of Solomon the divine wisdom is represented as the power which penetrates into everything, stretches from one boundary of the universe to the other, and rules over it.[6] As to Philo, he openly maintains that the Logos

[1] This is the reason why Clement maintains that God comprehends everything in himself without being comprehended by anything: see *Strom.* ii. 6. 2 (ii. 116. 4–5), v. 73. 3 (ii. 375. 20–1), and v. 81. 3 (ii. 380. 13–14).

[2] On the Stoic doctrine of the τόνος or τονικὴ κίνησις see *SVF* ii. 448 and 450 and also *Strom.* v. 48. 2, vol. ii. 358. 16–17 (= *SVF* ii. 447).

[3] *NGA*, phil.-hist. Kl. (1943), 158 ff., and *Die Stoa* i. 417–18.

[4] *Tim.* 34 b 3–4, ψυχὴν δὲ εἰς τὸ μέσον αὐτοῦ θεὶς διὰ παντός τε ἔτεινεν καὶ ἔτι ἔξωθεν τὸ σῶμα αὐτῇ περιεκάλυψεν, and 36 e 2–3, ἡ δ᾽ ἐκ μέσου πρὸς τὸν ἔσχατον οὐρανὸν πάντῃ διαπλακεῖσα κύκλῳ τε αὐτὸν ἔξωθεν περικαλύψασα.

[5] *Tim.* 36 a 6–37 a 1, αὐτὴ... λογισμοῦ δὲ μετέχουσα καὶ ἁρμονίας ψυχή; *Laws* x. 897 b, νοῦν μὲν προσλαβοῦσα ἀεὶ θεῖον ὀρθῶς θεὸς οὖσα ὀρθὰ καὶ εὐδαίμονα παιδαγωγεῖ πάντα (I follow the text established by A. Diès, *Platon, Œuvres complètes*, Paris, Les Belles Lettres, 1956), and 897 c, τὴν ἀρίστην ψυχὴν φατέον ἐπιμελεῖσθαι τοῦ κόσμου παντὸς καὶ ἄγειν αὐτὸν τὴν τοιαύτην ὁδὸν ἐκείνην; cf. also *Philebus* 28 d, νοῦν καὶ φρόνησιν... διακυβερνᾶν, 28 e, τὸ δὲ νοῦν πάντα διακοσμεῖν αὐτὰ φάναι, and 30 d, ἀεὶ τοῦ παντὸς νοῦς ἄρχει.

[6] vii. 24, διήκει δὲ καὶ χωρεῖ διὰ πάντων διὰ τὴν καθαρότητα (cf. *SVF* i. 533, ii. 416, 441, 442, 473, and 638); viii. 1, διατείνει δὲ ἀπὸ πέρατος ἐπὶ πέρας εὐρώστως καὶ διοικεῖ τὰ πάντα χρηστῶς.

is also immanent in the sensible world and holds it together, as can be seen from *Quis Rer. div. Her.* 188 (iii. 43. 17), *De Fuga et Inv.* 110 (iii. 133. 20–1), and 112 (iii. 133. 26–134. 2). Philo also adopts the Stoic and Platonic doctrine according to which the Logos (or world-soul) is spread from the centre up to the extreme boundaries of the universe. The correspondence between him and Clement is very close:

Clement, *Protr.* 5. 2 (i. 6. 7–8):	Philo, *De Plant.* 9 (ii. 135. 4–5):
ἔρεισμα τῶν ὅλων . . . ἀπὸ τῶν μέσων ἐπὶ τὰ πέρατα καὶ ἀπὸ τῶν ἄκρων ἐπὶ τὰ μέσα διαταθέν.	ἔρεισμα τῶν ὅλων ἐστίν. οὗτος ἀπὸ τῶν μέσων ἐπὶ τὰ πέρατα καὶ ἀπὸ τῶν ἄκρων ἐπὶ τὰ μέσα διαταθεὶς δολιχεύει τὸν τῆς φύσεως δρόμον.[1]

Like Clement (*Strom.* ii. 5. 4) Philo also maintains that the δύναμις of God (namely his Logos) comprehends the universe in itself: ἐγκεκόλπισται δὲ τὰ ὅλα καὶ διὰ τῶν τοῦ παντὸς μερῶν διελήλυθε, *De Conf. Ling.* 137 (ii. 255. 4–5).[2] It naturally follows that Philo also, like Clement, regards God as comprehending everything in himself without being comprehended by anything.[3]

As to Middle Platonism, Plutarch believes in the existence of a power or Logos which goes through the whole universe, holds it together and is the cause of its harmony:

Quaest. Plat. 1001 b (vi. 123. 17–18): δύναμις ἐγκέκραται τῷ τεκνωθέντι καὶ συνέχει τὴν φύσιν.

De Is. et Os. 373 d (ii. 529. 14–16): τὸ πᾶν ὁ λόγος διαρμοσάμενος σύμφωνον ἐξ ἀσυμφώνων μερῶν ἐποίησε.

De An. Procr. in Tim. 1026 c (vi. 178. 8–9): καὶ γὰρ ἀνάγκη καὶ νοῦς ἐστιν ἡ διήκουσα διὰ πάντων δύναμις.[4]

---

[1] This correspondence between Clement and Philo, of which Stählin, app. crit., vol. i. 6, makes no mention, has been noticed by Daniélou, *Mess. év. et cult. hell.* (Tournai, 1961), 335.

[2] Cf. Clement, *Strom.* ii. 5. 4, . . . δυνάμει, ᾗ τὰ πάντα ἐγκεκόλπισται.

[3] See, for instance, *De Post. C.* 7, *De Migr. Abr.* 182, *De Sobr.* 63, *De Somn.* i. 63 and i. 185. These passages of Philo should be compared with Clement's passages quoted in footnote 1, p. 210 above, and also with Gospel of Truth 22. 25–7, 'the profundity of Him who encircles all spaces, whereas there exists nothing which encircles Him'.

[4] It must be remembered that Plutarch's world-soul cannot be identified entirely with the third stage of the Logos of Clement and of Philo. For Plutarch the world-soul is formed by an evil, irrational element which is prior to the origin of the world and is the cause of the unruly movement of matter and by a rational part

The world-soul of Albinus is extended from the centre up to the extremities of the universe, comprehends it in itself, and holds it together (*Did.* 170. 3–6); moreover, its νοῦς (namely the second νοῦς, the first νοῦς being the highest divinity) accomplishes a function analogous to that which Clement and Philo allot to the third stage of their Logos: it is the cause of the order of the universe, διακοσμεῖ σύμπασαν φύσιν ἐν τῷδε τῷ κόσμῳ, *Did.* 165. 3–4. Numenius compares his demiurge (namely the δεύτερος θεός) to the helmsman, in so far as he guides the universe exactly as the helmsman guides his ship, Eus. *Praep. Ev.* xi. 18. 24 (= fr. 27 Leemans).[1] The ideas which occur in the passages of Plutarch and Albinus quoted above are also characteristic of Atticus' conception of the world-soul:

> Eusebius, *Praep. Ev.* xv. 12. 1 (= fr. viii Baudry): ἔτι τοῦ Πλάτωνος λέγοντος τὴν ψυχὴν διακοσμεῖν τὰ πάντα, διήκουσαν διὰ πάντων ...
> Ibid. xv. 12. 3 (= fr. viii Baudry): δύναμις ἔμψυχος διήκουσα διὰ τοῦ παντὸς καὶ πάντα συνδοῦσα καὶ συνέχουσα.

5. *The Doctrine of the Transcendence of God*

That Clement depends upon Philo in his conception of the highest divinity has already been observed by modern scholars.[2] It is, however, necessary to examine some points to which little attention has been paid so far. First, there are many correspondences between the doctrine of God's transcendence as it appears both in Clement and in Philo and the theology characteristic of Middle Platonism which, as A. J. Festugière has shown,[3] goes ultimately back to some passages of Plato. Secondly, some

(namely the νοῦς, δύναμις, or λόγος) which derives from God: see, for instance, *De An. Procr. in Tim.* 1016 c–d (vi. 165. 8–16), 1027 a (vi. 179. 25–180. 2), and 1029 e (vi. 204. 24–205. 3). This conception of Plutarch finds its explanation in the fact that he identified the irrational part of his world-soul with the evil world-soul which Plato mentions in *Laws* x. 897 d 1 and with what he thought to be the cause of the unruly movement prior to the origin of the world of which Plato speaks in *Timaeus* 30 a 4–5. Plutarch expressly refers to the evil world-soul of the tenth book of the *Laws* in *De An. Procr. in Tim.* 1014 e (vi. 160. 23–161. 2).

[1] The term οἰακίζων used by Numenius is the same term which Clement uses in *Strom.* vii. 5. 4 (see p. 210 above).

[2] See footnote 6, p. 199 above.

[3] A. J. Festugière, *Révélation d'Hermès Trismégiste* iv. 79–91; see also H. Dörrie, *Entr. Hardt* v. 195.

doctrines which connect Clement, Philo, and Middle Platonism closely with one another occur also in some gnostic systems of the second century A.D. Thirdly, it is also necessary to inquire into the position of Clement's theology in the development of the theology of Neoplatonism from Ammonius Saccas up to Plotinus by specifying to what extent Clement's conception of the highest divinity agrees with that of Plotinus or differs from it. Accordingly, we shall first examine the points on which the agreement between Clement, Philo, Middle Platonism, and Gnosticism is particularly evident[1] and then proceed to draw a comparison between Clement, Plotinus, and Ammonius Saccas.

Clement's doctrine of the transcendence of God is mainly based on the following points:

1. God is incorporeal, formless, and without any attribute;
2. he is very difficult to reach, far away from the sensible world, above space and time;
3. he is above the μονάς;
4. he is above virtue;
5. he cannot be comprehended by the human mind: in other words, he is 'unknown';
6. he is ineffable;
7. the best way to approach him which the human mind possesses is the negative process κατ᾽ ἀφαίρεσιν.

1. Clement lays a strong emphasis on the fact that God has no human shape and is also devoid of any human quality. In this idea he is closely dependent on Philo, as the correspondence between *Strom.* v. 68. 3 and *De Sacr. Ab. et C.* 96 clearly shows.[2]

That God can have neither shape nor body nor parts nor dimensions is, however, also a Middle Platonic and Gnostic doctrine, which has its origin in Plato. The following parallels are worth noticing:

---

[1] J. Daniélou, *Mess. év. et cult. hell.*, 302, 303–4, 305–6, 308–9, 311–12, 314–16, has drawn attention only to some correspondences between Clement, the Jewish-Alexandrine philosophy, Middle Platonism, and Gnosticism; our inquiry aims at completing the evidence collected by him.

[2] This correspondence between Philo and Clement has been observed by Stählin, app. crit., vol. ii. 371. See also *Strom.* v. 71. 4 (ii. 374. 15 ff.) and cf. *De Somn.* i. 235 and *De Sacr. Ab. et C.* 95.

Plato	Albinus	Apuleius
Parmenides 137 d: ἄ-πειρον καὶ ἄνευ σχή-ματος.	*Did.* 164. 14–15: ὡς μέγεθος συνεπινοεῖν καὶ σχῆμα καὶ χρῶμα	*De Plat.* i. 190: *sed haec de deo sensit, quod sit incorporeus.*
Ibid., 138 a: ἐπείπερ οὐδὲ μέρη ἔχει.	πολλάκις οὐ καθαρῶς τὰ νοητὰ νοοῦσι.	*De Plat.* i. 204: *incorporeus.*
Symp. 211 a: οὐδ᾽ αὖ . . . οἷον πρόσωπόν τι οὐδὲ χεῖρες.¹	*Did.* 165. 33: μέρη γε μὴν οὐκ ἔχων. *Did.* 166. 6–7: ὥστε ἀσώματος ἂν εἴη ὁ θεός.	

Maximus of Tyre	Numenius	Celsus
Or. xi. 60 a: οὐδὲ χρό-αν λέγει, οὐ γὰρ εἶδεν· οὐδὲ μέγεθος λέγει, οὐ γὰρ ἥψατο.	Eus. *Praep. Ev.* xi. 22. 1 (= *fr.* 11 Lee-mans): ἔνθα μήτε τις ἄνθρωπος μήτε τι ζῷ-ον ἕτερον μήτε σῶμα μέγα μήτε σμικρόν.	vi. 64: οὔτε μετέχει σχήματος ὁ θεὸς ἢ χρώματος.²

Corpus Hermeticum	Gnosticism	Gnosticism
iv. 9: οὐ γὰρ μορφὴ οὐδὲ τύπος ἐστὶ αὐτοῦ . . . ἀδύνατον γὰρ ἀσώματον σώματι φα-νῆναι. xi. 8: τοῦ ἀσωμάτου. xiii. 6: τὸ ἀχρώματον, τὸ ἀσχημάτιστον . . . τὸ ἀσώματον.	Apocryphon of John, 24. 16–18 (p. 89): He is neither corporeal nor incorporeal, nei-ther big nor small; he has no dimensions which can be mea-sured.	Treatise on the three natures: He has no aspect, no form which can be perceived by means of senses.³

Being without any body and formless, God is also devoid of any attribute. A close parallel, which already Früchtel has observed,⁴ can be established between Clement and Albinus:

¹ Cf. Festugière, op. cit., 85.   ² Cf. Festugière, op. cit. 115.
³ Some passages of this treatise have been translated by H. C. Puech and G. Quispel in *VC* 9 (1955), 65–102. On this passage see p. 84.
⁴ *BPhW* 57 (1937), 592; see also the apparatus in the reprint of Stählin's edition, vol. ii. 380.

Clement, *Strom.* v. 81. 5–6 (ii.
380. 18–22) : ὃ μήτε γένος ἐστὶ
μήτε διαφορὰ μήτε εἶδος . . . ἀλλὰ
μηδὲ συμβέβηκός τι μηδὲ ᾧ συμβέβηκέν τι. οὐδ' ἂν δὲ ὅλον εἴποι
τις αὐτὸν ὀρθῶς . . . οὐδὲ μὴν μέρη
τινὰ αὐτοῦ λεκτέον.

Albinus, *Did.* 165. 6 ff. : ἐπεὶ οὔτε
γένος ἐστὶν οὔτε εἶδος οὔτε διαφορά,
ἀλλ' οὐδὲ συμβέβηκέν τι αὐτῷ . . .
οὔτε μέρος τινὸς οὔτε ὡς ὅλον ἔχον
τινὰ μέρη.

2. The transcendence of God necessarily implies his aloofness.
He is very difficult to reach, and always keeps himself far away
from those who want to approach him. For this topic also Philo
is Clement's direct source, as can be seen from the correspondence between *Strom.* ii. 5. 3 (ii. 115. 19–21), *De Post. C.* 18 (ii.
4. 22–4),[1] and *De Post. C.* 13 (ii. 3. 16). It necessarily follows from
this that God cannot be situated in a determined place, but is
above space and time. Clement follows Philo very closely :

Strom. ii. 6. 1 (ii. 116. 2 ff.) : οὐ γὰρ
ἐν γνόφῳ ἢ τόπῳ ὁ θεός, ἀλλ'
ὑπεράνω καὶ τόπου καὶ χρόνου καὶ
τῆς τῶν γεγονότων ἰδιότητος. διὸ
οὐδ' ἐν μέρει καταγίνεταί ποτε.
Cf. *Strom.* vi. 71. 5 (ii. 374. 18–20):
οὔκουν ἐν τόπῳ τὸ πρῶτον αἴτιον,
ἀλλ' ὑπεράνω καὶ τόπου καὶ χρόνου.

De Post. C. 14 (ii. 4. 1–2) : οὐ γὰρ
ἐν γνόφῳ τὸ αἴτιον οὐδὲ συνόλως ἐν
τόπῳ, ἀλλὰ ὑπεράνω καὶ χρόνου
καὶ τόπου.
De Post. C. 7 (ii. 2. 12–13) : τὰς
τῶν γεγονότων ἰδιότητας ἁπάντων
ἐκβεβηκὼς μήτε ἐν μέρει κατα-
γίνεται.
Cf. *De Conf. Ling.* 136 (ii. 254.
23–6) : οὐδαμοῦ συμβέβηκεν εἶναι
μόνῳ . . . τὸ δὲ πεποιηκὸς ἐν οὐδενὶ
τῶν γεγονότων θέμις εἰπεῖν περι-
έχεσθαι.

That God is far away from the sensible world is also a Middle
Platonic doctrine, as can be seen from the following evidence :

Plutarch, *De Is. et Os.*
382 f (ii. 553. 20–1) :
ἔστι μὲν αὐτὸς ἀπω-
τάτω τῆς γῆς ἄχραν-
τος καὶ ἀμίαντος.

Albinus, *Did.* 164.
15–16: θεοὶ δὲ ἀπηλ-
λαγμένως τῶν αἰσθη-
τῶν εἰλικρινῶς τε καὶ
ἀμιγῶς.

Maximus of Tyre,
Or. xi. 59 a : ἐν ἀπηλ-
λαγμένη [sc. φύσει]
τοῦ ῥεύματος τούτου
καὶ μεταβολῆς.

[1] On this parallel between Clement and Philo see also Stählin, app. crit., vol.
ii. 115.

The view according to which God is above space and time has its origin in the first hypothesis of Plato's *Parmenides* and occurs also in Apuleius and in Gnosticism:

Plato	Apuleius	Gnosticism
Parm. 138 a: οὐδαμοῦ ἄν εἴη. Cf. *Symp.* 211 a: οὐδέ που ἐν ἑτέρῳ τινί.[1]	*Apol.* 64. 7: *neque loco neque tempore neque vice ulla comprehensus.*[2]	Hippol. *Ref.* vi. 29. 5: Πατὴρ δὲ ἦν . . . οὐ τόπον ἔχων, οὐ χρόνον (about the Valentinians). Apocryphon of John 25. 2–3 (p. 91): Time does not suit him. Treatise on the three natures: There is no place in which he dwells, or from which he comes, or to which he returns.[3]

3. Since, as we have seen (p. 207 above), the Logos as second hypostasis is for Clement identical with the μονάς, it necessarily follows that God, being the origin of the Logos, is above the μονάς itself. Clement completely agrees on this point with Philo. In the *Corpus Hermeticum* also it is possible to find the same doctrine. Attention should be paid to the following correspondences:

Clement	Philo	*Corpus Hermeticum*
Paed. i. 71. 1: ἐν δὲ ὁ θεὸς καὶ ἐπέκεινα τοῦ ἑνὸς καὶ ὑπὲρ αὐτὴν μονάδα.[4]	*De Vita cont.* 2: τὸ ὄν, ὃ καὶ ἀγαθοῦ κρεῖττόν ἐστι, καὶ ἑνὸς εἰλικρινέστερον καὶ μονάδος ἀρχεγονώτερον. Cf. *De Praem. et Poen.* 40.	v. 2: εὖξαι πρώτῳ τῷ κυρίῳ καὶ πατρὶ καὶ μόνῳ καὶ οὐχ ἑνὶ ἀλλ' ἀφ' οὗ ὁ εἷς.[5]

---

[1] Cf. Festugière, op. cit. 85.   [2] Cf. Festugière, op. cit. 105.
[3] Cf. H. C. Puech–G. Quispel, art. cit. 82.

[4] That Clement places God above the μονάς can also be inferred from the passage of *Strom.* v. 71. 1–3 describing the *via negativa*: the end of this process κατ' ἀφαίρεσιν is the μονάς, which is connected with Christ, the Logos. In order to reach God, it is necessary to go even beyond the μονάς.

[5] On the conception of the number one in the *Corpus Hermeticum* see especially Festugière, op. cit., chapter III, pp. 18 ff.

4. We have seen in the chapter on ethics (p. 66 above) that virtue, for Clement, is the product of the personal effort of man who, by means of training and instruction, attempts first to control, and then to destroy completely his irrational πάθη. This is, however, not the case of God, who, being ἀπαθής by his own nature, has no need of virtue: he is neither ἐγκρατής nor σώφρων, since both ἐγκράτεια and σωφροσύνη presuppose the control of the πάθη. This idea appears in the following passages:

Strom. ii. 81. 1 (ii. 155. 14–15): ὅθεν οὐδὲ ἐγκρατὴς κυρίως· οὐ γὰρ ὑποπίπτει πάθει ποτέ, ἵνα καὶ κρατήσῃ τοῦδε.

Strom. iv. 151. 2 (ii. 315. 8): οὐδὲ μὴν σώφρων ᾗ τῶν ἐπιθυμιῶν ἄρχει.

A similar conception occurs in Philo and in Albinus. Both of them maintain that the highest divinity is above virtue:

Philo

De Opif. M. 8 (i. 2. 20): κρείττων ἢ ἀρετή.

Albinus

Did. 181. 36–7: τῷ . . . ὑπερουρανίῳ, ὃς οὐκ ἀρετὴν ἔχει, ἀμείνων δ᾽ ἐστὶ ταύτης.

5. God's transcendence implies also that he is beyond any thought and cannot be comprehended by the human intellect. This idea occurs very frequently in Clement:

Strom. ii. 6. 1 (ii. 115. 27–8): ὅθεν ὁ Μωυσῆς οὔποτε ἀνθρωπίνη σοφίᾳ γνωσθήσεσθαι τὸν θεὸν πεπεισμένος.

Strom. iv. 156. 1 (ii. 317. 21–2): ὁ μὲν οὖν θεὸς ἀναπόδεικτος ὢν οὐκ ἔστιν ἐπιστημονικός.

Strom. v. 65. 2 (ii. 369. 26 f.): ὁ γὰρ τῶν ὅλων θεὸς ὁ ὑπὲρ πᾶν νόημα καὶ πᾶσαν ἔννοιαν . . .

Strom. v. 71. 5 (ii. 374. 19–20): ὑπεράνω . . . νοήσεως.

Strom. v. 81. 4 (ii. 380. 16–17): πάντως που καὶ ἡ πρώτη ἀρχὴ δύσδεικτος.

Strom. v. 82. 4 (ii. 381. 8): τὸ ἄγνωστον νοεῖν.

The idea that God is difficult to know leads both Philo and Clement to interpret the expression εἰς τὸν γνόφον of Exod. 20: 21 as hinting at the darkness which surrounds the knowledge of God. Here also Clement follows Philo:

218   PISTIS, GNOSIS, COSMOLOGY, AND THEOLOGY

Clement, *Strom.* ii. 6. 1 (ii. 115. 28–116. 2): καὶ εἰς τὸν γνόφον... εἰσελθεῖν βιάζεται, τουτέστιν εἰς τὰς ἀδύτους καὶ ἀειδεῖς περὶ τοῦ ὄντος ἐννοίας.

Philo, *De Post. C.* 14 (ii. 3. 19–20): ἤδη γοῦν εἰς τὸν γνόφον ὅπου ἦν ὁ θεὸς εἰσελεύσεται, τουτέστι εἰς τὰς ἀδύτους καὶ ἀειδεῖς περὶ τοῦ ὄντος ἐννοίας.

Cf. *De Gig.* 54 (ii. 52. 18): καὶ εἰς γνόφον, τὸν ἀειδῆ χῶρον, εἰσελθών.

That for Philo God cannot be known by the human mind is shown also by the following evidence:

De Post. C. 169 (ii. 37. 23–4): αὐτὸς δὲ μόνος ἀκατάληπτος.
De Somn. i. 67 (iii. 219. 15): καὶ κατὰ πάσας ἰδέας ἀκαταλήπτου θεοῦ.
Quod D. sit imm. 62 (ii. 70. 16–17): ὁ δ' ἄρα οὐδὲ τῷ νῷ καταληπτός.
De Mut. Nom. 15 (iii. 159. 13): καὶ ἀπερινόητον καὶ ἀκατάληπτον.

H. A. Wolfson has maintained that Philo was the first philosopher who clearly formulated the doctrine of the absolute unknowability of God and that he found the sources of this doctrine only in some passages of the Old Testament.[1] It is certainly true that these Scriptural passages had a relevant influence on Philo, but Wolfson goes too far when he denies the presence of this conception in any Greek philosopher prior to the Jewish author. E. R. Dodds and A. J. Festugière have drawn attention to the doctrine of the unknowability of the 'one' of the first hypothesis of Plato's *Parmenides* and of the idea of beauty as it appears in the *Symposium*;[2] E. R. Dodds especially has pointed out the fundamental importance which the passage of *Parmenides* 142 a had for the growth of the Neoplatonic conception of the highest divinity.[3] Moreover, the 'one' of the first hypothesis of the *Parmenides* was the object of a particular interpretation in the Neopythagorean schools of the first two centuries A.D., which identified it with the first principle.[4] It is therefore very likely that Philo, though

[1] *Philo* ii. 119–21. Wolfson has drawn attention especially to Exod. 6:3, καὶ τὸ ὄνομά μου κύριος οὐκ ἐδήλωσα αὐτοῖς, and Exod. 33:23, τὸ δὲ πρόσωπόν μου οὐκ ὀφθήσεταί σοι.
[2] E. R. Dodds, *Proclus. The Elements of Theology*, 311–13 (Dodds criticizes here the view expounded by E. Norden in his book *Agnostos Theos*, according to which the Neoplatonic idea that the supreme principle is unknown can only be explained by assuming oriental influences); A. J. Festugière, *Contemplation et vie contemplative selon Platon*, 227 n. 3, and *Révélation d'Hermès Trismégiste* iv. 85.
[3] Op. cit. 311. Dodds has drawn attention also to *Epist.* vii. 341 c–d, ῥητὸν γὰρ οὐδαμῶς ἐστιν. The passage of *Tim.* 28 c, τὸ μὲν οὖν ποιητὴν καὶ πατέρα τοῦδε τοῦ παντὸς εὑρεῖν τε ἔργον, should also be taken into account.
[4] See p. 206 above and footnote 1 on the same page.

having in mind the scriptural passages to which Wolfson has drawn attention, took into account also the speculations on the 'one' of the first hypothesis of the *Parmenides* which were current in the Neopythagorean schools of his time. The same can be said about Clement: what he says in *Strom.* iv. 156. 1 (ii. 317. 21–2), ὁ μὲν οὖν θεός . . . οὐκ ἔστιν ἐπιστημονικός, should be compared with the expression οὐδέ τις ἐπιστήμη which occurs both in *Parmenides* 142 a and in *Symp.* 211 a. The same doctrine of the unknowability of God occurs also in Numenius; similar views are expounded by Apuleius. The following correspondences are worth noticing:

Plato	Apuleius	Numenius
Tim. 28 a: τὸν μὲν οὖν ποιητὴν καὶ πατέρα τοῦδε τοῦ παντὸς εὑρεῖν τε ἔργον. *Parm.* 142 a: οὐδέ τις ἐπιστήμη οὐδὲ αἴσθησις οὐδὲ δόξα . . . οὐδὲ γινώσκεται, cf. *Symp.* 211 a.	*De Plat.* i. 191: cuius naturam invenire difficile est., Cf. *Apol.* 64. 7.	Eus. *Praep. Ev.* xi. 18. 22 (= fr. 26 Leemans): τὸν μέντοι πρῶτον νοῦν . . . παντάπασιν ἀγνοούμενον παρ' αὐτοῖς.[1]

The doctrine of the unknowability of God represents also a fundamental feature of the theology of Gnosticism:

Exc. ex Theod. 7. 1: ἄγνωστος οὖν ὁ Πατὴρ ὤν . . .
Exc. ex Theod. 29: ἡ Σιγὴ . . . ὃ δὲ κατέλαβεν, τοῦτο ἀκατάληπτον προσηγόρευσεν.
Irenaeus, *Adv. Haer.* i. 1. 1 (about the Valentinians): ὑπάρχοντα δ' αὐτὸν ἀχώρητον.
Id., *Adv. Haer.* i. 2. 1 (about the Valentinians): τοῖς δὲ λοιποῖς πᾶσιν . . . ἀκατάληπτον ὑπάρχειν.
Treatise on the three natures: It is impossible for the mind to know him. If he is incomprehensible, it follows that he is unknown.[2]
Apocryphon of John 24. 2–4 (p. 89): He cannot be described, since nobody comprehends him, in order to describe him.
Ibid., 24. 19–20 (p. 89): Nobody can comprehend him.

---

[1] The view of Albinus (*Did.* 165. 4) and of Maximus of Tyre (*Or.* xi. 60 a), according to which the highest divinity can be comprehended only by the νοῦς, is not the same conception as that which appears in Clement, Philo, and Numenius, who clearly maintain that God is above any knowledge.
[2] See H. C. Puech–G. Quispel, art. cit. 83–4.

Apocryphon of John, 26. 4 (p. 93) : Who will be able to comprehend him?

Gospel of Truth 17. 7–8: That incomprehensible, inconceivable one who is superior to all thought.[1]

Ibid., 17. 22: That incomprehensible, inconceivable one.[2]

6. Being beyond the reach of the human intellect, the highest divinity is also ineffable. No name, no word is sufficiently adequate to express its nature: the passages *Strom.* ii. 5. 3 (ii. 115. 21), *Strom.* v. 71. 5 (ii. 374. 19), *Strom.* v. 71. 5 (ii. 374. 22), *Strom.* v. 78. 3 (ii. 378. 2), *Strom.* v. 79. 1 (ii. 378. 17), *Strom.* v. 81. 5 (ii. 38. 18), *Strom.* v. 82. 1 (ii. 380. 24 ff.) are particularly worth noticing in this respect. The same idea occurs also in Philo (see *De Mut. Nom.* 14, vol. iii. 159. 4–5, and 15, vol. iii. 159. 12).[3]

Plato	Albinus	Apuleius
Parm. 142 a: οὐδ᾽ ἄρα ὄνομα ἔστιν αὐτῷ, οὐδὲ λόγος . . . οὐδ᾽ ὀνομάζεται ἄρα οὐδὲ λέγεται.	*Did.* 164. 7: ἦν μικροῦ δεῖ καὶ ἄρρητον ἡγεῖται ὁ Πλάτων. Cf. 164. 28 and 165. 4.	*De Plat.* i. 190: *quem quidem pronuntiat indictum, innominabilem.*
Symp. 211 a: οὐδέ τις λόγος.		*Apol.* 64. 7: *nemini effabilis.*
Epistle vii. 341 c: ῥητὸν γὰρ οὐδαμῶς ἐστιν.		

Maximus of Tyre	Numenius	Celsus
Or. xi. 60 a: τούτου ὄνομα μὲν οὐ λέγει, οὐ γὰρ οἶδεν . . . Ibid.: ἄρρητον φωνῇ.	Eus. *Praep. Ev.* xi. 22. 1 (= fr. 11 Leemans): ἀλλά τις ἄφατος καὶ ἀδιήγητος ἀτεχνῶς ἐρημία.	vi. 65: οὐδὲ λόγῳ ἐφικτός ἐστιν ὁ θεός, οὐδ᾽ ὀνομαστός.[4]

[1] To this passage of the Gospel of Truth attention has been drawn also by Daniélou, op. cit., 312.

[2] See also 18. 32 and 30. 34 (cf. Daniélou, op. cit. 312). Further evidence on the presence of this conception in Gnosticism can be found in Daniélou, op. cit. 310–11.

[3] H. A. Wolfson, *Philo* ii. 119–21, traces the Philonic conception of the ineffability of God also back to the Old Testament.

[4] Cf. Festugière, *Révélation* . . ., iv. 116.

Corpus Hermeticum	Gnosticism	Gnosticism
i. 31 : ἀνεκλάλητε, ἄρρητε, σιωπῇ φωνούμενε.	Basilides in Hipp. *Ref.* vii. 20 (iii. 196. 2–4 = p. 46 Völker) : ἐκεῖνο δὲ οὐδὲ ἄρρητον . . . ἀλλ' ἔστι, φησίν, ὑπεράνω παντὸς ὀνόματος ὀνομαζομένου.¹	Apocryphon of John 24. 4 (p. 89) : He is he, whose name cannot not be expressed.

Gnosticism	Gnosticism
Gospel of Truth 39. 11–13: For, indeed, the ungenerated has no name. For what name could one give to him?	Treatise on the three natures : He cannot be expressed by means of any word.²

7. Clement agrees with Middle Platonism also in the adoption of the analytical process κατ' ἀφαίρεσιν, which consists in depriving the object of knowledge of any sensible attribute and quality. This logical process is expounded by him in the well-known section of *Strom.* v. 71. 2–3 (ii. 374. 4–15). The same process occurs in Albinus, *Did.* 165. 14,³ in Celsus vii. 42. 10 (p. 188 Bader),⁴ and in Maximus of Tyre, *Or.* xi. 61 a (p. 143. 11–18 Hobein). Philo also seems to hint at it in *Quod D. sit imm.* 55–6.

Clement's God recalls, under many aspects, the 'one' of Plotinus. Like the highest divinity of the Alexandrine theologian, the Plotinian 'one' has no shape,⁵ is absolutely transcendent,⁶ escapes those who want to reach it,⁷ is not situated in any

¹ The words ὑπεράνω παντὸς ὀνόματος ὀνομαζομένου go back to St. Paul, Eph. 1:21.
² See H. C. Puech–G. Quispel, art. cit. 84.
³ The correspondence between Clement and Albinus in the adoption of this process has been noticed also by J. Wytzes, *VC* 14 (1960), 144 n. 72.
⁴ The whole passage of Celsus has been translated by C. Andresen, *Logos u. Nomos*, 133.
⁵ *Enn.* v. 5. 11 (4–5), οὐδὲ σχῆμα τοίνυν ὅτι οὐδὲ μέρη οὐδὲ μορφή. Cf. *Parmenides* 137 d 2, οὔτε μέρη ἕξει, and 137 d 9–e 1, καὶ ἄνευ σχήματος ἄρα.
⁶ *Enn.* v. 5. 13 (35–6), ἀλλ' ἀμιγὲς πάντων καὶ ὑπὲρ πάντα καὶ αἴτιον τῶν πάντων.
⁷ *Enn.* v. 5. 10 (9), κἂν τύχῃς, ἐκεῖνός σε ἐκφεύξεται.

place,[1] is above virtue,[2] cannot be the object of science,[3] and is ineffable;[4] moreover, Plotinus also, like Clement, maintains that the best way to get some idea of it is the negative process κατ' ἀφαίρεσιν.[5] And yet there are two important differences between the Plotinian 'one' and Clement's God which deserve some attention. First, Clement regards the highest divinity as a νοῦς which comprehends the ideas in itself: νοῦς δὲ χώρα ἰδεῶν, νοῦς δὲ ὁ θεός, Strom. iv. 155. 2 (ii. 317. 11). Plotinus, on the contrary, makes it clear that the 'one' is above the νοῦς itself since it is its source.[6] Secondly, Clement's God, being a νοῦς, is also endowed with a thought,[7] whereas Plotinus excludes that the 'one' can have any noetical activity.[8]

[1] Enn. v. 5. 9 (33), οὐκ ἐν ὁτῳοῦν ἄρα. ταύτῃ οὖν οὐδαμοῦ. Cf. Parmenides 138 a 2, καὶ μὴν τοιοῦτόν γε ὂν οὐδαμοῦ ἂν εἴη.

[2] According to Plotinus, the highest class of virtues is represented by the paradigmatic virtues which are contained in the νοῦς (Enn. i. 2. 6. 14; i. 2. 6. 16–17) and which are not real virtues but the act and the essence of the νοῦς (Enn. i. 2. 6. 15, ἐνέργεια αὐτοῦ καὶ ὅ ἐστιν). The 'one', being above the νοῦς (see footnote 6), is therefore also above virtue.

[3] Enn. v. 3. 14 (2–3), οὐδὲ γνῶσιν οὐδὲ νόησιν ἔχομεν αὐτοῦ; v. 3. 14 (18), καὶ αὐτὸς κρείττων νοῦ καὶ αἰσθήσεως; v. 4. 1 (9), οὗ μηδὲ ἐπιστήμη: cf. Parmenides 142 a 3–4, οὐδέ τις ἐπιστήμη οὐδὲ αἴσθησις οὐδὲ δόξα, 142 a 5–6, οὐδὲ δοξάζεται οὐδὲ γιγνώσκεται, and E. R. Dodds, Proclus. The Elements of Theology, 311.

[4] Enn. v. 3. 13 (1), διὸ καὶ ἄρρητον, v. 3. 13 (4), οὔτε ὄνομα αὐτοῦ, v. 3. 14 (18), καὶ αὐτὸς κρείττων λόγου, v. 4. 1 (9), οὗ μὴ λόγος. Cf. Plato, Parmenides 142 a 2, οὐδ' ἄρα ὄνομα ἔστιν αὐτῷ οὐδὲ λόγος, 142 a 5, οὐδ' ὀνομάζεται ἄρα οὐδὲ λέγεται, Epist. vii. 341 c 5–6, ῥητὸν γὰρ οὐδαμῶς ἐστιν, and Dodds, op. cit. 311.

[5] See the references collected by R. E. Witt, CQ 25 (1931), 197 n. 16, who has pointed out the correspondence between Clement and Plotinus in the adoption of this negative process.

[6] Enn. v. 1. 8 (6–7), τοῦ δὲ αἰτίου νοῦ ὄντος πατέρα φησὶ τἀγαθὸν καὶ τὸ ἐπέκεινα νοῦ καὶ ἐπέκεινα οὐσίας, v. 3. 11 (20), ἀλλὰ καὶ πρὸ πάντων, ὥστε καὶ πρὸ νοῦ, v. 3. 11 (28–9), δεῖ τὸ πάντη ἁπλοῦν καὶ πρῶτον ἁπάντων καὶ ἐπέκεινα νοῦ εἶναι, v. 3. 12 (48), τὸ δὲ ὥσπερ ἐπέκεινα νοῦ, v. 3. 16 (38), δεῖ τοίνυν ἐκεῖνο . . . εἶναι κρεῖττον καὶ νοῦ, v. 4. 2 (3), ἐπέκεινα νοῦ τὸ γεννῶν, v. 4. 2 (44), ἐπέκεινα ἄρα τι νοῦ, v. 5. 6 (20), τὸ ἐπέκεινα τοῦ νοητοῦ. Aristotle, though regarding the highest principle as νοῦς, had hinted at the possibility that it was something above the νοῦς: ὁ θεὸς ἢ νοῦς ἐστιν ἢ ἐπέκεινά τι νοῦ, fr. 46 Rose in Bekker, v. 1483ª27. What Aristotle had considered a simple hypothesis becomes a fundamental doctrine in the metaphysical system of Plotinus.

[7] The thought of God produces the ideas: see the passage of Strom. v. 16. 3 on p. 202 above.

[8] Enn. v. 3. 13 (35–6), οὐχ ἕξει νόησιν αὐτοῦ . . . οὔτ' οὖν αὐτὸ νοεῖ, v. 6. 2 (2), τὸ ἐπέκεινα νοῦ πρώτως νοούντος οὐκ ἂν ἔτι νοοῖ, v. 6. 2 (16), οὐκ ἄρα νοήσει. τὸ μὲν ἄρα οὐ νοεῖ, v. 6. 3 (21–2), δεῖ ἐν τῷ μὴ πλήθει τὸ νοεῖν μὴ εἶναι, v. 6. 4 (1–2), οὐδ' ἂν τοῦ νοεῖν δέοιτο, v. 6. 5 (4–5), καὶ πάσης κρείττων νοήσεως, v. 6. 6 (30–1), ἀλλ' ἐπέκεινα οὐσίας ὄντι καὶ ⟨τὸ⟩ τοῦ νοεῖν ἐπέκεινα εἶναι. Under this aspect, Basilides' God resembles much more the 'one' of Plotinus: Basilides denies that God is endowed with any thought or will: see Hipp. Ref. vii. 21 (iii. 196. 20 ff. = W. Völker,

Clement's God, though having many of the attributes which
are characteristic of the 'one' of Plotinus, is therefore not entirely
identical with it. He is still the νοῦς of the *Timaeus*, of the *Philebus*,
of the tenth book of the *Laws*,[1] and of book *Λ* of Aristotle's
Metaphysics,[2] and, being the source and the dwelling-place of the
ideas in the first stage of their existence, he corresponds also
substantially to the Plotinian νοῦς:[3] more exactly, he is the
Plotinian νοῦς with the addition of some of the attributes which
Plotinus allots to the 'one'.

The identification of the highest divinity with the νοῦς ap-
proximates Clement to the teaching of Ammonius Saccas and to
one of the main branches of Neoplatonism, namely to that represented by Origen the Neoplatonist and by Hierokles.[4] Proclus,
in Plat. Theol. 2. 4 (= Origen the Neoplatonist, fr. 7 Weber),[5]
criticizes *all* the interpreters of Plato and, among them, particularly Origen the Neoplatonist for refusing to place the 'one'
above the νοῦς and for considering the νοῦς itself as the highest
being: θαυμάζω δ' ἔγωγε τούς τε ἄλλους ἅπαντας ⟨τοὺς⟩ τοῦ
Πλάτωνος ἐξηγητάς, ὅσοι τὴν νοερὰν βασιλείαν ἐν τοῖς οὖσιν
προσήκαντο, τὴν δὲ τοῦ ἑνὸς ἄρρητον ὑπεροχὴν καὶ τῶν ὅλων ἐκβεβη-
κυῖαν ὕπαρξιν οὐκ ἐσέφθησαν καὶ δὴ διαφερόντως 'Ωριγένην τὸν τῷ
Πλωτίνῳ τῆς αὐτῆς μετασχόντα παιδείας· καὶ γὰρ αὖ καὶ αὐτὸς εἰς
τὸν νοῦν τελευτᾷ καὶ τὸ πρώτιστον ὄν, τὸ δὲ ἓν τὸ παντὸς νοῦ καὶ
παντὸς ἐπέκεινα τοῦ ὄντος ἀφίησι. Proclus does not speak here only
of Origen the Neoplatonist but of *all* the interpreters of Plato,
excluding only Plotinus. Among these interpreters of Plato
Ammonius Saccas also must be included. He aimed, in his lectures, at conciliating the teaching of Plato with that of Aristotle;[6]

Quellen zur Gesch. der christl. Gnosis, 47). A. F. Daehne, *De γνώσει Clementis Alexandrini* . . ., 79–95, and R. E. Witt, art. cit. 197–8 ('Clement's God . . . has
a close resemblance with the one of Plotinus'), have not noticed the important
differences between Plotinus and Clement.
  [1] See the Platonic passages quoted in chapter II, footnote 3, p. 115 above.
  [2] Aristotle calls the highest principle νοῦς: see, for instance, *Met. Λ* 1072^{b}19–20,
αὐτὸν δὲ νοεῖ ὁ νοῦς, and the whole of chapter 9 (1074^{b}15–1075^{a}10).
  [3] Actually the Plotinian νοῦς can be compared both with Clement's God and
with the Logos in the second stage of its existence, when it is the sum of the powers
or ideas of God (see p. 205 above).
  [4] See, on this point, K. O. Weber, *Zetemata* 27. 162.   [5] See Weber, 5–6.
  [6] Photius, *Bibl. Cod.* 214. 172 a (*PG* 103. 701 c 9 ff.) and 251. 461 a (*PG* 104.
77 D 1 ff.). Cf. also E. R. Dodds, 'Numenius and Ammonius', *Entr. Hardt* v. 25;
K. O. Weber, 160, and W. Theiler, *Ammonios der Lehrer des Origenes, Forschungen
zum Neuplatonismus*, 2.

in this connection, he must certainly have drawn attention to the fact that both the Plato of the *Timaeus*, the *Philebus*, and the tenth book of the *Laws*, and the Aristotle of book *Λ* of the *Metaphysics*, regarded the highest principle as a νοῦς.[1] Origen the Neoplatonist who, like Plotinus, had been a pupil of Ammonius,[2] kept himself closer than Plotinus to the views of his teacher since he also, as Proclus tells us in the passage quoted above, identified the νοῦς with the highest being without placing the 'one' above the νοῦς.[3]

A further interesting correspondence can be observed between Clement and Ammonius Saccas. Maximus the Confessor, in a passage of his work *De variis difficilibus locis Dionysii et Gregorii* (= Clement, fr. 48 Stählin, vol. iii. 224), tells us that the followers of Pantaenus regarded the creation of all things as the result of the will of God: εἰ γὰρ θελήματι τὰ πάντα πεποίηκε ... ἕκαστον δὲ τῶν γεγονότων θέλων πεποίηκε (Stählin iii. 224. 23–5). These words of Maximus have a striking similarity with what Hierokles says in a fragment preserved by Photius in *Bibl. Cod.* 214. 172 a and 251. 461 b:

Bibl. Cod. 214. 172 a (= *PG* 103. 704 A 8–9): ἀρκεῖν γὰρ αὐτῷ εἰς ὑπόστασιν τῶν ὄντων τὸ βούλημα.

Bibl. Cod. 251. 461 b (*PG* 104. 80 A 9–10): ἀρκεῖν γὰρ ἐκείνου βούλημα εἰς ὑπόστασιν τῶν ὄντων.[4]

F. Heinemann, K. O. Weber, W. Theiler, and H. Langerbeck are strongly inclined to consider Ammonius as the source of the fragment of Hierokles.[5] Particularly Heinemann has pointed out that Hierokles' sentence in *Bibl. Cod.* 214 (*PG* 103. 704 c 6–7), οὐκ ἄλλην νομίζειν αὐτὸν εἱμαρμένην ἀλλ' ἣν Ἀριστοτέλει καὶ Πλάτωνι νομίζειν δίδωσι, is perfectly in keeping with Ammonius' tendency to harmonize the teaching of Plato with that of Aris-

---

[1] See chapter II, p. 115 n. 3 and p. 116 n. 1 above. Whereas H. Dörrie, *Hermes* 83 (1955), 457, prefers to leave without a definite answer the question whether Ammonius separated the one from the νοῦς or not ('bei diesem Zeugnis muss es als zweifelhaft erscheinen, ob Ammonius ausdrücklich das Eine vom Sein sonderte'), K. O. Weber, 160, and W. Theiler, 10 and 41, are inclined to believe that for Ammonius the highest principle was the νοῦς.

[2] Photius, *Bibl. Cod.* 251. 461 a (*PG* 104. 77 D ff.) (= fr. 6 Weber, p. 5).

[3] The agreement between Origen the Neoplatonist and Ammonius has been pointed out by Weber, 160 and 162, and by Theiler, art. cit. 10.

[4] The complete text of Hierokles' fragment as it appears in *Bibl. Cod.* 214 and 251 is reproduced by F. Heinemann, *Hermes* 61 (1926), 7–9.

[5] See Heinemann, 6 and 10, Weber, 91–3, Theiler, art. cit. 9, and H. Langerbeck, *AAWG*, phil.-hist. Kl. 69 (1967), 148–9.

totle.[1] E. R. Dodds, on the contrary, sees no sufficient reason to trace Hierokles' fragment back to Ammonius but, on the other hand, does not exclude the possibility that its source is represented by Origen the Neoplatonist, one of the pupils of Ammonius.[2] The close correspondence between Hierokles' words and what Maximus the Confessor says about Pantaenus and his followers proves, however, that the doctrine expounded by Hierokles in the two passages of the *Bibl. Cod.* quoted above is much earlier than Origen the Neoplatonist and goes back to Pantaenus, i.e. to the end of the second century A.D. In this connection, it should not be forgotten that both Ammonius and Pantaenus lived in Alexandria in the last years of the second century A.D. and that Ammonius had originally been a Christian;[3]

---

[1] See Heinemann, art. cit. 10.

[2] 'Numenius and Ammonius', *Entr. Hardt* v. 25–6.

[3] See the Introduction, footnote 1, p. 4 above. The fact that Ammonius had originally been a Christian does not, however, prove at all Langerbeck's view, according to which he remained a Christian throughout his life (*JHS* 77 (1957), 68–9 and 74, and *AAWG*, phil.-hist. Kl. 69 (1967), 149 f. and 166). Langerbeck bases his thesis mainly on what Eusebius, after quoting Porphyry, says about Ammonius in *HE* vi. 19. 10, vol. ii. 560. 25–562. 2 (Ammonius preserved his divine philosophy pure from any contamination till the end of his life and wrote a treatise 'About the Agreement between Moses and Jesus') and denies that Porphyry in Eusebius, *HE* vi. 19. 7 (ii. 560. 4–7) hints at the conversion of Ammonius from Christianity to paganism. But Langerbeck's construction is wrong, since: (*a*) Porphyry, who obviously aims at pointing out the contrasting behaviour of Ammonius and of Origen the Christian, *does* say that Ammonius abandoned Christianity: according to him, whereas Ammonius, after starting reasoning and coming across the study of philosophy, converted himself to a way of life which was in keeping with the law (πρὸς τὴν κατὰ νόμους πολιτείαν μετεβάλετο), Origen the Christian followed the exactly opposite way since he, though having received a Greek education, embraced the barbarian philosophy (Porphyry is, however, wrong in assuming that Origen the Christian was a convert from paganism: see E. R. Dodds, 'Numenius and Ammonius', 31 n. 1); (*b*) Porphyry's account about Ammonius is much more reliable than that of Eusebius: as a pupil of Plotinus, Porphyry was most probably much better informed than Eusebius about Ammonius' life. As to the existence of the treatise 'About the Agreement between Moses and Jesus', which Eusebius attributes to Ammonius in *HE* vi. 19. 10, it can be explained in two ways: (*a*) either it was written by Ammonius in his youth, before he abandoned Christianity; or (*b*) Eusebius confused Ammonius the founder of Neoplatonism with another homonymous Christian author (H. Dörrie, *Hermes* 83 (1955), 468, believes in the existence of a Christian Ammonius who must be distinguished from the founder of Neoplatonism; this view is shared also by E. R. Dodds, 'Numenius and Ammonius', 31 n. 1, W. Theiler, *Ammonios der Lehrer des Origenes, Forsch. zum Neuplat.*, 1, and J. Quasten, *Patrology* ii. 101). Langerbeck's view, which is entirely adopted by his pupil, K. O. Weber (p. 38), is rightly rejected by A. H. Armstrong in his review of Weber's book, *JHS* 83 (1963), 185, E. R. Dodds, art. cit. 31, and H. Chadwick, *Early Christian Thought* ..., 149 n. 8.

Q

it is therefore very likely that the doctrine contained in the passage of Maximus and in the fragment of Hierokles was adopted not only by Pantaenus but also by Ammonius, and that Ammonius actually represents the source of Hierokles.[1]

[1] From Hierokles' words διακοσμήσεως ἦν ἐκ μηδενός φησιν ὑποκειμένου προαγαγεῖν τὸν τεχνίτην (*Bibl. Cod.* 214. 172 a) and διακοσμήσεως ἐκ μηδενὸς προυποκειμένου γεγενημένης (*Bibl. Cod.* 251. 461 b) it can be inferred that Hierokles' source (namely Ammonius) did not believe in the existence of an original matter (cf., for instance, A. Theiler, art. cit. 42: 'Ammonius kennt keine mit Gott gleich ewige Materie; sie ist von Gott geschaffen'). Like Clement (*Strom.* v. 89. 6–7) Ammonius may have held the view that matter was μὴ ὄν and that, therefore, it could not be regarded as one of the ἀρχαί of things (cf. Clement, *Strom.* v. 89. 7), thus rejecting the view of school-Platonism, which considered matter as one of the ἀρχαί (see, for instance, Albinus, *Did.*, c. viii, p. 162, and Hipp., *Ref.* i. 19. 1, vol. iii. 19. 4–6, Πλάτων ἀρχὰς εἶναι τοῦ παντὸς θεὸν καὶ ὕλην καὶ παράδειγμα... ὕλην δὲ πᾶσιν ὑποκειμένην). By refusing to see in matter an ἀρχή (or, in other words, the cause *from* which sensible things originate) Ammonius could easily deny that it was a ὑποκείμενον (in the passage of Hippolytus quoted above the two ideas of ἀρχή and ὑποκείμενον are clearly connected with each other) and come to the conclusion that 'the craftsman did not bring forward the universe out of any substratum' (*Bibl. Cod.* 214) or that 'the universe did not originate from any substratum' (*Bibl. Cod.* 251): the will of God suffices to bring things into existence (*Bibl. Cod.* 214 and 251) since he is the sole, real ἀρχή (cf. *Strom.* v. 89. 7, μίαν τὴν ὄντως οὖσαν ἀρχήν). If our interpretation of Hierokles' words is correct, i.e. if Ammonius really believed in the existence of a matter which was μὴ ὄν, no real ἀρχή and no substratum, we have discovered a further correspondence between Ammonius and Clement.

CONCLUSION

WE are now in a position to propose a solution for the two problems to which we have drawn attention in the introduction. Concerning the determination of Clement's cultural background, our inquiry into the various aspects of Clement's system has shown that it represents the meeting-point of three distinct streams: the Jewish-Alexandrine philosophy, the Platonic tradition (which includes both the school-Platonism of the second century A.D. and Neoplatonism), and Gnosticism. No part of Clement's thought can actually be adequately understood without taking these three factors duly into account.

Clement's views on the origin of Greek philosophy show a close analogy with doctrines characteristic of the Jewish-Alexandrine philosophy, of Justin, and of Celsus.[1] The way in which Clement judges the individual philosophical systems is, as in the case of Justin, entirely dependent on the school-Platonism of his time.[2] The function which Clement attributes to philosophy in the allegorical interpretation of Scripture and consequently also in the preparation of *gnosis*—this function is according to him closely parallel to that which philosophy has accomplished in history—is based on Philo's conception of the relationship between philosophy and theology or wisdom as well as on the tendency of the Jewish author to interpret the Old Testament in terms of Greek philosophy.[3] Clement's 'eclecticism' finds its natural explanation in his views on the origin of Greek philosophy and in the cultural syncretism which was characteristic of the Jewish-Alexandrine philosophy and of some of the Platonic schools of his time.[4]

The ethical views of the Alexandrine theologian rest upon a syncretism of Platonic, Stoic, and also Aristotelian doctrines, the main features of which appear also in Philo and in Middle Platonism. However, by adopting the conception of the twofold ethical stage, by considering ἀπάθεια as the highest ethical ideal, and by identifying it with ὁμοίωσις θεῷ Clement surpasses the limits of the school-Platonism of the second century A.D. which

---

[1] Chapter I, pp. 12–41 above.   [2] Chapter I, pp. 41–51 above.
[3] Chapter I, pp. 56–9 above.   [4] Chapter I, pp. 51–6 above.

CONCLUSION

is known to us and situates himself in the line of the Alexandrine tradition which, starting from Philo, goes up to Neoplatonism.[1]

Clement's conception of *pistis* aims at giving an answer to the criticism of the heathen philosophers who strongly attacked the Christian idea of faith, to the followers of Valentine, who attributed *pistis* to an inferior class of people who, according to them, had no possibility, owing to their own natures, of reaching *gnosis*, and also to some members of the Christian community of Alexandria (the *simpliciores*) who were afraid of developing their faith into a higher form of knowledge by dedicating themselves to the study of Greek philosophy.[2] In order to build up his theory of *pistis* Clement resorted to Peripatetic logical doctrines which were also current in the school-Platonism of his time as well as to some epistemological doctrines of Antiochus of Ascalon who, in some respects, can be considered as the father of Middle Platonism.[3] But Clement's conception of *pistis* is important, first of all, for a right appreciation of his idea of *gnosis*. He applies the twofold epistemological *pistis*—i.e. the *pistis* consisting in the immediate knowledge or acceptance of the principles of demonstration and the *pistis* consisting in the firm conviction of mind after the apprehension of the result of scientific demonstration—to the study and interpretation of Scripture: since this study is for him the equivalent of scientific demonstration, the inner meaning which it discloses produces a *pistis* which is one and the same thing with the *pistis* produced by scientific demonstration and consequently also with *gnosis*.[4] Clement could not have brought his theory of *pistis* into connection with the question of the study of Scripture if he had not inherited from Philo the conception of the existence of an inner meaning of Scripture, which must be disclosed by means of an allegorical interpretation of the sacred text.[5]

Clement's idea of *gnosis* represents the central point of his Christian philosophy. The contemplation of the highest divinity which can only be attained by means of an allegorical interpretation of Scripture, in which philosophy plays an important role, represents the object of an esoteric knowledge, which can be

[1] Chapter II, pp. 109–11 above.
[2] Chapter III, pp. 118–19 and 141–2 above.
[3] Chapter III, pp. 120–36 above.
[4] Chapter III, pp. 137–40 above.
[5] Chapter III, pp. 140–1 above.

communicated only to a select few. The combined influence of
Philo, of Platonism, and of heretical Gnosticism on this aspect of
Clement's *gnosis* is particularly evident. The source of this
esoteric knowledge is, according to Clement, the divine Logos
both as a metaphysical principle and as a historical person: if
Clement owes to the Jewish-Alexandrine philosophy, to Justin,
and partly also to Celsus the conception that the knowledge of
the divinity which the philosophers possessed is due to the inspiration of the divine wisdom or Logos,[1] the idea according to
which the incarnation of the Logos, i.e. the historical person of
Jesus, is the teacher of an esoteric tradition which was transmitted by the apostles to their successors and came down to
Clement shows the unmistakable mark of Gnosticism.[2]

During the life of man upon the earth *gnosis* consists mainly
in separation from material things (or purification) and in
close communion with Christ, or, in other words, in the contemplation of the intelligible ideas which form all together the
divine Logos;[3] to this contemplation the study of the encyclical
disciplines greatly contributes. By adopting Plato's ideal of
purification and of contemplative life and also his views on the
role of the encyclical disciplines Clement is perfectly in keeping
with the Platonic tradition and with Philo.[4]

It is, however, only after the death of the body that this communion with Christ, which the γνωστικός had realized to some
extent during his life on the earth, reaches its climax: the gnostic
soul, after leaving behind the seven inferior heavens and the
angels who watch its ascent, reaches the eighth heaven and the
dignity of the seven πρωτόκτιστοι who are closely connected with
the Logos, becomes a god, and enjoys the contemplation 'face to
face' and a perpetual rest. This topic of the *Himmelsreise* of the
gnostic soul, of its deification, and of its ἀνάπαυσις—it is clearly
adumbrated in the allegorical interpretation of the entry of the
High Priest into the Holy of Holies—represents a very close link
between Clement and Gnosticism.[5] In the idea of the deification of the soul and of the direct contemplation of the divinity
the Platonic influence, however, should also be taken into
account.[6]

[1] Chapter I, pp. 16 ff. above and chapter III, pp. 158–9 above.
[2] Chapter III, pp. 161–3 above.   [3] Chapter III, pp. 163 ff. above.
[4] Chapter III, pp. 163–73 above.   [5] Chapter III, pp. 173–88 above.
[6] Chapter III, pp. 186, 187, 188–9 above.

Clement's views on the origin of the world—the study of which represents for him a preliminary step towards *gnosis*—connect him very closely with Philo, with the school-Platonism of the second century A.D., and also with Neoplatonism. The Alexandrine theologian follows the Jewish author in interpreting the beginning of Genesis by resorting to the Platonic distinction between the sensible and the intelligible world and, in this way, agrees also with the school-Platonism which had also regarded the sensible world as a copy of the intelligible.[1] In the doctrine of matter Clement, like Philo and Middle Platonism, seems to believe in its pre-existence and considers it as devoid of any form and quality.[2] The agreement between Clement, Philo, and Middle Platonism is, however, in this case only partial. Clement rejects the view of the school-Platonism according to which matter is one of the ἀρχαί, maintains that God is the only true ἀρχή, and considers matter as μὴ ὄν (for Philo and Plutarch, on the contrary, matter was still an οὐσία).[3] In regarding matter as μὴ ὄν Clement agrees with Neopythagoreanism, with Plotinus, and perhaps also with Ammonius Saccas.[4] As to the question whether the world was generated or ungenerated, Clement, like Philo and such exponents of Middle Platonism as Plutarch and Atticus, is openly in favour of the first solution, but at the same time, following Philo, maintains that creation did not take place in time since time itself is directly dependent on the sensible world.[5]

In the doctrine of the Logos as a metaphysical principle Clement adopts Philo's theory, according to which the Logos is first one and the same thing with the reason of God and only afterwards becomes a distinct being, i.e. the second hypostasis.[6] Following the view characteristic of Philo and of Middle Platonism, which perhaps goes back to the Old Academy, Clement regards the ideas as the thoughts of God and as contained first in his mind (according to him there is an identity between the ideas, the mind of God, and the Logos in the first stage of his existence).[7] After becoming a distinct being the Logos—who is now the Son of God—contains all the ideas or divine powers in itself. In this doctrine also Clement is closely dependent upon

[1] Chapter III, p. 192 above.   [2] Chapter III, pp. 193–4 above.
[3] Chapter III, pp. 193, 195–6 above.
[4] See chapter III, pp. 195–6 above and footnote 1, p. 226 above.
[5] Chapter III, pp. 198–9 above.   [6] Chapter III, pp. 203 ff. above.
[7] Chapter III, p. 201 above.

Philo; but his conception according to which the Son is the
composite unity, since all powers are united in him (πάντα ἕν)
exactly as the radii of the circle are united in its centre, approxi-
mates him both to the Neopythagorean speculations on the
'one' of the second hypothesis of Plato's *Parmenides* and to the
Plotinian doctrine of the νοῦς.[1] In the definition of the Logos as
principle of creation and in his identification with the divine
wisdom Clement is closely dependent on the Jewish-Alexandrine
philosophy.[2] In the third stage of his existence the Logos is the
supreme *Weltvernunft*, the power which administers the universe
and holds it together: the Jewish-Alexandrine philosophy also
had allotted this function to the divine wisdom or Logos, which
is closely parallel to the function of the Stoic Logos and of the
world-soul of the Platonic tradition.[3]

The doctrines to which Clement resorts in order to describe the
transcendence of God occur also in Philo, in the Platonic tradition, and in the gnostic systems of the second century A.D., and
go ultimately back to some passages of Plato.[4] Particularly important is the doctrine of the absolute unknowability of the first
principle, which connects Clement very closely with Philo, with
Gnosticism, and with Neoplatonism;[5] it derives from the Neopythagorean interpretation of the 'one' of the first hypothesis of
Plato's *Parmenides*, although in the case of Philo and of Clement
the influence of some Scriptural passages cannot be excluded.[6]
Clement's God is similar, in many respects, to the 'one' of
Plotinus, but differs from it in two points: whereas for Clement
God is a νοῦς endowed with thought and a will, Plotinus places
his 'one' above the νοῦς and denies that it can think.[7] Clement's
conception of God resembles therefore more that of Ammonius
Saccas who, most probably, had not separated the 'one' from
the νοῦς.[8]

As to the second problem—namely the problem of the determination of the relationship between Clement's cultural background and his Christianity—we can divide our answer into
three parts, which correspond to the question formulated in the
Introduction (p. 7 above):

[1] Chapter III, p. 205 above.   [2] Chapter III, pp. 207–9 above.
[3] Chapter III, pp. 209–12 above.   [4] Chapter III, pp. 212 ff. above.
[5] Chapter III, pp. 217–20 above.   [6] Chapter III, pp. 218–19 above.
[7] Chapter III, p. 222 above.   [8] Chapter III, pp. 223–4 above.

1. Clement's use of Greek philosophical doctrines goes far beyond the borrowing of some terms which do not influence his Christianity at all and which represent only a superficial tinge: in ethics, in the theory of *pistis*, in *gnosis*, in the question of the origin of the world, and in theology Clement has produced a process of Hellenization of Christianity which is closely parallel to the process of Hellenization of Judaism which is characteristic of Philo's work. Clement does not borrow a few doctrines or 'terms' of Greek philosophy simply because he wants to speak with the heathen philosophers in their own language in order to convert them to his own religion; this aim, though present in Clement's intentions, is neither the sole nor the most important reason for his use of Greek philosophy. He wanted to transform his religious faith into a monumental philosophical system, to which he allotted the task of reflecting the absolute truth.[1] He was well aware of the fact that he could not have built up such a system without making use of the materials represented by the Platonism of Philo and of the second century A.D. He could easily resort to Hellenism since he did not see between it and Christianity that radical opposition which some modern theologians like to see between these two forces but, on the contrary, considered the best doctrines of Greek philosophy as practically one and the same thing with the highest aspect of Christianity, since they, according to him, had been originated by the divine Logos. It is exactly the theory of the derivation of philosophy from the Logos that enables Clement to consider it as the clue for the interpretation of Scripture, i.e. as the instrument which enables the ψιλὴ πίστις to become the philosophical system represented by *gnosis*.[2]

The deep influence of Clement's cultural background on his Christianity appears particularly evident in two cases: neither the way in which Clement judges the individual philosophical systems nor his 'eclecticism' is due to the fact that he, as a Christian, is able to separate the good from the evil, to choose the former and to reject the latter. In the first chapter we have seen that Clement's utterances on the individual philosophical

[1] Cf. A. von Harnack, *Lehrbuch der Dogmengeschichte*, Erster Band, 642: 'Dem Clemens ist also die Gnosis ... nicht nur ein Mittel, um das Heidentum und die Häresie zu widerlegen, sondern sie ist ihm zugleich das Mittel, um das höchste und innerste des Christentums erst zu erreichen und darzulegen.'
[2] Chapter I, pp. 56-7 above.

systems and his 'eclecticism' can only be explained by taking
into account the cultural milieu to which he belongs.[1]

2. *Gnosis*, as we have seen, consists in the contemplation of
intelligible realities and in the separation from sensible things.
But this contemplation is not possible if man has not reached
complete ἀπάθεια and ὁμοίωσις θεῷ and has not received an
esoteric teaching. Only Christ, according to Clement, can enable
man to reach the moral perfection represented by ἀπάθεια and
by ὁμοίωσις θεῷ and impart to him the esoteric teaching of *gnosis*.
Christ is therefore the source of *gnosis*. The Neoplatonic ideals
of ἀπάθεια, ὁμοίωσις θεῷ, and contemplation are completely
adopted by Clement but they find, in his system, their integration
in the Christian idea of the direct intervention of the Son of
God.[2] This is the element which sharply separates Clement from
Neoplatonism. In Neoplatonism also the ultimate aim of the
human soul is the knowledge of the highest principle; but, as
E. R. Dodds has clearly pointed out, Neoplatonism knows no
mediator between the 'one' and man, i.e. no intermediate being
which transmits the knowledge of the 'one' to man or which
enables him to attain it.[3] In Clement, on the contrary, this intermediate being is represented by the Son of God, who acts both
as a metaphysical principle and as a historical person.

3. It is necessary, therefore, to admit that Clement gives a
'Christian' solution to Neoplatonic problems. The adjective
'Christian' cannot, however, remain general or abstract. The
Christianity which Clement found in the teaching of Pantaenus
in Alexandria at the end of his long journeys could not be exempt
from the manifold influences of the various gnostic systems which
were so flourishing in Egypt in the second half of the second
century A.D.: in this period, the dividing line between orthodoxy
and heresy had not yet been clearly established but 'was still
in process of being drawn.'[4] That the highest divinity was completely unknown and that Jesus had come down on the earth
to reveal it to a select few, to teach *gnosis*, and to give origin to
an esoteric tradition was a fundamental idea of all Christian
gnostic systems. Clement adopted it entirely. If we remember

[1] Chapter I, pp. 51–6 above.
[2] See chapter II, pp. 113–17 above and chapter III, p. 173 above.
[3] *Proclus. The Elements of Theology*, 312, and *JRS* 50 (1960), 4 and 6.
[4] H. Chadwick, 'Clement of Alexandria', *Encyclopaedia Britannica* (1964), 899.

that he considered his teacher Pantaenus as one of the deposi-
taries of this esoteric tradition going back to the apostles and to
Christ,[1] we can easily infer that Pantaenus himself, though not
adhering to any particular gnostic system, was under the direct
influence of these gnostic ideas.[2] In fact, Christian Gnosticism
must be regarded as the source of the Christian element which
enabled Clement to give a satisfactory solution to his Neoplatonic problems.

[1] *Strom.* i. 11. 2–3 (ii. 9. 1–8).

[2] The evidence about Pantaenus which has come down to us has been collected
by A. von Harnack, *Geschichte der altchristlichen Literatur bis Eusebius*, Erster Theil,
291–6, and G. Bardy, *RSR* 27 (1937), 66 ff. Bardy rightly draws attention to the
gnostic character of Alexandrine Christianity and brings Pantaenus into connection with it (see especially pp. 72–4 and 78).

BIBLIOGRAPHY

AALL, A., *Geschichte der Logosidee in der griechischen Philosophie* (Leipzig, 1896).
—— *Geschichte der Logosidee in der christlichen Literatur* (Leipzig, 1899).
ALEITH, E., *Paulusverständnis in der alten Kirche*, Beiheft 18 zur *ZNW*, 1937.
ANDRES, F., *Die Engel und Dämonenlehre des Klemens von Alexandrien*, *RQ* 34 (1926), 13–27, 129–40, 307–29.
ANDRESEN, C., 'Justin und der mittlere Platonismus', *ZNW* 44 (1952/3), 157–95.
—— *Logos und Nomos* (Berlin, 1955).
ARMSTRONG, A. H., 'The Theory of the non-Existence of Matter in Plotinus and the Cappadocians', *TU* 80 (Berlin, 1962), 427–9.
—— review of Weber's book *Origenes der Neuplatoniker* in *JHS* 83 (1963), 184–5.
ARNIM, VON I., *De octavo Clementis Stromateorum libro* (Rostock Progr., 1894).
ARNOU, R., 'Platonisme des Pères', *DThC* 12 (1932–5), 2258–2392.
BAERT, E., 'Le thème de la vision de Dieu chez S. Justin, Clément d'Alexandrie et S. Grégoire de Nysse', *FZPhTh* 12 (1965), 439–97 (especially 460–80).
BAILEY, C., *Epicurus. The Extant Remains* (Oxford, 1926).
BARDENHEWER, O., *Geschichte der altkirchlichen Literatur*, Erster Band (Freiburg, 1913); Zweiter Band (Freiburg, 1914).
BARDY, G., *Clément d'Alexandrie* (Paris, 1926).
—— 'La spiritualité de Clément d'Alexandrie', *VSAM* 39 (1934), Suppl. 81–104, 129–45.
—— 'Aux origines de l'école d'Alexandrie', *RSR* 27 (1937), 65–90.
BARTH, P., and GOEDECKEMEYER, A., *Die Stoa* (Stuttgart, 1941).
BASILAKES, G., Κλήμεντος Ἀλεξανδρέως ἡ ἠθικὴ διδασκαλία (Erlangen, 1892).
BAUDRY, J., *Atticos. Fragments de son œuvre avec introduction et notes par J. Baudry* (Paris, Les Belles Lettres, 1931).
BAUER, W., *Rechtgläubigkeit und Ketzerei im ältesten Christentum* (Tübingen, 1934).
BÄUMKER, C., 'Die Ewigkeit der Welt bei Plato', *PhM* 23 (1887), 513–29.
—— *Das Problem der Materie in der griechischen Philosophie* (Münster, 1890).
BAUR, F. C., *Die christliche Gnosis oder die christliche Religionsphilosophie in ihrer geschichtlichen Entwicklung* (Tübingen, 1835).
BÉKÉS, G., 'De continua oratione Clementis Alexandrini doctrina', *SA* 14 (Romae, 1942).
BIELCKE, I. A., *Dissertatio de Clemente Alexandrino eiusque erroribus* (Ienae, 1737).
BIGG, C., *The Christian Platonists of Alexandria* (Oxford, 1913, 2nd ed.).
BLUCK, R. S., *Meno, edited with Introduction and Commentary* (Cambridge, 1961).
BÖHLIG, A., and LABIB, P., 'Koptysch-gnostische Apokalypsen aus Codex V von Nag-Hammadi', *Wissenschaftliche Zeitschrift der Martin-Luther Univ. Halle-Wittenberg* (1963).

Bousset, W., 'Die Himmelsreise der Seele', *ARW* 4 (1901), 136–69 and 229–73 (reprinted as a separate book, Darmstadt, 1960).

—— *Jüdisch-christlicher Schulbetrieb in Alexandria und Rom* (Göttingen, 1915).

Boyancé, P., 'Philon d'Alexandrie selon le P. Daniélou', *REG* 72 (1959), 377–84.

Bratke, 'Die Stellung des Clemens Alexandrinus zum antiken Mysterienwesen', *ThStK* 60 (1887), 647–708.

Bréhier, E., *Les Idées philosophiques et religieuses de Philon d'Alexandrie* (Paris, 1925).

Butterworth, G. W., 'Clement of Alexandria's Protrepticus and the Phaedrus of Plato', *CQ* 10 (1916), 198–205.

—— 'The Deification of Man in Clement of Alexandria', *JTS* 17 (1916), 157–69.

Camelot, P., 'Les idées de Clément d'Alexandrie sur l'utilisation des sciences et de la littérature prophane', *RSR* 21 (1931), 38–66.

—— 'Clément d'Alexandrie et l'utilisation de la philosophie grecque', *RSR* 21 (1931), 541–69.

—— *Foi et Gnose. Introduction à l'étude de la connaissance mystique chez Clément d'Alexandrie* (Paris, 1945).

Capitaine, W., *Die Moral des Clemens von Alexandrien* (Paderborn, 1903).

Casey, R. P., 'Clement and the two Divine Logoi', *JTS* 25 (1924), 43–56.

—— 'Clement of Alexandria and the Beginning of Christian Platonism', *HThR* 18 (1925), 39–101.

—— *The 'Excerpta ex Theodoto' of Clement of Alexandria* (London, 1934).

Chadwick, H., 'Clement of Alexandria', *Encyclopaedia Britannica* (1964), 899–900.

—— *Early Christian Thought and the Classical Tradition* (Oxford, 1966).

—— 'Clement of Alexandria', *The Cambridge History of Later Greek and Early Medieval Philosophy*, ed. by A. H. Armstrong (Cambridge, 1967), 168–81.

Champomier, J., 'Naissance de l'humanisme chrétien', *BAGB* n.s. 3 (1947), 58–96 (especially 85–96).

Chase, F. H., *Clement of Alexandria* (Church Leaders in Primitive Times) (London, 1909).

Christ, W., 'Philologische Studien zu Clemens Alexandrinus', *ABAWM*, philos.-philol. Kl. 21, Abt. iii (München, 1901), 457–526.

Cognat, J., *Clément d'Alexandrie: sa doctrine et sa polémique* (Paris, 1959).

Collomp, P., 'Une source de Clément d'Alexandrie et des homélies pseudo-clémentines', *RPh* 37 (1913), 11–46.

Colson, F. H., "Ἀπαρέμφατος", *JTS* 22 (1921), 156–9.

Conybeare, F. C., *Philo about the Contemplative Life* (Oxford, 1895).

Courdaveaux, V., 'Clément d'Alexandrie', *RHR* (Annales du Musée Guimet) 25 (1892), 287–321.

Daehne, A. F., *De γνώσει Clementis Alexandrini et de vestigiis neoplatonicae philosophiae in ea obviis* (Lipsiae, 1831).

—— *Geschichtliche Darstellung der jüdisch-alexandrinischen Religionsphilosophie* (Stuttgart, 1835).

Daniélou, J., 'Typologie et allégorie chez Clément d'Alexandrie', *TU* 79 (Berlin, 1961), 50–7.

—— *Message évangélique et culture hellénistique* (Tournai, 1961).
—— 'Les traditions secrètes des Apôtres', *EJ* 21 (1962), 199–215.
DASKALAKIS, M., 'Die eklektischen Anschauungen des Clemens von Alexandria und seine Abhängigkeit von der griechischen Philosophie' (Diss. Leipzig, 1908).
DEDEN, P., 'Le "mystère" Paulinien', *ETL* 13 (1936), 405–42.
DE FAYE, E., *Clément d'Alexandrie* (Paris, 1906, 2nd ed.).
—— 'De l'originalité de la philosophie chrétienne de Clément d'Alexandrie', *AEHE* (Section des sciences religieuses, 1919), 1–20.
DE LA BARRE, A., 'Clément d'Alexandrie', *DThC* 3 (1908), 133–99.
DELATTE, A., 'Un fragment d'arithmologie dans Clément d'Alexandrie' (*Études sur la littérature pythagoricienne*), *BEHE*, Sciences historiques et philologiques (Paris, 1915), 231–45.
DEMETRESKOS, D., Κλήμεντος Ἀλεξανδρέως ὁ Προτρεπτικὸς πρὸς Ἕλληνας λόγος (Boucarest, 1890).
DIBELIUS, O., 'Studien zur Geschichte der Valentinianer', *ZNW* 9 (1908), 230–47, 329–40.
DIELS, H., *Doxographi graeci* (Berolini et Lipsiae, 1929).
DIHLE, A., 'Indische Philosophen bei Clemens Alexandrinus', Festschr. Th. Klauser, *JACh*, Ergänzungsband 1 (Münster, 1964), 60–9.
DODDS, E. R., 'The *Parmenides* of Plato and the Origin of the Neoplatonic One', *CQ* 22 (1928), 129–42.
—— *Proclus. The Elements of Theology* (Oxford, 1933).
—— 'Numenius and Ammonius', *Entretiens Hardt* v (Genève, 1960), 3–32.
—— 'Tradition and personal Achievement in the Philosophy of Plotinus', *JRS* 50 (1960), 1–7.
DODS, M., *Clement of Alexandria* (Prophets of the Christian Faith) (London, 1897).
DORESSE, J., 'Trois livres gnostiques inédits', *VC* 2 (1948), 137–60.
—— 'Nouveaux documents gnostiques coptes découverts en Haute-Égypte', *CAIBL* (1949), 176–80.
—— 'Une bibliothèque gnostique copte découverte en Haute-Égypte', *BAB* (1949), 435–49.
—— 'Sur les traces des papyrus gnostiques: recherches à Chénoboskion' *BAB* (1950), 432–9.
—— *Les Livres secrets des gnostiques d'Égypte* (Paris, 1958).
—— and MINA, T., 'Nouveaux textes gnostiques coptes découverts en Haute-Égypte. La bibliothèque de Chénoboskion', *VC* 3 (1949), 129–41.
DÖRRIE, H., 'Ammonios der Lehrer Plotins', *Hermes* 83 (1955), 439–77.
—— 'Die Frage nach dem Transzendenten im Mittelplatonismus', *Entretiens Hardt* v (Genève, 1960), 193–223.
EIBL, H., 'Die Stellung des Klemens von Alexandrien zur griechischen Bildung', *ZPhuphK* 164 (1917), 33–59.
ELTER, A., *De gnomologiorum graecorum historia atque origine* (Bonn Universitätsprogr., 1893–5).
ERMONI, V., 'The Christology of Clement of Alexandria', *JTS* 5 (1904), 123–6.

ERNESTI, K., *Die Ethik des Titus Flavius Clemens von Alexandrien* (Paderborn, 1900).

ERNST, W., *De Clementis Alexandrini Stromatum libro octavo qui fertur* (Diss. Göttingen, 1910).

FALLER, O., 'Griechische Vergottung und christliche Vergöttlichung', *Gregorianum* 6 (1925), 405–35.

FASCHER, E., 'Epoptie', *RACh*, 973–83.

—— 'Der Logos-Christus als göttlicher Lehrer bei Clemens von Alexandrien' (Studien zum Neuen Testament und zur Patristik E. Klostermann zum 90. Geburtstag dargebracht) *TU* 77 (Berlin, 1961), 193–207.

FESTUGIÈRE, A.-J., *Contemplation et vie contemplative selon Platon* (Paris, 1936).

—— *La Révélation d'Hermès Trismégiste*:
  I. *L'Astrologie et les sciences occultes* (Paris, 1950).
  II. *Le Dieu cosmique* (Paris, 1949).
  III. *Les Doctrines de l'âme* (Paris, 1953).
  IV. *Le Dieu inconnu et la gnose* (Paris, 1954).

FRANK, E., *Philosophical Understanding and Religious Truth* (London, 1945).

FREPPEL, E., *Clément d'Alexandrie* (Cours d'éloquence sacrée fait à la Sorbonne pendant l'année 1864–5) (Paris, 1866).

FRÜCHTEL, L., 'Klemens von Alexandria und Albinus', *BPhW* 57 (1937), coll. 591–2.

—— review of Witt's book *Albinus and the history of Middle Platonism* (Cambridge, 1937) in *BPhW* 58 (1938), coll. 996–1003.

GEFFCKEN, J., *Zwei griechische Apologeten* (Leipzig u. Berlin, 1907).

GERCKE, A., 'Eine platonische Quelle des Neuplatonismus', *RMPh* 41 (1886), 266–91.

GFRÖRER, A. F., *Philo und die jüdisch-alexandrinische Philosophie* (Stuttgart, 1835).

GÖRGEMANNS, H., 'Beiträge zur Interpretation von Platons Nomoi', *Zetemata* 25 (1960).

GOODENOUGH, E. R., *By Light, Light* (New Haven, 1935).

GRANT, R. M., *Gnosticism and Early Christianity* (New York, 1959).

—— 'Notes on Gnosis', *VC* 11 (1957), 145–51.

GRONAU, K., *Poseidonios und die jüdisch-christliche Genesisexegese* (Leipzig, 1914).

GUERIKE, H. F., *De schola quae Alexandriae floruit catechetica* (Halae, 1824).

GUILLOUX, P., 'L'ascétisme de Clément d'Alexandrie', *RAM* 3 (1922), 282–300.

HACKFORTH, R., 'Plato's Theism', *CQ* 30 (1936), 4–9.

HANSON, R. P. C., *Origen's Doctrine of Tradition* (London, 1954).

HARNACK, VON A., *Geschichte der altchristlichen Literatur bis Eusebius*, Erster Theil, Erste Hälfte (Leipzig, 1893).

—— *Lehrbuch der Dogmengeschichte*, Erster Band (Tübingen, 1931).

HÉBERT-DUPERRON, V., *Essai sur la polémique et la philosophie de Clément d'Alexandrie* (Paris, 1855).

HEGERMANN, H., 'Die Vorstellung vom Schöpfungsmittler im hellenistischen Judentum und Urchristentum', *TU* 82 (Berlin, 1961).

HEINEMANN, F., 'Ammonios Sakkas und der Ursprung des Neuplatonismus', *Hermes* 61 (1926), 1–27.

HEINISCH, P., *Der Einfluß Philos auf die älteste christliche Exegese* (Münster, 1908).

HEINZE, R., *Xenocrates* (Leipzig, 1892).

HEUSSI, C., 'Die Stromateis des Clemens Alexandrinus in ihrem Verhältnis zum Protrepticus und Pädagogus', *ZWTh* 45 (1902), 465–512.

HIRZEL, R., *Untersuchungen zu Ciceros philosophischen Schriften*, III. Theil (Leipzig, 1883).

HITCHCOCK, F. R., *Clement of Alexandria* (London, 1899).

HOFSTEDE DE GROOT, P., *Disputatio de Clemente Alexandrino philosopho Christiano* (Gröningen, 1826).

HOLTE, R., 'Logos spermatikos', *STh* 12 (1958), 109–68.

HOLZCLAU, T., *Dissertatio de Clemente Alexandrino eiusque morali doctrina* (Wirceburg, 1779).

HOROWITZ, J., *Das platonische νοητὸν ζῷον und der philonische κόσμος νοητός* (Diss. Marburg, 1900).

—— *Untersuchungen über Philons und Platons Lehre von der Weltschöpfung* (Marburg, 1900).

HORT, J. A., and MAYOR, J. B., *Clement of Alexandria. Miscellanies, Book VII.* The Greek Text with Introduction, Translation, Notes, Dissertations and Indices (London, 1892).

HUBER, J., *Die Philosophie der Kirchenväter* (München, 1859).

IVANKA, VON E., *Plato Christianus* (Übernahme und Umgestaltung des Platonismus durch die Väter) (Einsiedeln, 1964).

JAEGER, W., *Aristoteles* (Berlin, 1955, 2nd ed.).

—— *Aristotle*, English translation by R. Robinson (Oxford, 1948).

—— review of Merki's book 'Ὁμοίωσις θεῷ (Freiburg in der Schweiz, 1952) in *Gnomon* 27 (1955), 573–81 (= *Scripta Minora* (Roma, 1960), ii. 469–81).

—— *Early Christianity and Greek Paideia* (Cambridge, Massachusetts, 1965).

JONES, R. M., 'The Ideas as the Thoughts of God', *CPh* 21 (1926), 317–26.

KAYE, J., *Some Account of the Writings and Opinions of Clement of Alexandria* (London, 1835).

KLING, 'Bedeutung des alexandrinischen Klemens für die Entstehung der christlichen Theologie', *ThSK* (1841), Heft 4, 857–908.

KNITTEL, 'Pistis und Gnosis bei Clemens von Alexandrien', *TQ* 55 (1873), 171–219, 363–417.

KOCH, A., 'Clemens von Alexandrien als Lehrer der Vollkommenheit', *ZAM* 7 (1932), 363–4.

KRAUSE, M., and LABIB, P., 'Die drei Versionen des Apokryphon des Johannes im Koptischen Museum zu Alt-Kairo', *Abhandlungen des Deutschen archäologischen Instituts Kairo*, Band I (1962).

KROLL, J., 'Die Lehren des Hermes Trismegistos', *BGPhM*, Band XII, Heft 2–4 (Münster, 1914).

LAEMMER, H., *Clementis Alexandrini de λόγῳ doctrina* (Lipsiae, 1855).

LANGERBECK, H., 'The Philosophy of Ammonius Saccas', *JHS* 77 (1957), 67–74.

—— 'Die Verbindung aristotelischer und christlicher Elemente in der Philosophie des Ammonius Saccas', *AAWG*, phil.-hist. Klasse 69 (1967), 146–66.

240 BIBLIOGRAPHY

LAZZATI, G., *Introduzione allo studio di Clemente Alessandrino* (Milano, 1939).

LEBRETON, J., 'Le désaccord de la foi populaire et de la théologie savante dans l'Église chrétienne du III siècle', *RHE* 19 (1923), 481–506; 20 (1924), 5–37.

—— 'La théorie de la connaissance religieuse chez Clément d'Alexandrie' *RSR* 18 (1928), 457–88.

—— 'La théologie de la Trinité chez Clément d'Alexandrie', *RSR* 34 (1947), 55–76, 142–79.

LEEMANS, E. A., 'Studien over den wijsgeer Numenius van Apamea met vitgave der fragmenten', *MAB*, Classe des Lettres 27 (1937).

LIETZMANN, H., *Geschichte der alten Kirche* (Berlin u. Leipzig, 1936).

LOENEN, J. H., 'Albinus' Metaphysics. An Attempt at Rehabilitation', *Mnemosyne*, Series iv, 10 (1957), 35–56.

LUCK, G., 'Der Akademiker Antiochos' (*Noctes Romanae* 7) (Bern, 1953)

LUEDER, A., *Die philosophische Persönlichkeit des Antiochos von Askalon* (Diss. Göttingen, 1940).

MARROU, H.-I., 'Humanisme et christianisme chez Clément d'Alexandrie d'après le Pédagogue', *Entretiens Hardt* iii (Genève, 1958), 183–200.

MARSH, H. G., 'The Use of μυστήριον in the Writings of Clement of Alexandria with special reference to his sacramental Doctrine', *JTS* 37 (1936), 64–80.

MÉHAT, A., 'Les ordres d'enseignement chez Clément d'Alexandrie et Sénèque', *TU* 64 (Berlin, 1957), 351–7.

—— *Étude sur les Stromates de Clément d'Alexandrie* (Paris, 1966).

MERK, C., *Clemens Alexandrinus in seiner Abhängigkeit von der griechischen Philosophie* (Diss. Leipzig, 1879).

MERKI, H., "Ὁμοίωσις θεῷ. Von der platonischen Angleichung an Gott zur Gottähnlichkeit bei Gregor von Nyssa', *Paradosis* 7 (Freiburg in der Schweiz, 1952).

MERLAN, PH., 'The later Academy and Platonism', *The Cambridge History of Later Greek and Early Medieval Philosophy*, ed. by A. H. Armstrong (Cambridge, 1967), 53–83.

MEYER, A., *Das Gottesbild im Menschen nach Clemens von Alexandrien* (Romae, 1842).

MINA, T., 'Le papyrus gnostique du Musée Copte', *VC* 2 (1948), 129–36.

MÖHLER, I. A., *Patrologie* I (Regensburg, 1840).

MOINGT, J., 'La gnose de Clément d'Alexandrie dans ses rapports avec la foi et la philosophie', *RSR* 37 (1950), 195–251, 398–421, 537–64; and 38 (1951), 82–118.

MOLLAND, E. 'Clement of Alexandria on the Origin of Greek Philosophy', *SO* 15–16 (1936), 57–85.

—— *The Conception of the Gospel in the Alexandrian Theology* (Oslo, 1938).

MONDÉSERT, C., 'Le symbolisme chez Clément d'Alexandrie', *RSR* 26 (1936), 158–80.

—— *Clément d'Alexandrie. Introduction à l'étude de sa pensée religieuse à partir de l'Écriture* (Paris, 1944).

MORESCHINI, C., 'La posizione di Apuleio e della scuola di Gaio nell'ambito del medioplatonismo', *ASNSP*, Serie II, 33 (1964), 17–56.

—— *Studi sul 'De dogmate Platonis' di Apuleio* (Studi di lettere, storia e filosofia pubblicati dalla Scuola Normale Superiore di Pisa, 29) (Pisa, 1966).
MUCKLE, J. T., 'Clement of Alexandria on Philosophy as a divine Testament for the Greeks', *Phoenix* v (1951), 79–86.
MÜLLER, G., 'Studien zu den platonischen Nomoi', *Zetemata* 3 (1951).
MUNCK, J., *Untersuchungen über Clemens von Alexandrien* (Stuttgart, 1933).
NOCK, A. D., review of Goodenough's book *By Light, Light* (New Haven, 1935), in *Gnomon* 13 (1937), 156–65.
—— 'A Coptic Library of Gnostic Writings', *JTS* n.s. 9 (1958), 314–24.
ORBE, A., 'Los primeros herejes ante la persecución', *AG* 83 (Romae, 1956).
—— 'Hacia la primera teología de la Procesión del Verbo', *AG* 100 (Romae, 1958).
—— 'La Unción del Verbo', *AG* 113 (Romae, 1961).
OSBORN, E. F., *The Philosophy of Clement of Alexandria* (Cambridge, 1957).
OUTLER, A. C., 'The Platonism of Clement of Alexandria', *JR* 20 (1940), 217–40.
OVERBECK, F., and BERNOUILLI, C. A., *Titus Flavius Klemens von Alexandria: die Teppiche* (Basel, 1936).
PADE, P. B., *Λόγος Θεός. Untersuchungen zur Logoschristologie des Titus Flavius Clemens von Alexandrien* (Rom, 1939).
PARKER, C., 'Musonius Rufus in Clement', *HStCPh* 12 (1901), 191–200.
PATRICK, J., *Clement of Alexandria* (Edinburgh, 1914).
PERETTI, A., *Teognide nella tradizione gnomologica* (Pisa, 1953).
PFÄTTISCH, I. M., *Der Einfluß Platos auf die Theologie Justins des Märtyrers* (Paderborn, 1910).
PHRANKOULÈS, J. D., "'Η συμβολικὴ τῶν ἀριθμῶν παρὰ τῷ Κλήμεντι τῷ Ἀλεξανδρεῖ'', *Θεολογία* 13 (1935), 5–21.
POHLENZ, M., 'Das dritte und vierte Buch der Tusculanae', *Hermes* 41 (1906), 321–35.
—— review of Strache's dissertation *De Arii Didymi in morali philosophia auctoribus* in *BPhW* 31 (1911), coll. 1497–1500.
—— 'Philo von Alexandreia', *NGA*, phil.-hist. Klasse (1942), 409–87.
—— 'Klemens von Alexandreia und sein hellenisches Christentum', *NGA*, phil.-hist. Kl. (1943), 103–80.
—— *Die Stoa* (Göttingen, 1959).
PRAECHTER, K., 'Hierax der Platoniker', *Hermes* 41 (1906), 593–618.
—— 'Zum Platoniker Gaios', *Hermes* 51 (1916), 510–29.
—— article on Gaios in *RE*, Supplementband III (Stuttgart, 1918), coll. 535–7.
—— 'Nikostratos der Platoniker', *Hermes* 57 (1922), 481–517.
—— article on Tauros in *RE*, Zweite Reihe, Neunter Halbband (Stuttgart, 1934), coll. 58–68.
—— in Überweg–Heinze, *Grundriss der Geschichte der Philosophie*, Band I, 'Die Philosophie des Altertums' (Basel, 1953, 13th ed.).
PREISCHE, H., *De γνώσει Clementis Alexandrini* (Jenae, 1871).
PRÜMM, K., 'Glaube und Erkenntnis im zweiten Buch der Stromata des Klemens von Alexandrien', *Scholastik* 12 (1937), 17–57.
—— 'Mysterion von Paulus bis Origenes', *ZKT* 61 (1937), 391–425.

PRUNET, O., *La Morale de Clément d'Alexandrie et le Nouveau Testament* (Paris, 1966).

PUECH, H. C., 'Numénius d'Apamée et les théologies orientales au second siècle', *AIO*, Mélanges Bidez, 2 (1934), 745–78.

—— 'Les nouveaux écrits gnostiques découvertes en Haute-Égypte (premier inventaire et essai d'identification)', *Coptic Studies in honour of W. E. Crum*, (Boston, Massachusetts, 1950), 91–154.

—— and DORESSE, J., 'Nouveaux écrits gnostiques découverts en Égypte', *CAIBL* (1948), 87–95.

—— and QUISPEL, G., 'Les écrits gnostiques du Codex Jung', *VC* 8 (1954), 1–51.

—— —— 'Le quatrième écrit gnostique du Codex Jung', *VC* 9 (1955), 65–102.

QUASTEN, J., *Patrology*, vol. ii (Utrecht–Antwerp, 1953).

QUATEMBER, F., *Die christliche Lebenshaltung des Clemens von Alexandrien nach seinem Pädagogus* (Wien, 1946).

RECHEIS, A., *Engel, Tod und Seelenreise* (Roma, 1958).

REDEPENNING, E., *Origenes* (Bonn, 1841).

REID, J. S., *Cicero: Academica* (London, 1885).

REINKENS, H. J., *De Clemente presbytero Alexandrino homine scriptore philosopho atque theologo* (Vratislaviae, 1851).

REITZENSTEIN, R., *Die hellenistischen Mysterienreligionen* (Darmstadt, 1956; reprint of the third edition of 1927).

RICH, A. N. M., 'The Platonic Ideas as Thoughts of God', *Mnemosyne*, Series iv, 7 (1954), 123–33.

RITTER, H., *Geschichte der altchristlichen Literatur* (Hamburg, 1841).

RÜTHER, T., *Die sittliche Forderung der ἀπάθεια in den beiden ersten christlichen Jahrhunderten und bei Klemens von Alexandrien* (Freiburg, 1949).

SAGNARD, F., *Clément d'Alexandrie: extraits de Théodote* (Paris, 1948).

—— *La Gnose valentinienne et le témoignage de saint Irénée* (Paris, 1947).

SCHERER, W., *Clemens von Alexandrien und seine Erkenntnisprinzipien* (München, 1908).

SCHMEKEL, A., *Die Philosophie der mittleren Stoa* (Berlin, 1892).

SCHMIDT, C., and WAINBERG, J., 'Gespräche Jesus mit seinen Jüngern nach der Auferstehung. Ein katholisch-apostolisches Sendschreiben des 2. Jahrhunderts', *TU* 43 (Berlin, 1919).

SCHMIDT, P. J., 'Klemens von Alexandreia in seinem Verhältnis zur griechischen Religion und Philosophie' (Diss. Wien, 1939, typescript).

SCHÜRER, E., *Geschichte des jüdischen Volkes im Zeitalter Jesu Christi*, Band III (Leipzig, 1909).

SCHÜRMANN, H., *Die hellenische Bildung und ihr Verhältnis zur christlichen nach der Darstellung des Clemens von Alexandrien* (Münster, 1859).

SIEGFRIED, C., *Philo von Alexandria als Ausleger des Alten Testamentes* (Jena, 1875).

SINKO, T., *De Apuleii et Albini doctrinae platonicae adumbratione*, Rozprawy Akademii Umiejętności, Wydział Filologiczny, Serya II, Tom 31 (Cracoviae, 1906).

—— 'Apuleiana', *Eos* 18 (1912), 137–67.

SODEN, VON H., 'Μυστήριον und Sacramentum in den ersten zwei Jahrhunderten der Kirche', ZNW 12 (1911), 188–227.

SOULIER, H., La Doctrine du Logos chez Philon d'Alexandrie (Turin, 1876).

SPANNEUT, M., Le Stoicisme des Pères de l'Église (Paris, 1957).

STÄHLIN, O., Geschichte der altchristlichen Literatur (Handbuch der Altertumswissenschaft) 2/ii (München, 1924, 6th ed.).

STELZENBERGER, J., Die Beziehungen der frühchristlichen Sittenlehre zur Ethik der Stoa (München, 1933).

STRACHE, H., De Arii Didymi in morali philosophia auctoribus (Diss. Berlin, 1909).

—— Der Eklektizismus des Antiochos von Askalon (Philologische Untersuchungen herausgegeben von A. Kiessling und U. von Wilamowitz-Moellendorff) (Berlin, 1921).

TAYLOR, A. E., A Commentary on Plato's Timaeus (Oxford, 1928).

TELFER, W., 'Bees in Clement of Alexandria', JTS 28 (1926/7), 167–78.

THEILER, W., review of Delatte's book Études sur la littérature pythagoricienne (Paris, 1915) in Gnomon 2 (1926), 147–50.

—— 'Die Vorbereitung des Neuplatonismus', Problemata 1 (Berlin, 1930).

—— 'Philo von Alexandria und der Beginn des kaiserzeitlichen Platonismus', Parusia, Festgabe für J. Hirschberger (Frankfurt/M, 1965), 199–218.

—— Ammonios der Lehrer des Origenes, Forschungen zum Neuplatonismus (Berlin, 1966), 1–45.

TILL, W. C., 'Die Gnosis in Ägypten', LPP 4 (1949), 230–49.

—— 'Die gnostischen Schriften des koptischen Papyrus Berolinensis 8502', TU 60 (Berlin, 1955).

—— Das Evangelium nach Philippos (Berlin, 1963).

TOLLINTON, R. B., Clement of Alexandria (London, 1914).

TREU, U., 'Etymologie und Allegorie bei Klemens von Alexandrien', TU 79 (Berlin, 1961), 191–211.

TRIBBECHOVIUS, F., Dissertatio historica de vita et scriptis Clementis Alexandrini (Halae, 1706).

UNNIK, VAN W. C., 'The Origin of the recently discovered "Apocryphon Iacobi"', VC 10 (1956), 149–56.

VACHEROT, E., Histoire critique de l'école d'Alexandrie (Paris, 1846).

VIELHAUER, PH. 'Ἀνάπαυσις. Zum gnostischen Hintergrund des Thomasevangeliums', Festschrift für Ernst Haehnchen, Beiheft 30 zur ZNW (1964), 281–99.

VÖLKER, W., Quellen zur Geschichte der christlichen Gnosis (Tübingen, 1932).

—— 'Fortschritt und Vollendung bei Philo von Alexandrien', TU 49 (Leipzig, 1938).

—— 'Die Vollkommenheitslehre des Clemens Alexandrinus in ihren geschichtlichen Zusammenhängen', TZ 3 (1947), 15–40.

—— 'Der wahre Gnostiker nach Clemens Alexandrinus', TU 57 (Berlin, 1952).

WAGNER, W., Wert und Verwertung der griechischen Bildung im Urteil des Clemens von Alexandrien (Diss. Marburg, 1902).

WALZER, R., Aristotelis Dialogorum Fragmenta (Testi della Scuola Normale Superiore di Pisa, vol. ii) (Firenze, 1934).

WALZER, R., 'New Light on Galen's moral Philosophy', *CQ* 43 (1949), 82–96.
—— *Galen on Jews and Christians* (Oxford, 1949).
—— *Galeni Compendium Timaei Platonis* (Plato Arabus, vol. i) (Londinii, 1951).
WASZINK, J. H., article on Basilides in *RACh*, Band I (1950), coll. 1217–23.
—— 'Der Platonismus und die altchristliche Gedankenwelt', *Entretiens Hardt* iii (Genève, 1955), 139–78.
—— 'Bemerkungen zu Justins Lehre vom Logos Spermatikos', Festschrift Theodor Klauser, *JACh*, Ergänzungsband 1 (Münster, 1964), 380–90.
WEBER, K. O., 'Origenes der Neuplatoniker', *Zetemata* 27 (1962).
WEISS, H. F., 'Untersuchungen zur Kosmologie des hellenistischen und palästinischen Judentums', *TU* 97 (Berlin, 1966).
WENDLAND, P., *Quaestiones Musonianae* (Berlin, 1886).
—— *Philos Schrift über die Vorsehung* (Berlin, 1892).
—— *Philo und die kynisch-stoische Diatribe* (Beiträge zur Geschichte der griechischen Religion und Philosophie von P. Wendland und O. Kern (Berlin, 1895).
—— 'Die Therapeuten und die philonische Schrift vom beschaulichen Leben', *JCPh*, Supplementum 22 (1896), 695–770.
—— 'Philo und Clemens Alexandrinus', *Hermes* 31 (1896), 435–56.
WILSON, R. McL., *The Gospel of Philip*. Translated from the Coptic Text with an Introduction and Commentary (London, 1962).
WINTER, F. J., *Die Ethik des Clemens von Alexandrien* (Leipzig, 1882).
WITT, R. E., 'The Hellenism of Clement of Alexandria', *CQ* 25 (1931), 195–204.
—— *Albinus and the History of Middle Platonism* (Cambridge, 1937).
WLOSOK, A., 'Laktanz und die philosophische Gnosis', *AHAW*, phil.-hist. Kl. (1960), especially 143–79.
WOLFSON, H. A., *Philo* (Cambridge, Massachusetts, 1947).
—— *The Philosophy of the Church Fathers* (Cambridge, Massachusetts, 1956).
—— 'Plato's pre-existent Matter in Patristic Philosophy', *The Classical Tradition* (Ithaca, N.Y., 1966), 409–20.
WYTZES, J., 'Paideia and Pronoia in the Work of Clemens Alexandrinus', *VC* 9 (1955), 148–58.
—— 'The Twofold Way (I): Platonic Influences in the Work of Clement of Alexandria', *VC* 11 (1957), 226–45.
—— 'The Twofold Way (II): Platonic Influences in the Work of Clement of Alexandria', *VC* 14 (1960), 129–53.
ZAHN, T., *Forschungen zur Geschichte des neutestamentlichen Kanons und der altkirchlichen Literatur*, III. Theil, Supplementum Clementinum (Erlangen, 1884).
ZELLER, E., *Die Lehre des Aristoteles von der Ewigkeit der Welt. Vorträge und Abhandlungen* iii (Leipzig, 1884), 1–36.
—— *Die Philosophie der Griechen in ihrer geschichtlichen Entwicklung*, II/1 (Leipzig, 1889, 4th ed.); II/2 (Leipzig, 1879, 3rd ed.); III/1 (Leipzig, 1923, 5th ed.); III/2 (Leipzig, 1903, 4th ed.).
ZIEGERT, P., 'Über die Ansätze zu einer Mysterienlehre aufgebaut auf den antiken Mysterien bei Philo Iudäus', *ThStK* 7 (1894), Heft 4, 706–32.

ZIEGLER, K., article on Plutarchos in *RE*, 41 Halbband (Stuttgart, 1951),
coll. 636–962.

N.B. Titles of books and papers are usually omitted in the footnotes: the
name of the author is immediately followed by the indication of the page in
case of a book, by the *sigla* of the journal in case of a paper. In case of two
or more works by the same author, however, the title of the book or of the
paper is entirely or partially reproduced.

ADDENDA

p. 152, *footnote* 1. See also B. Gärtner, *The Theology of the Gospel of Thomas* (London, 1961), pp. 109–10.

p. 158 *and p.* 163, *footnote* 2. R. Wagner, *Die Gnosis von Alexandria*, Stuttgart 1968, p. 109, also hinted at Clement's dependence on Gnosticism in the doctrine of the existence of a 'secret tradition', but did not work out this most important point.

p. 162. That the view according to which Jesus taught the true knowledge to his disciples after his resurrection was widespread in Gnosticism has been pointed out also by B. Gärtner, *The Theology of the Gospel of Thomas*, pp. 98 ff.

p. 199, *footnote* 6. As to the dependence of Clement on Philo in his theological system see also H. J. Krämer, *Der Ursprung der Geistmetaphysik* (Amsterdam, 1967), p. 282.

p. 202, *footnote* 3. On the derivation of the ideas as thoughts of God from Xenocrates see also H. J. Krämer, *Der Ursprung der Geistmetaphysik*, pp. 41–2, and 'Grundfragen der aristotelischen Theologie' (II), *Theologie und Philosophie*, 44 (1969), pp. 486–96.

p. 207. As to Clement's dependence on Philo in the identification between the intelligible world, the μονάς, and the Logos see also H. J. Krämer, *Der Ursprung der Geistmetaphysik*, p. 283.

p. 221. As to the sentence τὸ γὰρ ὑπολειφθὲν σημεῖόν ἐστι μονάς, ὡς εἰπεῖν, θέσιν ἔχουσα of *Strom.* v. 71. 2 (ii. 374. 9–10) see the exact parallels produced by J. Whittaker, 'Neopythagoreanism and Negative Theology', *SO* 44 (1969), pp. 114–15.

p. 221, *footnote* 3. H. A. Wolfson, 'Negative Attributes in the Church Fathers and in the Gnostic Basilides', *Harv. Theol. Rev.* 50 (1957), thinks of a direct dependence of Clement on Albinus; against this view see Whittaker's criticism, *SO* 44 (1969), pp. 113–14.

INDEX

n. 0 indicates continuation of footnote from previous page